Campus Crusade for Christ Library

D1435367

CHRISTIAN MISSIONS
IN BIBLICAL PERSPECTIVE

CHRISTIAN MISSIONS
IN
BIBLICAL PERSPECTIVE

by

J. HERBERT KANE

School of World Mission
Trinity Evangelical Divinity School
Deerfield, Illinois

Baker Book House
Grand Rapids, Michigan

Copyright 1976 by
Baker Book House Company

ISBN: 0-8010-5370-6

First Printing, June 1976

Printed in the United States of America

The Scripture quotations in this publication are from the Revised Standard Version of the Bible, copyright 1946, 1952, 1971, 1973 by the National Council of the Churches of Christ in the U.S.A. and are used by permission of the copyright holder.

The following chapters, with adaptations, are taken from the author's earlier volume, *Understanding Christian Missions,* published by Baker Book House in 1974: "The Sovereignty of God," "The Missionary Mandate," "The Fate of the Heathen," and "The Uniqueness of the Christian Faith."

Campus Crusade for Christ Library

BV
2061
K 16

to

PAMELA, KAREN, AND SCOTT

10560

Campus Crusade for Christ Library

Foreword

The only book that does not need to be revised or rewritten is the Bible. All other books must be revised, updated, and rewritten in the light of new information, changing circumstances, new insights, and better solutions. J. Herbert Kane in *Christian Missions in Biblical Perspective* takes an old subject much written about and gives to all of us a persuasive, cogent, and illuminating work that evangelicals will find useful for years to come.

Certainly the Church today is swept by rising tides of syncretism and universalism. Who can avoid asking questions: Is Christianity the *only* way to life everlasting? Can or does God ever allow *anyone* to go at last into the lake of fire? Are the "heathen" really lost? Professor Kane answers these questions. But he goes far beyond this.

The Trinitarian basis of God's salvatory mission in Christ, the Bible's own witness to the missionary task of the Church, and the important theological doctrines pertinent to an adequate missiology are all discussed.

It is to be hoped that, at a time when the churches in the West are faltering in their missionary outreach, this book will help to clear the air, show Christians their unchanging duty, get them to be about the Father's business, and let them know they have divine guidance, light, help, and hope when they take the Great Commission seriously.

I recommend this volume highly both to those who are vitally interested in missions and to those who are not but who ought to be and, indeed, will be if they read what Professor Kane has written.

Harold Lindsell

May 1976

Preface

The missionary enterprise has always been under scrutiny by both its friends and its enemies. In former times the questions raised pertained to motives, methods, purposes, and goals; but in recent years the very idea of mission has been called into question. Some even suggest that the missionary era has ended and the greatest contribution any missionary can now make is to come home and leave the churches in the Third World to fend for themselves. As for the 2.7 billion human beings who have never heard the gospel, they are already part of the "new humanity" inaugurated by Christ at the Resurrection and need cause us no concern.

As a result, potential candidates are wondering if the Christian mission is any longer a viable option, and not a few veteran missionaries are going through an identity crisis. Little wonder that missionary dropouts have increased significantly in the past ten years. It is precisely at such a time as this that we need once again to go back to the Holy Scriptures to ascertain what they have to say about the most important obligation of the Christian church.

To begin with, I should state clearly that I take a high view of both the Written Word and the Living Word. The Scriptures I regard as reliable, authentic, and authoritative. They *alone* contain all revealed truth concerning God, man, sin, and salvation. They *alone* are able to make one wise unto salvation (2 Tim 3:16). As for Jesus Christ, I believe that He is the Son of God, who in the Incarnation became the Son of Man, that through His death, resurrection, and ascension He might become the only Savior and Sovereign of the world (1 Tim 6:15); and sooner or later all men must come to terms with Him (Jn 12:48; Acts 17:31).

I also take a high view of the church. In spite of all her blunders and blemishes, she is still the finest institution in the world. She is the salt of the earth and the light of the world (Mt 5:13-16). It is pre-eminently through the church that God is working out His purposes today. That is not to deny that God is at work in the world. Obviously He is; but it must be affirmed that there is an essential difference between the church and the world, and that the former, not the latter, is the paramount vehicle for the realization of God's redemptive purposes in history.

No attempt has been made to deal with the many theologies of development, liberation, or revolution; nor is anything said about Black theology, African theology, or Indian theology. Those and other theologies—of death, hope, pain, woman, etc.—like the "Death of God" theology in the 1960s are fads that come and go and leave hardly a trace of their former existence. Rather an attempt has been made to re-examine the Scriptures to see what they have to say concerning the *unchanging* aspects of the Christian mission.

The Christian church, the Christian mission, and the Christian missionary all stand under the judgment of God. All are required to operate according to the principles of Scripture. We are grateful for the contribution that anthropology and sociology have made to the discipline of missiology. They should not, however, become a substitute for the clear teachings of the Word of God. If we must choose between the insights of the social sciences and the teachings of Scripture, we shall have to opt for the latter.

In this, as in my other books, I am greatly indebted to my wife for the wise counsel, constructive criticism, and patient endurance that went into the preparation of the manuscript, to say nothing of the many tedious hours devoted to proofreading.

J. HERBERT KANE

June 1976

Contents

PART ONE

The Biblical Basis of Missions

The Christian mission is rooted in the Holy Scriptures. They and they alone are able to make man "wise unto salvation" (2 Tim 3:15). From them we derive our message, our mandate, our motivation, and our methodology. Apart from the Word of God the missionary movement has neither meaning nor sanction.

It is imperative that today's missionary have an adequate grasp of Christian theology, especially as it relates to the worldwide proclamation of the gospel in a cross-cultural situation in a rapidly changing world. In the nineteenth century almost all missionaries held to a conservative interpretation of Scripture. This is no longer true. The ancient landmarks are being removed. As a result we have a "new theology" and a "new evangelism," both of which threaten to change the force and thrust of the Christian mission.

In our day the ideas of men are being substituted for the Word of God. Anthropology and sociology are rapidly replacing theology, with disastrous results. The vertical dimension of the Christian mission has been lost and all that remains is the horizontal.

According to the "new theology" man is not eternally lost, for the simple reason that a loving heavenly Father would never consign even a Hitler to hell. His all-conquering love and His irresistible grace will finally win the day, and all men will be saved. Indeed, they are already saved by virtue of the universal application of the saving merit of Jesus Christ to humanity en masse, regardless of their attitude or understanding. The task of today's missionary, then, is simply to inform

15

the non-Christian world that, without their knowledge or consent, all men are "in Christ," and as such are part of the new humanity of which He is the Head.

This gives salvation an altogether new twist. Salvation today is no longer personal but societal. Humanization, not redemption, is the watchword. Man needs to be delivered, not from the penalty and power of his own sins, but from the demonic power structures that have destroyed his authentic manhood and alienated him from his neighbor. Hence the emphasis on the theology of development, the theology of liberation, and even the theology of revolution.

Missionaries, pastors, and all who have a vital interest in the evangelization of the world have an obligation to search the Scriptures in order to come to an understanding of the biblical basis of the Christian mission.

1

Missions in the Old Testament

Some Bible scholars claim they find missionary purpose, message, and activity in the Old Testament. Other scholars fail to find any of these. Much depends on one's definition of "mission." If by "mission" is meant the crossing of political or cultural boundaries to take the message of the one true God to those who know nothing about Him, then, with the exception of Jonah, we will not find much about "mission" in the Old Testament.

This does not mean the *idea* is not there. To be sure, it is stated implicitly rather than explicitly in the doctrine of universalism, for which there is ample evidence in the Old Testament. Liberal scholars trace the development of Old Testament thought from polytheism through monotheism to universalism, and finally to mission. Conservative scholars reject this approach and insist that both monotheism and universalism are found in the earliest chapters of Genesis. Mission, as distinct from universalism, is a later development, and does not really come to full bloom until the New Testament. H. H. Rowley has no difficulty in finding the concept of mission in the Old Testament and suggests that Moses was the first missionary. At the same time he reminds us that Israel never became a missionary community in the modern sense of that term.

> Enough has been said to demonstrate that the Old Testament is a missionary book. Yet it is undeniable that Judaism is not essentially and notably a missionary religion. That it knew some missionary impetus, and some proselytising zeal, may be allowed without

contradicting this. Yet there never has been the slightest likelihood of its becoming a world religion, in the sense in which Christianity has been a world religion from the first century of its existence.[1]

God's Missionary Role in the Old Testament

The Old Testament is a missionary book because Jehovah is a missionary God. From the very beginning God has been desperately concerned for the spiritual and material welfare of the world. Long before our Founding Fathers coined the phrase, God was interested in "life, liberty, and the pursuit of happiness" for all His creatures. This comes out clearly in the revelation of God as described in the Old Testament.

1. God is the Creator and Sustainer of the physical universe. The Old Testament opens with the magnificent declaration: "In the beginning God created the heavens and the earth." If that were the only statement we had, it would be sufficient grounds for the Christian mission.

Matter is not eternal; nor is the universe the result of electrical impulses or mechanical forces operating on their own, apart from any plan or purpose. Whether we examine the nucleus of the atom or study the stars in their courses we come to the same conclusion: The hand that made them is divine.

Because God made the world, He owns it. "In his hand are the depths of the earth; the height of the mountains are his also. The sea is his, for he made it; for his hands formed the dry land" (Ps 95:4-5). And because He owns it, He controls and sustains it (Is 40:28). He opens His hand and supplies the need of every living thing, be it man or beast (Ps 145:16). Man especially sustains a unique relationship to God. He was made by God, for God, and to this day bears the image of his Creator (Gen 1:26; Jas 3:9). It was God's intention that man should find his highest happiness, not in himself or his environment or his achievements, but in God (Mt 22:37). We are His people and the sheep of His pasture (Ps 100:3). In Him we live and move and have our being (Acts 17:28). His lovingkindness is better than life (Ps 63:3) and His tender mercies are over all His works (Ps 145:9). His goodness

---

1. H. H. Rowley, *The Missionary Message of the Old Testament* (London: Cary Kingsgate Press, 1944), p. 76.

is extended without discrimination to all His creatures without respect to merit (Mt 5:45).

The entire universe is a manifestation of the power and wisdom of its Creator. "The heavens are telling the glory of God; and the firmament proclaims his handiwork. Day to day pours forth speech, and night to night declares knowledge. There is no speech, nor are there words; their voice is not heard; yet their voice goes out through all the earth, and their words to the end of the world" (Ps 19:1-4). Speaking of God's creative power, Paul says: "Ever since the creation of the world his invisible nature, namely, his eternal power and deity, has been clearly perceived in the things that have been made" (Rom 1:20). Again he says that God "did not leave himself without witness for he did good and gave you from heaven rains and fruitful seasons, satisfying your hearts with food and gladness" (Acts 14:17).

2. God is the Governor and Judge of the moral universe. The Scriptures portray God as a moral Being. His outstanding characteristic is holiness. "I, the Lord your God, am holy" (Lev 19:2). Moreover, He demands holiness in His people (1 Pet 1:16). Without it no man will see the Lord (Heb 12:14). Man, created in God's image, is likewise a moral being. God endowed him with a rational mind, a free will, and a moral nature. God invested man with immense authority, giving him dominion over the entire animal kingdom (Gen 1:28). He was placed in the Garden of Eden with instructions to cultivate it (Gen 2:15). He was also told to be fruitful and multiply and replenish the earth (Gen 1:28). In this way God's rule was to be extended throughout the earth.

Man was responsible only to God, his Maker. Only one prohibition was laid on him—a prohibition he violated with devastating consequences. Chaos was introduced into every part of man's constitution. His mind was darkened (Eph 4:18), his emotions were vitiated (Jn 3:19), and his will was enslaved (Rom 7:19-21). In a word, he became totally depraved. He was told by Satan that it wouldn't happen, but it did; and man learned the hard way that the laws that govern the moral universe are just as inexorable as those that govern the physical universe. No one can escape the consequences of his wrongdoing. Man is a free moral agent and may choose to sin if he wishes, but he cannot sin with impunity. Sin brings its own punishment. Moses warned the children of Israel: "Be sure your sin will find you out" (Num 32:23). Paul declared: "The wages of sin is death" (Rom 6:23). This is not a human law, much less a tribal law. It is a universal law, built into the moral fabric of the universe. Therefore it has universal validity (Rom 5:12).

Sin always exposes the one who commits it to the judgment of God. This goes for cities and nations as well as individuals, since they too belong to God and come under His judgment. When the iniquity of the Amorites was full, judgment fell (Gen 15:16). When the moral decadence of Sodom and Gomorrah reached unprecedented heights, they were destroyed with fire and brimstone from heaven (Gen 19). The first-born in Egypt fell under the sword of the destroying angel (Ex 12). When Daniel stood before Belshazzar he rebuked him for exalting himself against the Lord of heaven, "in whose hand is your breath, and whose are all your ways" (Dan 5:23). And when he pronounced doom on his empire, Daniel declared: "God has numbered the days of your kingdom and brought it to an end" (Dan 5:26). Nineveh was warned of impending doom if it did not repent (Jon 3).

Because God is righteous in all His ways and holy in all His works (Ps 145:17) He has no favorites (Deut 10:17)—not even the children of Israel. They too came under His judgment when idolatry became rampant. Indeed, judgment *begins* at the house of God (1 Pet 4:17). God is often more tolerant with strangers than with His own children. To Israel He said: "You only have I known of all the families of the earth: *therefore* I will punish *you* for all your iniquities" (Amos 3:2).

On the other hand we must bear in mind that God is not vindictive. He does not take pleasure in the death of the wicked (Ezek 18:23). Judgment is His "strange" work (Is 28:21). He prefers to heal, not hurt. And when He does act in judgment it is always with the hope that men and nations will repent. Judgment is not simply punitive, it is remedial as well. Nineveh is a classic example of this. When the king and people of that great, wicked city repented, God withheld judgment, much to Jonah's disgust. In wrath He remembers mercy (Hab 3:2), and whenever possible provides a way of escape for those willing to avail themselves of it. He destroyed the world with the Flood, but provided salvation in the form of the Ark; and for 120 years Noah tried to persuade the people to avoid disaster.

Because all men have been created in the image of God all men are ultimately responsible to Him (Rom 1:18). The human race is one (Acts 17:26), and all its members are part of God's great family (Eph 3:14-15). As such they are the object of God's love and care. He is not willing that *any* should perish (2 Pet 3:9), but that *all* should come to a knowledge of the truth (1 Tim 2:4).

God prefers salvation to judgment. Herein lies the missionary element. God's wrath makes the gospel necessary: His love makes it possible. This is made plain in the Old Testament by God's dealings with Israel and the heathen nations.

3. God is the King and Ruler of the Gentile nations. The word "nation" appears first in Genesis 10:20. The Hebrew word *goyyim,* as used in the Old Testament, is identical with "heathen." It carries with it a religious rather than a political connotation. It would appear that God's original intention was that the human race should remain one; but when the postdiluvians disobeyed God's command to "replenish" the earth and instead built the Tower of Babel, God confounded their language. In the resulting confusion they went their separate ways and soon became scattered over the face of the earth.

At the same time there is a sense in which God *created* these nations. They are the work of *His* hands (Ps 86:9). The Dispersion of the nations is described by Moses as an act of God and was arranged according to the number of the children of Israel (Deut 32:8). And whenever the nations are mentioned in the Old Testament it is usually in relation to Israel.

> Because the God of Israel has been the God of all nations in the past, so *also* is He in the present and will be in the future. Because the God of Israel is the Creator not only of all nations, but also of heaven and earth, man and beast, therefore He will reveal Himself in the future as Creator and more particularly as *Redeemer* also of the whole world.[2]

When the sons of Shem, Ham, and Japheth were scattered abroad they soon forgot the lessons of the Flood. In their attempt to throw off the rule of God they gave up the worship and service of Jehovah and proceeded to worship gods of their own making (Rom 1:21-25). In an effort to compensate for the loss of their spiritual heritage, they built cities and castles and founded empires and dynasties—all without God. By the time of Abraham their moral and spiritual declension was complete. They were in every sense of the word *goyyim*—heathen nations.

But their rejection of Jehovah in no way removed them from His rule. Even as heathen nations, with their false gods and pagan practices, they were still under Jehovah's universal control. They belonged to Him and were accountable to Him whether or not they acknowledged the fact.

The rule of God extends to all the world. "The Lord has established his throne in the heavens, and his kingdom rules over all" (Ps 103:19). "The earth is the Lord's and the fulness thereof, the world and those who dwell therein" (Ps 24:1). Psalm 47 is very clear on this point: "For the Lord, the Most High, is terrible, a great king over all the earth" (v. 2) and "God reigns over the nations" (v. 8).

---

2. Johannes Blauw, *The Missionary Nature of the Church* (New York: McGraw-Hill, 1962), p. 36.

In many passages of the Old Testament we find God speaking of the nations as belonging to Him. After laying claim to Gilead, Manasseh, Ephraim, and Judah, God goes on to say: "Moab is my washbasin; upon Edom I cast my shoe; over Philistia I shout in triumph" (Ps 108:9). Daniel declared that Nebuchadnezzar's kingdom, majesty, glory, and honor were all a gift from God (Dan 5:18).

Nowhere is Jehovah's lordship over the nations more clearly seen than in the prophecies of Isaiah and Amos. In the first two chapters of Amos God pronounces judgment on Damascus, Tyre, and Moab, saying: "For three transgressions and for four I will not revoke the punishment." Isaiah, in chapters 13–23, takes up the "oracle" of one heathen nation after another: Babylon, Moab, Damascus, Egypt, and Tyre. They, as well as Samaria and Judah, are subject to God's law, therefore exposed to His wrath. Indeed, in one passage Egypt and Assyria are mentioned in the same category with the nation of Israel: "Blessed be Egypt my people, and Assyria the work of my hands, and Israel my heritage" (Is 19:25).

Even more striking is Jehovah's reference to Cyrus. As the pagan king of a pagan nation, Cyrus had no clear knowledge of the one true God (Is 45:4); yet God used him as an instrument to accomplish His purpose for Israel. In this capacity Cyrus is referred to as God's "shepherd" (Is 44:28) and God's "anointed" (Is 45:1).

4. God is the Father and Redeemer of Israel. Up to this point we have been concerned with universalism—God's sovereign and universal dominion over all the earth. Now we turn to particularism. The former relates to God's worldwide purpose; the latter has to do with the method whereby God achieves that purpose. "No doubt the Old Testament is 'particularistic,' in the sense that salvation and the service of God are confined to one special people; but this 'particularism' is the instrument for the universal ends of God with the world."[3]

Among all the nations of the earth, Israel sustained a unique relationship to Jehovah. The other nations were made by Him (Ps 86:9) and ruled by Him (Ps 103:19), but only Israel is said to have been "redeemed" by Him: "Thus says the Lord, who created you, O Jacob, he who formed you, O Israel: 'Fear not, for I have redeemed you; I have called you by name, you are mine'" (Is 43:1). Thirteen times in the second half of Isaiah Jehovah is referred to as the "Redeemer" of Israel.

Beginning with Genesis 12, history in the Old Testament is the history of Israel; and the history of Israel is the history of redemption.

---

3. Ibid., p. 24.

The other nations are neither ignored nor forgotten, but they are brought into the picture only in relation to Israel (Deut 32:8). "The nations come into view variously in the Old Testament, but always *in their relation to Israel* as the people of God. It is out of the question, then, to speak of a uniform judgment on the nations; on the contrary, it is always a question of their *concrete relation* to Israel."[4]

The call of Abraham in Genesis 12 marks a turning point in God's dealings with the world. Campbell Morgan divides the book of Genesis into three parts: Generation (1–2), Degeneration (3–11), and Regeneration (12–50). Abraham and Israel were not chosen by God for their own sakes, but for a much wider purpose—the salvation of the world. The promise "In thee shall all the nations of the earth be blessed" (KJV) was made twice to Abraham (Gen 12:3 and 22:18) and once to Jacob (Gen 28:14). Though weaker and smaller than the other nations, Israel was indispensable to God's overall scheme of redemption. God's plan to redeem the world centered on Israel. The history of redemption began not with Adam or Noah or Moses, but with Abraham. Even Jesus acknowledged that "salvation is from the Jews" (Jn 4:22).

God had a threefold purpose in the election of Israel. *First,* Israel was to be the recipient and the guardian of God's special revelation to the world (Heb 1:1-3). *Second,* Israel was to be the channel through which the Redeemer was to enter the stream of human history. He was to be the Son of Abraham (Mt 1:1), of the tribe of Judah (Gen 49:10), of the house of David (Rom 1:3). *Third,* Israel was to be God's servant (Is 44:1-2) and witness (Is 43:10) in the midst of the nations.

Too often election is regarded as conferring privilege and preeminence.

> It would be a grave misunderstanding to see in the election of Israel only an arbitrary act of the autonomous God, who in His sovereignty leaves all other nations to themselves in order to select a nation and show preference to it. Precisely the election of Israel is a service of God toward the nations. It was part and parcel of His *mission.* Through this election the other nations were also included in His promise (Gen 12:1ff.). Israel was for them the bearer of the promise and the mediator of the blessing, lofty sign of the fact that they, too, could be saved and partake of salvation.[5]

The election of Israel was not an end in itself, but a means to an end. God chose Israel not primarily for her own sake but for the sake

---

4. Ibid., p. 25.
5. Georg F. Vicedom, *The Mission of God* (St. Louis: Concordia Publishing House, 1965), p. 48.

of the world, and the purpose was not to confer privilege but to impose responsibility. Of course, election does involve privilege; but there is no such thing as privilege without responsibility. "The purpose of the election is service, and when service is withheld the election loses its meaning, and therefore fails."[6] We know from Israel's later history that this is precisely what happened. Because of her unbelief Israel was rejected and only a very small remnant survived (Is 1:9; Rom 11:5).

As we have already mentioned, the outstanding attribute of God as revealed in the Old Testament was righteousness or holiness. God's earliest word to Israel was: "You shall be holy; for I the Lord your God am holy" (Lev 19:2). It was God's intention that Israel should become a "kingdom of priests and a holy nation" (Ex 19:6). As such they were to offer sacrifices of righteousness (Deut 33:19), and were to worship Him in the beauty of holiness (Ps 29:2). In their daily contact they were to do justice, to love kindness, and to walk humbly with their God (Mic 6:8). Israel's monotheism and moral purity would be in stark contrast to the idolatry and immorality of the Gentile nations; in this way the glory of the Lord would be made known throughout the world (Is 62:2).

The historic event which signaled the redemption of Israel as a people was, of course, their deliverance from Egypt, the house of bondage (Deut 13:5). Without doubt this was the greatest event in Israel's history, one that is mentioned repeatedly throughout the Old Testament. It was the supreme event by which God forever separated His people from the rest of the nations and made them His own peculiar treasure (Ex 19:5). The Exodus culminated in the Red Sea episode, which had a twofold effect: the death and destruction of their enemies as well as deliverance and freedom for themselves. That it marked a decisive turning point in their history seems clear from the words of Paul: "Our fathers were all under the cloud, and all passed through the sea, and all were baptized into Moses in the cloud and in the sea" (1 Cor 10:1-2).

While the Exodus went forth from Egypt and involved only the Israelites and the Egyptians, it was designed by God to serve a world-wide purpose. This comes out clearly in God's warning to Pharaoh through Moses: "For by now I could have put forth my hand and struck you and your people with pestilence, and you would have been cut off from the earth; but for this purpose have I let you live, to show you my power, *so that my name may be declared throughout all the earth*" (Ex 9:15-16). Paul develops the same theme in Romans 9.

God dealt with His covenant people in a twofold way: in grace

---

6. H. H. Rowley, *The Biblical Doctrine of Election* (London: Lutterworth, 1952), p. 52.

and in judgment. In either case Israel became a witness to the nations. The Psalmist said: "May God be gracious to us and bless us and make his face to shine upon us, that thy way may be known upon the earth, and thy saving power among all nations" (Ps 67:1-2). As long as Israel remained faithful and obedient she was the recipient of God's grace. God promised to prosper and protect her against all her enemies (Deut 28:1-14). "The Lord shall cause your enemies who rise up against you to be defeated before you; they shall come out against you one way, and flee before you seven ways" (v. 7). "And all the people of the earth shall see that you are called by the name of the Lord; and they shall be afraid of you" (v. 10).

Through the centuries God kept His promises. His warning to all potential enemies was: "Touch not my anointed ones, do my prophets no harm" (Ps 105:15). And anyone who dared to touch Israel touched the apple of His eye (Zech 2:8). On more than one occasion Israel came to the brink of national disaster, only to be delivered at the eleventh hour. Pharaoh tried to drown them (Ex 1); Haman tried to hang them (Esther 3–7); Nebuchadnezzar tried to burn them (Dan 3). In each case they proved to be indestructible. God in His grace intervened and delivered them from the hands of their enemies. In this way Israel became a witness to the other nations of the saving power of Jehovah (Ps 66:1-7; Is 52:10).

But Israel did not always remain faithful. Throughout her entire history she was surrounded by hostile Gentile nations whose political power posed a threat to Israel's sovereignty and whose pagan practices presented a temptation to idolatry. The latter often proved more disastrous than the former. Many times Israel succumbed to the temptation and lapsed into idolatry. Did she then cease to be God's witness? Not at all.

Moses foresaw this contingency and warned Israel of the dire consequences of disobedience (Deut 28). It is worth noting that Moses takes only fourteen verses to enumerate the blessings of obedience but fifty-four verses to describe the calamities of disobedience; and in verse 37 he warns: "You shall become a horror, a proverb, and a byword, among all the people where the Lord will lead you away." When Israel disobeyed, God dealt with her in judgment, ultimately allowing her to be carried away captive by her enemies. But even in exile she was a reminder to the Gentile nations of the moral character of Jehovah, who is righteous in all His ways and holy in all His works, who will not tolerate sin, even in His own chosen people.

Whether obedient or disobedient, Israel remained God's witness to pagan nations round about her. The emphasis, of course, is on presence, not proclamation. Israel by her very presence in the world was a witness

25

to the one true God, Creator of heaven and earth and the Judge and Ruler of the world. In this passive way she was filling her "missionary" role.

Israel's Missionary Role Before the Captivity

While God is revealed in the Old Testament as the Father and Redeemer of Israel, it is obvious that His salvation was not to be restricted to Israel. As His covenant people, Israel was to remain separate from the Gentile nations. She was not to worship their gods (Deut 11:16) nor marry their children (Deut 7:3). At the same time it was God's intention that she should be a "light to the nations" (Is 42:6) in order that His salvation "may reach to the end of the earth" (Is 49:6). This twofold assignment was difficult to perform. Prior to the Captivity Israel's missionary activity (what there was of it) was centripetal. The nations came to Israel but she did not go out to them. The sole exception was Jonah's mission to Nineveh; and his message was one of judgment, not salvation. During this period Israel's missionary activity developed in three stages.

1. **"Strangers" were permitted to enter the congregation of Israel.** Some of these instances date back to the days of the Exodus when a "mixed multitude" joined the children of Israel in their departure from Egypt (Ex 12:38). Other strangers were permitted to join later on. In the time of Solomon the strangers numbered 153,600 (2 Chron 2:17), and were hired by Solomon in the building of the Temple. In some cases certain restrictions were laid down. The Edomites, for example, had to wait until the third generation (Deut 23:7-8); others, such as the Ammonites and the Moabites, were not permitted to enter the congregation even to the tenth generation (Deut 23:3).

On the other hand, once these strangers were admitted into the congregation they enjoyed considerable favor. They were permitted to keep the Passover (Num 9:14) and were required to observe the Sabbath (Ex 20:10). They could even offer sacrifices (Lev 17:8). They could not, however, become kings (Deut 17:15). Israel was given strict instructions regarding the treatment of these strangers in their midst. The Israelites were expressly forbidden to oppress them (Ex 22:21), the reason being that they themselves had been strangers in Egypt (1 Chron 16:19-20). Moreover, they were required to treat them generously, purposely leaving the gleanings for them at harvest time (Lev 19:9-10). God's warning on this point was clear: "When a stranger sojourns among you in your land, you shall not do him wrong.

The stranger that sojourns with you shall be to you as the native among you, and you shall love him as yourself; for you were strangers in the land of Egypt" (Lev 19:33-34).

The book of Ruth is a beautiful example of the way in which these strangers were assimilated into the congregation. Ruth, a Moabite widow, was so impressed with her mother-in-law, Naomi, that she refused to leave her on her return to the land of Judah. In vain did Naomi try to dissuade her. In words as precious as they are poetic Ruth clinched the matter by saying to Naomi: "Entreat me not to leave you or go to return from following you; where you go I will go, and where you lodge I will lodge; your people shall be my people, and your God my God; where you die I will die, and there will I be buried" (Ruth 1:16-17). And Ruth was not only accepted as a full member of the congregation, she became the great-grandmother of King David (Ruth 4:21-22) and an ancestress of our Lord (Mt 1:5).

In the stories of Ruth and Rahab we get a glimpse of the missionary concern of Israel even before the days of the prophets. "Long before the diaspora there had been a certain inclination towards missionary activities. . . . Accepting foreigners into the Israelitic community can rightly be considered to be the first stage, or rather a stage leading up to the Jewish mission."[7]

The clearest passage in the Old Testament dealing with the spiritual plight of the strangers and their relationship to the God of Israel is found in Solomon's prayer at the dedication of the Temple.

> Likewise when a foreigner, who is not of thy people Israel, comes from a far country for the sake of thy great name, and thy mighty hand, and thy outstretched arm, when he comes and prays toward this house, hear thou from heaven thy dwelling place, and do according to all for which the foreigner calls to thee; in order that all the peoples of the earth may know thy name and fear thee, as do thy people Israel (2 Chron 6:32-33).

Doubtless Solomon hoped that the fame of this strikingly beautiful and costly building would attract strangers from faraway places; and he was concerned that their prayers be answered, not simply for their own sake but also that the nations might come to know and fear Jehovah.

Later on Isaiah expressed the same hope in even clearer terms:

> And the foreigners who join themselves to the Lord, to minister to him, to love the name of the Lord, and to be his servants, every one who keeps the sabbath, and does not profane it, and holds fast my covenant—these will I bring to my holy mountain, and make them joyful in my house of prayer; their burnt offerings and

---

7. Blauw, *Missionary Nature of the Church*, p. 56.

sacrifices will be accepted on my altar; for my house shall be called a house of prayer for all peoples (Is 56:6-7).

2. Entire nations were to be attracted to the God of Israel. The prophets, especially Isaiah, foresaw the day when not only individuals but entire nations would come to a knowledge of Jehovah and flock to Jerusalem to hear the words of the Lord:

> It shall come to pass in the latter days that the mountain of the house of the Lord shall be established as the highest of the mountains, and shall be raised above the hills; and all nations shall flow to it, and many peoples shall come and say: "Come let us go up to the mountain of the Lord, to the house of the God of Jacob; that he may teach us his ways and that we may walk in his paths." For out of Zion shall go forth the law, and the word of the Lord from Jerusalem (Is 2:2-3).

We find the same emphasis in Jeremiah: "At that time Jerusalem shall be called the throne of the Lord, and all nations shall gather to it, to the presence of the Lord in Jerusalem, and they shall no more stubbornly follow their own evil heart" (Jer 3:17).

In none of these passages is there any reference to Israel's going out to the nations to spread the knowledge of God. The nations come of their own accord, drawn by the centripetal force of Israel's ethical monotheism and the glory and power of her God and King.

> It is quite plain that He who *made* the nations (Ps 86:9) and who has made them as *His* nations (Ps 87) is also the only one who can call them to himself. That which will bring the world of nations to Him is *not* Israel's calling them, *not* her going out to them, but exclusively the visible manifestation of the deeds of God in and with Israel; only so will they recognize Yahweh as *their* God, i.e. confess that Israel's God is *their* God, the God of the whole earth, the *only* God.[8]

Jehovah, unlike the gods of the other nations, is not a tribal god or a nature God. He is not a god of the hills or the valleys. He is the God of the whole earth who chose one nation, Israel, through whom to reveal Himself to the rest of the world. He is the Lord of history, and through His elect people He is working out His gracious purposes for them and for the Gentile nations. Because He is omnipotent, He is able to make the wrath of man to praise Him (Ps 76:10); therefore He is not frustrated by the vicissitudes of history nor thwarted by the machinations of the nations.

Israel, in the midst of the nations, functioned on their behalf as both priest and prophet. It was in Jerusalem that worship was offered

---

8. Ibid., p. 37.

to Jehovah. That was the place He chose to put His name (1 Kings 11:36). Every devout Jew recognized that Jerusalem was the place "where men ought to worship" (Jn 4:20). Jerusalem was also the place from which the word of the Lord was to go forth. It was God's word and He had promised: "So shall my word be that goes forth from my mouth; it shall not return to me empty, but it shall accomplish that which I purpose, and prosper in the thing for which I sent it" (Is 55:11).

The vision conjured up by Isaiah and the other great prophets depicted the Gentile nations making their way to Jerusalem to hear the word of the Lord and to call on His name in prayer. Jerusalem was the only place on earth where they could do this.

3. All the nations would know and worship the Lord. A third stage in the development of Israel's missionary activities would be reached when a knowledge of the one true God would become universal. Habakkuk predicted a day when "the earth will be filled with the knowledge of the glory of the Lord, as the waters cover the sea" (2:14). An identical passage is found in Isaiah (11:9). The same thought is expressed in Malachi. He foresaw the time when the Lord's name would be great among the Gentiles; and *in every place,* not simply Jerusalem, incense would be offered to His name (1:11).

In this connection a new expression comes into use: "the ends of the earth." No longer will the nations have to repair to Jerusalem to worship Jehovah. "All the ends of the earth shall remember and turn to the Lord; and all the families of the nations shall worship before him" (Ps 22:27). Israel was given as a light to the nations that God's salvation might reach to the ends of the earth (Is 49:6). Jehovah makes a direct appeal to the nations: "Turn to me and be saved, all the ends of the earth! For I am God and there is no other" (Is 45:22).

Israel's Missionary Role During the Exile

The Captivity was God's judgment on Israel for her continued disobedience. It marked a turning point in her history second only to the Exodus. Jerusalem was destroyed by Nebuchadnezzar, and the Jews were carried away captive to Babylon about 600 B.C. After seventy years in captivity only 42,000 returned to Palestine under Zerubbabel. The majority preferred to remain in exile, eventually representing about 7 per cent of the Roman Empire. In A.D. 70 Strabo reported: "It is hard to find a single place on the habitable earth that has not admitted this tribe of men, and is not possessed by it."[9] They were particularly numerous in Mesopotamia, Syria, and Egypt.

Known as the Diaspora, they continued to regard Jerusalem as their common religious center and maintained close contact with the Jewish authorities there. They sent generous offerings to maintain the Temple services and were represented by numerous synagogues in the city (Acts 6:9). Year after year the chief festivals attracted large numbers of Jews from all parts of the Mediterranean world (Acts 2:9-11).

During their long and lonely exile the Jews were forever cured of their idolatrous tendencies. Never again did they lapse into idolatry. Wherever they went in the Greco-Roman world they strenuously maintained the integrity of their religious faith, so much so that they were known as the "second race"—quite distinct from the Greeks and Romans. For this reason they were admired and detested at the same time.

It was during this period that Israel's missionary role completely changed and became centrifugal. Instead of the nations flocking to Jerusalem to learn the law of the Lord, the law was taken by the Jews of the Diaspora literally to the ends of the earth. For the first time in her history Israel became actively engaged in winning converts from the Gentile nations. Indeed, one of the chief characteristics of the Diaspora was proselytism. Judging from the words of our Lord, their proselytizing activities must have been both intensive and extensive (Mt 23:15). "From the first the Jews in Rome exhibited such an aggressive spirit of proselytism that they were charged with seeking to infect the Romans with their cult, and the government expelled the chief propagandists from the city in 139 B.C."[10]

There were two kinds of converts—the proselyte and the God-fearer. The former adopted Judaism *in toto,* including the rite of circumcision; consequently he was accepted as a full member of the Jewish community. The God-fearer, on the other hand, stopped short of the surgical rite and remained a second-class citizen. Both, however, had access to the synagogue.

Six characteristics of Jewish religious life in the Diaspora contributed directly to the making of converts and indirectly to the spread of Christianity later on.

1. **The institution of the synagogue.** It is difficult to overestimate the importance of the synagogue in the religious life of the Diaspora. Only a handful of Jews could attend the Temple services in Jerusalem,

9. Josephus, *Antiquities of the Jews* xiv. 7.
10. *The Interpreter's Dictionary of the Bible* (Nashville: Abingdon Press, 1962), 3:925.

and then only on festive occasions. Without the synagogue it is doubtful if the Jews of the Diaspora could have long retained their religious heritage. Wherever ten male leaders could be found, the Jewish community built a synagogue, which became the religious and social center of the Jewish life. The main service of the week fell on the Sabbath, at which time there was the recitation of the Shema (Deut 6:4-5), prayer, and the reading of Scripture, followed by an exhortation and a benediction.

The synagogue could never be a substitute for the Temple. It was primarily a teaching institution; hence its leader was a rabbi, not a priest. No sacrifices were ever offered in the synagogue. For that the Jews had to make the pilgrimage to the Temple in Jerusalem. While the Gentiles were excluded from the Temple (Acts 21:29), they had free access to the synagogue. It was there that they received instruction in the Jewish faith. So the synagogue became the chief means of making converts.

2. **The observance of the Sabbath.** The institution of the Sabbath goes back beyond Moses and Abraham to the very beginning, when God rested on the seventh day of creation and hallowed it. The keeping of the Sabbath was reinforced by its inclusion in the Decalogue. The Jews attached enormous importance to this fourth commandment in the law. Circumcision was the only kind of "work" permitted on the Sabbath (Jn 7:22-23). The Jews would sooner be slaughtered by the thousands than engage in battle on the Sabbath. Such strict adherence to a public rite must have made a deep and lasting impression on outsiders, for nearly everyone respects a person who takes his religion seriously and is not afraid to practice it in public.

3. **The translation of the Scriptures into Greek.** After centuries of exile the Jews forgot their Hebrew, in which the Old Testament was written. Instead they spoke Greek, the *lingua franca* of the Mediterranean world. It was necessary that the Scriptures be translated into Greek for the benefit of the Jews of the Diaspora. This was done sometime in the third century B.C. in Alexandria. The translation came to be known as the Septuagint (LXX) because it was supposed to have been the work of seventy scholars. The LXX soon became a very potent missionary tool in the hands of the Jews of the Diaspora. It was the Bible of Jesus and the apostles, and was read every Sabbath in the synagogues throughout the Greco-Roman world (Acts 15:21). It is doubtful if the Greeks in any large numbers would have frequented the synagogues had the Scriptures and the services been in Hebrew instead of Greek. The LXX and the Wisdom of Solomon and other

31

noncanonical literature, all in the Greek language, were of immense help to Philo of Alexandria and others who took it on themselves to make the Jewish religion intellectually respectable to the philosophical Greeks.

4. The concept of monotheism. The Greco-Roman world was honeycombed with polytheism. The Greeks were reputed to have 30,000 gods, most of them gods of lust. In fact, the gods were more immoral than the men who worshiped them. By the time of Plato the idea of one supreme God was discussed by the philosophers, but the common people continued with their idolatry. Many a seeking Greek, fed up with the immorality of the Olympian gods and disillusioned with the speculations of the pagan philosophers, turned with a sigh of relief to the ethical monotheism of Judaism, which preached the doctrine of one true God, Creator of heaven and earth, immanent and yet transcendent, mighty and yet merciful, who punishes sin and rewards virtue. No other religion had such an exalted doctrine. This was an immense stimulus toward attracting converts.

5. The practice of morality. Immorality ranked with idolatry as the two great sins of the pagan world. Its large cities were cesspools of iniquity. Divorce was widespread; infanticide was common. Paul's description of pagan society in Romans 1 is an accurate picture of the moral decadence of the Roman Empire. Tenney describes it graphically:

> Paganism was devoid of any power to lift it above itself, and the growing consciousness of its own impotence brought upon it a pessimism and a depression that it could not escape. Corruption in politics, debauchery in pleasure, fraud in business, deceit and superstition in religion made life in Rome depressing for the many and unendurable for the few.[11]

In contrast to this corruption was the wholesome domestic life of the Jewish people. Divorce was a rare occurrence. Children were regarded as a gift from God; consequently family life was sacred. Fathers taught the Law to their families, and every boy became a Son of the Law at thirteen years of age. Fathers also taught their sons a trade. Immorality was frowned on, with adultery punishable by death. Heathen families desirous of escaping the moral pollution of pagan society found a warm and welcome change in the high moral standards of Judaism. This too was a great drawing card.

6. The promise of a coming Savior. In the closing centuries of the

11. Merrill C. Tenney, *New Testament Survey* (Grand Rapids: Eerdmans Publishing Company, 1961), p. 59.

pre-Christian era there was in the Greco-Roman world an almost universal longing for a deliverer. The Greeks gave the world its greatest philosophers and Rome provided its greatest statesmen; but neither the lucubrations of the one nor the machinations of the other could solve the problems of society. Plato had suggested in *The Republic* that philosophers should be kings and kings should be philosophers; but there were few takers for his recipe, because as a rule philosophers don't make good kings and kings don't make good philosophers. Confucius tried it and failed. And even the philosophers were unable to live up to their own high standards. Consequently the man in the street, far removed from both philosopher and statesman, looked in vain for someone who could promise—and provide—the abundant life both here and hereafter.

Into this vacuum stepped the Jews with their centuries-old expectation of a coming Messiah. There was nothing vain or vague about this Figure. Both His person and His program were clearly outlined in the Hebrew Scriptures. He would be Prophet, Priest, and King, all in one. He would succeed where others had failed. Possessed of divine power and knowledge, He would establish a kingdom of universal peace based on absolute justice—something the world had dreamed of but never seen.

The Greco-Roman world listened, and liked what it heard. Thus Judaism became a missionary religion and helped prepare the way for Christianity.

2

Missions in the Gospels

At first sight there appears to be little missionary emphasis in the Gospel records. In the First Gospel Jesus is portrayed as the King of Israel, and the genealogy in chapter 1 traces His ancestry back through David to Abraham. In the first verse He is referred to as the "Son of David" and the "Son of Abraham." The emphasis is on Christ's mission to the Jewish people, not to the great Gentile world.

This is quite understandable. Paul tells us that Jesus was "descended from David according to the flesh" (Rom 1:3); consequently He was "born under the law" (Gal 4:4). He was circumcised according to the law (Lk 2:21); and when the time came for Mary's purification according to the law of Moses, they brought Him to Jerusalem to present Him to the Lord (Lk 2:22). They did not return to Nazareth until "they had performed everything according to the law of the Lord" (Lk 2:39). Thus He lived under the law; He also died under the law (Gal 3:13). In His teachings He both exalted and expounded the law, declaring that He had come not "to abolish the law and the prophets but to fulfil them" (Mt 5:17); and He warned His disciples against relaxing "one of the least of these commandments."

Even Paul, the great apostle to the Gentiles, declared that "Christ became a servant to the circumcision to show God's truthfulness, in order to confirm the promises given to the patriarchs" (Rom 15:8). Jesus told the woman of Samaria that "salvation is from the Jews" (Jn 4:22). To a Canaanite woman in the borders of Tyre and Sidon He said He was sent "only to the lost sheep of the house of Israel"

34

(Mt 15:24). Most of His public ministry was confined to the narrow limits of Palestine, Galilee in particular, and directed to the Jews there. When He sent out the Twelve on their first preaching mission He gave them strict instructions: "Go nowhere among the Gentiles, and enter no town of the Samaritans, but go rather to the lost sheep of the house of Israel" (Mt 10:5-6).

This was only right and proper, for as God's Messiah His first responsibility was to Israel. To them belonged "the sonship, the glory, the covenants, the giving of the law, the worship, the promises . . . and the patriarchs" (Rom 9:4-5). But they failed to recognize Him and rejected both Him and the offer of the kingdom He made to them. "He came to his own home, and his own people received him not" (Jn 1:11).

To substantiate His messianic claims Jesus performed many miracles in which He demonstrated His complete power over men, demons, and the powers of nature. Though His mighty works were unique in both number and quality (Jn 15:24), they failed to move the nation to repentance (Mt 11:20-24); whereupon He pronounced His woes on the cities of Galilee in which most of His mighty works were done. "Woe to you, Chorazin! woe to you, Bethsaida, for if the mighty works done in you had been done in Tyre and Sidon, they would have repented long ago in sackcloth and ashes" (Mt 11:21).

That marked the turning point in His relationship with Israel. *"From that time* Jesus *began* to show his disciples that he must go to Jerusalem and suffer many things from the elders and chief priests and scribes, and be killed, and on the third day be raised" (Mt 16:21). Later on in the same Gospel, Jesus in three striking parables—the two sons (21:28-32), the householder (21:33-45), and the marriage feast (22:1-14)—openly and officially rejected Israel, warning that the kingdom would be taken from them and given to others. And His enemies got the point, for they went about to kill Him.

While all this is perfectly true, it is also a fact that from the very beginning the ultimate worldwide mission of Jesus was known to Himself and a few chosen ones to whom this great mystery was revealed. This worldwide missionary thrust of the life and ministry of Christ may be seen in several ways.

The Purpose of the Incarnation

The New Testament clearly teaches a threefold purpose of the Incarnation.

The first purpose was to reveal God the Father. This comes out most clearly in John's Gospel. "The Word became flesh and dwelt among us, full of grace and truth; we have beheld his glory, glory as of the only Son from the Father. . . . No man has ever seen God; but the only Son, who is in the bosom of the Father, he has made him known" (Jn 1:14, 18). We have the same idea expressed even more precisely in the words of Jesus Himself: "I am the way, and the truth, and the life; no one comes to the Father but by me. If you had known me, you would have known my Father also; henceforth you know him and have seen him" (Jn 14:6-7).

The second purpose of the Incarnation was to destroy the devil. Man is not only a sinner in bondage to sin (Rom 7:14-20), he is also a slave to Satan and a captive in his kingdom of darkness (Mt 12:25-29). Before he can be delivered from that sinister power, Satan's kingdom must be invaded and his power destroyed. John in his first epistle says: "The reason the Son of God appeared was to destroy the works of the devil" (3:8). This He did on the cross. "Since therefore the children share flesh and blood, he himself likewise partook of the same nature, that through death he might destroy him who has the power of death, that is, the devil, and deliver all those who through fear of death were subject to life-long bondage" (Heb 2:14-15). Paul says virtually the same thing in Colossians 2:13-15.

The third purpose of the Incarnation was to save the world, not just the Jewish people. "For God so loved the *world* that he gave his only Son, that whoever believes in him should not perish but have eternal life. For God sent the Son into the world, not to condemn the world, but that the *world* might be saved through him" (Jn 3:16-17). John in his first epistle says: "We have seen and testify that the Father has sent the Son as the Savior of the *world*" (4:14). Paul insists that Christ "died for all" (2 Cor 5:14). Jesus Himself regarded His impending death as having universal appeal. "I, when I am lifted up from the earth, will draw *all men* to myself" (Jn 12:32). Again He said, "The Son of Man came not to be served but to serve, and to give his life a ransom for many" (Mt 20:28). Paul goes further and declares that the death of Christ had cosmic significance (Col 1:19).

The Circumstances Surrounding Christ's Birth

The birth of Christ is recorded by Luke in nineteen words: "She

[Mary] gave birth to her first-born Son and wrapped him in swaddling clothes and laid him in a manger" (Lk 2:7). Unlike the stories surrounding the birth of Buddha and Laotze, there is nothing vulgar or grotesque about the birth of Jesus. The miraculous element is reduced to an irreducible minimum. Only the act of conception was supernatural. The birth itself was quite natural. No one but an inspired writer would have been so brief in his description of so momentous an event.

The prenatal events contain two statements of great significance. In the *Magnificat* Mary begins by rejoicing in God her Savior and ends with a reference to God's covenant with Abraham in Genesis 12:1-3: "By you all the families of the earth shall bless themselves" (Lk 1:55). Zacharias, on the birth of his son, John the Baptist, uttered a prophetic word regarding the redemption of Israel, and tied it in with the covenant made by God to Abraham (Lk 1:72-75).

The first mention of the Good News of the gospel occurred when the angel of the Lord announced the birth of Christ to the shepherds: "Be not afraid; for behold I bring you good news of great joy which will come to all the people" (Lk 2:10). And the doxology voiced by the multitude of the heavenly host ascribed "glory to God in the highest, and on earth peace among men with whom he is pleased" (Lk 2:14).

At the presentation of Jesus in the Temple, Simeon makes reference to the universal scope of the coming kingdom and the inclusion of the Gentiles in the purposes of God (Lk 2:25-32). The Messiah is to be not only the glory of Israel but also a light to the Gentiles. And Matthew, whose Gospel was written primarily for the Jews, included in his record an account of the visit of the Wise Men from the East, who doubtless were Gentiles.

The Life and Ministry of Christ

As the promised Messiah of the nation of Israel, Jesus Christ was born of Jewish stock (Rom 1:3) and was known as the Son of David (Mt 1:1). Nevertheless it is not without significance that Jesus spent several years as a "displaced person" in Egypt. On His return He settled in Nazareth, a despised little town in the foothills of Galilee. Later on He moved to Capernaum, a more Gentile city than Nazareth. Even the synagogue there was built by a Roman centurion (Lk 7:5). Most of His public ministry was spent in "Galilee of the Gentiles" (Mt 4:15), which was not supposed to produce any prophets (Jn 7:52), much less the Messiah (Jn 1:46).

Unlike His compatriots, Jesus was free from racial prejudice. The fact that the Jews had no dealings with the Samaritans in no way deterred Him from preaching in that part of the country meticulously avoided by the Jews. Openly and unashamedly He conversed with the woman of Samaria, offering her the water of life. Following the conversation He remained two days and during that time many Samaritans believed (Jn 4:39-42).

On another occasion Jesus healed ten lepers, only one of whom returned to give glory to God, and he was a Samaritan (Lk 17:11-19). On still another occasion we find Him in Samaria on His way to Jerusalem. When the villagers refused to extend hospitality to Jesus and His disciples, James and John made the fantastic suggestion that they call down fire from heaven to consume the village. Jesus would have none of it. He simply rebuked His disciples, saying: "The Son of Man came not to destroy men's lives but to save them" (Lk 9:55).

His healing ministry went beyond the Samaritans, who were half-Jews, to the Romans, who were outright Gentiles. Mark informs us that His teaching and healing ministry extended far beyond the confines of Galilee and Judea to Idumaea, Transjordan, Tyre, and Sidon (Mk 3:7-8). Matthew speaks of His fame as having spread throughout all Syria, with great crowds following Him from Galilee and Decapolis (Mt 4:24-25).

According to the Gospels at least three recorded healings involved Gentiles. The first was the healing of the centurion's servant in Capernaum (Mt 8:5-13). So great was this man's faith that Jesus declared He had not found such faith among His own people. The second was that of the demon-possessed maniac in the country of the Gerasenes (Mk 5:1-20). Since he lived in a predominantly Gentile country, it is safe to assume that this man was a Gentile. In addition, the presence of a large number of swine would argue against a Jewish identification. The fact that Jesus was addressed not as the "Son of David" but as the "Son of the Most High God" further strengthens the argument.

The third case is that of the Syrophoenician woman whose daughter was healed in answer to the cry of faith. That this woman was a Gentile is made clear by the dialogue that took place between her and Jesus. Here again, Jesus was impressed with the remarkable faith of a Gentile (Mt 15:21-28).

The Teachings of Christ

Even before Jesus Christ began His public ministry in Galilee John the Baptist, whose mission it was to prepare the way of the Lord, was preaching his baptism of repentance. With thoughts that breathed and words that burned he called the Jewish people to an act of national repentance in preparation for the coming of their Messiah. He solemnly warned against a spiritual complacency that took for granted their standing before God. It was not enough to be "children of Abraham." They must possess the faith and do the works of Abraham; otherwise they would fare no better than anyone else. "Even now the axe is laid to the root of the trees; every tree therefore that does not bear fruit is cut down and thrown into the fire" (Mt 3:10). Was John here referring to the ultimate rejection of Israel and the inclusion of the Gentiles in the purposes of God? It could well be.

Particularly significant is the title that Jesus chose for Himself. Jesus' favorite title was not "Son of David" or "Son of Abraham," but "Son of Man." Socrates is always the Greek. Cicero is always the Roman. Confucius is always the Chinese. But Jesus is not to be identified with any one race or culture. Because He is the Lord from heaven He is the Universal Man. All others are from beneath; He alone is from above (Jn 8:23). As such He is forever above culture and beyond history. By adopting this title Jesus intended to make clear the universality of both His mission and His message.

> Jesus' promise of salvation to the nations, however, becomes fully clear only if we see it in the light of His Messianic declarations. We must consider here, first, the self-designation "Son of Man," which is borrowed from Daniel 7:13. It is a Messianic title which indicates universal dominion, though it also probably serves to *hide* Jesus' Messianic character during His ministry through Israel.... But it has been demonstrated beyond doubt that the Son-of-Man title is certainly intended to reflect the universal claims and the eschatological character of Jesus' Messianic commission, which first becomes fully clear during the trial before Caiaphas and *after* the resurrection.[1]

Nowhere is the universal nature of Christ's mission clearer than in His teachings. In His first sermon in the synagogue in Nazareth He claimed to fulfill the messianic prophecy of Isaiah 61 (Lk 4:16-21). The hearers were surprised and pleased. "All spoke well of him, and wondered at the gracious words which proceeded out of his mouth." But when He began to expound the passage, their pleasure turned to anger; for He had the temerity to make honorable mention of two well-known Gentiles in the Old Testament, the widow of Zarephath and Naaman the Syrian, both of whom were preferred by God over the Jews. Such "heresy" had never been heard in that synagogue before.

---

1. Johannes Blauw, *The Missionary Nature of the Church* (New York: McGraw-Hill, 1962), p. 69.

Their reaction was sullen and swift. Filled with anger they thrust Him out of the city and sought to destroy Him by pushing Him over the brow of the hill.

It seems perfectly clear from the Gospel of John that Jesus conceived of His mission in worldwide terms. The word *kosmos* (world) is used seventy-seven times, mostly by Jesus Himself. The opening verses set the tone for the entire book. "He was in the world, and the world was made through him, yet the world knew him not" (1:10). John the Baptist points Him out as the "Lamb of God who takes away the sin of the world" (1:29). The Samaritans acknowledge Him not simply as the Messiah of Israel but as the Savior of the world (4:42).

Equally clear are the sayings of Jesus Himself. He said, "God sent his Son into the world, not to condemn the world, but that the world might be saved through him" (3:17). He claimed to be "the light of the world" and promised that all who follow Him would never again walk in darkness (8:12). He offered men "the bread of life" and promised that He would give this bread "for the life of the world" (6:51). Speaking of the Crucifixion, He said, "I, when I am lifted up from the earth, will draw all men to myself" (12:32). He promised to send the Holy Spirit, declaring that when He came He would "convince the world of sin and of righteousness and of judgment" (16:8). In His last prayer for His disciples He prayed that through their witness the world might come to a knowledge of the one true God (17:21-23).

Even in the Synoptic Gospels there are clear indications of a wider dimension to the gospel as preached by Jesus. His immediate audience was made up almost exclusively of Jews and it was to them that His words were addressed, but the truths He proclaimed were as good for the Gentiles as for the Jews. He laid down principles that have universal application: "*Man* shall not live by bread alone" (Mt 4:4). "No *man* can serve two masters" (Mt 6:24). "The sabbath was made for *man,* not *man* for the sabbath" (Mk 2:27). "What can a *man* give in return for his life?" (Mk 8:37).

In His parable of the wheat and the tares He declared that "the field is the world" (Mt 13:38), not just Palestine or even the Roman Empire. When He cleansed the Temple He took the opportunity to remind the people that it was God's intention that the Temple should be a house of prayer not only for the Jews, but for "all the nations" (Mk 11:17). He said, "I have other sheep, that are not of this fold; I must bring them also, and they will heed my voice. So there shall be one flock, one shepherd" (Jn 10:16). This is an obvious reference to the Gentiles who, after His death and resurrection, would hear and accept the gospel of the grace of God and become part of His great family. It is not without significance that a despised Samaritan is singled

40

out by Jesus as the hero in one of His greatest parables (Lk 10:25-37). And the contrast is between the compassion of the Samaritan and the callous indifference of a priest and a Levite!

From first (Mt 4:23) to last (Acts 1:3), Jesus' teaching centered in the kingdom of God; but His concept of the kingdom differed radically from that of the Jews or even that of His own disciples. They looked for an earthly kingdom based on temporal power whose boundaries would have been no larger than those of Palestine. This comes out quite clearly in the very last question addressed to Jesus on the day of the Ascension: "Lord, will you at this time restore the kingdom to Israel?" (Acts 1:6). They expected the Messiah to be a political figure, a conquering Messiah who would deliver them from their enemies (Lk 1:73-74), not a suffering Messiah who would save them from their sins (Mt 1:21).

But the kingdom as defined by Jesus was to be an inner, spiritual kingdom (Lk 17:21), virtually closed to the worldly-wise (Mt 11:25) and the wealthy (Lk 18:25), but wide open to the meek (Mt 5:5), the poor (Lk 6:20), and even the publicans and harlots, if they repented (Mt 21:32). It was to be spiritual in character (Rom 14:17), universal in scope (Mt 25:31-36), cosmopolitan in composition (Mt 8:11), and eternal in duration (Lk 1:33). It was to be founded on truth, not power (Jn 8:31-32); governed by love, not law (Rom 13:8-10); dedicated to peace, not war (Jn 18:33-38). Its rulers were to be servants, not lords (Mt 20:25-28). Its citizens were to be meek, merciful, pure, peaceful, and forgiving (Mt 5:5-11). Above all they were to possess a new kind of righteousness greater than that of the scribes and Pharisees (Mt 5:20).

Two incidents in the ministry of Christ call for comment, for they appear to contradict what has been said up to this point. The first is His instructions when sending out the Twelve and the other is His treatment of the Syrophoenician woman.

His instructions to the Twelve were clear: "Go nowhere among the Gentiles, and enter no town of the Samaritans, but go rather to the lost sheep of the house of Israel" (Mt 10:5-6). At first glance this appears to completely preclude the Gentiles, but we must bear in mind that this was a particular mission with an immediate purpose and a limited goal. He had to begin *somewhere,* and the most natural place to begin was with His own people. Moreover, the time was short. Not all the centers of Jewish life could be covered in the allotted time before the "coming" of the Son of Man (Mt 10:23). To have sent the disciples *at that time* on a worldwide preaching mission would have served no purpose. What message did they have *at that time* for the Gentile world? Obviously none. The offer of the messianic kingdom must first be made to God's covenant people. If they rejected the offer, they would forfeit their prior claim to both the covenant and the promises. What is more, their rejection of the kingdom was to involve the death of the King, at which time "all men" would be drawn to Him (Jn 12:32).

> Jesus at first kept this universality of the new community relatively hidden, as He did with the power and authority given Him [Mt 28:18], and with the name of Messiah (Mt 16:20). Why? The previous, historical Israel had not yet run its course before Jesus' death. His life had not yet been spent as a ransom for many. Not everything was ready yet. The table had not been set. The guests could not yet be invited. Israel was not yet fully prepared to fulfill its eschatological mission. Aware of this "not yet," Jesus understood His mission to be—temporarily—to the lost sheep of the house of Israel.[2]

Jesus' treatment of the Syrophoenician woman is the strangest episode in His ministry. On the surface it seems that here Jesus was completely out of character. Instead of responding to the woman's plea for help, He callously remarked: "It is not fair to take the children's bread and throw it to the dogs." But the woman took the rebuke in her stride: "Yes, Lord, yet even the dogs eat the crumbs that fall from their master's table" (Mt 15:27). Greatly pleased with the woman's response, Jesus answered, "O woman, great is your faith! Be it done for you as you desire." And the daughter was healed.

Mark in his Gospel adds a significant statement not found in Matthew: "Let the children *first* be fed" (Mk 7:27). This places the whole episode in an entirely different light. Even here Jesus implies that the Gentiles were to be included. It was simply a matter of time.

In the Old Testament God's covenant was with Israel and all His blessings were promised to them. But here and there exceptions were found—the widow of Zarephath and Naaman the Syrian, to say nothing of Jonah's preaching to Nineveh.

> The so-called exceptions in Jesus' ministry to the Jews fit into the same category as those mentioned above. He came as the last messenger under the old covenant dispensation, and though His mission was primarily to Israel He shewed mercy to Gentiles as well. This was an indication of how the blessing promised to Abraham was indeed to flow to the Gentiles, as well as being a warning to Israel that the kingdom was to be taken away from her and given to a nation bringing forth the fruits thereof.[3]

2. Karl Barth, "An Exegetical Study of Matthew 28:16-20," *The Theology of the Christian Mission,* ed. Gerald H. Anderson (Nashville: Abingdon Press, 1961), p. 65.
3. A. M. Harman, "Missions in the Thought of Jesus," *The Evangelical Quarterly* (July-September 1969), p. 140.

The Post-Resurrection Teaching

The significant turning point in the ministry of Jesus was His death by crucifixion and His resurrection. Both events were part of God's original plan—not simply an incident, much less an accident, of human history (Acts 4:27-28). That Jesus from the beginning was aware of His impending death is clear from His frequent references to His "hour" as not yet come (Jn 2:4; 7:30; 8:20) and later on as having come (Jn 12:23; 13:1; 17:1). The Crucifixion was regarded by the disciples as a great disaster (Lk 24:21), but the Resurrection transformed it into a glorious victory (Col 2:13-15). He is no longer simply Jesus of Nazareth; He is also the Prince of life (Acts 3:15) and the Lord of glory (1 Cor 2:8), the "blessed and only Potentate, the King of kings and Lord of lords" (1 Tim 6:15). All authority in heaven and on earth is given to Him (Mt 28:18), including authority to forgive sins (Acts 5:31), to bestow life (Jn 17:2), and to execute judgment (Jn 5:22; Acts 17:31).

Having obtained by His death and resurrection eternal redemption (Heb 9:12) for the sins of the whole world (1 Jn 2:2), Jesus Christ is now the "Savior of the world" (1 Jn 4:14) and the "heir of all things" (Heb 1:2). As a reward for His life of perfect obedience He was exalted by God to His own right hand (Phil 2:9-11; Heb 1:3), "far above all rule and authority and power and dominion" (Eph 1:21). And God the Father said to God the Son: "Ask of me and I will make the nations your heritage, and the ends of the earth your possession" (Ps 2:8).

It is quite possible that Jesus had Psalm 2 in mind when He gave His disciples the Great Commission: "Go into all the world and preach the gospel to the whole creation" (Mk 16:15), "and make disciples of all nations" (Mt 28:19).

The Great Commission is recorded in all four Gospels and Acts 1. It is expressed in five different forms but the substance is the same. It is not necessary to believe that these passages are five different versions of one isolated command. Jesus spent forty days with His disciples between the Resurrection and the Ascension, during which time He gave them further instructions concerning the kingdom of God (Acts 1:3). It is safe to assume that the Great Commission was a major part of those instructions. The earliest announcement came on Easter Day (Jn 20:19-23); the last one occurred on Ascension Day (Acts 1:6-8).

There are many reasons why the church should engage in world evangelism, but the paramount reason is the command of Christ. "We engage in evangelism today not because we want to or because we choose to or because we like to, but because we have been told to. The

43

Church is under orders. The risen Lord has commanded us to 'go,' to 'preach,' to 'make disciples,' and that is enough for us."[4]

Jesus Christ is both the Head of the church and the Commander-in-chief of the army of occupation that He left behind to bring the nations of the world to the obedience of faith (Rom 1:5). The Great Commission represents His marching orders to the church for all time to come. This is her supreme task. When the church ceases to be a missionary church she has denied her faith and betrayed her trust.

The earliest and shortest form of the Great Commission is summed up in a single sentence: "As the Father has sent me, even so I send you" (Jn 20:21). The worldwide mission of the church is nothing new, it is an extension of Christ's mission. As Christ was the incarnation of God, the church is the incarnation of Christ. Jesus Christ remains with the church (Mt 28:20), lives in the church (Col 1:27), and works through the church (Mk 16:20). Her mission is simply a continuation of His. To persecute the church is to persecute Christ (Acts 9:4). The church, Christ, and God are all linked together in the work of mission: "He who receives you," said Jesus, "receives me, and he who receives me receives him who sent me" (Mt 10:40).

It is pertinent to ask: "How did God send Christ?" If our mission is an extension of His, then His mission should set the pattern for ours. Three things were true of His mission and should be true of ours.

(1) *The principle of identification.* Although in His own person He was "holy, blameless, unstained and separated from sinners" (Heb 7:26), yet in His ministry He deliberately and consistently identified Himself with sinners. Over the protest of John the Baptist He insisted on submitting to the baptism of repentance when He knew full well He had nothing for which to repent (Mt 3:13-17). To the despair and disgust of the scribes and Pharisees He fraternized with publicans and sinners (Lk 15:1-2). And on the cross He hung between two malefactors (Lk 23:32-33). All who would engage in the Christian mission must have the mind of Christ and be willing to do the same (Phil 2:5-9).

(2) *The threefold pattern of service: preaching, teaching, and healing.* Jesus "went about all Galilee teaching in their synagogues and preaching the gospel of the kingdom and healing every disease and every infirmity among the people" (Mt 4:23). Man as created by God is a unity made up of body, mind, and soul. All three parts of man were involved in the Fall. All three must be included in redemption. Jesus was not content to save a man's soul without at the same time offering him healing for body and mind. He recognized that sorrow,

---

4. John R. W. Stott, "The Great Commission," *One Race, One Gospel, One Task* (Minneapolis: World Wide Publications, 1967), I:37.

suffering, disease, and death are all part of the kingdom of Satan that He came to destroy (Mt 12:22-29; Heb 2:14; 1 Jn 3:8). Therefore He offered healing for the whole man: body, mind, and soul. Only when all three forms of healing were received, was the person "made whole." This is why the modern missionary movement has not only built churches, but has maintained hospitals and schools as well. All are an integral part of the missionary program.

(3) *The power of the Holy Spirit.* At the baptism of Jesus the Holy Spirit descended in the form of a dove and rested on Him (Mt 3:16). This special anointing was to prepare Him for His public ministry (Lk 4:18). It was in the power of the Holy Spirit that He "went about doing good and healing all that were oppressed by the devil" (Acts 10:38). It was through the Holy Spirit that He offered Himself to God on the cross (Heb 9:14). It was in the power of that same Holy Spirit that He rose from the dead (Rom 1:4). If Jesus' mission was carried out from first to last in the power of the Holy Spirit, it stands to reason that our mission is equally dependent on the same power (Acts 1:8).

The Great Commission

The longest, best-known, and most quoted form of the Great Commission is that found in Matthew 28. It begins with a declaration, continues with a commission, and concludes with a promise.

Jesus begins by claiming to possess all authority in heaven and on earth. This is a clear reference to His exalted position as King of kings and Lord of lords, an honor conferred on Him by God the Father (Jn 17:1, 5) in recognition of His obedience as the Son of Man in the days of His flesh (Phil 2:5-11). By His death on the cross He destroyed Satan and all his emissaries (Col 2:15). By His resurrection He robbed death of its sting and the grave of its victory (1 Cor 15:55-56). Chronologically the Ascension was still a few days away, but in the thought of Jesus it was already an accomplished fact. By His exaltation to the right hand of the Majesty on high (Heb 1:3) He became the undisputed Ruler of the universe. All things have been put under His feet. He is now the Head of the church (Eph 1:21-23) and the King of the ages (Rev 15:3-4). There is no conceivable power—human or demonic, natural or supernatural—that is not subject to His absolute rule.

He is now the sole Sovereign and Savior of the world. He purchased their redemption with His blood; hence all peoples rightly belong to Him and owe Him the obedience of faith. He has destroyed the demonic power structures of this present evil world system; hence all nations are now under His dominion and all men are subject to His law. He is the universal Lord; He is the cosmic Christ. Sooner or later all men (Rom 14:11) and all nations (Rev 11:15) must come to terms with Him (Ps 2:7-12).

It was in the light of these great facts that Jesus announced the Great Commission. This is clear by the use of the word "therefore." It is His person and His power that form the basis of the worldwide mission of the church. There is a direct and necessary connection between the universal lordship of Jesus Christ and the worldwide mission of the Christian church. Without the first the second would be cultural imperialism. Without the second the first would be little more than an empty cliché on the lips of a presumptuous church. Jesus is not a Jewish Messiah. Christianity is not a Western religion. The peoples of the world, East and West, are not asked to join *us* but to follow *Him*.

Four important words are found in the Great Commission: "go," "make disciples," "baptize," and "teach."

It is generally assumed that the word "go" is an imperative verb and constitutes the last command of Christ. This is not correct. The word "go" is not an imperative. It is an aorist participle and should be translated "having gone" or "as you go." This in no way diminishes the full force of the statement. It was not really necessary for Jesus to command the disciples to "go" into the world. He took for granted that in the ordinary course of events or as a result of persecution they would soon find themselves scattered to all parts of the empire. This is exactly what happened (Acts 8:4; 11:19-21). The geographical location was not important. Wherever they went they were expected to be the salt of the earth and the light of the world.

It was not long before the early Christians were scattered abroad. They resided for the most part in the cities, where they lived their lives, reared their children, and plied their trades side by side with their pagan neighbors. Little by little, without fuss or fanfare, these simple, wholesome, joyous Christians made their presence felt and their secret known. The light was shining. The salt was penetrating. The leaven of the gospel was working its way through the fabric of society. By the year 200 the Christian presence had become so pervasive that Tertullian could write: "We are a new group but have already penetrated all areas of imperial life—cities, islands, villages, towns, market-places, even the camp, tribes, palace, senate, the law-court. There is nothing left for you but your temples."[5]

The second word, "make disciples," is the only imperative in Mat-

---

5. Tertullian, *Apology* 37.

thew's version of the Great Commission. The word is usually found in noun form. Only here in the New Testament is the verb form used. In the Greek only one word is used, and should be translated "disciple" the nations.

Actually there was nothing new in the concept of discipleship. Some years before, Jesus had made disciples by calling them to follow Him. "Follow me," He said, "and I will make you fishers of men" (Mt 4:19). Having been intimately associated with Christ in His public ministry, they knew exactly what was involved in making disciples. They had by this time been with Him for three years; their period of discipleship training was over. He was about to return to heaven and they would be on their own.

The act of making disciples was not to be confined to Israel, but was to extend to "all nations." The entire world is His by right of creation (Jn 1:3) and redemption (Jn 3:17). It now became their task to win that world for Christ.

As His ambassadors (2 Cor 5:20) they were invested with His power (Acts 3:12-16) and authorized to act in His name (Acts 3:6; 4:10). Everywhere they went they announced the advent of the new age. In former times God "allowed all nations to walk in their own ways" (Acts 14:16), but now He "commands all men everywhere to repent" (Acts 17:30) and "confess that Jesus Christ is Lord" (Phil 2:11).

Two words remain to be examined: "baptizing" and "teaching." These two words are participles and not, therefore, to be understood as a command. Rather they indicate the method by which disciples are to be made.

The New Testament has more to say about teaching than about baptizing. Jesus engaged extensively in the former; the latter He delegated to His disciples (Jn 4:2). Paul spent much of his time in teaching (Col 1:28) and had very little to say about baptizing. Apparently he too left that to his disciples (1 Cor 1:14-16). (This is not to suggest that baptism is not important.)

In the New Testament there are two kinds of baptism: water baptism and baptism in or by the Holy Spirit. By the latter form of baptism the believer is united to Christ and becomes part of His body, the church (1 Cor 12:13). This transaction is spiritual, invisible, irrevocable, and infallible. It has nothing to do with water baptism, which is administered by man, not God.

Water baptism is the sign or symbol of a change of heart leading to a change of life. By this act the believer is identified with Christ. By participation in the death of Christ the "old self" is said to have "died with Christ." By participation in the resurrection of Christ, the believer is said to "walk in newness of life" (Rom 6:1-6). Baptism represents a radical break with the past and the promise of a new life to come.

Baptism is a public act by which the new believer openly identifies himself with Jesus Christ and confesses before the world his allegiance to his new King. The New Testament knows nothing of *secret* believers. Confession of Christ is always "before men" (Mt 10:26-33). For a time Joseph of Arimathaea was a secret disciple, but the cross put an end to that (Jn 19:38-40).

Teaching is the second method by which disciples are made. Those who practice infant or household baptism make much of the fact that baptism precedes teaching in the Great Commission. Those who practice adult or believers' baptism insist that teaching comes first and prepares the way for baptism.

One thing is certain: Baptism is a single transaction; teaching is an endless process. In the New Testament, teaching comes both before and after baptism. It was after a clear presentation of the truth that Peter on the day of Pentecost called on his compatriots to "repent and be baptized" (Acts 2:38). Even the Ethiopian eunuch was asked by Philip: "Do you understand what you are reading?" Only after Philip had "told him the good news of Jesus" was he baptized (Acts 8:26-38).

But teaching does not stop with baptism. Jesus said to the Jews who had believed in Him: "If you continue in my word, you are truly my disciples, and you will know the truth, and the truth will make you free" (Jn 8:31-32). And the teaching-learning process was to continue after the Ascension, for Jesus said: "When the Spirit of truth is come, he will guide you into all the truth" (Jn 16:13). It was said of the early church that they "devoted themselves to the apostles' teaching and fellowship" (Acts 2:42). We think of Paul as the great missionary, but much of his missionary work involved teaching. Toward the end of his life he wrote: "Him [Christ] we proclaim, warning every man and teaching every man in all wisdom, that we may present every man mature in Christ" (Col 1:28). The teaching process continues "until we all attain to the unity of the faith and of the knowledge of the Son of God, to mature manhood, to the measure of the stature of the fullness of Christ" (Eph. 4:13).

Two things are worth noting about teaching in the Great Commission. *First,* the disciples were to include in their teaching *all* that Jesus had imparted to them. That included the "hard sayings" (Jn 6:60) that offended so many of His disciples. It included not only John 3:16 and Matthew 11:28, but Matthew 10:37-39 and Mark 9:43-50. It included not only the parable of the Prodigal Son (Lk 15:11-32), but also the parable of the Last Judgment (Mt 25:31-46). It included His teaching on sin, death, judgment, and hell as well as His teaching on forgiveness, love, heaven, and eternal life. It included the Sermon on the Mount with its high ethical standards as well as His talks with Nicodemus and the woman of Samaria. In short, it included *all* the teachings of Jesus.

Second, the teachings of Jesus must be regarded as commandments. The disciples were to pass on to others all that Jesus had "commanded" them. As far as the treatment of the world was concerned, there was little difference between Master and disciple. Both would receive the same harsh treatment (Mt 10:24-25). But when it came to their relationship to one another, there was no doubt who was in charge. He spoke with a full understanding of God (Mt 11:27) and man (Jn 2:24), and taught with complete authority (Mt 7:28-29). He declared that His words were "spirit and life" (Jn 6:63), that they would outlast heaven and earth (Mt 24:35), and would rise up in the last day to judge all men (Jn 12:48). His sayings are the very foundation of all Christian life and truth, and the person who takes his stand on them is building on solid rock (Mt 7:24-27).

The disciple then is not at liberty to pick and choose. He does not have the right to accept what he likes and reject what he does not. Jesus does not peddle platitudes or offer advice, He issues commands. He does not plead for patronage or solicit support, He demands utter and complete allegiance. Because His truths are eternal, His claims are absolute. He is the King of truth and always speaks with authority.

Campus Crusade for Christ Library

3

Missions in the Acts
of the Apostles

The Acts of the Apostles occupies a strategic place in the canon of the New Testament. It forms a bridge between the Gospels, which are biographical, and the Epistles, which are hortatory. The Acts of the Apostles is the only historical book in the New Testament. Without it we would know nothing of the churches to which the Epistles were written. We would also know nothing of the apostle Paul, who was the author of thirteen books, not including Hebrews. Without the book of Acts we would be completely in the dark regarding the spread of the gospel from Galilee—where it began—to Antioch, Ephesus, Corinth, and Rome.

As a historian Luke was careful to ascertain and evaluate his facts before committing them to writing (Lk 1:1-4). He was careful to point out the direct connection between his Gospel and the Acts. In the preface to his second book Luke says: "In the first book, O Theophilus, I have dealt with all that Jesus began to do and teach, until the day when he was taken up" (Acts 1:1-2). The Gospel of Luke ends and the Acts of the Apostles begins with the same event—the Ascension. In the former Luke deals with what Jesus *began* to do and teach when He was here in person. The book of Acts is the account of what the risen Christ *continued* to do and teach through the twelve apostles whom He had trained for the purpose.

Another connecting link between the Gospels and the Acts is the statement of Jesus in John 20:21: "As the Father has sent me, even so I send you." Jesus Christ launched the Christian mission; the

50

apostles were to carry it on. Their mission was to be a continuation of His—designed for the same purpose, endowed with the same power, entrusted with the same message.

The key verse is Acts 1:8: "But you shall receive power when the Holy Spirit has come upon you; and you shall be my witnesses in Jerusalem, and in all Judea and Samaria, and to the end of the earth." It is obvious that Luke built his entire book around that verse. The book divides into three clearly defined parts and traces the expansion of Christianity in concentric circles, beginning with Jerusalem (1–7), progressing to Judea and Samaria (8–12), extending ultimately to the ends of the earth (13–28).

The two important words in verse 8 are "power" and "witnesses." These two words form the motif for the entire book. The Resurrection made the disciples witnesses; Pentecost provided the power to make their witness effective.

Graham Scroggie in his book, *Know Your Bible,* finds four important concepts in Acts 1:8: (1) The central theme of the Christian witness is Christ. (2) The exclusive medium of the Christian witness is the church. (3) The ultimate scope of the Christian witness is the world. (4) The unfailing secret of the Christian witness is the Holy Spirit.

From Disciples to Apostles

When we pass from the Gospels to the Acts of the Apostles we find ourselves in a new world. The disciples are the same, and yet they are not the same. They are new men. In the Gospels they are disciples, in the Acts they have become apostles. It is true that they are sometimes referred to as apostles in the Gospels. Certainly Jesus endowed them with apostolic power when He sent them out to preach (Mt 10:1). But to the end they continued to act more like disciples than apostles.

In the Gospels they were timid, uncertain, selfish, quarrelsome, and disobedient. They were followers, not leaders; learners, not teachers. And even as learners they didn't do very well. Time and again Jesus had to rebuke them for their lack of faith. On more than one occasion they were nonplussed by His teaching. As followers, they walked more by sight than by faith. Their sense of security depended to a large measure on the physical presence of Jesus. When that was missing they were fearful and uncertain. And when the end came and Jesus was arrested, all but John forsook Him and fled.

We turn the page to the book of Acts and discover that a mighty transformation has taken place. The disciples are now full-fledged apostles with all the rights and privileges that belong to that high office.

1. Events that contributed to the change. It is a law of nature that in any change the cause must be commensurate with the effect. This was certainly true in the case of the apostles. Such a dramatic transformation could be brought about only by events of the first magnitude. Three such events occurred during a fifty-day period.

(1) *The Resurrection.* The resurrection of Jesus Christ from the dead is the greatest event in the history of mankind. As a historic event it is unique in the annals of religion. No other person, before or since, ever rose from the dead in the power of an endless life. This one event, more than anything else, places Jesus Christ in a class by Himself. It was the supreme event that changed the course of history, by changing the men most immediately concerned. The fact that the event was totally unexpected on the part of the disciples only served to enhance its significance in their eyes. For the first time it dawned on them that Jesus was in truth what He claimed to be—the resurrection and the life. Thus the apostles in the Acts refer to Him as the "Prince" or "Author" of life (Acts 3:15).

(2) *The Ascension.* This epochal event took place forty days after the Resurrection and marked the climactic end of the earthly life of Jesus. By means of the Ascension Jesus of Nazareth is exalted to the "right hand of the Majesty on high" (Heb 1:3), far above "all rule and authority and power and dominion" (Eph 1:21). No longer is He the Man of Galilee, He is now the "Lord of glory" (1 Cor 2:8). The apostles witnessed this event and knew something of its significance (Acts 1:9-11), and it became an essential part of their message (Acts 2:33).

(3) *Pentecost.* Ten days after the Ascension the risen and exalted Christ sent the Holy Spirit to indwell the disciples, to unite them into one body, and to empower them for their worldwide ministry. This is the most important event recorded in the Acts of the Apostles. Indeed, the book would not make sense without the experience of Pentecost. It was that singular event that made possible the presence and power of the Holy Spirit, without which the early church would have been impotent.

2. The change in the disciples. The transformation from disciples to apostles was in some ways more profound than their first encounter with Christ in the beginning of His public ministry. In the book of Acts these men act, think, and work like apostles, fully conscious of their new role. This is seen in several ways.

(1) *A new insight into Scripture.* In the Gospels the disciples

were very slow to comprehend the teaching of Jesus. After hearing the parable of the tares they required further instruction (Mt 13:36). When He foretold His impending death, they refused to entertain the idea (Mt 16:21-22). To the very end the Old Testament remained a closed book so far as their spiritual understanding was concerned (Lk 24:25-27). No such spiritual blindness characterizes them now. On the day of Pentecost Peter has no hesitation in explaining the phenomenon of Pentecost. Quoting the prophecy of Joel (2:28-32), he declares with authority: "This is what was spoken by the prophet Joel" (Acts 2:16). In that same discourse he interprets David's words in Psalm 16 as referring not to David but to Christ (Acts 2:25-31). This kind of insight into the Old Testament was something new.

(2) *A new initiative in action.* While Jesus was with the disciples they were content to have Him give the orders. They worked alongside of Him but were reluctant to initiate any work of their own. Now that is all changed. When the early church faces its first major problem, relating to the distribution of food, the apostles, instead of being content to "pray about the matter," rise to the occasion and come up with a practical solution that solves the problem and sets them free for the more spiritual ministry to which they were called. When the Samaritans respond to the preaching of Philip, the apostles in Jerusalem take it on themselves to send Peter and John to investigate the situation to make sure it is something to which they can give their sanction (Acts 8:14-25). When the controversy between law and grace threatens to divide the church, the apostles gather in Jerusalem to consider the matter; and they agree on a formula that is satisfactory to all (Acts 15).

(3) *A new power in service.* In the Gospels the disciples were given power to heal the sick and cast out demons (Mt 10:1), but they were not always successful (Mt 17:14-21). No such problem appears in the Acts. They always speak and act with conscious power. They heal the sick (Acts 3:1-10) and cast out demons (Acts 16:16-18). One word from Peter, and Ananias and Sapphira fall dead at his feet (Acts 5:1-10). Peter pronounces a curse on Simon Magus in Samaria (Acts 8:20-23) and Paul does the same with Elymas on the island of Cyprus (Acts 13:10-12). In Joppa Peter raises Dorcas from the dead (Acts 9:36-42). At the first church council in Jerusalem the whole assembly listens to Paul and Barnabas as they relate "what signs and wonders God had done through them among the Gentiles" (Acts 15:12). It is no exaggeration to say with J. B. Phillips that the book of Acts throbs with power.

(4) *A new courage in witnessing.* While Jesus was still with them, the disciples boasted of their courage and declared that they would

follow Him even to death; but no sooner was their Master arrested than they took to their heels and fled for their lives. The first Easter Day found them huddled together in the upper room "for fear of the Jews" (Jn 20:19). Following Pentecost they are still in the upper room, but the fear is gone. The danger has not lessened—indeed, it has increased; but they are unperturbed. Their one concern is to preach the Good News of the death and resurrection of Jesus Christ. When the Sanhedrin forbids them to teach or preach in the name of Jesus, they simply reply: "Whether it is right in the sight of God to listen to you rather than to God, you must judge; for we cannot but speak what we have seen and heard" (Acts 4:19-20). Later, when asked why they failed to comply with the prohibition imposed by the Sanhedrin, the apostles reply: "We must obey God rather than man" (Acts 5:29). After their first encounter with the Sanhedrin the apostles return to the upper room and resort to prayer; and in their prayer they ask, not for deliverance from persecution, but for boldness to preach the Word without fear (Acts 4:29).

The Content of the Witness

One of the qualifications of an apostle was personal identification with Christ in the days of His flesh, as well as being an eye-witness of the Resurrection (1 Cor 9:1; Acts 1:22). Both Peter and John make much of the fact that their intimate association with Christ made it possible for them to speak with integrity and authority (2 Pet 1:16-18; 1 Jn 1:1-3).

These twelve men spent three full years with Jesus, during which they saw Him under every conceivable circumstance of life; and at the end of that time even doubting Thomas came to the conclusion that He was the Son of God (Jn 20:28). They witnessed every major miracle He performed; they heard every major address He gave. They were persuaded that both His words and His works were from God. Consequently they had no need to invent a story or propound a theory, still less to concoct a lie. As for the Resurrection, it was no "Easter story" that they believed. So far as they were concerned it was an indisputable fact that Jesus Christ rose from the dead. They saw the empty tomb. They met the risen Lord and were completely transformed as a result of that experience. They were there when it happened, and it happened to them.

The apostles did not regard themselves as ecclesiastical bureaucrats, nor had they any ambition to become eloquent preachers or erudite theologians. They were simple, open-minded, warmhearted individuals who had seen the glory of God in the face of Jesus Christ and had a consuming passion to share their faith with the rest of the world. To the very end they regarded themselves as witnesses—no more, no less. Even Paul, the greatest theologian of all time, could say at the close of his life: "To this day I have had the help that comes from God, and so I stand here *testifying* both to small and great, saying nothing but what the prophets and Moses said would come to pass: that Christ must suffer, and that, by being the first to rise from the dead, he would proclaim light both to the people and to the Gentiles" (Acts 26:22-23).

The witness of the apostles revolved around a central theme: Jesus Christ. Peter at Pentecost said: "This Jesus God raised up, and of that we all are witnesses" (Acts 2:32). Philip went down to the city of Samaria and "proclaimed to them the Christ" (Acts 8:5). When he met the Ethiopian eunuch he told him "the good news of Jesus" (Acts 8:35). Paul summed it all up when he said: "For what we preach is not ourselves, but Jesus Christ as Lord" (2 Cor 4:5). Their witness included four important truths regarding Christ.

1. The identity of His person. Jesus presented Himself to the Jewish people as their Messiah, but they rejected both Him and His offer of the kingdom because they expected a different kind of Messiah. They were looking for a powerful political figure who would break the yoke of Rome and restore the kingdom to Israel. Instead, Jesus ended His life on a cross between two malefactors. The Jewish leaders could not bring themselves to believe that Jesus, the carpenter of Nazareth, was their long-expected Messiah. His humble origin, His mild manner, His pacific purpose—all these combined to render Him totally unacceptable to the Jewish leaders bent on the overthrow of Roman power in Palestine. It was unthinkable that such a person could possibly be the Messiah.

When the apostles, barely fifty days after the Resurrection, stood up in Jerusalem and preached the gospel to the Jews, they were fully aware of the millstone that was round their necks. How could they possibly persuade the Jews that this despised Jesus of Nazareth really *was* their Messiah? The task was enormously difficult. Humanly speaking, there wasn't one chance in a thousand that they would make any converts. The offense of the cross, as Paul called it, was a stumbling block of major proportions. Nevertheless the apostles went ahead anyway and preached the truth as they understood it. They refused to dodge the issue or soften the blow. They were convinced that Jesus *was* the Christ and they proceeded to bear witness to that fact.

And how did they do it? They based their approach on two considerations: the prophecies of the Old Testament and the mighty works that accompanied Jesus' ministry.

(1) *The prophecies of the Old Testament.* In dealing with the Jews it was absolutely essential that any new doctrine be in line with the teaching of their Holy Scriptures. If the Jews were to acknowledge Jesus as their Messiah, it would have to be on the basis of their own Scriptures. This the apostles understood, and acted accordingly. They remembered their own unbelief and the Bible lesson the risen Lord gave them on the way to Emmaus, when He said: "O foolish men, and slow of heart to believe all that the prophets have spoken! Was it not necessary that the Christ should suffer these things and enter into his glory?" And Luke adds: "And beginning with Moses and all the prophets, he interpreted to them in all the scriptures the things concerning himself" (Lk 24:25-27).

That last verse is very important. It throws light on the method used by the apostles in the book of Acts. They too began with Moses and all the prophets and proved from the Scriptures that Jesus was the Christ (Acts 3:18; 13:29; 17:2-3).

They made no attempt to conceal the guilt of the Jews in the Crucifixion. In terms that were unmistakably clear they accused the Jewish leaders of crucifying their own Messiah (Acts 3:13-15), but they went on to say that in that very act they fulfilled their own Scriptures (Acts 13:27). The death of Christ was part of God's eternal plan (Acts 2:23); and all that Pilate, Herod, and Caiaphas were able to do was to help God accomplish His own purpose (Acts 4:27-28).

If the Jews had read their Scriptures correctly they would have expected a suffering, not a conquering, Messiah, and would not have considered Jesus to be an impostor.

(2) *The mighty works in the ministry of Jesus.* On one occasion the Jews asked Jesus: "How long will you keep us in suspense? If you are the Christ, tell us plainly." Jesus replied: "I told you and you do not believe. The works that I do in my Father's name they bear witness to me" (Jn 10:24-25). The apostles adopted the same approach. They appealed to the miracles as a sign of God's approval of Jesus. Peter in his sermon at Pentecost said: "Men of Israel, hear these words: Jesus of Nazareth, a man attested to you by God with mighty works and wonders and signs which God did through him in your midst, as you yourselves know—this Jesus, delivered up according to the definite plan and foreknowledge of God, you crucified and killed by the hands of lawless men" (Acts 2:22-23).

The works of Christ were in a class by themselves (Jn 15:24). They were works of grace and power, sufficient to convince any open, honest mind that He was a "prophet mighty in deed and word before

God and all the people" (Lk 24:19). Even Nicodemus, a ruler of the Jews, had to acknowledge: "Rabbi, we know that you are a teacher come from God; for no one can do these signs that you do, unless God is with him" (Jn 3:2).

When John the Baptist in prison had second thoughts about the mission of Jesus, he sent two of his disciples to ask Him: "Are you he who is to come [the Messiah], or shall we look for another?" Jesus replied: "Go and tell John what you hear and see: the blind receive their sight and the lame walk, lepers are cleansed and the deaf hear, and the dead are raised up, and the poor have the good news preached to them. And blessed is he who takes no offense at me" (Mt 11:2-6). Jesus did not do what the Jews expected Him to do, but He did do what their own Scriptures had foretold He would do (Is 35:4-6) and thus had God's seal of approval on Him.

The apostles in their teaching hammered home the truth that in spite of His humble origin and His refusal to speak out against Roman rule, Jesus of Nazareth was indeed the King of the Jews; and their failure to recognize Him as such was due to ignorance (Acts 3:17). They hoped to dispel this ignorance by proving from the Scriptures and from the miracles that Jesus was their Messiah.

2. The nature of His death. That Jesus died under Pontius Pilate about the year A.D. 30 is a matter of history. That He died for the sins of the world is a matter of revelation (1 Cor 15:3). For clearly, we would not have known it had it not been revealed to us in the Scriptures.

When Jesus first announced His impending death, the idea was strenuously rejected by the disciples. Peter went so far as to rebuke Him, saying: "God forbid, Lord! This shall never happen to you" (Mt 16:22). After it had taken place they regarded it as a dire calamity (Lk 24:21), and decided to return to their fishing business (Jn 21:3). But the Resurrection changed all that, and we find the apostles in their preaching and writings declaring the great truth of the atonement through the death of Christ.

Far from being a tragedy, the death of Christ was the atoning death of the Lamb of God foreordained from before the foundation of the world (1 Pet 1:18-20). Because of His sacrificial death on the cross, His flesh is meat indeed and His blood is drink indeed (Jn 6:55). The death of Christ is spoken of as a sacrifice (Heb 9:26) and compared to the paschal lamb mentioned in Exodus (1 Cor 5:7). Paul says He died "for our sins" (1 Cor 15:3). Peter says He died "the righteous for the unrighteous, that he might bring us to God" (1 Pet 3:18). Again he says: "He himself bore our sins in his body on the tree that we might die to sin and live to righteousness" (1 Pet 2:24). John tells us that "the blood of Jesus his Son cleanses us from all sin" (1 Jn 1:7). One of the most profound statements in the New Testament bears on this subject. It comes from the pen of Paul: "For our sake he [God] made him [Christ] to be sin who knew no sin, so that in him we might become the righteousness of God" (2 Cor 5:21).

The death of Christ by its sacrificial nature made possible the forgiveness of sins. In the death of Christ, God's righteous claims against sin have been satisfied. His law has been vindicated (Rom 3:31); His righteousness has been preserved (Rom 3:25). He can now dispense mercy without doing violence to His holiness. He can be just and at the same time the Justifier of all those who believe in Jesus (Rom 3:26).

It is because of this that Peter is able to close his Pentecost address with this appeal: "Repent and be baptized every one of you in the name of Jesus Christ for the forgiveness of your sins" (Acts 2:38). Paul closes his message in the synagogue in Antioch with even stronger words: "Let it be known to you, therefore, brethren, that through this man [Christ] forgiveness of sins is proclaimed to you, and by him every one that believes is freed from everything from which you could not be freed by the law of Moses" (Acts 13:38-39).

The Jews, of course, knew very well that "without the shedding of blood there is no forgiveness of sins" (Heb 9:22). What they needed to be told was that all the Old Testament sacrifices pointed as it were with prophetic finger to "the Lamb of God who takes away the sin of the world" (Jn 1:29).

3. The fact of the Resurrection. Without the Resurrection the death of Christ would have no more meaning than the death of Socrates. This was clear to the apostles; hence their insistence on the fact of the Resurrection. Paul says: "If Christ has not been raised, your faith is futile and you are still in your sins" (1 Cor 15:17). If the Resurrection is not a historical fact all our fine talk about the forgiveness of sins and the life everlasting is just so much theological poppycock.

Wherever the apostles went they preached "Jesus and the Resurrection," knowing well that the idea was repugnant to the Greeks and heresy to the Sadducees. This, however, did not deter them. They were eyewitnesses of the unique event and they knew it to be a fact. Moreover, they were aware of its theological implications, and, therefore, made it the burden of their testimony. They preached it to the Jews in Jerusalem (Acts 4:2), the Gentiles in Caesarea (Acts 10:40), and the philosophers in Athens (Acts 17:31). It was the central issue in

Paul's defense before Felix (Acts 24:15, 21), Festus (Acts 25:19), and Agrippa (Acts 26:8, 23).

That Jesus Christ was alive (Lk 24:34) and lived in their hearts (Eph 3:17) was the most dynamic fact in their entire experience (Eph 1:19-20). By virtue of their relationship with Him they had become new creatures (2 Cor 5:17), with a new purpose in life (Phil 1:21) and a new concern for the welfare of others (Rom 9:3). To know Christ and the power of His resurrection was their highest ambition (Phil 3:10). To preach the unsearchable riches of Christ to Jew and Gentile was the greatest of all privileges (Eph 3:7-10). By His law of love they were determined to live (2 Cor 5:14-15), and for His name they were prepared to die (Acts 21:13).

4. The hope of His return. In His last discourse in the upper room Jesus told His disciples that He was about to leave them and return to the Father; but He added: "When I go and prepare a place for you, I will come again and will take you to myself, that where I am you may be also" (Jn 14:3). That promise was confirmed by the angels at the time of His ascension. "This Jesus," they said, "who was taken up from you into heaven, will come in the same way as you saw him go into heaven" (Acts 1:11).

God's plan for the restoration of all things, summed up by Jesus in the concept of the kingdom of God, was not to be denied or delayed by the unbelief of the Jews or by the gathering in of the Gentiles. Jesus Christ will come again, with power and great glory (Lk 21:27), to rapture the church (1 Thess 4:14-18), to execute judgment (2 Thess 1:4-10), and to establish His kingdom (Mt 25:31-46).

The second coming will mean glory and gladness for the believer (1 Thess 2:19-20), but it will be a time of pain and punishment for the unbeliever. The righteous suffer now; but the day is coming when God Himself will make all things right, when Jesus Christ will be revealed from heaven "with his mighty angels in flaming fire, inflicting vengeance upon those who do not know God and upon those who do not obey the gospel of our Lord Jesus" (2 Thess 1:7-8).

Both Peter and Paul linked the preaching of the gospel and the call to repentance to God's intervention at the end of the age, which they thought was not far away. Peter said to the Jews in Jerusalem: "Repent therefore, and turn again, that your sins may be blotted out, that times of refreshing may come from the presence of the Lord, and that he may send the Christ appointed for you, Jesus, whom the heaven must receive until the time for establishing all that God spoke by the mouth of his holy prophets from of old" (Acts 3:19-21). Paul in his address to the philosophers in Athens warned that since the coming of Christ a drastic change had occurred in the economy of God. "The times of ignorance God overlooked, but *now* he commands all men everywhere to repent, because he has fixed a day on which he will judge the world in righteousness by a man whom he has appointed, and of this he has given assurance to all men by raising him from the dead" (Acts 17:30-31).

The Nature of the Witness

For the witness to be effective it must be powerful. This is precisely what we find in the apostolic witness as described in the book of Acts. Luke says: "With great power the apostles gave their testimony to the resurrection of the Lord Jesus, and great grace was upon them all" (Acts 4:33). When we analyze the apostolic witness we find that there were three ingredients:

1. It was verbal. The gospel centers around the person and the work of Jesus Christ and involves certain propositional truths that must be believed. Before one can exercise saving faith in Christ he must understand the meaning of those truths. Paul says: "Faith comes from what is heard, and what is heard comes by the preaching of Christ" (Rom 10:17); but he goes on to ask: "How are they to hear without a preacher?" (Rom 10:14).

When the angel of the Lord appeared to Cornelius he bade him send for Peter, saying: "Send to Joppa and bring Simon called Peter; he will declare to you a message by which you will be saved and all your household" (Acts 11:13-14). Referring to the same incident at a later period, Peter said: "Brethren, you know that in the early days God made choice among you, that by my mouth the Gentiles should hear the word of the gospel and believe" (Acts 15:7).

The apostles were not content to "live" the gospel, hoping that thereby certain interested persons might be attracted to Christ. The truths were too profound and the issues were too momentous to be left to the curiosity or the credulity of the crowds. The truths of the gospel had to be articulated, line upon line and precept upon precept, to make sure that the hearers understood what it was all about. Only then could they exercise genuine faith in Christ. Hence the emphasis in the book of Acts and in the epistles of Paul on the importance of preaching. Presence evangelism is right and proper and has its place, but it is no substitute for proclamation evangelism.

It is significant that when the Holy Spirit was poured out at Pentecost "there appeared to them tongues of fire, distributed and resting on each of them. And they were all filled with the Holy Spirit and began to speak in other tongues, as the Spirit gave them utterance" (Acts 2:3-4). The Holy Spirit is the Spirit of utterance and when He fills a person that person invariably begins to witness. When Peter and John were forbidden to speak in the name of Jesus, they replied: "We cannot but speak of what we have seen and heard" (Acts 4:20). When persecution drove the early Christians out of Jerusalem they went everywhere preaching the Word (Acts 8:4). Luke says of Peter and John after they had paid a visit to Samaria: "When they had testified and spoken the word of the Lord, they returned to Jerusalem, preaching the gospel to many villages of the Samaritans" (Acts 8:25). He says of Philip, following his encounter with the Ethiopian eunuch, "But Philip was found at Azotus, and passing on he preached the gospel to all the towns till he came to Caesarea" (Acts 8:40).

The same kind of verbal witness was prominent in the ministry of Paul. As soon as he was converted at Damascus, "immediately he proclaimed Jesus" (Acts 9:20). At the end of his life he admonished Timothy to "preach the word" (2 Tim 4:2). Between these two incidents, he said: "Woe to me if I do not preach the gospel" (1 Cor 9:16).

2. It was visible. As the revelation of God in Christ was both audible and visible (1 Jn 1:1), so was the witness of the early church. In addition to preaching the Word, the apostles performed miracles, thereby giving visible demonstration of the power of Christ both to heal and to save. Peter and John were accused of having "filled Jerusalem" with their teaching (Acts 5:28). This was accomplished not alone by preaching but by reason of the notable miracle performed by Peter on the lame man at the gate of the Temple (Acts 4:16). That, together with the miracle of tongues at Pentecost, caused the people to be "filled with wonder and amazement" (Acts 2:7; 3:10).

Both of these aspects—the verbal and the visible—were brought together when Philip was in the city of Samaria. "And the multitudes with one accord gave heed to what was said by Philip, when they *heard* him and *saw* the signs which he did" (Acts 8:6).

There are some people who are saved by the preaching of the Word. There are others who require a miracle to authenticate the Word. There are still others whose hearts and minds are so closed to spiritual truth that they will not be persuaded even though one rose from the dead (Lk 16:31). Fortunately these last-mentioned persons are few and far between. When genuine miracles accompany the preaching of the Word, converts are usually won in large numbers (Acts 5:14; 9:35; 19:20). At least, that's the way it worked in the early church; and there is no reason to believe it won't work that way today.

3. **It was vital.** One of the things that attracted the common people to Jesus was the vitality of His teaching. They were "astonished at his teaching, for he taught them as one who had authority, and not as their scribes" (Mt 7:28-29). The same thing can be said of the apostles in their teaching ministry in the book of Acts. By personal experience they knew both the truth and the power of the gospel they preached. To them the Resurrection was not simply a fact of history or even a tenet in their creed. In their own hearts and lives they had experienced the power as well as the truth of the Resurrection, for that power had been released in them (Eph 1:19-21). They knew what it was to be set free from the law of sin and death by the Spirit of life in Christ Jesus (Rom 8:2).

The apostles were a living demonstration of the power of the gospel. No honest person could watch them perform and not be impressed with the dynamic character of the Christianity they preached. Their enemies were completely nonplussed and didn't know how to cope with this new breed of men. Punish them with many stripes, and they rejoice that they are counted worthy to suffer for Christ's sake (Acts 5:41). Put them in prison and fasten their feet in the stocks, and at midnight they hold a prayer-and-praise meeting which results in an earthquake and the conversion of the jailor (Acts 16:19-34). Threaten to take their lives and they reply: "For to me to live is Christ, and to die is gain" (Phil 1:21).

Few persons entered more deeply into the sufferings of Christ than did the apostle Paul; yet he could say: "We are treated as impostors, and yet are true; as unknown, and yet well known; as dying, and behold we live; as punished, and yet not killed; as sorrowful, yet always rejoicing; as poor, yet making many rich; as having nothing, and yet possessing everything" (2 Cor 6:8-10). Little wonder that they were known as men who "turned the world upside down" (Acts 17:6).

The Dynamic of the Witness

Luke tells us that "with great power the apostles gave their testimony to the resurrection of the Lord Jesus, and great grace was upon them all" (Acts 4:33). Grace and power—what a beautiful combination! Stephen is described by Luke as being "full of grace and power" and doing "great wonders and signs among the people"—so much so that his enemies could not "withstand the wisdom and the Spirit with which he spoke" (Acts 6:8-10). So powerful was his defense before the Sanhedrin that when he finished, his enemies were so enraged that they "ground their teeth . . . stopped their ears . . . rushed upon him . . . cast him out of the city, and stoned him" (Acts 7:54-58).

What was the secret of such a powerful witness? Three factors were involved:

1. The historic event of the Resurrection. The Crucifixion was a catastrophic blow to the disciples. Their whole world fell apart at the seams. They had staked their all on the belief that Jesus was the Christ, but now their hopes were shattered. Instead of establishing an earthly kingdom based on temporal power, as they had anticipated, He ended His life on a Roman cross between two malefactors. They could not have made a greater blunder. Moreover, they did not expect to see Him alive again. They were certain that everything was lost.

Then came Easter morning with the empty tomb and the angelic announcement: "He is not here for he is risen, as he said" (Mt 28:6). Jesus of Nazareth, their Lord and Master, was alive! Everything He had ever said was really true! He *was* the resurrection and the life. He *was* their own Messiah who had conquered death and was alive forevermore. This stupendous event completely revolutionized their life and their thinking. They could never be the same again. This was the greatest event in the history of the world. The Good News of the Resurrection was too good to keep to themselves. At any cost, they must share it with all—friend and foe alike. The whole world must be informed of this cosmic event.

2. The coming of the Spirit at Pentecost. Like the Resurrection, Pentecost was a unique event. The Ascension marked the end of one age, Pentecost the beginning of another. Certainly the Holy Spirit had been present in the world prior to Pentecost; nevertheless Pentecost was the historic occasion when the Holy Spirit was "poured out" on God's people in a unique way, for a unique purpose.

The Resurrection restored and strengthened the apostles' faith in Jesus as their Messiah. Pentecost provided the spiritual power which made effective their witness to the Resurrection. Only the Holy Spirit could equip the church for her worldwide missionary task. He alone could prepare the world for the church's missionary message. To announce the Good News of the Resurrection is one thing; to get a sophisticated world to believe it is another matter.

Without Pentecost the apostles, left to their own resources, would never have been able to make disciples of all nations. The Resurrection story was so incredible that no man in his right mind would readily believe it. Only as the Spirit of power filled the messengers would they be able to witness effectively (Acts 1:8). Only as the Spirit of truth illuminated the minds of the hearers would they be able to confess Jesus Christ as Lord (1 Cor 12:3).

3. The indwelling presence of the living Christ. The Ascension removed the physical presence of Jesus from the world. The disciples who had known Him after the flesh would know Him that way no more. But before His departure He promised He would not leave them comfortless (Jn 14:18); He would come to them. Indeed, He would be with them (Mt 28:20) and make His home in them (Jn 14:23). He went so far as to say that it would be to their advantage for Him to leave them (Jn 16:7). And this is precisely what happened.

While His physical presence was no longer available, He was present with them in the person of the Holy Spirit. The spiritual presence of Jesus was to the disciples a living, bright reality. His transforming friendship, which had meant so much to them while He was still with them, was a continuing experience. Their fellowship with Him was more immediate and more precious than when He was with them in the flesh. Then they could have His presence only if they occupied the same geographical location. Now they enjoyed His presence wherever they went because He lived in their hearts (Eph 3:17). And He had promised never to leave them.

His abiding presence, then, was the inspiration of their service (Acts 27:21-25), their protection in life (Acts 18:10), and their solace in death (Acts 7:54-60). Without Him they could do nothing (Jn 15:5), but with Him they could do anything (Phil 4:13). No power in heaven, earth, or hell could ever separate them from His love (Rom 8:38-39). With that assurance they went out to win the world for Christ, and in doing so were "more than conquerors" (Rom 8:37).

The Extent of the Witness

For an account of the expansion of Christianity in the first century we are dependent almost entirely on the Acts of the Apostles, which does not by any means tell the whole story. There are hints in Paul's epistles that the gospel had a much wider proclamation than that described by Luke. Nevertheless, the book of Acts gives us the broad outlines and from these we can draw certain conclusions.

1. It involved the entire church. The missionary enterprise of the early church was not the responsibility of the Women's Missionary

Society or the Foreign Mission Board. Nor was the work of witnessing left to professionals like elders, deacons, or even apostles. Laity and clergy alike were all involved. In those early days the church *was* mission. The missionary program of the early church was based on two assumptions: (1) The chief task of the church is world evangelization. (2) The responsibility for carrying out this task rests with the entire Christian community. During the early times there was no organized missionary endeavor such as characterized later periods. The gospel was spread by laymen. "Nearly every convert, with the ardor of a revolutionary, made himself an office of propaganda."[1]

A superficial reading of the Acts of the Apostles might give the impression that in the early church all the evangelistic work was done by professionals—the apostles and their colleagues; but that is not so. Here and there we find suggestions that the Good News of the gospel was carried far and wide by laymen, many of them displaced persons fleeing from persecution (Acts 8:4; 19:19-20). Wherever they went they "gossiped the gospel" with friends, neighbors, and even strangers.

2. It extended to the ends of the earth. Prior to Pentecost the disciples were provincial in their outlook and would gladly have settled for a "kingdom" no larger than Palestine. Jesus, on the other hand, thought in terms of the "world." After Pentecost they began in Jerusalem, to be sure; but from there they took the gospel to Judea and Samaria, and ultimately to the "ends of the earth." Philip took the gospel to Samaria (Acts 8); Peter did the same for Judea (Acts 9); while Paul and his companions covered the whole eastern half of the Roman Empire (Rom 15:19) and had plans for penetrating as far west as Spain (Rom 15:24).

Difficulties and dangers beset them on every hand (2 Cor 11:23-28), imprisonment and afflictions awaited them in every city (Acts 20:23), and hundreds of them sealed their testimony with their blood (Acts 26:10). Nevertheless they continued to bear witness to the person of Christ and the power of the gospel, until in the words of Paul the message had been "preached to every creature under heaven" (Col 1:6).

3. It included all classes of men. Christianity began as a reform movement within Judaism, and to the end (A.D. 70) the church in Jerusalem remained more Jewish than Christian in flavor (Acts 21:20-26). It took some years for Christianity to develop its own theology, chart its own course, and project its own image. Paul, more than anyone else, was responsible for this development.

---

1. Will Durant, *Caesar or Christ* (New York: Simon and Schuster, 1944), p. 602.

In the beginning the gospel was preached to the Jews only (Acts 11:19). It was with the greatest reluctance that the church leaders, Peter included, finally agreed to include the Gentiles in their plans (Acts 10:9-20). Philip broke the ice by going to the city of Samaria (Acts 8). Peter set a precedent when he preached the gospel to Cornelius (Acts 10). But it wasn't really until Paul came on the scene that the gospel was made available to the Gentiles on anything like a universal scale, and even then it created a controversy which led to the first church council (Acts 15). Fortunately Paul and his companions won out (Gal 2), and the Gentiles were accepted into the church without having to become Jews in the process. So Paul declares himself to be a debtor to the "Greeks and the barbarians, the wise and the foolish" (Rom 1:14).

Not only did the gospel solve the racial issue, it solved the social issue as well. Jews and Gentiles in all walks of life and all levels of society were welcomed as full members of the Christian church. So Paul could boast that in the church "there is neither Jew nor Greek, there is neither slave nor free, there is neither male nor female; for you are all one in Christ Jesus" (Gal 3:28). The church in Philippi was a microcosm of the universal church. Its charter members included a wealthy businesswoman (Lydia), the Roman jailor, the slave girl, and the members of their households.

The enemies of Christianity faulted it for gathering converts from the dregs of humanity. Celsus described the Christians as "worthless, contemptible people, idiots, slaves, poor women and children."[2] This was the glory, not the shame, of the Christian church. Jesus led the way by fraternizing with publicans and sinners and appealing to all "who labor and are heavy laden" (Mt 11:28). The church was the only institution in the empire whose doors were open to high and low, rich and poor, slave and free.

The Techniques of the Witness

The witness of the early church, carried out under the guidance of the Holy Spirit, was neither halting nor haphazard. There was a definite plan of action designed to produce certain desirable results.

1. They preached the gospel. The apostles believed that in the gospel of Christ they possessed the only panacea for the ills of mankind. There was no uncertainty in their minds concerning the nature

---

2. Origen, *Contra Celsum* iii. 49-55.

or importance of the gospel. God had acted decisively in the death and resurrection of Jesus Christ, thereby reconciling the world to Himself. This gospel must be understood and accepted before a person can partake of its benefits. Hence the importance of preaching.

Paul and the other apostles recognized that the gospel was a "stumbling block to the Jews and folly to the Gentiles" (1 Cor 1:23); nevertheless it is "the power of God unto salvation to all who believe" (Rom 1:16). Jesus Christ is Lord of all and bestows His riches on all who call on Him, and everyone who calls on Him will be saved. But Paul goes on to ask four pertinent questions: "How are men to call upon him in whom they have never believed? How are they to believe in him of whom they have never heard? How are they to hear without a preacher? How can men preach unless they are sent?" (Rom 10:14-15).

2. They called for a response. The apostles were not content to present the gospel on a take-it-or-leave-it basis. It was not enough to announce the Good News concerning Christ, it was imperative that the hearers understand the nature of their own fate. God loved the world and Christ died for all, but this does not mean that all men everywhere are already saved and only need to be advised of the fact. The salvation provided in Christ is *sufficient* for the whole world, but it is *efficient* only for those who respond.

Repentance and faith are both required for salvation. The first is negative and involves a change of mind. The second is positive and includes an intellectual, emotional, and volitional commitment to Jesus Christ as Savior and Lord. Repentance in the New Testament is always repentance toward God (Acts 26:20), and faith is always faith in Jesus Christ (Acts 16:31). Both are brought together by Paul in Acts 20:21.

Repentance and faith are not two separate and distinct experiences; rather they are two aspects of one experience whereby the sinner is reconciled to God. There can be no genuine faith in Christ without a concomitant repentance toward God. Sin must be renounced at the same time that faith is exercised. The command to "repent" comes through loud and clear in the preaching of the apostles (Acts 2:38; 3:19; 8:22; 17:30; 26:20). The exhortation to "believe" is equally clear (Acts 4:4; 10:43; 13:39; 16:31). The gospel is the power of God unto salvation *only* for those who repent (Lk 13:3) and believe (Rom 1:16).

3. They promised forgiveness. After the Resurrection Jesus said to His disciples: "If you forgive the sins of any, they are forgiven; if you retain the sins of any, they are retained" (Jn 20:23). Acting on the authority granted to them by Jesus, the apostles promised forgiveness to all who would repent and believe. Even the Jewish leaders, who were morally responsible for the murder of Jesus, were included in the offer (Acts 2:38; 5:31; 13:38; 26:18). No sin is too great to be forgiven on the basis of the atoning death of Jesus Christ.

God took man's most heinous deed and turned it to man's salvation. "Where sin increased, grace abounded all the more" (Rom 5:20).

> He died that we might be forgiven;
> He died to make us good,
> That we might go at last to heaven,
> Saved by His precious blood.

Forgiveness, as preached by the apostles, was a present possession, not a future expectation. Sinners of the deepest dye can all be forgiven on the basis of the atoning work of Jesus Christ on the cross. And God is more willing to bestow the gift than man is to receive it (Is 55:7). There was no doubt in the minds of the apostles that it is possible for the sinner to be exonerated in the eyes of a holy God simply and solely on the basis of repentance and faith. No one stated it more clearly than the apostle Paul: "Let it be known to you, therefore, brethren, that through this man [Jesus Christ] forgiveness of sins is proclaimed to you, and by him every one that believes is freed from everything from which you could not be freed by the law of Moses" (Acts 13:38-39).

4. They warned of judgment. Salvation was for all—Jew and Gentile alike. Forgiveness was free for the taking. But what if some preferred sin to salvation? Like Jesus before them, the apostles recognized that there is such a thing as recalcitrant sin; and like Him they were too honest to dodge the issue. Man can repent or he can rebel, but he can't do both at the same time. To repent is to receive forgiveness, full and free, for time and eternity; but to continue in rebellion is to encounter judgment. To accept Christ is to choose life, to reject Christ is to choose death. There is no third alternative. God's love is a reality; His wrath is likewise a reality. Both are an essential part of His character. To preach forgiveness without judgment is to deceive men; to preach judgment without forgiveness is to defame God. The apostles preached both forgiveness and judgment. They implored men to accept forgiveness and be reconciled to God (2 Cor 5:20). At the same time they warned men against storing up wrath for themselves on the day of wrath when God's righteous judgment will be revealed (Rom 2:5).

This comes out time and again in the book of Acts (3:23; 13:41; 17:31; 24:25).

5. They practiced baptism. Both John the Baptist and Jesus practiced it before them. When Jesus announced the Great Commission He indicated that teaching and baptism were the two methods to be used in making disciples (Mt 28:18-20). Peter was the first to mention baptism in the Acts of the Apostles. Following his address at Pentecost the hearers were cut to the heart and cried out, "What must we do?" Peter replied: "Repent and be baptized every one of you in the name of Jesus Christ for the forgiveness of your sins and you will receive the gift of the Holy Spirit" (Acts 2:37-38). It is noteworthy that baptism as practiced by the apostles always followed repentance and faith (Acts 8:36-38).

It was administered by Peter (Acts 2:41), by Philip (Acts 8:38), by Ananias (Acts 9:18), and by Paul (Acts 16:15, 33; 19:5). Included in the rite were Jews (Acts 2:41), Samaritans (Acts 8:12), Gentiles (Acts 10:47-48), and even the disciples of John the Baptist (Acts 19:5). Baptism was the outward sign and symbol of an inward change of heart leading to a change of life. It was the one visible and public act by which a convert openly and irrevocably identified himself with the Christian faith.

6. They established churches. The apostles were not content to sow the seed, or even to reap a harvest; they established local churches as centers of worship, teaching, fellowship, and service. The rallying center was the person and presence of Jesus Christ (Mt 18:20). They were drawn together by their common attachment to Him (Jn 12:32). Their fellowship with one another grew out of their fellowship with the Father and the Son (1 Jn 1:3).

In the early days the groups were small and the service simple. The Jerusalem church met in an upper room (Acts 1:13-15). As the numbers increased, problems arose and organization was developed (Acts 6:1-4). The first officers, after the apostles, were deacons (Acts 6:5-7). Later on elders were appointed (Acts 14:23). The organizational structure was by no means rigid, at least not in the beginning. In Jerusalem the Christians continued to frequent the Temple (Acts 3:1; 21:26). Elsewhere they worshiped in the synagogues (Acts 22:19) until they were driven out (Acts 19:9). In many places they simply met for the breaking of bread and prayers in their own homes (Acts 2:46; 11:12; 20:8). The place was not important (Jn 4:20-21), the building had no particular significance (Acts 17:24-25), money was no problem (Acts 3:6), and numbers were not essential to success (Mt 18:19).

The two outstanding characteristics of the early Christians were their faith in Christ and their love for the brethren (Col 1:4; 1 Thess 1:3; 2 Thess 1:3). They were a closely knit group that shared not only a common faith and hope but also their earthly goods (Acts 2:44-45; 4:32). "Behold, how these Christians love one another," was the comment of the world.

What, in the final analysis, made the church a unique institution? It was the presence of Jesus Christ (Jn 20:19; Mt 28:20). He was the center of their fellowship (Mt 28:20). He was the theme of their teaching and preaching (Acts 5:42). He was the motive for their service (Mk 9:41; Col 3:24). He was the object of their worship (Mt 28:17; Rev 5:11-14).

The Results of the Witness

The apostles expected results and got them. They believed that a powerful gospel (Rom 1:16), preached in the power of the Holy Spirit (1 Cor 2:4), would always produce results. Referring to his impending visit to Rome, Paul could say: "I know that when I come to you I shall come in the fullness of the blessing of Christ" (Rom 15:29). He had no desire to "run in vain or labor in vain" (Phil 2:16). Moreover, he was certain that his converts likewise would not labor in vain (1 Cor 15:58).

What kind of results did the apostles achieve?

1. They were immediate. They did not spend long, weary years sowing the seed, hoping some day for a harvest. The first sermon in Acts produced three thousand converts and baptism was administered on the spot! In the average church today the ratio is usually the other way round—it takes three thousand sermons to produce one convert! Philip (the deacon, not the apostle) preached in the city of Samaria and the "multitudes with one accord gave heed to what was said." As a result, "there was much joy in that city" (Acts 8:6-8). The Ethiopian eunuch believed the gospel the first time he heard it, and was baptized. Cornelius the Roman centurion, the governor of Cyprus, the Philippian jailor, Lydia the wealthy businesswoman—all these became converts on the first contact.

2. They were impressive. It was not just one convert here and another there. They were converted in large numbers—three thousand at one time (Acts 2:41) and five thousand at another (Acts 4:4). Such words as "many," "great numbers," "multitudes," occur repeatedly throughout the Acts of the Apostles. The witness was so successful in Jerusalem that the Christians were accused of "filling Jerusalem with their doctrine" (Acts 5:28). In Antioch "the hand of the Lord was with them and a great number that believed turned to the Lord" (Acts 11:21). In Antioch in Pisidia "the whole city gathered together to hear the word of God" (Acts 13:44). In Ephesus, the religious center of the Roman world, Paul's preaching was so successful that the silver-smiths found their image-making trade in jeopardy (Acts 19:23-27). And a large number of those who practiced magic arts brought their books together and consigned them to the fire. The total value of the books was fifty thousand pieces of silver (Acts 19:19).

3. They were permanent. The apostles didn't have to sacrifice quality for quantity. The converts were really *converted!* They preached repentance as well as faith, and before the convert "decided for Christ" he knew what was involved. It was not a case of "easy believism." The issues were clear: it was God or mammon (Mt 6:24), Christ or Belial (2 Cor 6:15), life or death (2 Cor 2:16), salvation or damnation (Mk 16:16). From a worldly point of view the convert had everything to lose by accepting Christ. The only way into the kingdom in those days was "through many tribulations" (Acts 14:22), and not a few converts became martyrs for the faith (Acts 26:10). The early Christians were not perfect, nor was the church without its problems; but one problem it didn't have was the presence of "rice" Christians. This is all the more remarkable when we remember that there was no long probationary period between conversion and baptism. They were baptized immediately on their confession of faith.

There were, of course, backsliders and even apostates in the early church; but their numbers were comparatively small. The convicting power of the Holy Spirit was so strong that the work of grace was deep and lasting. Moreover, the converts were taught to cleave to the Lord with purpose of heart. The vast majority did just that.

4

Missions in the Ministry of Paul

By any definition the apostle Paul was an unusual person. He would stand out in any crowd, not because of his physical stature but because of his intellectual, moral, and spiritual qualities. He ranks with the great personalities of the Old Testament: Abraham, Moses, David, Elijah, Isaiah, Daniel. He did for Christianity what Moses did for Judaism. Indeed, the two men had much in common. Both were carefully reared in the faith of their fathers. Both were familiar with the wisdom of the world. Both were chosen by God to become men of destiny. Both had a dramatic confrontation with God in preparation for their life's work. Both became dynamic leaders, mighty in word and deed.

God saw in Paul qualities not found in any other man of that generation, not even Peter, James, or John. He had the mind of a scholar, the heart of an evangelist, the discipline of a soldier, the devotion of a lover, the vision of a seer, the zeal of a reformer, and the passion of a prophet. By the grace of God Saul of Tarsus, once the chief of sinners, became Paul, the greatest of all the apostles.

Peter, the prince of the apostles, is the dominant character in Acts 1–12; but he suddenly passes out of the picture and is replaced by Paul in Acts 13–28. This is all the more remarkable when we remember that Paul was not one of the twelve apostles chosen by Christ. Nor was he the only missionary in the early church. At least a score of others are mentioned by Luke; doubtless there were hundreds more. Why then was he singled out by Luke and given such prominence in the Acts of the Apostles?

The expansion of Christianity under Paul was the fact of chief importance. Luke followed it, not because he was ignorant of others, nor merely because he had been associated with the apostle. It was through Paul's work that Christianity was established in the chief cities of the empire, and thus obtained the significance it had when Luke wrote. This line of progress was historically the most portentous. In Paul's Epistles, moreover, which are the index of his teaching, the Christian system of belief was completely unfolded, so that under him Christianity evolved its content as well as extended its area.[1]

It is fair to say that without the immense influence of Paul, Christianity would not have thrown off the swaddling clothes of Judaism and become a truly universal religion.

Paul's Missionary Strategy

We might begin by asking: Did Paul have a missionary strategy? Some say yes; others say no. Much depends on one's definition of strategy. If by strategy is meant a deliberate, well-formulated, duly executed plan of action based on human observation and experience, then Paul had little or no strategy; but if we take the word to mean a flexible *modus operandi* developed under the guidance of the Holy Spirit and subject to His direction and control, then Paul did have a strategy.

Our problem today is that we live in an anthropocentric age. We imagine that nothing of consequence can be accomplished in the Lord's work without a good deal of ecclesiastical machinery—committees, conferences, workshops, seminars; whereas the early Christians depended less on human wisdom and expertise, more on divine initiative and guidance. It is obvious that they didn't do too badly. What the modern missionary movement needs above everything else is to get back to the missionary methods of the early church.

Michael Green at the Lausanne Congress on World Evangelization made a point of saying: "Many of you commented that my paper was thin on the strategy of the early Christians. You are right. You see, I don't believe they had much of a strategy. . . . The Gospel spread out in an apparently haphazard way as men obeyed the leading of the Spirit, and went through doors he opened."[2]

Roland Allen took a similar position: "It is quite impossible to

---

1. George T. Purves, *Christianity in the Apostolic Age* (Grand Rapids: Baker Publications, 1975), p. 174.
2. *Let the Earth Hear His Voice,* ed. J. D. Douglas (Minneapolis: World Wide Publications, 1975), p. 174.

maintain that St. Paul deliberately planned his journeys beforehand, selected certain strategic points at which to establish his churches and then actually carried out his designs."[3]

With these introductory thoughts in mind we will proceed to discuss Paul's missionary strategy.

1. He maintained close contact with the home base. Paul received his missionary call directly from the Lord at the time of his conversion, but this was later confirmed by action of the church in Antioch where Paul was a teacher. The Holy Spirit directed the church to consecrate Barnabas and Paul for the work to which He had called them. The church concurred, and after prayer and fasting sent the two men away with its blessing.

That Paul attached great importance to this contact is evident from the fact that at the end of his missionary journeys he always returned to Antioch. Luke is careful to remind his readers that Antioch was the church by which Paul and Barnabas had been recommended to the grace of God for the work which they had now fulfilled, as if there was some necessary connection between the success of the mission and the prayers of the church. On their return the two missionaries called a meeting of the entire church and reported in detail what God had accomplished through them, especially how He had opened the door of faith to the Gentiles. After this they stayed on in Antioch "no little time" (Acts 14:28), during which, we may well conclude, they ministered the Word as they had done in years past.

This had one great advantage. It eliminated the custom in modern missions that obliges the missionary on furlough to travel from Maine to California to pay a week-end visit to scores of churches to thank them for their past support and solicit their continuing support. Furlough, which is supposed to be a time for rest and relaxation, turns out to be a rat race. After an exhausting year of travel and turmoil, the missionary, weary in mind and body, returns to the field with a sigh of relief. In the meantime he has not remained in any one church long enough to do himself or anyone else much good.

Paul was also concerned to maintain contact with the church in Jerusalem, without whose blessing his mission to the Gentiles might have been in jeopardy. For at least two decades the church in that city was regarded as the mother church. Some of the twelve apostles were still there, and so were many of the original elders, who by this time had acquired an influence second only to that of the apostles. Paul was wise enough to see the importance of maintaining con-

---

3. Roland Allen, *Missionary Methods: St. Paul's or Ours?* (Grand Rapids: Eerdmans Publishing Co., 1962), p. 10.

tact with that influential church. On at least five occasions he visited Jerusalem and each time he conferred with the leaders there. This became increasingly crucial as the rift between the Jewish and Gentile branches of the Christian church widened. On his last visit to Jerusalem he took with him a love offering from the Gentile churches of Macedonia and Achaia. The immediate reason for the offering was the depressed economic condition of the poor saints in Jerusalem, but no doubt he hoped the gift would serve another purpose—to bring the two branches of the church together in the bonds of Christian love. In this way he sought to ensure the success of his mission to the Gentiles.

Later on, when his work in the eastern part of the empire was drawing to a close, he wrote to the church in Rome to solicit support for his mission to Spain (Rom 15:15-24). If he was to launch a mission in the western part of the empire he would need a base in Italy. His real reason, then, for writing his Epistle to the Romans was missiological rather than theological. He was convinced that the world-wide Christian mission must have a strong support base at home.

2. He confined his efforts to four provinces. Any one missionary has only so much time and energy. He cannot cover *all* the ground. If he tries he will surely meet with failure or frustration or both. Paul's original commission called on him to take the gospel "far away to the Gentiles" (Acts 22:21). How far is "far away"? Mesopotamia? Egypt? India? China? Africa? Obviously he could not visit all these places; so under the leading of the Holy Spirit he ended up by concentrating on four of the most populous, prosperous provinces: Galatia, Asia, Macedonia, and Achaia. The first two were in Asia, the other two in Europe. Rather than wandering all over the world and scattering the seed in great profusion, Paul preferred to labor in a much smaller field, where he and others could water the seed, cultivate the soil, and produce a harvest (1 Cor 3:6). His aim was not simply to cover territory but to plant churches. To accomplish this it was necessary not only to sow the seed but also to reap a harvest. This could best be done by confining his efforts to a fairly restricted area.

It is interesting to note in this connection that Paul and Luke thought in terms of provinces rather than cities. Reference is made to the churches in Judea, Galilee, and Samaria (Acts 9:31), Syria and Cilicia (Acts 15:23), Macedonia and Achaia (2 Cor 9:2). Seldom is a church identified with a city.

Paul's active missionary career lasted twelve to fifteen years; yet in that comparatively short time he succeeded in planting strong, thriving, autonomous churches in all four of the provinces mentioned. So thorough was his work that at the end of this period he could write to the Christians in Rome: "From Jerusalem and as far round as Illyricum I have fully preached the gospel of Christ. . . . But now, since I no longer have any room in these regions, and since I have longed for many years to come to you, I hope to see you in passing as I go to Spain" (Rom 15:19-24).

Modern missions could learn from Paul at this point. Many boards, instead of placing thirty missionaries in one country and leaving them there until the job is done, have spread their missionaries over twenty or thirty countries, with not enough in any one to raise up a strong indigenous church. Proliferation, not concentration, seems to be the name of the game. In Japan there are ninety-seven North American mission agencies. Fifty-seven of them have fewer than ten workers in the country! One wonders if there isn't a certain amount of spiritual pride in some forms of missionary work which prompts a board to do what looks good on paper but what in reality makes for weakness rather than strength. We can easily spread ourselves so thin that there is little or no depth to our work. Paul did not make that mistake. He was content to confine his labors to four major regions, in all of which he did a solid piece of work.

3. He concentrated on the large cities. Paul chose to work in the cities of the empire, not because they afforded more comforts or larger crowds, but because they were strategic centers from which the light of the gospel could spread to the surrounding regions. He began in Antioch, where he and Barnabas spent a whole year teaching the disciples (Acts 11:26). A glance at the map will immediately indicate the strategic importance of Antioch for the Christian missionary.

> The third city of the empire, outranked in size only by Rome and Alexandria, crowded with a mixed population and connected commercially with both East and West, Antioch was the most important place for the faith, advancing from Jerusalem, to occupy. From it the new religion would be carried by report in every direction. It lay just beyond the confines of Palestine, and thus was not so far from the original center as to lose touch with the mother church. At the same time it was the door from Palestine to the Graeco-Roman world. No place was so well suited to be the base of operations for the progress of Christianity into the empire.[4]

In his three missionary journeys Paul kept pretty well to the famous Roman roads built and maintained by the state. Along these roads were situated the most important cities of the empire. All of them were the centers of Roman administration and Greek civilization.

---

4. Purves, *Christianity in the Apostolic Age,* p. 102.

Some of them, such as Philippi, were Roman colonies; others, such as Thessalonica, were busy commercial centers. All except Philippi had a sizable Jewish population. Athens was the cultural center and Ephesus the religious center of the empire.

Paul did not preach in *all* the cities along the way. He chose those which, for one reason or another, were important to his plan for the speedy evangelization of the empire. He passed through—but evidently did not preach in—Amphipolis and Apollonia on his way from Philippi to Thessalonica (Acts 17:1). Nor was his stay in each city of equal duration. In some he remained only a few weeks; in others he stayed two or three years.

Without doubt Ephesus was the most important of all the cities in which Paul labored. It was not only the capital of the province of Asia but, being the site of the famous temple of Diana, it was the religious center of the empire. Every year tens of thousands of pilgrims visited the city. Indeed, the merchants derived much of their wealth from the tourist trade (Acts 19:25-27). So important was Ephesus that Paul remained there for the best part of three years (Acts 20:31), longer than in any other city. On his departure he left Timothy in charge of the work (1 Tim 1:3). Priscilla, Aquila, and Apollos all labored in Ephesus (Acts 18:24-26). Later on the apostle John took up residence there. In the Acts of the Apostles Luke records four major addresses given by Paul. One of these was his farewell address to the elders of the church in Ephesus (Acts 20), which affords valuable insights into his missionary methods. Paul spent the first three months in Ephesus preaching in the synagogue, "arguing and pleading about the kingdom of God" (Acts 19:8). When opposition drove him from the synagogue he moved to the hall of Tyrannus, where he carried on a daily dialogue with all who would listen.

Some idea of the effectiveness of Paul's ministry there can be seen from Luke's comment: "This continued for two years so that all the residents of Asia heard the word of the Lord, both Jews and Greeks" (Acts 19:10). This is one of the most remarkable statements in the book of Acts. It shows clearly the enormous influence that Paul was able to exercise when situated in a strategic center. When Luke says that "all the residents of Asia heard the word of the Lord," we need not assume that it refers only to a widespread sowing of the seed with no concerted effort to secure a harvest. We know from Revelation 2 and 3 that later on there were seven well-established churches in the province of Asia, each one identified by name. How, when, and by whom were they founded? Is it not reasonable to suppose that they were the result of Paul's three-year stay in the capital?

Did Paul confine his personal ministry during that time to the city of Ephesus, or did he make short visits to other cities nearby? Luke does not tell us, nor is it necessary for us to know. It is, of course, possible that Paul himself did make brief trips into the province, but there is nothing to confirm the suggestion.

How then were the churches in Asia founded? Two possibilities are open. Paul had many fellow workers who came and went constantly. Some of these were probably with him in Ephesus. If so, he doubtless sent them to the outlying cities and towns while he supervised the total operation from the capital. In the second place, Ephesus would attract a large number of merchants, officials, soldiers, and others from the surrounding territory. Many of these would have heard the Word from Paul in the hall of Tyrannus, and on their return home they would have carried the gospel with them. In time churches sprang up in all parts of the province. This is church planting by multiplication, not by addition.

That the above is not altogether conjecture can be seen by a glance at Paul's Epistle to the Colossians. Colossae, just ninety miles east of Ephesus, had a church. Two of its leaders are identified by name, Epaphras and Tychicus. Epaphras was a native of Colossae and the founder of the work there (Col 1:7). He became one of Paul's fellow workers. But Paul had never been to Colossae (Col 2:1). How then did they meet? If Paul didn't go to Colossae, Epaphras must have gone to Ephesus. The suggestion is not only intriguing but highly probable. On his return home he went to work and started a church there.

4. He made the synagogue the scene of his chief labors. Although he was chosen by God to be the apostle to the Gentiles (Gal 2:8) and took special pride in the office (Rom 11:13), Paul followed the principle "to the Jew first" (Rom 1:16). When he entered a city he made a beeline for the synagogue. Only in Philippi did he fail to find such an institution. There he had to settle for a "place of prayer" because it was a Roman colony. Still regarding himself as belonging to the seed of Abraham and an heir of the promises (Gal 3:29), Paul on entering the synagogue immediately felt at home. Its order of service and mode of worship were familiar to him. In the synagogue he found three distinct classes: Jews, proselytes, and God-fearing Gentiles, all of whom already had a knowledge of the one true God, an acquaintance with the Old Testament, and an expectation of the coming Messiah.

Moreover, it was the custom in the synagogue to invite a visiting rabbi to give a "word of exhortation" to the assembled worshipers (Acts 13:15). This meant that wherever Paul went he had an opportunity to give his witness to an attentive, devout, intelligent audience in a made-to-order situation. And he took full advantage of it every time.

Only when expelled from the synagogue did he go elsewhere (Acts 18:7; 19:9); and when he moved on to the next city, back he went to the synagogue. Most of Paul's opposition came from the synagogue; nevertheless it afforded the very best opportunity for the proclamation of the gospel in the Roman world. If the Jews turned against him, and they usually did, he always found a ready response on the part of the proselytes and the God-fearing Gentiles. If his epistles are any criterion, most of his converts came from these two classes. It is difficult to exaggerate the strategic importance of the synagogue to the spread of the Christian faith in the first century. Paul was exceedingly wise to avail himself of this unique opportunity.

5. He preferred to preach to responsive peoples. Not all peoples are equally responsive to the gospel. This was made clear by Christ in the parable of the Sower in Matthew 13. In that parable there were four kinds of soil and four kinds of harvest. In each case the harvest did not depend on the sower or the seed, for both were the same in all four cases, but on the soil. Good soil produced a good harvest, poor soil produced a poor harvest or none at all. And even in the case of the good soil the harvest was not *uniformly* good. In one case it was a hundredfold, in another sixtyfold, and in still another only thirtyfold.

Paul was interested in results. He was very conscious of the fact that he had been "entrusted with a commission" (1 Cor 9:17) and would one day have to account for the manner in which he carried out his commission (1 Cor 3:10-15). The Christian worker is required to be faithful (1 Cor 4:2), and he is also required to be fruitful (Jn 15:2). Some missionaries who are not very fruitful take comfort from the fact that they are faithful. Others are so enamored of fruitfulness that they care little about faithfulness. Paul was determined to be both faithful and fruitful.

Most of Paul's preaching was done in the synagogues of the Roman world, where he soon discovered that every congregation was divided into two parts: those who accepted the Word and followed him, and those who opposed the truth and fought him. The former were made up mostly of the proselytes and God-fearing Gentiles. The latter were Jews who listened most attentively as long as Paul spoke of Israel's glorious history, but the moment he tried to prove that Jesus of Nazareth was Israel's long-promised Messiah they turned against him and raised a riot in an attempt to destroy him. More than once the timely intervention of his followers saved him from a violent death. On one occasion he was actually left for dead (Acts 14:19).

After that incident Paul took decisive action. It occurred first in Antioch in Pisidia. Paul and Barnabas spoke out boldly, saying: "It was necessary that the word of God should be spoken first to you. Since you thrust it from you, and judge yourselves unworthy of eternal life, behold, we turn to the Gentiles" (Acts 13:46). And to prove his case Paul quoted from Isaiah 49:6. The performance was repeated, with even harsher words, in Corinth. When the Jews opposed and reviled him, Paul shook out his garments and said to them: "Your blood be upon your heads! I am innocent. From now on I will go to the Gentiles" (Acts 18:6).

This must have been an agonizing decision on Paul's part; for he loved his own people with a passion rare, if not unique, in missionary annals. On one occasion he said: "I have great sorrow and unceasing anguish in my heart. For I could wish that I myself were accursed and cut off from Christ for the sake of my brethren, my kinsmen by race" (Rom 9:2-3). But the spread of the gospel and the extension of the kingdom were of paramount importance; and so nothing, not even his love for his own people, could be permitted to stand in the way. He believed that every ethnic group has the right to hear the gospel and he would gladly preach it to them; but if they adamantly and consistently refused the message and persecuted the messenger, no further purpose could be served by continuing to preach to them. Better far to move on to another group who would respond. Only in this way could the command to "make disciples of all nations" be fulfilled.

All too often has this principle been denied or ignored by the modern missionary movement. Burdened with land, buildings, and institutions of one kind and another, we have stayed year after year in places where there has been no visible fruit, while other areas ready to harvest are neglected for lack of suitable manpower. We have lacked the moral courage to pull up our stakes and move on to more fruitful fields. Roland Allen has a pertinent comment on this matter:

> The possibility of rejection was ever present. St. Paul did not establish himself in a place and go on preaching for years to men who refused to act on his preaching. When once he had brought them to a point where decision was clear, he demanded that they should make their choice. If they rejected him, he rejected them. . . . It is a question which needs serious consideration whether the Gospel can be truly presented if this element is left out. Can there be true teaching which does not involve the refusal to go on teaching? The teaching of the Gospel is not a mere intellectual instruction; it is a moral process, and involves a moral response. If we go on teaching where that moral response is refused, we cease to preach the Gospel; we make the teaching a mere education of the intellect.[5]

---

5. Allen, *Missionary Methods,* p. 75.

6. He baptized converts on confession of their faith. There are many differences between first century and twentieth century missions. One of the greatest is the matter of baptism. In modern missions we have usually required a fairly long period of probation during which the convert undergoes religious indoctrination. Only when he has acquired some degree of understanding of Christian doctrine and achieved a certain degree of sanctification is the candidate "ready" for baptism. In some parts of the world social customs and religious practices were a major stumbling block. In India it was caste; in China, ancestral worship; in Africa, polygamy. Only when all vegetarian vows were broken and all fetishes burned was the convert accepted for baptism.

There is no evidence in the New Testament that the early church required a waiting period, long or short, between conversion and baptism. The three thousand Jews and proselytes who responded to Peter's message at Pentecost appear to have been baptized immediately without additional instruction of any kind. The Philippian jailor, who must have come from a heathen background, was baptized on the spot (Acts 16:33). Moreover, his entire household, which almost certainly included slaves as well as children, were baptized with him. This does not mean that Paul was interested in numbers at the expense of quality. No one acquainted with Paul's epistles could possibly accuse the apostle of that kind of folly. It is, however, a matter of record that Paul and the other apostles baptized their converts immediately on confession of their faith in Christ (Acts 8:12; 8:36-38; 9:18).

One important factor must be borne in mind, however, before we throw all caution to the winds and baptize every Tom, Dick, and Harry who applies. The preaching of the gospel in the apostolic age was always accompanied by the power of the Holy Spirit (1 Cor 2:1-5; 1 Thess 1:5), and that made all the difference in the world. Only when the Holy Spirit is present in power is it possible for the sinner to pass from death to life (Jn 5:24). He alone has the power to regenerate the human soul (Jn 3:5-6; Tit 3:5). Paul's entire ministry was carried out in the power of the Holy Spirit (Rom 15:19); hence his converts were *really* converted. Under these conditions the risk of the new believer reverting to his old manner of life was small indeed. Paul had good reason to believe that God who began the good work in his converts would "bring it to completion at the day of Jesus Christ" (Phil 1:6).

It was not until the post-apostolic period, when the church was beginning to substitute ecclesiastical power for spiritual power, that candidates for baptism were required to undergo a period of probation and instruction. It is fair to ask: Was there any connection between the diminution of spiritual power and the addition of extrabiblical safeguards?

7. He remained long enough in one place to establish a church. Like every good missionary, Paul had two goals in mind. His immediate goal was the speedy evangelization of the world. His ultimate goal was the establishing of local churches. The latter could not be accomplished by a ten-day crusade; so Paul made a practice of remaining in each city long enough to establish a church.

In most cities his stay was cut short when the unbelieving Jews stirred up the populace to drive him out of town. Doubtless Paul would have remained longer had it not been for this kind of opposition. In spite of the difficulties and dangers, however, he usually managed to remain for at least two or three months. In some cases, such as Corinth and Ephesus, he stayed much longer. But in every city, with the possible exception of Athens, he left behind a strong and growing church that could carry on after his departure.

The churches founded by Paul were not only self-governing and self-supporting, they were self-propagating as well. In other words, they were missionary-minded churches, concerned—as Paul was—for the evangelization of the world. They could not move about as Paul did, but they could and did make themselves responsible for the total evangelization of their own regions. In his earliest epistle, written to a young, persecuted mission church, Paul congratulated the new Christians on becoming an example to all the believers. "For not only has the word of the Lord sounded forth from you in Macedonia and Achaia, but your faith in God has gone forth everywhere, so that we need not say anything" (1 Thess 1:8).

Paul's strategy paid off handsomely. After only fifteen years of missionary work he could say: "From Jerusalem and as far round as Illyricum I have fully preached the gospel of Christ. . . . But now, since I have no longer any room for work in these regions . . . I hope to see you in passing as I go to Spain" (Rom 15:19-24). Does Paul mean that he himself had preached in every city in the eastern part of the empire? Certainly not. It was never Paul's intention to preach in *every* city. That was neither possible nor desirable. He established missionary churches in the major centers of population and they in turn engaged in "saturation evangelism" in their own areas. The eastern part of the empire could safely be left to them. He would head for Spain to begin the evangelization of the western half of the empire.

Here again the modern missionary has failed to follow Paul's example. We establish churches that are supposed to be self-supporting, self-governing, and self-propagating. The missions stress self-support while the churches demand self-government. Neither the churches nor the missions pay much attention to self-propagation. Consequently in countries where missions have operated for well over a hundred years there are still large areas that are completely unevangelized. In a word, we have failed to establish *missionary* churches.

8. He made ample use of fellow workers. Paul was no lone eagle. He had no desire to go his own way or do his own thing. He believed wholeheartedly in teamwork.

Before he began his missionary work he was associated with Barnabas in a team-teaching ministry in Antioch. On his first missionary journey he had Barnabas and John Mark as his companions. After his falling out with Barnabas over John Mark, he chose another partner, Silas. In Lystra he picked up Timothy. Luke joined the party in Troas. Other fellow workers included Sopater, Aristarchus, Secundus, Gaius, Tychicus, and Trophimus (Acts 20:4). In his epistles reference is made to others: Epaphras, Demas, Epaphroditus, Archippus, Priscilla, Aquila, Apollos, Titus, and Phoebe among others. In Romans 16 he sends greetings to twenty-seven persons he mentions by name, many of whom had been fellow workers.

We tend to think of Paul as a strong, courageous, dynamic, self-sufficient personality who could fight and fend for himself; but such was not the case. Paul had a great capacity for friendship and did his best work in association with others. When he arrived in Athens he sent word back to Berea for Timothy and Silas to join him with all haste (Acts 17:15). When he sent Timothy back from Athens to Thessalonica he spoke of being "left alone" in Athens (1 Thess 3:1). He wrote to the Corinthians: "When I came to Troas to preach the gospel of Christ, a door was opened for me in the Lord; but my mind could not rest because I did not find my brother Titus there. So I took leave of them and went on to Macedonia" (2 Cor 2:12-13).

But Paul's preference for fellow workers was not dictated solely by his desire for companionship. It was part of his strategy as a "skilled master builder" (1 Cor 3:10). He heartily agreed with the Old Testament dictum that if five can chase a hundred, a hundred can put ten thousand to flight (Lev 26:8). Also, he remembered that Jesus sent out His disciples two by two. In any event, Paul was a confirmed believer in teamwork, and by temperament and training he was marked for leadership. "He [Paul] was not a solitary evangelist, but rather the commanding officer of a large circle of missionaries; and the number of his co-laborers increased with the progress of the work."[6]

---

6. Purves, *Christianity in the Apostolic Age*, p. 177.

It is obvious that Paul in his capacity of "commanding officer" was in full charge of the operation. Under the leading of the Holy Spirit he moved his workers around as occasion required. Some, like Luke and Timothy, were associated with him over a long period of time. Others, like Priscilla and Aquila, worked with him sporadically. Still others came and went, some of their own accord (1 Cor 16:17) and others at his behest (Phil 2:23). They brought him news from the churches (1 Thess 3:6) and took back his instructions to the churches (Col 4:7). In this way Paul was able to multiply himself many times, thereby increasing his effectiveness as an apostle to the Gentile world. Of all his fellow workers, Timothy served him longest and loved him best (2 Tim 4:9; Phil 2:19-23).

9. He became all things to all men. When it came to the content of the gospel message Paul was both adamant and dogmatic. The message could never be changed, not even by an angel from heaven (Gal 1:6-9). But in everything else he was flexible. To the Jews he became as a Jew, to the Gentiles he became as a Gentile. And all this for one supreme purpose—that by all means he might win men to Christ (1 Cor 9:19-23).

This appears all the more remarkable when Paul's background and training are taken into consideration. At one time he had been "a Hebrew born of Hebrews" (Phil 3:5), "a Pharisee, a son of Pharisees" (Acts 23:6), and "extremely zealous . . . for the traditions" of his fathers (Gal 1:14). But his lofty religious pedigree he counted "as loss for the sake of Christ" (Phil 3:7). Indeed, he counted everything as loss because of the surpassing worth of knowing Christ Jesus the Lord. Thereafter it was his inestimable privilege to "preach to the Gentiles the unsearchable riches of Christ" (Eph 3:8). In order to fulfill that high and holy calling he was willing to become all things to all men that by all means he might win some.

The church in Paul's day was divided into two distinct camps: the Jewish Christians who wanted to retain their Jewish culture, and the Gentile Christians who wanted to develop a Christian culture. The cleavage between these two groups was so great that a special council had to be called in Jerusalem to discuss and define the status of the Gentile believers in the Christian church (Acts 15). Paul, the apostle to the Gentiles, was caught in the crossfire of this controversy.

The burning issue among Jewish believers was circumcision (Acts 15:1). Paul's own position on the matter was clear. "In Christ Jesus neither circumcision nor uncircumcision is of any avail, but faith working through love" (Gal 5:6). Again he wrote: "For he is not a real Jew who is one outwardly, nor is true circumcision something external and physical. He is a Jew who is one inwardly, and real circumcision is a matter of the heart, spiritual and not literal" (Rom 2:28-29).

How then do we explain Paul's decision to circumcise Timothy (Acts 16:3) and his refusal to do the same for Titus (Gal 2:3-4)? The answer is: the good of the work. Paul knew that not everyone shared his lofty views regarding circumcision; therefore he would gladly go along with them in their ignorance or prejudice. He was prepared to fight the world, the flesh, and the devil; but he refused to fight his brothers in Christ over matters which, to him at least, were not a fundamental part of the gospel. He even rejoiced over those who preached Christ "from envy and rivalry," thinking to afflict him in his imprisonment (Phil 1:15-17). Paul's understanding of the gospel in Galatians 1 should not be divorced from his attitude toward the gospel preachers in Philippians 1.

In the Gentile church the major issue was idolatry, in particular food offered to idols (1 Cor 8). Paul's knowledge that an idol has no real existence solved the problem for him, but he realized that not all believers possessed his knowledge. Therefore he advised sympathy and understanding on the part of the strong. For himself, he was willing to go the whole way for the sake of the weaker brother and not touch the stuff. "If food is a cause of my brother's falling, I will never eat meat, lest I cause my brother to fall" (1 Cor 8:13).

Does that mean that if Paul was a missionary to the Muslims he would not eat pork, and if he was a missionary to the Hindus he would not eat beef? What else *could* it mean? How many present-day missionaries are that flexible? Some American missionaries feel obliged to defend capitalism and the free enterprise system in a socialist country, even though they know they will alienate the very people they are seeking to win. Others give the impression that the kingdom of God is to be equated with the American way of life. The missionary movement of our day operates in a highly complex international situation whose political, economic, social, and racial problems defy solution. The Christian missionary, especially the American missionary, should be as wise as a serpent and as harmless as a dove (Mt 10:16), and as far as possible give no offense to the Jews or the Gentiles or the church of God (1 Cor 10:32).

Factors in Paul's Success

Few missionaries have been as successful as the apostle Paul. Whatever he did, the blessing of God rested on his labors. Everywhere,

85

the gospel proved to be the power of God unto salvation. Souls were saved, believers were edified, churches were founded, entire communities were changed. But not all reaction was positive. Some people followed him, while others fought him tooth and nail and ran him out of town. At least he had the satisfaction of not being ignored. As a matter of fact, his reputation for causing excitement was such that he and his companions were known as men who "turned the world upside down" (Acts 17:6).

Paul was a success-oriented person in the best sense of the term. He played to win (1 Cor 9:26-27), and he played for keeps (2 Cor 5:9-10). He was a high-minded person (Phil 4:8) with the purest of motives (1 Cor 13:1-3) and the noblest of goals (Phil 1:21). He sought nothing for himself (1 Thess 2:5-9) but wanted everything for Christ (Phil 1:20). For him, success involved two things—the glory of God (1 Cor 10:31) and the good of his fellow men (Rom 15:1-2). He brings both ideas together in one passage: "He who serves Christ is acceptable to God and approved by men" (Rom 14:18). He believed in success (2 Cor 2:14), he prayed for success (Rom 1:10), he expected success (Rom 15:29), and he achieved success (2 Tim 4:6-8).

How are we to account for his amazing success?

1. His deep conviction regarding his call. In this postcolonial period many missionaries have an identity crisis. They are not quite sure who they are or how they are to fit into the new scheme of things on the mission field. Paul had no such problem. He knew himself to be an apostle and frequently referred to himself as such. He was many other things as well: author, preacher, teacher, traveler, organizer, tentmaker; but these were incidental to his main calling, that of an apostle.

He refers to himself as having been "called" to be an apostle (Rom 1:1; 1 Cor 1:1) "by the will of God" (2 Cor 1:1; Eph 1:1; Col 1:1; 1 Tim 1:1; 2 Tim 1:1). He speaks of having been "set apart" to the gospel ministry before he was born (Gal 1:15). At the time of his conversion God referred to him as a "chosen instrument of mine to carry my name before the Gentiles and kings and the sons of Israel" (Acts 9:15).

Following his conversion he "did not confer with flesh and blood," nor did he go up to Jerusalem to those who had been apostles before him. Instead he went into Arabia for a time of reflection and orientation (Gal 1:16-17).

More specifically, he was called to be an apostle to the Gentiles (Eph 3:7-8). This too was not his doing. Given a choice, Paul doubtless would have preferred to be an apostle to his own beloved people, for whose salvation he so ardently longed (Rom 9:1-5). On at least one occasion God had to remind him of his mission to the Gentiles and order him out of Jerusalem (Acts 22:17-21).

One thing Paul never doubted or forgot was his relationship to Jesus Christ. If he was a prisoner, he was not a prisoner of Rome but of Jesus Christ (Eph 3:1). Rome might immobilize him, neutralize him, victimize him, but even in chains he remained an ambassador for Christ (Eph 6:20). He might lose his Roman citizenship but never his apostolic credentials. These remained intact, quite beyond the reach of hostile forces, political or religious. Nothing could dampen his spirits or blur his vision. Even from his prison cell in Rome he could write: "I rejoice. Yes, and I shall rejoice. For I know that through your prayers and the help of the Spirit of Jesus Christ this will turn out for my deliverance, as it is my eager expectation and hope that I shall not be at all ashamed, but that with full courage now as always Christ will be honored in my body, whether by life or by death. For to me to live is Christ, and to die is gain" (Phil 1:18-21).

2. His complete dedication to the will of God. To many people the will of God is something to be avoided; if not avoided, then endured. Not so with Paul. Like his Master before him, he had a high regard for the will of God and could say: "Lo, I have come to do thy will, O God" (Heb 10:7). Just as David served his generation by the will of God, so did Paul.

From the day he first acknowledged the lordship of Christ on the Damascus road to the end of his long and fruitful career, Paul's chief concern was to do the will of God. All his plans were focused on that one great goal. He desired greatly to see Rome, and prayed to that end; but he would proceed there only if God prospered him (Rom 1:10). When pressed to remain in Ephesus he declined, saying: "I will return to you if God wills" (Acts 18:21). On his last visit to Jerusalem his friends did their best to dissuade him from exposing himself to danger. When he refused to take their advice, they desisted, saying, "The will of the Lord be done" (Acts 21:14). Some expositors have thought Paul was wrong at that point and should have heeded their advice and thus avoided imprisonment, but there is no hint of this in Paul's writings. When referring to the matter later on he said: "I want you to know, brethren, that what has happened to me has really served to advance the gospel" (Phil 1:12). There is no suggestion that his imprisonment, which began in Jerusalem, had taken him out of the will of God.

Paul's thorn in the flesh must have been exceedingly bothersome. Three times he requested that it be removed; but when he discovered that such was not God's will for him, he acquiesced, saying: "I will all the more gladly boast of my weakness, that the power of Christ may rest upon me" (2 Cor 12:9). It never entered Paul's mind to question the will of God once he knew it. He would have said a hearty amen to the words of the hymn writer:

> He always wins who sides with God,
>   To him no chance is lost;
> God's will is sweetest to him
>   When it triumphs at his cost.
>
> Ill that He blesses is our good,
>   And unblest good is ill;
> And all is right that seems most wrong
>   If it be His sweet will.

3. His complete dependence on the Holy Spirit. Paul was an unusual man with great natural gifts, and the temptation to depend on those gifts must have been a perennial problem. Did he succumb to that temptation in Athens? If so he corrected the situation when he got to Corinth, for he said: "When I came to you, brethren, I did not come proclaiming to you the testimony of God in lofty words or wisdom. For I decided to know nothing among you except Jesus Christ and him crucified. And I was with you in weakness, and in much fear and trembling; and my speech and my message were not in plausible words of wisdom, but in demonstration of the Spirit and power, that your faith might not rest in the wisdom of men but in the power of God" (1 Cor 2:1-5).

This power is variously referred to as the power of God (Rom 1:16), the power of Christ (2 Cor 12:9), and the power of the Spirit (Rom 15:19). These are not three kinds of power, but one divine power communicated to (Rom 8:11), and mediated through, the believer (Rom 15:18-19).

The Holy Spirit is the Spirit of life (Rom 8:2), the Spirit of truth (Jn 14:17), and the Spirit of power (Acts 1:8). In this threefold capacity He is quite indispensable to God's total scheme of redemption. It is the Holy Spirit who imparts the life of God to the soul dead in trespasses and sins (Eph 2:1; Rom 8:11). It is the Holy Spirit who reveals the truth of God to the mind darkened by sin and Satan (1 Cor 2:11-15; 2 Cor 4:4). It is the Holy Spirit who communicates the power of God to the life dedicated to the service of God (Rom 15:15-20). Without the presence and power of the Holy Spirit the Christian worker labors in vain. All his best efforts are doomed to abject failure. It is not by might nor by power, but by the Holy Spirit that the work of God is accomplished (Zech 4:6). For the missionary (or anyone else for that matter), to try to live and work in the energy of the flesh, without the power of the Holy Spirit, is an act of consummate folly. No one knew this better than the apostle Paul.

4. His fearless presentation of the gospel. If today's missionary in his presentation of the gospel thinks he has problems with paganism, humanism, nationalism, communism, syncretism, or universalism, he should remember the predicament in which Paul found himself in the first century.

The world of Paul's day was divided into three major groups: Jews, Greeks, and Romans. Paul preached to all three groups, and they all found his message offensive. The Jews demanded signs, the Greeks sought after wisdom, the Romans were interested only in power.

The Jews listened politely as long as Paul preached from the Old Testament; but the moment he shifted gears and declared that Jesus, the despised carpenter of Nazareth, was their Messiah they were ready to stone him (Acts 14:19).

The Greeks were an intellectual people who loved nothing more than philosophical debate. They equated civilization with wisdom. The mind, not the body, was important. For them salvation would come at death when the *nous* (mind) would be liberated from the prison house of the body. Consequently they had no interest whatever in the Resurrection and laughed Paul to scorn when he mentioned it (Acts 17:32).

The Romans were the great empire builders of the day. Their cities, roads, libraries, palaces, and colosseums were symbols of imperial might. They equated civilization with power. Imagine their reaction when they were asked to believe that a Jewish criminal, crucified in weakness on a Roman cross, was the Sovereign and Savior of the world.

Obviously Paul had his problems. But never once did he flinch in his proclamation of the gospel. Regardless of who was in his audience—Jews, Greeks, Romans, or all three—he never failed to declare the whole counsel of God. It is true that his approach was different with different groups, and with each he endeavored to build bridges of understanding. He was considerate and conciliatory. He always began with what was familiar to his audience and from there proceeded to the new and unfamiliar truths of the gospel, knowing that some of those truths were totally unacceptable to them.

This took both faith and courage, but Paul had his full share of both. He really believed in both the *truth* (Col 1:5) and the *power* (Rom 1:16) of the gospel. He likewise believed in the ability of the Holy Spirit to apply the gospel to the minds and hearts of the hearers (Jn 16:8).

As for courage, Paul was living proof that when God becomes

The Biblical Basis of Missions

real, others become shadows. And to Paul, God was real. The fear of man was the least of his worries; his chief concern was to please God (Gal 1:10). He was persuaded that nothing could separate him from the love of God (Rom 8:39) or the life of Christ (Phil 1:21-23). He believed, as John Wesley did, that he was immortal till his work was done. To live or die was all the same to him (Phil 1:20). And if perchance his enemies succeeded one day in killing him, he would simply go home to heaven in a blaze of glory!

5. His emphasis on the autonomy of the local church. Nowhere were Paul's methods and ours so far apart as in the matter of church planting. Roland Allen says:

> If there is a striking difference between St. Paul's preaching and ours there is a still greater difference between his method of dealing with his converts and that common among us today. Indeed, I think we may say that it is in his dealing with his converts that we come to the heart of the matter and may hope to find one secret of his amazing success.[7]

How do we treat our converts? Allen goes on to say:

> We have done everything for them. We have taught them, baptized them, shepherded them. We have managed their funds, ordered their services, built their churches, provided their teachers. We have nursed them, fed them, doctored them. We have trained them, and have even ordained some of them. We have done everything for them except acknowledge any equality. We have done everything for them, but very little with them. We have done everything for them except give place to them. We have treated them as "dear children," but not as "brethren."[8]

Many changes have come about since those words were written, but not always with our approval and seldom with our initiative. We dragged our feet until we became the unwilling allies of the historical unfolding of history or, worse still, the unfortunate victims of the upheaval of politics. Our greatest single blunder was to hold on to power too long. Much of the church-mission tension today is due to that melancholy fact.

How did Paul treat his converts? Each local church was a part of the universal church, but each was expected to stand on its own feet and administer its own affairs without any control from him or anyone else. It was to be independent of all outside influence, relying solely on the Holy Spirit. To get the church established Paul appointed the first group of elders. After that they appointed their own elders. From

7. Allen, *Missionary Methods*, p. 82.
8. Ibid., p. 143.

then on everything was under their control—baptism, the Lord's Supper, teaching, training, discipline, finances, and so forth.

Paul did not leave his converts to fend for themselves alone. He committed them to the tender ministry of the Holy Spirit, knowing that He could take care of His own. After all, it was the Holy Spirit who consecrated the first group of elders (Acts 20:28), and He would not desert them. In the case of the church in Ephesus, Paul knew that after his departure "fierce wolves" would attack the flock; but he did not delay his departure on that account. He simply commended them to God and the Word of His grace (Acts 20:32). God, who had purchased the church with His own blood, was well able to protect His own property in the face of all potential enemies, within or without.

To the apostle Paul the Holy Spirit was a living, bright reality, a person as well as a power. He possessed all the prerogatives of Godhead, along with the Father and the Son. He had become incarnate in the church at Pentecost. Throughout this entire dispensation He would be the Executive Director of the Triune God in full charge of the church's affairs. He would guide the church into all truth. He would energize the church for witness and service. He would control, teach, purify, and protect the church. Paul taught his converts to depend on the Holy Spirit. If they followed that course, they would have no need to depend on anyone else.

6. His wise policy regarding money. Money is the *sine qua non* of modern missions—or so it would seem. Probably no other one thing has done so much harm to the Christian cause. And the problem is still with us.

Money did not loom very large in the thinking of Jesus or the practice of the early church. It is true that Jesus and His disciples paid for their food (Jn 4:8), and Judas acted as treasurer for the Twelve (Jn 12:6). Nevertheless, neither Jesus nor the apostles attached much importance to money. Jesus warned against laying up treasures on earth (Mt 6:19) and stated clearly that it is impossible to serve God and mammon (Mt 6:24). He also taught that a man's life does not consist in the abundance of things that he possesses (Lk 12:15). When He sent out the Twelve He told them: "Take no gold, nor silver, nor copper in your belts, no bag for your journey, nor two tunics, nor sandals, nor a staff; for the laborer is worthy of his hire" (Mt 10:9-10).

It would seem that the apostles followed Jesus' instructions; for on one occasion, when asked for alms, Peter was obliged to say: "I have no silver and gold, but I give you what I have; in the name of Jesus Christ of Nazareth, walk" (Acts 3:6). Apparently lack of money didn't hamper Peter. He had something that money could not buy.

Paul's policy with regard to money was threefold. (1) He supported himself and his colleagues by working with his own hands. (2) He expected the churches founded by him to be self-supporting from the beginning. (3) He encouraged those churches, poor though they were, to contribute to the needs of others.

As an apostle, Paul had every right to expect his converts to support him. It was a recognized principle laid down by the Lord Himself that those who "proclaim the gospel should get their living by the gospel" (1 Cor 9:14). This was the general practice among the apostles (1 Cor 9:1-7). Paul, however, refused to assert his right in this matter. He preferred to pay his own way, thus making the gospel "free of charge" (1 Cor 9:18). He reminded the Thessalonians that he worked "night and day" that he might not be a "burden" to any of them (1 Thess 2:9), and he reminded the Ephesian elders that he had "coveted no one's silver or gold or apparel" (Acts 20:33).

This was important for both the reputation of the preacher and the success of the gospel, for the Roman world of that day was full of peripatetic teachers who lived off the "offerings" of gullible listeners whose ears it was not difficult to tickle. Paul would do everything in his power to avoid the charge of money-making, thus bringing the gospel into disrepute.

On the other hand Paul did not refuse to accept personal gifts when they were an expression of Christian love. Several such gifts were received from the church at Philippi, and Paul's Epistle to the Philippians is a beautiful and tactful acknowledgment of those gifts. He was grateful for the gifts, not only because they met his need but also because they represented fruit that increased to their credit (Phil 4:17).

Even more important was Paul's practice of establishing self-supporting churches. There is no mention of Paul giving money to the churches. He expected them to manage their own affairs and pay their own way even though many of them were extremely poor (2 Cor 8:2). Poverty was no hindrance to progress. They were to live within their means and support the local work, including works of charity. They bought no land, erected no buildings, and endowed no institutions. Hence their annual budget was modest enough to be sustained by local means.

All this is in stark contrast to the methods employed by modern missions. Missionaries from the affluent West had plenty of money but didn't always use it wisely. They bought valuable property and proceeded to erect costly buildings that the national churches were unable to maintain. Pastors, teachers, evangelists, and others were hired by the missionaries and paid with foreign funds. Once the pattern was established it was almost impossible to change it. Some of the oldest churches on the mission field have been the last to achieve self-support.

Paul not only taught the Gentile churches to stand on their own feet, he encouraged them on at least one important occasion to take up a special offering for the poor saints in Jerusalem. So important was this task that he and his colleagues devoted several years to the project. This gesture was much more than an act of charity; it was, at least in Paul's mind, an expression of Christian love and a demonstration of Christian unity. Doubtless Paul entertained the hope that this generous gift, given out of deep poverty, would help to cement relations between the Jewish and Gentile segments of the Christian church.

7. The example of his life. In all Christian work the character of the messenger is as important as the content of the message. There are two dimensions to Christian work—the divine and the human. Nobody knew this better than Paul. In explaining his success in Thessalonica he mentioned both dimensions. The divine was equated with the power of the Holy Spirit. The human had to do with the character of the messengers, including Timothy and Silas. Paul declared: "For our gospel came to you not only in word, but also in power and in the Holy Spirit and with full conviction. You know what kind of men we proved to be among you for your sake" (1 Thess 1:5). Then he devoted the first twelve verses of the second chapter to a description of the three men. "You are witnesses, and God also, how holy and righteous and blameless was our behavior to you believers" (1 Thess 2:10).

He also reminded them: "You became imitators of us and of the Lord" (1 Thess 1:6). The order here is important. They were won first to Paul, then to Christ. Paul's converts were attracted to him because he was a living example of the loveliness of Christ, and through him they came to know the Lord. Modern pedagogy has shown how important the character of the teacher is. If the student is "turned off" by the teacher, he is not likely to accept his teaching.

Time and again in his epistles, especially in his Second Epistle to the Corinthians, Paul, in all honesty and modesty, reminds his converts of the kind of life he lived among them. To an unusual degree he exemplified in his own character the virtues he tried to inculcate in them. There is no doubt this had much to do with his phenomenal success.

PART TWO

The Trinitarian Dimension of Missions

Too often we have thought of the Christian mission as relating predominantly, if not exclusively, to the person and work of Jesus Christ. His incarnation is at the heart of the Christian faith. We celebrate His birth at Christmas, His death on Good Friday, and His resurrection on Easter Sunday. He is the Head of the church and the Author of the Great Commission. The earliest and simplest of all creeds is "Jesus Christ is Lord." One early creed of the church contains six phrases (1 Tim 3:16), and all six of them pertain to the person of Christ. This being so, it is very easy to allow the role of the second person of the Trinity to overshadow, if not obliterate, that of the other two.

The church in our day has paid scant attention to the trinitarian dimension of the Christian mission. "The point has several times been made that a true doctrine of missions must make a large place for the work of the Holy Spirit; but it is equally true that a true doctrine of missions will have much to say about God the Father."[1]

---

1. Lesslie Newbigin, *Trinitarian Faith and Today's Mission* (Richmond: John Knox Press, 1963), p. 31.

5

The Sovereignty of God

One of the great doctrines of the Bible is the sovereignty of God. The Scriptures clearly teach that God is the Creator, Sustainer, and Ruler of the universe. Heaven is His throne and earth is His footstool (Is 66:1). The earth is the Lord's and the fullness thereof, the world and they that dwell therein (Ps 24:1). He is the Giver of every good and perfect gift (Jas 1:17). Day by day He opens His hand and satisfies the desire of every living thing (Ps 145:16). In Him we live and move and have our being (Acts 17:28). He has a plan and a purpose for the church and the world (Eph 1:9-10). He knows the end from the beginning (Is 46:10) and is working all things after the counsel of His own will (Eph 1:11), not only among the hosts of heaven but also among the inhabitants of the earth (Dan 4:35). Paul expresses it in these majestic words: "O the depth of the riches and wisdom and knowledge of God! How unsearchable are his judgments and how inscrutable his ways! 'For who has known the mind of the Lord, or who has been his counselor?' 'Or who has given a gift to him that he might be repaid?' For from him and through him and to him are all things. To him be glory for ever. Amen" (Rom 11:33-36).

The sovereignty of God is based on three outstanding attributes which in their fullness belong only to God: His almighty power (Is 40:12-31), His perfect wisdom (Rom 11:33-36), and His intrinsic goodness (Ps 145:17). All three of these great attributes are essential to the concept of sovereignty. It is not enough to say, "I believe in God the Father Almighty." If God were all-powerful but not all-wise,

The Trinitarian Dimension of Missions

He might conceivably use His power in foolish and futile pursuits. If He were all-powerful but not all-good, He might abuse His power to the everlasting detriment of His helpless creatures. This means that in the moral character of God there are built-in checks and balances which make Him a perfect Supreme Being worthy of our love and trust. His wisdom ensures that His power will always be used in a safe and sane manner. His goodness ensures that all His plans and purposes will be not only for His own glory but also for the ultimate and everlasting good of His creatures.

The sovereignty of God is seen in all three of His divine activities: creation (Rev 4:11), redemption (Eph 1:5-9), and judgment (Rev 15:3-4; 16:5-7; Rom 9:18-23). Everything God does is done according to His own plan and purpose, on His own initiative, by His own power, for His own glory. When human history has run its course and mankind stands before God, the unanimous verdict of a moral universe will be, "He has done all things well."

The Christian mission is part of God's sovereign activity in the realm of redemption. From first to last the Christian mission is God's mission, not man's. It originated in the heart of God. It is based on the love of God. It is determined by the will of God. Its mandate was enunciated by the Son of God. Its rationale is explained in the Word of God. For its ultimate success it is dependent on the power of God. Nowhere is the sovereignty of God more clearly seen than in the Christian mission, and this in several ways.

God's Dealings with the Missionary

1. **God's choice of the man.** We are accustomed to speaking of missionary "volunteers," and everyone knows what is meant by the expression. Is it biblically correct? What about the great prophets of the Old Testament? Were any of them "volunteers"? Did Abraham, Moses, David, or Jeremiah volunteer for the service of God? The answer is no. At forty years of age Moses was a "volunteer" and offered his services to his people in slavery. His self-initiated attempt at saving his people ended in disaster and he had to flee for his life. Forty years later, when God's time had come, Moses was anything but a volunteer. He offered all kinds of excuses why God should get someone else.

Jeremiah was no better: he too tried to beg off. At first sight it looks as if Isaiah was a volunteer, for he said, "Here am I; send me" (Is 6:8); but a closer look at the passage will reveal the fact that he

98

was simply responding to God's call, "Whom shall I send, and who will go for us?"

Jesus made it very plain: "You did not choose me, but I chose you and appointed you that you should go and bear fruit" (Jn 15:16). He found Peter and Andrew by the Sea of Galilee and issued the command, "Follow me." He did the same with James and John (Mt 4:18-22). There is no reason to believe that these four fishermen, left to themselves, would have abandoned their fishing business and followed Jesus. It was His idea, not theirs.

Paul is most emphatic on this point. He insisted that he was an apostle "by the will of God" (Col 1:1). It is unthinkable that the arch persecutor of the church would ever have volunteered to become its chief apostle. He would never have capitulated to the hated Nazarene unless he had been "apprehended" on the road to Damascus. At the beginning of his Christian life God spoke of him as a "chosen instrument" (Acts 9:15). And writing about his apostolic ministry Paul said: "For I take no special pride in the fact that I preach the Gospel. I feel compelled to do so; I should be utterly miserable if I failed to preach it. If I do this work because I choose to do so then I am entitled to a reward. But if it is no choice of mine, but a sacred responsibility put upon me, what can I expect in the way of reward?" (1 Cor 9:16-17, Phillips).

In the four Gospels only one person ever "volunteered" to follow Christ, and he was dissuaded by the hardships involved (Lk 9:57-58). "Don't be a missionary if you can possibly avoid it" was the advice given to a young man by a veteran missionary. Taken at face value it sounds like strange advice, but there is enough truth in the statement to make us sit up and take notice.

Every Christian is called on to be a witness for Christ in his daily life and work. Not everyone is called to be a full-time missionary in the professional sense of that term. Not all were apostles in Paul's day, not all are missionaries in our day; and whether or not a person becomes a missionary depends on the will of God, not the inclination of the individual.

2. The kind of ministry. Not only does God make sovereign choice of the man, He also decides on the kind of ministry in which the messenger will engage. One's ministry depends on the spiritual gifts he possesses. There is a necessary connection between the two. The gift equips the man for the ministry and the ministry depends for its success on the gift. And how does one acquire the gift? The spiritual gifts are bestowed on the believer by the Holy Spirit in His own sovereign way. After enumerating the various gifts of the Spirit Paul

99

goes on to say, "All these are inspired by one and the same Spirit, who apportions to each one individually as he wills" (1 Cor 12:11). The same teaching is found in Ephesians 4.

Peter and Paul were both apostles by the will of God, but one was an apostle to the Jews and the other to the Gentiles. Who was responsible for the choice? Was the choice left to them or was it made for them? Paul makes bold to suggest that God Himself was responsible for this division of labor (Gal 2:8). It was God who ordained that he should be an apostle to the Gentiles, and on more than one occasion He had to remind Paul of this fact (Acts 9:15; 22:21).

Even though Peter was officially known as an apostle to the Jews, it was he who preached the gospel to the Gentile, Cornelius. Was this left to Peter's discretion? Indeed not. Speaking at the council in Jerusalem when the fate of the Gentile Christians was in the balance, Peter reminded the assembly of the historic event recorded in Acts 10. "Brethren, you know that in the early days God made choice among you, that by my mouth the Gentiles should hear the word of the gospel and believe" (Acts 15:7). Left to himself Peter would never have preached the gospel to Cornelius. But God chose Peter and the Spirit bade him go (Acts 11:12). Only then was he willing to preach the gospel to the Gentiles.

In both cases the choice was God's. Thankfully, the two men had the good sense to acquiesce in the will of God.

3. The sphere of the ministry. The field is the world, and the apostles were told to go into all the world and preach the gospel to every creature. They were to begin at Jerusalem and proceed from there to Judea and Samaria and ultimately to the ends of the earth. Obviously a person can work in only one place at a time. It would not be wise to have all the apostles in Judea or in Samaria. If the world is to be evangelized in an orderly fashion, there must be some overall plan of action.

Who decided on the plan of action? When Paul reached the western perimeter of Asia he tried to preach the gospel in the Roman province of Asia, but the Holy Spirit forbade him (Acts 16:6). He then tried to go to Bithynia, but again the Spirit interfered (Acts 16:7). In a nocturnal vision Paul saw a man of Macedonia saying, "Come over to Macedonia and help us" (Acts 16:9). Interpreting this to be the Lord's will for him at that time, Paul and his companions crossed over into Europe and planted the church in that continent. As a result Europe became a "Christian" continent and Asia remained "heathen."

What might have happened had Paul followed his own inclinations and gone east instead of west? It is intriguing to remember that Buddhism entered China from India about the time Paul arrived in Rome. There it took root and became one of the three great religions of China. Suppose Christianity instead of Buddhism had been taken to China at that time. Would Asia today be "Christian" and Europe "heathen"?

The fact remains that Paul in his missionary journeys was guided very definitely by the Lord, and the sphere of his ministry was necessarily restricted to those regions for which God had a purpose of grace. Wherever Paul went he knew that he would go "in the fulness of the blessing of Christ" (Rom 15:29). Paul was not left to make his own travel plans. It is true that he used common sense when he followed the Roman roads, concentrating on the large cities with their cosmopolitan populations. Nevertheless in all his travels he was conscious of the leading of the Lord, and no amount of danger could deter him from going forward if he conceived this to be the will of God for him (Acts 21:13). On the other hand, a city as large and strategic as Ephesus would merit a visit only "if God will" (Acts 18:21).

4. The duration of the ministry. Some missionaries, like William Axling (Japan) and Stanley Jones (India), rounded out sixty years in the service of Christ. Others, like John and Betty Stam (China), were cut down during their first term of service. Circumstances enter into the picture to be sure, but even the circumstances are under God's control. When Peter asked Jesus about the ministry of John, Jesus replied, "If it is my will that he remain until I come, what is that to you?" (Jn 21:22). Stephen became the first Christian martyr; but his fellow deacon, Philip, served Christ for a whole generation (Acts 21:8). The apostle James was beheaded by Herod; but Peter, slated for the same fate, was miraculously delivered (Acts 12).

5. The success of the ministry. Who is to say what is "success" in the service of Christ? Jesus Christ is the Lord of the harvest. It is He who deploys His workers in various parts of the vineyard. He ordains some to sow and others to reap (Jn 4:35-38). We identify success with those who reap. Every supporting church likes to hear a "success" story when the missionary returns on furlough. Given a choice, most missionaries would prefer to be among the reapers, not the sowers. Who wants to sow year after year and not see a harvest? But God has ordained that some of His servants will sow and others will reap. In the final analysis it is God who gives the increase (1 Cor 3:6-9). John the Baptist recognized this fact and was content to leave the results with God (Jn 3:25-27). When Jesus' messianic mission ended in failure, He fell back on the sovereignty of God and gave thanks for apparent failure (Mt 11:25-26). A thing is good only if it is good *in God's sight*.

God's Dealings with the Sinner

1. The fate of the sinner is decided by a judicial act of God. However difficult it may be for us to explain, the fact remains that God in His sovereignty opens the eyes of some (Mt 13:14-17) and closes the eyes of others (Rom 11:8). The Scriptures tell us that God hardened Pharaoh's heart (Ex 7:3) and opened Lydia's heart (Acts 16:14). The early church grew in strength and size not because people decided to join the church, but because they were added to the church by an act of God (Acts 2:47). The only ones who believed were those who were "ordained to eternal life" (Acts 13:48).

2. Only those who are drawn by the Father will ever come to Christ. The teaching of Christ is clear on this point. He said, "No one can come to me unless the Father who sent me draws him" (Jn 6:44). Left to himself, the ungodly sinner will never forsake his wicked way and seek after God (Rom 3:10-18). Therefore God must take the initiative. Jesus Christ came into the world to seek and to save that which is lost (Lk 19:10). The Holy Spirit came into the world to convict the world of sin, righteousness, and judgment (Jn 16:8). Without the seeking Shepherd the sheep would never be found. Without the convicting Spirit the sinner would never be saved.

3. The very faith by which a person believes is itself the gift of God. Paul is emphatic on this point. "For by grace you have been saved through faith, and this is not your own doing, it is the gift of God" (Eph 2:8).

> We must never forget that it is God who saves. It is God who brings men and women under the sound of the gospel, and it is God who brings them to faith in Christ. . . . If we forget that only God can give faith, we shall start to think that the making of converts depends, in the last analysis, not on God but·on us.[1]

If God of His own free will does not give this faith, man cannot by the independent exercise of his own intellect "believe" in Christ. He can give intellectual assent to certain historic facts concerning Christ, but saving faith is something else. The insight that enabled Peter to confess Jesus as the Son of God came as a revelation from

1. J. I. Packer, *Evangelism and the Sovereignty of God* (London: Inter-Varsity Fellowship, 1961), p. 27.

God (Mt 16:17). Paul informs us that no man can call Jesus "Lord" except by the Holy Spirit (1 Cor 12:3).

4. Only persons united to Christ by the Holy Spirit remain steadfast in the faith; the others fall away. The way to God is through Jesus Christ (Jn 14:6). The way to Christ is through the Holy Spirit (Jn 16:13-14). He and He alone unites the soul to Christ (1 Cor 12:13). Not all of Christ's disciples remained with Him to the end. In mid-career many of them left Him and went their way when they were introduced to His "hard sayings" (Jn 6:60, 66). Only those whose faith was God-given (Mt 16:17) and therefore genuine (Jn 6:69) remained with Him to the end (Jn 17:12).

The apostles were disturbed when the Pharisees took offense at the teachings of Christ. They feared that the "hard sayings" would alienate them, and so they expressed their fears to the Master. Jesus had no such fears. He replied: "Every plant which my heavenly Father has not planted will be rooted up" (Mt 15:13). Jesus had implicit faith in the sovereignty of God and refused to panic when the crowds began to dwindle. He believed that every soul "given" to Him by the Father would ultimately come to Him. None would be cast out (Jn 6:37), none would be uprooted (Mt 15:13). If they took offense and went away, that was proof that they had never been "given" or "planted" by the Father. If their roots were in God, they would remain no matter what happened. If their roots were not in God, sooner or later they were sure to be plucked up.

God's Ordering of World Events

God is the Creator and Sustainer of the universe. This world is *His* world. In spite of all the evidence to the contrary, God is in full charge of human affairs and world events (Dan 4:35). He is the God of history as well as the God of creation and redemption. The missionary movement is part of history and must continue to operate within the context of history regardless of how turbulent it may become. This is seen in the following ways:

1. The times and seasons are in God's control. The last question addressed to Christ by His disciples was, "Will you at this time restore the kingdom to Israel?" (Acts 1:6). Jesus replied, "It is not for you to know times or seasons which the Father has fixed by his own authority." In the course of church history there have been good times and bad. Indeed, we are informed that "for everything there is a season and a time for every matter under heaven" (Eccles 3:1). There is a time to plant and a time to pluck up what is planted. There is a time to break down and a time to build up. There is a time to keep and a time to cast away. There is a time for war and a time for peace (Eccles 3:2-8). These times and seasons—bad as well as good—are fixed by the authority of God.

2. The opening and the closing of doors are the prerogative of God. We have heard much in this postwar period about closing doors. The assumption is that these doors were closed by the nationalists, or the Communists, or the revolutionists; and behind all these, of course, was the devil. It is true that the devil delights in closing doors. It is also true that human agents are usually employed. The fact remains that when doors are closed they are closed by God and not by man or the devil.

This may sound like heresy but it has the sanction of Holy Scripture. In His letter to the church in Philadelphia Jesus Christ describes Himself as the One who opens and no man shuts, and shuts and no man opens (Rev 3:7). Most of us prefer open doors. We don't like closed doors. We tend to identify the former with God and His purposes; we associate the second with the devil and his diabolical schemes. This is because, like Peter, we have man's point of view and not God's (Mt 16:23).

The greatest reverse ever suffered by the modern missionary movement was the evacuation of mainland China in the early 1950s. In the 1840s the Christian church, like a mighty army, moved into China with its banners flying. On those banners were inscribed the words of Scripture: "I am he that openeth, and no man shutteth." One hundred years later the church was on the march again, but this time it was coming out of China. Its banners, tattered and torn, were dragging in the dust. But on those banners were inscribed the words of Scripture: "I am he that shutteth, and no man openeth." By purely human definition the first event was a victory, the second a tragedy. But both were engineered by God. It was He who opened the door in the 1840s and it was He who closed the door in the late 1940s. If it had not been for the permissive will of God, all the armies of Red China could not have chased the missionaries out of that country. One can only conclude that when doors open, they open at His command; and when they close, they close at His behest. Closed doors are just as much a part of His plan as open doors.

3. Open and closed doors involve a great mystery, but God has explained the mystery in the Scriptures. After his great discourse on the history of Israel—past, present, and future—the apostle Paul exclaims, "O the depth of the riches and wisdom and knowledge of God! How unsearchable are his judgments and how inscrutable his ways! ... For from him and through him and to him are all things. To him be glory for ever" (Rom 11:33-36).

We are living in an anthropocentric world where man is the measure of all things. The whole world, so we think, revolves around a center of gravity called man. Little by little God has been pushed from the center to the perimeter. What the church needs today is a fresh look at what the Scriptures have to say about the sovereignty of God. Surely He knows the end from the beginning and is even now working all things after the counsel of His own will (Eph 1:11). He has a plan and purpose for the Jews, the Gentiles, and the church of God (1 Cor 10:32). And when things get out of hand, He is able to make even the wrath of man to praise Him (Ps 76:10). When his sanity returned after seven years, King Nebuchadnezzar had to acknowledge that the Most High does "according to his will in the host of heaven and among the inhabitants of the earth; and none can stay his hand, or say to him 'What doest thou?' " (Dan 4:35).

If we have difficulty in accepting this point of view we should not be surprised. God has already warned us: "My thoughts are not your thoughts, neither are your ways my ways, says the Lord. For as the heavens are higher than the earth so are my ways higher than your ways and my thoughts than your thoughts" (Is 55:8-9). Should we be surprised if now and then Almighty God, Maker of heaven and earth, does something that our puny, finite minds cannot fully understand? To understand everything God does, we would have to be God.

It doesn't require much faith to believe in the sovereignty of God when the world situation is under control and everything is to our liking. It is when things go wrong and life breaks down that the Christian must take his stand on the Holy Scriptures and believe that in some mysterious way, which he cannot fully understand, the purposes of God are being worked out according to His perfect plan.

The China debacle in the late 1940s was a heartbreaking experience for the thousands of missionaries there at the time. It was unthinkable that Chiang Kai-shek, a devout Christian, should be defeated by Mao Tse-tung, an avowed atheist whose hatred for religion was well known. Had God taken a poll of missionary opinion, almost to a man the missionary body would have supported Chiang Kai-shek and the Kuomintang. But God acted on His own without consulting the missionaries. And the result? By 1953 all of the missionaries were out of China. It was a bitter pill to swallow. The missionaries shook their heads. They could not believe their eyes. At least one mission leader had a nervous breakdown. The largest single mission field in all the world was closed to Christian missionaries. Worse than that, the institutional church has all but been destroyed. It takes great faith to believe that God has been in control of the situation in China during the last twenty-five years. But that is the verdict of Holy Scripture, and we had better believe it.

4. God's command to us is to get on with the job of world evangelization whether the circumstances are favorable or unfavorable. He was a wise Preacher who said, "He who observes the wind will not sow; and he who regards the clouds will not reap. . . . In the morning sow your seed, and at evening withhold not your hand; for you do not know which will prosper, this or that, or whether both alike will be good" (Eccles 11:4-6).

World evangelization cannot wait for fair skies and calm seas. The King's business requires haste (1 Sam 21:8). In the world we will always have tribulation (Jn 16:33). Bonds and afflictions awaited Paul in every city (Acts 20:23), but he never allowed them to delay or deter him (Acts 21:13). He was always ready for service (Rom 1:15) or sacrifice (Phil 2:17). To live or die was all the same to him (Phil 1:20). His only concern was that he might glorify God (1 Cor 10:31) and finish his course with joy (Acts 20:24; 2 Tim 4:7).

Some of the greatest events in mission history occurred when the times were least propitious. William Carey was pleading the cause of world missions during the French Revolution, which threatened to engulf the whole of Europe. The first American missionaries sailed for India in 1812, the year that war broke out between Britain and the United States. Hudson Taylor first arrived in China in 1853 as the Taiping Rebellion was getting under way—a rebellion that lasted fifteen years and took at least twenty million lives. In 1930, at the depth of the Depression, the China Inland Mission, now the Overseas Missionary Fellowship, called for two hundred new workers in two years—and got them.

In Ephesus Paul found "a wide door for effective work." He also discovered that there were "many adversaries" (1 Cor 16:9). The one often accompanies the other. And certainly Paul had a very turbulent career. In nearly every city his preaching precipitated a citywide riot. Time and again he barely escaped with his life. Sometimes he was told to remain where he was in spite of danger, as in the city of Corinth (Acts 18:9-10). At other times he was told to flee, as was the case in Jerusalem (Acts 22:17-18). But whether he stayed or went was inconsequential. His chief concern was to preach Christ. He never allowed circumstances—good or bad—to determine his course of action. He got his guidance from God. Once he received the green light he pressed forward without hesitation, knowing that God would hold Himself responsible for all the consequences that flowed from his obedience. He realized that safety and security are no guarantee of success. On the other hand he recognized that difficulty and danger do not necessarily spell disaster.

Missionary work must be carried on in fair weather and foul. The real tragedy does not lie in the closed countries we can't enter but in the open countries we don't enter. Closed countries are God's responsibility and we can safely leave them with Him. Open countries are our responsibility and we neglect them at our peril. We should be up and doing. The time *is* short, the fields *are* white, the laborers *are* few. It is both foolish and futile to spend our time lamenting the few doors that are closed while we refuse to enter the many doors that are open.

6

The Lordship of Christ

The lordship of Christ is an established fact, not a wish or hope on the part of the church. Preachers have been known to exhort their hearers to "make Jesus Lord." They mean well and think they are speaking biblically, but they are not. Nobody can "make" Jesus Lord. He *is* Lord. The lordship of Christ was established once and for all by an act of God the Father. Peter said: "Let all the house of Israel therefore know assuredly that God has made him both Lord and Christ, this Jesus whom you crucified" (Acts 2:36). Jesus Christ is universal Lord, not by an act of man but by an act of God.

Through the centuries the church has developed many creeds, some short and simple, others long and complicated. The earliest of all creeds was the simple declaration: "Jesus Christ is Lord" (Phil 2:11). For the early church that simple four-word confession was sufficient. Jesus Christ is Lord—period! That settled everything. That put Jesus where He belongs—on the throne. The life, work, witness, and worship of the church revolve around the person and power of the risen and exalted Christ.

This high honor was conferred on Christ by God the Father as a reward for His life of obedience during the days of His incarnation. After describing the complete obedience of Jesus to the will of the Father, Paul goes on to say: *"Therefore* God has highly exalted him and bestowed on him a name which is above every name, that at the name of Jesus every knee should bow, in heaven, and on earth, and under the earth, and every tongue confess that Jesus Christ is Lord, to the glory of God the Father" (Phil 2:9-11).

At no point did Christ exalt Himself, or arrogate the glory once renounced. He prayed, when the hour was come: "Now Father, *glorify Thou me* with Thine own self, with the glory which I had with Thee before the world was." It was for the Father to say, as He raised and enthroned Him: "Thou art my Son; I today have begotten Thee!"[1]

This act of exaltation involved two historic events: the Resurrection (Acts 3:15) and the Ascension (Acts 5:31). In Paul's epistles the Resurrection and the Ascension are regarded not as two separate events, but as two stages of one event, whereby God raised Jesus from the dead and set Him at His own right hand in glory (Eph 1:20-22). The forty-day period between the two events was simply a stopover on Jesus' triumphal march from the grave to the throne, during which He rounded up His disillusioned disciples, encouraged their hearts, strengthened their faith, and gave them their marching orders for the days to come.

The lordship of Christ is exercised in three main spheres: over the individual, the church, and the world.

Over the Individual

The claims of Christ on the individual Christian have not been adequately presented. In our preaching of the gospel we have emphasized the saviorhood of Christ but said little or nothing about His lordship. We have created the impression that it is possible to accept Christ as Savior without *at the same time* acknowledging Him as Lord. By so doing we have set up a dichotomy that is wholly foreign to New Testament teaching. We have preached a gospel of "easy believism," encouraging young people to "give their hearts to Christ" without saying anything about His claim on their lives. The results have been all too obvious in the life of the church. We end up with two kinds of Christians: the "converted" Christian and the "committed" Christian. Little wonder that so much of modern Christianity is nominal rather than vital.

There is nothing in the New Testament to suggest that a person can accept Christ as Savior at one stage in life, and five or ten years later accept Him as Lord. Jesus Christ cannot be divided. He is both Savior and Lord *in one person*. To really accept Christ is to acknowledge both His saviorhood and His lordship. When the Philippian jailor asked Paul what he must do to be saved, Paul replied: "Believe in the

1. George G. Findlay, *The Expositor's Bible* (Grand Rapids: Eerdmans, 1943), VI:27.

Lord Jesus and you will be saved" (Acts 16:31). And baptism, which immediately ensued, was a sign of his total commitment to the Lord Jesus Christ.

Missionary recruits would be much easier to get if all Christians were committed Christians who acknowledge the lordship of Jesus Christ. The New Testament has a good deal to say about the claims of Christ on the individual Christian.

1. His claim on our persons. Paul asks: "Do you not know that your body is a temple of the Holy Spirit within you, which you have from God? You are not your own; you were bought with a price. So glorify God in your body" (1 Cor 6:19-20).

All men belong to Jesus Christ by right of creation (Jn 1:3) and providence (Col 1:17; Heb 1:3). But Christians belong to Him in a special way—by right of redemption as well (Eph 1:7; Col 1:14). Jesus Christ bought us with His own blood, not simply that He might redeem us from sin, but that He might have us for His own possession (Tit 2:14).

Because he belongs wholly to Christ, the Christian's chief aim in life is to please his Lord in all things. Paul, writing to Timothy, said: "Take your share of suffering as a good soldier of Christ Jesus. No soldier on service gets entangled in civilian pursuits, since his aim is to satisfy the one who enlisted him" (2 Tim 2:3-4). So complete is His lordship over the Christian that all horizontal relationships in life are subservient to this vertical relationship to Him. Children are to obey their parents in everything for this *pleases the Lord* (Col 3:20). Slaves are to obey their earthly masters, not with eyeservice, as men pleasers, but in singleness of heart, *fearing the Lord* (Col 3:22). Masters are to treat their slaves justly and fairly, knowing that *they also have a Master in heaven* (Col 4:1). Husbands are to love their wives *as Christ loved the church* (Eph 5:25), and wives are to be subject to their husbands as *the church is subject to Christ* (Eph 5:24).

The strongest of all words came from Christ Himself when He said: "He who loves father or mother more than me is not worthy of me; and he who loves son or daughter more than me, is not worthy of me; and he who does not take up his cross daily and follow me is not worthy of me. He who finds his life will lose it, and he who loses his life for my sake will find it" (Mt 10:37-39). No one knows the truth of these words better than the missionary, who is called on to leave friends and relatives to serve in a foreign land, and later on to send his children away to school at the tender age of six or seven.

There is no such thing as "cheap grace." Discipleship is a costly business. The fact that we are saved by grace doesn't alter the situation.

In fact, it only serves to add to our indebtedness to Christ. All that we have and are we owe to Him. He made us; He bought us with His blood; by His power He keeps us day by day. Spirit, soul, and body—our whole being belongs exclusively to Him. He is our Savior and our Lord. We are, therefore, entirely at His disposal. Paul summed it all up when he wrote: "None of us lives to himself, and none of us dies to himself. If we live, we live to the Lord, and if we die, we die to the Lord; so then, whether we live or die, we are the Lord's" (Rom 14:7-8).

One of the great pioneer missionaries of all time was the famous David Livingstone. On his fifty-ninth birthday, after a lifetime of incredible hardship and privation in central Africa, he wrote in his diary: "My Jesus, my King, my life, my all; I again dedicate my whole self to Thee. Accept me and grant that ere this year is gone I may finish my task."[2]

2. His claim on our possessions. God is the one who gives man the power to acquire (Deut 8:18) and to enjoy (Eccles 5:19) wealth. It is true that God "richly furnishes us with everything to enjoy" (1 Tim 6:17). At the same time we are said to be "stewards of the manifold grace of God" (1 Pet 4:10, KJV). All the good things of life that the Christian enjoys have been given to him by God, and are to be held in trust for Him. He is not to squander his wealth or to keep his possessions to himself. They have been given to him that he might share them with others.

This was one of the outstanding characteristics of the early Christians, of whom it was said: "Now the company of those who believed were of one heart and soul, and no one said that any of the things which he possessed was his own; but they had everything in common" (Acts 4:32). This was made possible by the recognition of the fact that their possessions in the first place belonged not to themselves but to the Lord. And if they belong to the Lord, they should be at the disposal of His people. E. Stanley Jones used to say: "If I have something that my brother needs more than I do, I am duty bound as a Christian to let him have it."

That is a very high standard, but no higher than that set by Jesus Himself. To His disciples He said: "Give to every one who begs from you; and of him who takes away your goods do not ask them again" (Lk 6:30). During His public ministry Jesus had few personal possessions. He acted on the assumption that His lordship guaranteed ready

---

2. Tim Jeal, *Livingstone* (New York: G. P. Putnam's Sons, 1973), p. 356.

access to anything the disciples possessed. Consequently, without hesitation He commandeered Peter's boat, the upper room in which He held the Last Supper, and the colt on which He rode into Jerusalem on Palm Sunday. "If anyone asks why you are taking the colt, just say: 'The Lord has need of it' " (Lk 19:31). When He fed the four thousand and again when He fed the five thousand, He commandeered their resources; and they gladly make them available.

In His teachings Jesus warned His disciples about the deceitfulness of riches and the danger of laying up treasure on earth. He stated quite plainly that "a man's life does not consist in the abundance of his possessions" (Lk 12:15). When He encountered the rich young ruler who professed to have an interest in eternal things, He said: "One thing you still lack. Sell all that you have and distribute to the poor, and you will have treasure in heaven; and come, follow me" (Lk 18:22). By so saying, Jesus once again established His lordship over all of life, material as well as spiritual.

And when He made that kind of demand, He was not asking of others what He Himself was unwilling to give. Paul says: "You know the grace of our Lord Jesus Christ, that though he was rich, yet for your sakes he became poor, so that by his poverty you might become rich" (2 Cor 8:9). Charles Studd, missionary to China, India, and Africa, said on one occasion: "If Jesus Christ be God and died for me, nothing that I can ever do for Him should be called a sacrifice."

As Lord of all life He has the right to say to His disciples: "Seek first his [God's] kingdom and his righteousness, and all these things shall be yours as well" (Mt 6:33). Far from impoverishing the individual, this kind of conduct brings its own reward; for Jesus said: "Give, and it will be given to you; good measure, pressed down, shaken together, running over, will men put into your lap" (Lk 6:38). And the person who gives up houses or lands for the sake of the kingdom will receive "manifold more in this time and in the age to come eternal life" (Lk 18:30). After the feeding of the five thousand they gathered up twelve baskets of leftovers, which doubtless went to the boy who furnished the loaves and fishes to begin with. No one can be a follower of Jesus Christ unless he is prepared to say with Frances Havergal: "Take my silver and my gold, not a mite would I withhold."

Raymond Lull, the first and greatest missionary to the Muslims, after selling all his property and possessions, dedicated himself to the service of Jesus Christ with these words: "To Thee, O Lord God, I offer myself, my children, and all that I possess. May it please Thee to accept all that I give to Thee, that I, and my wife and children, may be Thy lowly servants."

3. His claim on our vocation. Who decides whether the Christian will be a missionary or a merchant, a preacher or a plumber, a butcher or a banker? Does the Christian have the right to make up his own mind on such an important matter? If the lordship of Christ is anything more than a cliché, then He is the one who decides where the Christian will go and what he will do.

Jesus accepted the will of God for His life. Paul did the same for his. Time and again he described himself as an apostle "by the will of God." Left to himself, Saul of Tarsus would never have become a disciple—much less an apostle—of Jesus Christ. To his dying day he never ceased to be amazed at the grace of God that made him what he was (1 Cor 15:10).

When Jesus called His disciples He said: "Follow me, and I will make you fishers of men" (Mt 4:19). Toward the end of His ministry He reminded them of this fact: "You did not choose me, but I chose you and appointed you that you should go and bear fruit and that your fruit should abide" (Jn 15:16).

Jesus Christ has a plan and purpose for every life that He has redeemed with His own blood. "We are his workmanship, created in Christ Jesus for good works, which God prepared beforehand, that we should walk in them" (Eph 2:10). This applies across the board to all Christians, regardless of whether they are in so-called Christian service or secular employment. A Christian should be a philosopher or a farmer, a lawyer or a laborer, a mailman or a football coach only by the appointment of his Lord. It goes without saying that a missionary should be a missionary only by the will of God. If Jesus Christ has called a person into His service, he won't be able to be anything else. Moses, Gideon, Jeremiah, and a host of others all tried to be something else; but it didn't work out. The fire burned in their bones and they could not rest until they became what God willed them to be. Jesus Christ is God and has the right to do what He likes with His disciples.

4. His claim on our talents. Psychology, a comparatively young science, has given man a new understanding of himself. Beginning in junior high school, students are given aptitude tests designed to provide a profile of their behavioral traits, their strengths and weaknesses, their interests and talents. Every effort is made by the guidance counselors to relate the student's talents to his vocational goals. All of this is perfectly good. There is one danger, however. The Christian student may all unconsciously accept the results of the tests as final, and assume that because his talents don't seem to be particularly suited to a missionary career, he therefore is not "called" to full-time Christian service.

If the twelve apostles had been subjected to a modern aptitude

113

test, how would they have fared? Peter would have been turned down; he was a fisherman. Matthew would have been ruled out; he was a tax collector. Simon would have been sent home; he was a revolutionist.

No man can be a disciple unless he is prepared to acknowledge the lordship of Jesus Christ without any ifs, ands, or buts. He demands unconditional surrender followed by total obedience. When that matter has been taken care of, *He* decides what to do with the disciple's gifts and talents. And He makes no mistakes. He is in possession of all the facts. He doesn't need to consult the charts or graphs. He understands the disciple better than he understands himself. He knows not only where the disciple is most needed, but also in what capacity he will function best. If Jesus Christ decides to make a missionary out of a musician, or a preacher out of a plumber, or an evangelist out of an engineer, who are we to object?

Over the Church

The church is mentioned only twice in the Gospels, and both times the speaker is Christ (Mt 16:18; 18:17). It is not until we come to the epistles that we find anything like an adequate description of the church. Most of the New Testament teaching regarding the church is found in the Pauline epistles, particularly Ephesians and Colossians. In Ephesians the emphasis is on the unity of the body. In Colossians the emphasis is on the headship of Christ. Jesus Christ is both the Savior and the Head of the church, which is His body (Eph 5:23). He was constituted Head of the church by the act of God the Father when He "raised him from the dead and made him sit at his right hand in the heavenly places . . . and put all things under his feet and made him head over all things for the church, which is his body, the fullness of him who fills all in all" (Eph 1:20-23).

In His role as Head of the church Jesus Christ performs certain very important functions.

1. He appoints its ministers. The church as a living organism could not function without certain ministers, including apostles, prophets, evangelists, pastors, and teachers, who are described as Christ's gifts to the church (Eph 4:7-11). Other gifts are mentioned in 1 Corinthians 12, and these too are bestowed on the church by divine initiative. Paul was an apostle, not by his own choice but by the will of God, and he became Christ's gift to His church. Paul in turn appointed elders in the churches founded by him (Acts 14:23); but he recognized that in the final analysis it was Christ, through the Holy Spirit, who actually did the appointing (Acts 20:28).

Jesus said to Peter, "Feed my sheep" (Jn 21:17), and in so doing made Peter one of the shepherds of the flock. Peter, though often referred to as "the prince of the apostles," regarded himself simply as a fellow elder with all the other elders of the church (1 Pet 5:1). He and they were under the direction of the Chief Shepherd and derived both their position and power from Him.

2. He invests it with authority. On several occasions Jesus invested His disciples with special authority. When He sent out the Twelve He gave them authority over unclean spirits, to cast them out, and to heal every disease and every infirmity (Mt 10:1); and on their return they reported with delight that the demons were subject to them in His name (Lk 10:17). When Peter made his confession of Christ in Caesarea Philippi, Jesus said to him: "I will give you the keys of the kingdom of heaven, and whatever you bind on earth shall be bound in heaven, and whatever you loose on earth shall be loosed in heaven" (Mt 16:19). The third occasion immediately followed the Resurrection and seems to confirm the statement made earlier to Peter: "Jesus breathed on them and said to them, 'Receive the Holy Spirit. If you forgive the sins of any, they are forgiven; if you retain the sins of any, they are retained'" (Jn 20:22-23).

If the Roman Catholic Church has made too much of these two passages, the Protestant churches have gone to the other extreme and made too little. Doubtless the second was a reaction against the first. Either way, it is simply a matter of record that the church of Jesus Christ has never regained the spiritual power it obviously exercised in the first century as recorded in the Acts of the Apostles.

Jesus Christ intended that His church should be equipped with all the authority necessary to carry out successfully its several functions in the world. In the discourse in the upper room (Jn 13-17) Jesus had much to say about prayer. Obviously He expected that prayer, offered in His name, would provide them with a new and untapped source of power: "In that day you will ask nothing of me. Truly, truly, I say to you, if you ask anything of the Father, he will give it to you in my name. Hitherto you have asked nothing in my name; ask, and you will receive, that your joy may be full" (Jn 16:23-24).

One has only to turn to the Acts of the Apostles to discover how extensively the early church took advantage of the spiritual power invested in it by Jesus Christ. The gospel was preached (8:12), the sick were healed (3:6), the demons were cast out (16:18), and converts were baptized (2:38)—all in the name of Jesus Christ.

Nor did it stop there. Discipline was exercised and judgment pronounced in His name. Peter "retained" the sin of Simon Magus when he said to him: "I see that you are in the gall of bitterness and in the bond of iniquity" (Acts 8:23). Paul took similar action when he encountered demonic opposition on Cyprus (Acts 13:9-11). Ananias and Sapphira fell down dead at Peter's feet when he rebuked them for covetousness and hypocrisy (Acts 5:1-10). Paul advised similar drastic action in the church in Corinth (1 Cor 5:5).

Alas! the church in later ages, shorn of spiritual power, was obliged to substitute other forms of power: in the second century, ecclesiastical power; in the third century, economic power; in the fourth century, political power; and during the Crusades, military power. With the advent of the "post-Christian era" the church is now slowly but surely being robbed of these illegitimate forms of power. Instead of shedding tears on her behalf, we should do well to thank God for the new turn of events. Certainly the church has nothing to gain by adopting worldly ways and resorting to carnal means to achieve spiritual ends.

3. He receives its worship. This is most dramatically seen in Revelation 5, when no one in heaven or earth was found worthy to open the scroll or break its seals. John wept, until one of the elders said to him: "Weep not; lo, the Lion of the tribe of Judah, the Root of David, has conquered, so that he can open the scroll and its seven seals." Whereupon the four living creatures and the twenty-four elders fell down before the Lamb, saying: "Worthy is the Lamb who was slain to receive power and wealth and wisdom and might and honor and glory and blessing!"

And John added: "I heard every creature in heaven and on earth and under the earth and in the sea, and all therein, saying, 'To him who sits upon the throne and to the Lamb be blessing and honor and glory and might for ever and ever!' And the four living creatures said 'Amen!' and the elders fell down and worshipped" (Rev 5:13-14).

From time to time attempts to worship others have been made. Cornelius fell at Peter's feet and worshiped him; but Peter lifted him up, saying, "Stand up; I too am a man" (Acts 10:25-26). The primitive animists of Lycaonia, when they witnessed the miracle performed by Paul and Barnabas, regarded them as gods and were about to worship them; but the apostles would have none of it (Acts 14:8-18). When John the apostle, who should have known better, fell down to worship at the feet of the angel, he was rebuked by the angel: "You must not do that! I am a fellow servant with you and your brethren, the prophets. . . . Worship God" (Rev 22:8-9).

4. He evaluates its ministry. There is no such thing as privilege without responsibility, and responsibility always involves accountability. The church with all her power and privilege stands always under the judgment of the Lord Jesus Christ. The individual believer will one day stand before the Judgment Seat of Christ to be judged for the things done in the body (2 Cor 5:10). "Each man's work will become manifest; for the Day will disclose it, because it will be revealed with fire, and the fire will test what sort of work each one has done" (1 Cor 3:13).

The church as a corporate body is constantly under the judgment of Jesus Christ her Lord. In every age and in every place she is required to be a thing of beauty and glory in the earth (Eph 5:27), always showing forth the praises of Him who called her out of darkness into His marvelous light (1 Pet 2:9). Her worship and witness are all to be carried on in the power of the Holy Spirit, not in the energy of the flesh or the wisdom of man. When she fails in her responsibility, she is in danger of losing not only her future reward but also her present role as salt and light in the world.

The seven letters to the seven churches of Asia in Revelation 2 and 3 give ample evidence of the probationary status of the church in all ages. She is constantly under the all-seeing eye of her living Lord. It is He who evaluates her work and witness. Each letter begins with the expression: "I know your works." Rewards are promised to those who overcome, warnings are issued to those who are disobedient or delinquent. Indeed, one church—Ephesus—was in danger of having the candlestick removed altogether (Rev 2:5). Each letter ends with a solemn warning: "He who has an ear, let him hear."

Over the World

Jesus Christ is not only the Head of the church, He is also the Lord of history and the King of all nations. They may not recognize Him as their King, but that in no way alters the fact. The strongest statement to this effect comes from the pen of the apostle Paul, who refers to Christ as "the blessed and only Sovereign, the King of kings and Lord of lords" (1 Tim 6:15). He is now seated "at the right hand of the Majesty on high" and "upholds the universe by his power" (Heb 1:3). In another passage Paul describes His position at the right hand of God as "far above all rule and authority and power and dominion, and above every name that is named, not only in this age but also in that which is to come" (Eph 1:21).

The church, of which Christ is the Head, is part of the kingdom, of which Christ is the King. As now constituted, the kingdom exists in mystery form (Mt 13). It is yet to be fully revealed (Phil 3:20-21; Col 3:4; Tit 2:13; 1 Cor 15:24-25; 1 Jn 3:2). In the meantime, Jesus Christ *is* a king and He *has* a kingdom. His kingdom is different from all other kingdoms the world has ever seen (Jn 18:36). It is spiritual, not physical (Rom 14:17). It is eternal, not temporal (Heb 12:28; 2 Pet 1:11). It is internal, not external (Lk 17:21). It is not a matter of palaver, but of power (1 Cor 4:20). It is not "pie in the sky by and by," but a real kingdom, now existing in the hearts of men but one day to be revealed in all its power and majesty when Jesus comes again. It is the kingdom for which we pray (Mt 6:10), work (Acts 28:31), and wait (Rom 8:19-23).

Because Jesus Christ is the King of the nations He has instructed His followers to go into all the world and disciple the nations (Mt 28:19-20). The world for which Christ died is to be claimed for Him. The nations that have been "given" to Christ by God the Father (Ps 2:8) are to be possessed for Him through the proclamation of the gospel (Mk 16:15), in the power of the Holy Spirit (Acts 1:8).

If Jesus is a king, then His messengers are ambassadors (2 Cor 5:20). They go forth to represent Him (Mt 10:40), to deliver His message (Gal 1:8-11), to extol His name (Acts 4:8-12), and to extend His kingdom (Rom 15:15-20). To this end the King has given orders to His ambassadors. They are to go into all the world, preach the gospel to every creature, and make disciples of all nations (Mt 28:19). All men everywhere are required to repent and believe the gospel (Acts 17:30). Only by doing so can they be transferred from the kingdom of darkness to the kingdom of light (Col 1:13). Nothing short of world conquest is the ultimate goal, and the King has given assurance that one day the kingdoms of this world will become the kingdom of our Lord and of His Christ (Rev 11:15). There is no ambiguity about the plan, no uncertainty about the outcome.

The Christian missionary is the personal envoy of the Savior and Sovereign of the universe. His abode, even if it is a mud hut in Africa, a snow-covered house in Alaska, a cottage in the Amazon jungle, or a tent in the Sahara Desert, is the "residency over which waves the banner of the King and round which an angel keeps watch."[3]

While the missionary has none of the outward accoutrements usually associated with diplomatic protocol, nevertheless his credentials are impeccable. He is the bearer of a divine revelation enshrined in an infallible Book. He has the law of God in his mouth, the rod of God in his hand, and the power of God in his life.

---

3. Mildred Cable and Francesca French, *Ambassadors for Christ* (London: Hodder and Stoughton, 1935), p. 153.

What is the nature of the kingdom he represents and how does it differ from all other kingdoms?

1. It is a kingdom of truth. Pilate said to Jesus: "So you are a king?" Jesus answered, "You say that I am a king. For this I was born, and for this I have come into the world, to bear witness to the truth. Every one who is of the truth hears my voice" (Jn 18:37). Pilate knew what a "kingdom" is. He thought he knew what "truth" is. It didn't occur to him to put the two together. Truth and politics don't mix very well. It has been said that truth is the first casualty in time of war. One wonders whether this is not also the case in time of peace, especially in a democracy where the politician's chief concern is to remain in office. Usually he tells the truth only when it serves his purpose.

Not so with Jesus. He claimed to be "the way, and the truth, and the life" (Jn 14:6). He knew the truth, He spoke the truth, He lived the truth. In short, He *is* the truth. And His kingdom is a kingdom of truth. It is founded on an understanding of the truth (Jn 8:32). It is extended by the preaching of the truth (Col 1:5-6). It is maintained by the practice of the truth (1 Jn 1:6-7).

The missionary, as an ambassador for Christ, represents a kingdom of truth. As such he is a herald of the truth (Mt 10:26-27). The idea of a herald is that of a town crier (before the days of mass media). The town crier read a proclamation for the benefit of the populace. He did not write the message, he simply proclaimed it. This is an apt illustration of the missionary. He does not invent his message any more than Paul did (Gal 1:1-10). He is expected to teach and preach what Jesus commanded (Mt 28:19-20). His message is one of reconciliation (2 Cor 5:18). The wages of sin is death, but the gift of God is eternal life. Salvation is an accomplished fact. Forgiveness is man's for the asking, because God was in Christ reconciling the world to Himself.

The message then is a message of salvation. This message is called the truth of God (Rom 1:25), or the truth as it is in Christ (Eph 4:21). The missionary is a herald of the truth. His primary responsibility is to announce the Good News concerning God, Christ, man, sin, salvation, and judgment. All of this is what Paul called "the truth of the gospel" (Gal 2:5).

As men accept and believe the truth they are set free (Jn 8:32). They are translated from the kingdom of darkness to the kingdom of light (Col 1:13).

The modern missionary finds himself in an embarrassing situation. In a pluralistic world it is becoming increasingly difficult to maintain the truth of the gospel over against the other faiths. It is considered "cultural imperialism" to insist that one religion is true and other religions are partly or wholly false. No religion, we are told, has all the truth and nothing but the truth; and to cling to such an outmoded concept is to forfeit one's intellectual respectability.

At the risk of being misunderstood, the Christian missionary, in all humility and sincerity, must insist on the truth of the gospel. If other religions contradict Christianity they must be regarded as false, at least at the point of contradiction. Two contradictory statements on any subject cannot both be true. Both *may* be wrong. One *must* be wrong. The Christian faith is not true because the missionary says so, but because Jesus Christ, the King of truth, declared it to be so.

> The nature of the message constitutes our duty to proclaim it. It is "the word of *truth.*" If there be any doubt upon this, if our certainty of the Christian truth is shaken and we can no longer announce it with conviction, our zeal for its propagation naturally declines. Scepticism chills and kills missionary fervour, as the breath of the frost the young growth of spring.[4]

This question is of immense importance. Stephen Neill says: "The only reason for being a Christian is the overpowering conviction that the Christian faith is true."[5]

That expression, "overpowering conviction," describes perfectly the mentality of the early church. The apostles believed with all their hearts that in the gospel of Christ they possessed a body of truth not found anywhere else (Jn 6:67-69); that Jesus Christ is the way, the truth, and the life (Jn 14:6); and that apart from Him there is no salvation (Acts 4:12). There are many paths, but only one way; many prophets, but only one Savior; many religions, but only one gospel. Their creed was simple but it was sufficient: "Jesus Christ is Lord." He stands in a class all by Himself. He occupies a solitary throne. He has no equals, nor any rivals.

As a herald of the truth it is the missionary's high privilege to proclaim to the entire world the glorious news that Jesus Christ lived and died and rose again, and by so doing provided salvation for the entire human race. As a result, whosoever will call on the name of the Lord will be saved (Rom 10:13).

2. It is a kingdom of peace. Every empire known to man was founded on force and maintained by force; and when the force failed, the empire disintegrated. The twentieth century has witnessed the demise of the greatest empire of modern times—the British Empire.

---

4. Findlay, *Expositor's Bible,* VI:19.
5. Stephen Neill, *Call To Mission* (Philadelphia: Fortress Press, 1970), p. 10.

Bled white by two world wars, Great Britain had neither the economic strength nor the military might to support and protect her overseas colonies, and the empire collapsed.

How different it is with Jesus and His kingdom! Jesus said to Pilate: "My kingship is not of this world; if my kingship were of this world, my servants would fight" (Jn 18:36). When Jesus made that statement He wrote *Ichabod* over every empire founded on force. Jesus' kingdom is a kingdom of peace because He is a man of peace. One of His messianic titles is "Prince of Peace" (Is 9:6). At His birth the angels proclaimed "peace on earth" (Lk 2:14). Throughout His public ministry He preached peace (Eph 2:17). He would not resort to force, nor did He permit His disciples to do so (Jn 18:36). He extolled the virtues of peace, pronouncing a special blessing on all those who actively seek it (Mt 5:9). The only legacy He left to His disciples was a legacy of peace (Jn 14:27). By His death He achieved peace between God and man (Eph 2:13) and between man and man (Eph 2:14-15).

The kingdom He is now establishing on earth is a kingdom of peace (Rom 14:17) and His gospel is a gospel of peace (Eph 6:15). This peace has two dimensions, vertical and horizontal. Both are part of the gospel; both belong to the kingdom.

The missionary as an ambassador for Christ is an envoy of peace. He bids men be reconciled to God (2 Cor 5:20). He also encourages men to be reconciled to one another and to live in peace (Rom 12:18). Sin brought discord into the world and set man against God (Rom 1:21-23) and against his neighbor (Rom 3:15-18). The Fall not only separated Adam and Eve from God, it also produced enmity between Cain and Abel. Before man can be reconciled to his fellow man he must first be reconciled to God.

The missionary as an envoy of peace is the one person who by commission and conviction is dedicated to the proposition that the human race is one and therefore its various peoples and nations should live together in peace. He, better than anyone else, can bridge the gap between the Jew and the Gentile, the Arab and the Jew, the Hindu and the Muslim, to say nothing of the feuding tribes of Africa.

Missionary annals are replete with examples of missionaries who, at great cost to themselves, acted as envoys of peace and brought warring factions together. Before the coming of the missionary, the South Sea Islanders constantly engaged in cannibalistic wars that decimated the population. In fact, in that part of the world interisland warfare was a way of life and cannibalism was raised to the status of a cult. Those wars ceased completely with the coming of the missionary and his gospel of peace.

In the eighteenth century the subcontinent of India was torn with strife caused by the contending European powers. Only one man, Lutheran missionary Christian Schwartz, was trusted and respected by the British, the French, and the Dutch on the one hand, and the Hindu and Muslim leaders on the other. One of the Muslim princes, Hyder Ali, refused to deal directly with the British, saying: "Send me the Christian; he will not deceive me."

And what shall be said about China between 1910 and 1937, when the warlords ravaged the countryside? During those years scores of missionaries were carried off by bandits. Some were held for ransom that was never paid, others were killed, and still others died in captivity. Yet in the midst of all the turmoil the missionaries for the most part remained at their posts. On more than one occasion they offered their good services as mediators and effected a truce between the various warring factions, thus preventing further death and destruction. In 1923 at the height of the troubles a group of missionaries signed the following declaration:

> The undersigned, American missionaries, are in China as mes-
> sengers of the gospel of brotherhood and peace. . . . We therefore
> express our earnest desire that no form of military pressure . . . be
> exerted to protect us or our property; and that in the event of our
> capture by lawless persons or our death at their hands, no money
> be paid for our release, no punitive expedition be sent out, and no
> indemnity be exacted.[6]

In more recent years the missionaries have continued their mission of reconciliation and peace. In civil wars in Nigeria, India, Pakistan, Bangladesh, Burundi, Vietnam, Sudan, and other countries they have protected national leaders, political as well as religious, organized and supervised refugee camps, and engaged in relief and rehabilitation. Not a few of them have been decorated by the governments concerned.

3. It is a kingdom of love. In His last discourse with the disciples before He went to the cross, Jesus said: "By this all men will know that you are my disciples, if you have love for one another" (Jn 13:35). Paul wrote: "Owe no one anything, except to love one another; for he who loves his neighbor has fulfilled the law. . . . Love does no wrong to a neighbor; therefore love is the fulfilling of the law" (Rom 13:8-10). The true Christian is one who loves God with all his heart and his neighbor as himself (Mt 22:37-39). According to Paul, love is the highest good. Indeed, without love the other virtues count for nothing (1 Cor 13:1-3).

Jesus Christ was the embodiment of God's love, not only in word

---

6. R. Pierce Beaver, *Envoys of Peace* (Grand Rapids: Eerdmans, 1964), p. 29.

but in deed as well. Peter said: "He went about doing good, healing all that were oppressed by the devil" (Acts 10:38). He is the King of love, and the kingdom He is establishing on earth is a kingdom of love.

The missionary, as an ambassador for Christ, is an apostle of love. The successful missionary needs many qualifications, but the most indispensable of all is love. If he doesn't have love—real love—he might as well remain at home. And the nationals on the receiving end have an uncanny ability to discern the presence (or absence) of love. If they find love, they will forgive almost anything else. If they don't find love, nothing else is likely to impress them.

And it is not enough to love the *souls* of men; the missionary must love their *bodies* as well. He must love them as *persons,* not just potential converts. This is precisely what Jesus did. There were no strings attached to His service. He ministered to all people regardless of their attitude toward Him or their response to His message. He came to demonstrate the amazing, all-embracing, never failing love of His heavenly Father. This He did in deed as well as word. He was kind even to the ungrateful. On one occasion He healed ten lepers, knowing all the time that only one of them would return to give glory to God (Lk 17:17). In so doing He provided every missionary with a living example of the indiscriminate love of God, who loves the sinner, not because he is particularly lovable, but because it is His nature to love (1 Jn 4:16).

One of the outstanding features of the modern missionary movement has been the spirit of love manifested by the missionaries. Everywhere they went they sought out the poor, the weak, the sick, and the downtrodden. By word and deed they showed them the love of Christ.

For three centuries the iniquitous slave trade flourished between Africa and South America. Conditions aboard the slave ships were incredibly bad. Half of the human cargo died at sea. Jesuit missionaries ministered to the survivors on their arrival at Cartagena, feeding them, cleaning their sores, healing their bodies, telling them of Christ, and baptizing those near death. When the Moravians went to the West Indies in the early part of the eighteenth century they sold themselves into slavery in order to share the gospel with the slaves. The first Salvation Army workers in India became "untouchables," living with them and like them in order to bring them the Good News of the gospel. In our own day Mother Teresa has given a lifetime of loving service to the destitute people of Calcutta.[7]

By all odds the early missionaries were exceptional men and women. Singlehandedly and with great courage they attacked the social evils

---

7. See Malcolm Muggeridge, *Something Beautiful for God: Mother Teresa of Calcutta* (New York: Harper & Row, 1971).

of their time: child marriage, the immolation of widows, temple prostitution, and untouchability in India; the opium trade, gambling, footbinding, and infanticide in China; the slave trade, the liquor trade, and the destruction of twins in Africa. In all parts of the world they opened schools, hospitals, clinics, orphanages, and leprosaria. They gave succor and sustenance to the dregs of society cast off by their own people.

And what was their great motivating power? It was the love of Christ shed abroad in their hearts by the Holy Spirit (Rom 5:5). As apostles of love they went forth to serve the peoples of the world in the name and spirit of Christ, thus giving a tangible demonstration of *agape,* the self-giving love which lies at the heart of the Christian faith.

> Every missionary—be he ordained or a layman; be he minister, social worker, teacher, relief director—has the function of mediating the Fatherly love of God and the brotherly love of Christ to men. The love of God is actually mediated to a person through another person who has a genuine concern for him as an individual, estimates his value in the eyes of God, and loves him for Christ's sake.[8]

After he was banished to the island of St. Helena, Napoleon remarked to a friend: "Alexander, Caesar, Charlemagne, and I have founded empires. But on what did we rest the creations of our genius? Upon force. Jesus Christ founded his empire upon love; and at this hour millions of men would die for him."[9]

Jesus Christ is the King of truth, the Prince of peace, and the Lord of love; and the kingdom that He is building is a kingdom of truth, peace, and love. The day will come when this kingdom will be fully realized. Truth *will* triumph (Ps 85:11); peace *will* prevail (Is 9:6-7); love *will* endure (1 Cor 13:13).

---

8. Beaver, *Envoys of Peace,* pp. 78-79.
9. Frank S. Mead, *The Encyclopedia of Religious Quotations* (Westwood, N.J.: Fleming H. Revell, 1965), p. 56.

7

The Ministry of the Spirit

The most important single event in the Acts of the Apostles is the coming of the Holy Spirit at Pentecost. That event explains all the other events. Some fifty-five times the Holy Spirit is mentioned in the Acts. The book should really be called the Acts of the Holy Spirit.

The Christian mission is God's mission. It began with the coming of Christ. God became incarnate in Christ in the Gospels. In the Acts, the Holy Spirit became incarnate in the church. The mission of the church is simply an extension of the Incarnation. "As the Father has sent me, even so I send you" (Jn 20:21). Christ's ministry was performed in the power of the Spirit (Lk 4:16-18; Acts 10:38), and He indicated that the disciples were to be endued with the same power (Jn 7:38-39; 14:12-17). The church's mission could be carried out only in the power of the Holy Spirit (Acts 1:8).

The ten days between the Ascension and Pentecost were spent in Jerusalem, as Jesus had commanded. During that time the disciples were engaged in prolonged prayer, waiting for the promised Holy Spirit. On the day of Pentecost the Holy Spirit came. The historic event is described by Luke. "When the day of Pentecost had come, they were all together in one place. And suddenly a sound came from heaven like the rush of a mighty wind, and it filled all the house where they were sitting. And there appeared to them tongues as of fire, distributed and resting on each one of them. And they were all filled with the Holy Spirit and began to speak in other tongues, as the Spirit gave them utterance" (Acts 2:1-4).

The worldwide mission of the Christian church, stretching over nearly two thousand years, is unthinkable apart from the presence and power of the Holy Spirit. Without Him it would never have commenced. Certainly without Him it would not have continued to this day. What precisely is the role of the Holy Spirit in the worldwide mission of the Christian church?

He Creates the Missionary Spirit

Missionary work through the centuries has been incredibly difficult. Stephen Neill expresses it well: "Christian missionary work is the most difficult thing in the world. It is surprising that it should ever have been attempted."[1] Jesus recognized the situation when giving instructions before sending out the Twelve in Matthew 10, and warned them that they would be flogged, hated, persecuted, and even killed. Only those who could endure to the end would be saved.

Because missionary work is so difficult, only those endued with a missionary spirit can successfully engage in it. This the disciples did not understand. When Jesus asked them: "Are you able to drink the cup that I am to drink?" they answered blithely, "We are able!" (Mt 20:22). But when the test came they all forsook Him and fled. It was not until Pentecost that they acquired the ingredients that make up what is called the missionary spirit.

1. **The spirit of sacrifice.** In the light of Calvary it ill becomes us to speak of sacrifice. Charles Studd, a wealthy man who gave away his fortune and became a member of the famous Cambridge Seven that went to China under the China Inland Mission in the 1880s, once said, "If Jesus Christ be God and died for me, nothing that I can ever do for Him should be called a sacrifice." Isaac Watts felt the same way when he wrote his famous hymn:

> Were the whole realm of nature mine,
> That were an offering far too small;
> Love so amazing, so divine,
> Demands my life, my soul, my all.

One must confess that in Western Christianity today there is very little genuine sacrifice. We usually see to it that our own needs are well supplied before giving to the Lord's work. This goes for our time as well as our money. If there is any spirit of sacrifice in the

---

1. Stephen Neill, *Call to Mission* (Philadelphia: Fortress Press, 1970), p. 24.

Christian church it is found mostly in missionary ranks, and even there it differs from mission to mission and from field to field. But taking the long view, it is safe to say that missionary work, more than any other kind of Christian service, calls for sacrifice. How else are we to explain the paucity of missionary candidates as compared with candidates for other kinds of service? As the affluent West becomes more and more affluent and the poverty-stricken East becomes more and more poverty-stricken, the element of sacrifice becomes greater.

When Hudson Taylor arrived in China in 1853 he found no running water, no electric lights, and no telephone service. So what? He didn't have these back home either! Where then was the sacrifice? The economic gap between the United States and most parts of the Third World today is greater than the gap between England and China in the nineteenth century. Consequently young people going to the mission field today are called on to make a greater sacrifice than the pioneer missionaries of an earlier day.

There are mission hospitals that are woefully understaffed and others that have had to close their doors simply for lack of qualified medical staff. What is going to induce a doctor to give up a $100,000-a-year practice in the States and offer for missionary services overseas, where he and his family will have barely enough to keep body and soul together? Let no one imagine that sacrifice is no longer demanded in missionary service, nor should we lose sight of the fact that that kind of sacrificial spirit is created only by the Holy Spirit.

2. The spirit of courage. In the Gospels the disciples showed little courage. In the end they fled for their lives and left Jesus alone. But the story is different in the Acts of the Apostles. There they are men of supreme courage. They feared God and no one else. Time and again their enemies were astonished at their boldness (Acts 4:13). This was not natural boldness, but a form of boldness directly associated with the filling of the Holy Spirit (Acts 4:31). Their missionary service involved them in all kinds of danger, even death itself; but they were undeterred (Acts 15:26; 21:13). If tradition can be trusted, John was the only one of the apostles that died in bed. All the others suffered a violent death.

Courage is still a necessary ingredient in a missionary career. With the passing of the colonial era the dangers attendant on missionary life seem to be greater than ever before. Political instability in the emerging nations in the Third World has added greatly to the difficulties and dangers of missionary work. Civil wars in various countries have placed in jeopardy the lives of hundreds of missionaries and their children.

The Trinitarian Dimension of Missions

In 1960 Roy Orpin, on his way to Chiengmai to be with his wife
for the birth of their first child, was shot and killed by bandits in
north Thailand. Following the birth of the baby Mrs. Orpin was
encouraged by her family and friends to return home to New Zealand.
Instead she gathered up her baby and her few belongings and headed
back to the mountains, where she continued to serve the Lord. In
1964 Hector McMillan was killed by the Simbas in Zaire. His wife,
Ione, gathered the six sons around the body of their father and
exhorted them not to harbor any ill feeling against the Africans.
After a brief furlough in the States, Mrs. McMillan and the younger
children returned to Zaire to serve the people who had killed her
husband. That kind of courage is alien to the human spirit. It is made
possible only by the power of the Holy Spirit.

3. **The spirit of love.** Love is the hallmark of the Christian faith.
God so loved the world that He gave His only Son (Jn 3:16). Christ
loved the church and gave Himself for it (Gal 2:20). Jesus said to
His disciples, "By this all men will know that you are my disciples,
if you have love" (Jn 13:35). Paul wrote: "If I speak in the tongues
of men and of angels, but have not love, I am a noisy gong or a
clanging cymbal. And if I have prophetic powers, and understand all
mysteries and all knowledge, and if I have all faith, so as to move
mountains, but have not love, I am nothing" (1 Cor 13:1-2). Love
is the virtue that gives value to all the other virtues of the Christian
life. It is love that "binds everything together in perfect harmony"
(Col 3:14).

There are, of course, many motives for missionary service, but
the greatest of all is love.

> Missionary zeal does not grow out of intellectual beliefs, nor out of
> theological arguments, but out of love. If I do not love a person I
> am not moved to help him by proofs that he is in need; if I do love
> him I wait for no proof of special need to urge me to help him.
> Knowledge of Christ is so rich a treasure that the spirit of love
> must necessarily desire to impart it.[2]

Apart from the Peace Corps, which is of very recent vintage,
Christian missionaries have been the only ones who went to the Third
World to give and not to get. As Jesus Christ was the embodiment of
God's love, so the missionaries have been the embodiment of Christ's
love. Motivated by the love of Christ and serving in the name of Christ,
they gave succor and sustenance to the dregs of society cast off by
their own people. At great risk to themselves and their families they

2. Roland Allen, *The Ministry of the Spirit* (Grand Rapids: Eerdmans, 1962
reprint), p. 35.

fought famines, floods, pestilence, and plagues. They were the first to rescue unwanted babies, educate girls, and liberate women. In the conduct of their work they encountered indifference, suspicion, hostility, persecution, and imprisonment. Their homes were looted, their buildings burned, their churches destroyed, and their lives threatened. Thousands returned home broken in health. Other thousands died prematurely of tropical diseases. Hundreds became martyrs. And all this they endured without recognition, regret, or reward.

The missionaries came closer than anyone else to fulfilling the highest ethic expressed by Christ when He said: "Love your enemies, do good to those who hate you, bless those who curse you, pray for those who abuse you" (Lk 6:27-28). All this they were able to do, not in their own strength, but because the love of God was shed abroad in their hearts by the Holy Spirit (Rom 5:5).

4. The spirit of zeal. Whatever else a missionary has, he *must* have zeal. Indeed, the very term *missionary* is synonymous with zeal. A missionary without zeal is like a soldier without courage—he won't last long.

The apostle Paul was the greatest missionary of all time, and one of his outstanding characteristics was zeal. As a rabbinical student in Jerusalem he was "extremely zealous" of the traditions of the Jewish faith (Gal 1:14). Later on he showed his zeal for God by persecuting the church (Phil 3:6). His conversion by no means diminished his zeal. If anything, it strengthened and increased it. He spent the rest of his life preaching the unsearchable riches of Christ throughout the length and breadth of the Roman Empire. Everywhere he went he met with opposition and persecution. Times without number his life was in danger, but not once did he falter. When his friends tried to dissuade him from going to Jerusalem for fear of imprisonment, he replied: "What are you doing, weeping and breaking my heart? For I am ready not only to be imprisoned but even to die at Jerusalem for the name of the Lord Jesus" (Acts 21:13). His passion for souls knew no bounds. He could say: "I have great sorrow and unceasing anguish in my heart. For I could wish that I myself were accursed and cut off from Christ for the sake of my brethren, my kinsmen by race" (Rom 9:2-3).

No one can read missionary biography without being impressed with the zeal of the missionaries. Hudson Taylor said, "If I had a thousand lives, I would give them all to China." Count Zinzendorf said, "I have one passion. It is He and He alone." Henry Martyn, on his arrival in India, said, "Now let me burn out for God." Melville Cox, first American Methodist missionary to Africa, died after four months in Liberia; but before his death he said: "Let a thousand fall before Africa be given up." Such was the consuming zeal of the early missionaries.

Pearl Buck's biographies of her parents do not place them in a very favorable light, but she was impressed with her father's zeal:

> The early missionaries were born warriors and very great men, for in those days religion was still a banner under which to fight. No weak or timid soul could sail the seas to foreign lands and defy death and danger unless he did carry religion as his banner; under which even death would be a glorious end. To go forth, to cry out, to warn, to save others, these were frightful urgencies upon the soul already saved. There was a very madness of necessity—an agony of salvation.

5. **The spirit of conviction.** Here again Paul is the great example. He wrote to the little mission church in Thessalonica: "Our gospel came to you not only in word, but also in power and in the Holy Spirit and with much conviction" (1 Thess 1:5). Paul believed that in the gospel of Christ he possessed the truth about God, man, sin, and salvation. By that truth he was determined to live, and for that truth he was prepared to die. He believed that all men are lost and need to be saved (Rom 3:19-20) and that there is only one way of salvation (1 Tim 2:5). He also believed that in order to be saved men must hear and believe the gospel (Rom 10:9-15). He regarded himself as having been entrusted with the gospel (1 Tim 1:11). Consequently he was under solemn obligation to share the gospel with the rest of the world (Rom 1:14). He became all things to all men that by all means he might save some (1 Cor 9:22). So intolerable was his burden for the lost that he said: "Necessity is laid upon me. Woe to me if I do not preach the gospel!" (1 Cor 9:16).

Almost to a man the missionaries of the nineteenth century shared Paul's conviction regarding the nature of the gospel and the fate of the heathen. This is no longer true. In our day the lostness of man is by no means a universally held doctrine. The liberals have long since given up such a notion, and even some evangelicals are having second thoughts about the matter. Little wonder that the Christian mission is not the urgent matter it was in former days.

He Promotes Missionary Activities

The Christian mission is not a human enterprise. It is a divine operation from start to finish, directed and controlled by the Holy

Spirit. Robert Hall Glover has said: "Christian missions are no human undertaking, but a supernatural and divine enterprise for which God has provided supernatural power and leadership."[3] The same author has also said: "He [the Holy Spirit] came as the divine Commander-in-chief of the forces and the campaign, and was at once recognized and acknowledged as such. His coming imparted the divine character to every aspect of the enterprise."[4] John R. Mott said virtually the same thing: "Missionaries . . . are absolutely united in the conviction that world evangelization is a divine enterprise, that the Spirit of God is the great missioner, and that only as He dominates the work and workers can we hope for success in the undertaking to carry the knowledge of Christ to all people."[5]

Harry Boer maintains that the missionary mandate does not rest on the Great Commission but on the presence and power of the Holy Spirit. "At Pentecost the Church became a witnessing institute because the coming of the Spirit made Christ's mandate an organic part of her being, an essential expression of her life."[6] The Spirit-filled church is naturally and inevitably a witnessing church, not because of any external command but by reason of an inner compulsion that is both spontaneous and irresistible. As Adam was instructed to be fruitful and multiply and replenish the earth, so the church is commanded to engage in spiritual procreation by taking the life-giving gospel to the ends of the earth. The Spirit is the Spirit of life, and as such He imparts life wherever He goes.

How does the Spirit promote missionary activity?

1. He initiates the work of the missionary. The ascended Lord is the Head of the church, but the Holy Spirit is His Executive Director here on earth. It is He who directs and controls the church in all its various activities. All the gifts mentioned by Paul in 1 Corinthians 12 are said to be "inspired by one and the same Spirit who apportions to each one individually as he wills" (v. 11). In the Acts of the Apostles only men filled with the Holy Spirit were chosen to do God's work. Even the deacons in Acts 6 were required to be men full of the Holy Spirit and wisdom (v. 3). Elders were appointed to their office by the Holy Spirit (Acts 20:28). And when the apostles and elders in Jerusalem concluded the first church council, they wrote in their

3. Robert Hall Glover, *The Bible Basis of Missions* (Chicago: Moody Press, 1964), p. 70.
4. Ibid., p. 63.
5. John R. Mott, *The Decisive Hour of Christian Missions* (New York: Student Volunteer Movement, 1910), p. 103.
6. Harry R. Boer, *Pentecost and Missions* (Grand Rapids: Eerdmans Publishing Co., 1961), pp. 119-20.

official report: "It has seemed good to the Holy Spirit and to us" (Acts 15:28).

The clearest example of the Holy Spirit's control and direction is found in the church in Antioch in Acts 13. While the believers were assembled for worship, the Holy Spirit said, "Set apart for me Barnabas and Saul for the work to which I have called them" (v. 2). After a period of prayer and fasting, the church obeyed and the two men were sent out "by the Holy Spirit." When they returned home after their first missionary journey they called the church together and declared all that God had done with them, and how He had opened a door of faith to the Gentiles (Acts 14:27).

From beginning to end the administration of the church's affairs was under the Spirit's control.

> This administration of the Spirit is the key of the apostolic work. It alone explains the promise of remission of sins in the preaching of the apostles. It alone explains the assurance of forgiveness which filled the hearts of their converts. It alone explains the new power which was manifested in the life of the Christian church, the new striving after holiness, the new charity expressed in organized form for the amelioration of the sufferings of the poorer brethren. It alone explains the certainty of the hope of eternal life which filled the souls of the Christians and enabled them to face persecution and martyrdom. It alone explains the new sense of value and dignity of the body which led to a new enthusiasm for purity of life and created hospitals for the care of the diseased. It alone explains the zeal for the salvation of men, which carried the gospel of Christ throughout the then known world.[7]

The leading of the Holy Spirit is the key to *all* missionary endeavor, modern as well as ancient. Were it not for His gracious influence the modern missionary movement would never have gotten under way. In the early years the idea of foreign missions was opposed on every hand by the ecclesiastical leaders of the day. Justinian von Welz, August Francke, Bartholomew Ziegenbalg, William Carey—all of them ran into opposition when they tried to promote the cause of world missions. Dr. Ryland, who at first took a dim view of Carey's determination to be a missionary, afterward said: "I believe God Himself infused into the mind of Carey that solicitude for the salvation of the heathen which cannot be fairly traced to any other source."[8]

> The Holy Ghost calls out the missionary witnesses; and when He calls His chosen ones will hear, even though a dead church and secular clergy have no notification of their appointment. God de-

---

7. Allen, *Ministry of the Spirit*, pp. 42-43.
8. A. J. Gordon, *The Holy Spirit in Missions* (Harrisburg, Pa.: Christian Publications, 1968 reprint), p. 62.

clares no preference for an uncanonical ministry; but He constantly teaches that without the ordination of the Spirit men lay on hands in vain, and that with the ordination of the Spirit he is a veritable missionary on whom no hands have been laid.[9]

2. He inspires the words of the missionary. When Jesus sent out the twelve apostles He warned them of the kind of treatment they could expect at the hands of a hostile world. He compared them to sheep in the midst of wolves and warned that they would end up in prison. He added: "When they deliver you up, do not be anxious how you are to speak or what you are to say; for what you are to say will be given to you in that hour; for it is not you who speak, but the Spirit of your Father speaking through you" (Mt 10:19-20).

Jesus gave His disciples two commands: "go into all the world" (Mt 28:19) and "stay in the city" (Lk 24:49). The purpose of the latter was that they might wait for the promise of the Holy Spirit. On the day of the Ascension our Lord again referred to this matter: "You shall receive power when the Holy Spirit has come upon you; *and you shall be my witnesses*" (Acts 1:8). This was literally fulfilled on the day of Pentecost when the assembled disciples were all "filled with the Holy Spirit and began to speak with other tongues, *as the Spirit gave them utterance*" (Acts 2:4).

No one can doubt that when Peter delivered his great sermon at Pentecost (Acts 2) he was speaking under the inspiration of the Holy Spirit. His words came with such power and conviction that the hearers, former enemies of Jesus who were responsible for His death, were "cut to the heart, and said to Peter and the rest of the apostles, 'Brethren, what shall we do?' " (Acts 2:37).

When Stephen, filled with the Spirit, carried the gospel into the synagogues of Jerusalem, he met with stubborn opposition. Doubtless Saul of Tarsus was among his opponents. But the elders in these synagogues were "unable to withstand the wisdom and the Spirit with which he spoke" (Acts 6:10). When Stephen made his defense before the Sanhedrin, he charged his enemies with resisting not him but the Holy Spirit. When they heard these things they were enraged, and they ground their teeth at him. He said, "Behold I see the heavens opened, and the Son of Man standing on the right hand of God." This further infuriated them so that they "cried out with a loud voice and stopped their ears and rushed together upon him" (Acts 7:51-57).

It was because the apostles spoke in the power of the Holy Spirit that their words carried conviction to the hearers. In this way they

---

9. Ibid., p. 63.

were fulfilling the prediction of our Lord. Most often their words led to salvation, but at times they issued in judgment. Without doubt Peter's words were inspired when he said to Sapphira: "How is it that you agreed together to tempt the Spirit of the Lord? Hark, the feet of those that have buried your husband are at the door, and they will carry you out" (Acts 5:9). The same was true when Peter spoke to Simon Magus: "Your silver perish with you, because you thought that you could obtain the gift of God with money. You have neither part nor lot in this matter, for your heart is not right before God. . . . For I see that you are in the gall of bitterness and in the bond of iniquity" (Acts 8:20-23).

Throughout history, whenever the Spirit of God moved in an unusual way we find sinners coming under conviction. When Jonathan Edwards preached his famous sermon, "Sinners in the Hands of an Angry God," able-bodied men clung to the pillars of the church for fear of falling directly into hell.

3. He directs the steps of the missionary. In the Psalms we read that the steps of a good man are ordered by the Lord (37:23). Nowhere is this more clearly seen than in the movements of the apostles in the early church. Jesus told them they were to begin in Jerusalem, and from there to branch out into Judea and Samaria and to the ends of the earth (Acts 1:8). That was the general plan, but its outworking required special guidance. If Peter was to be the apostle to the Jews, then he would have to go where the Jews were; and if Paul was to be the apostle to the Gentiles, he would be required to go "far away to the Gentiles" (Acts 22:21).

On his second missionary journey, when he reached the western limits of Asia, Paul tried to speak the word in Asia but the Holy Spirit forbade him. Then he attempted to go into Bithynia; again the Holy Spirit intervened and directed his way to Macedonia (Acts 16:6-10). On one occasion when danger threatened, he was told to clear out of Jerusalem (Acts 22:18). On another occasion, equally dangerous, he was told to stay in Corinth (Acts 18:9-11). Obviously Paul did not plan his itinerary months ahead. Daily he walked and worked in the Spirit and looked to Him for guidance. In Acts 8 the Holy Spirit directed Philip to leave a citywide revival in Samaria to preach the gospel to the Ethiopian eunuch. The leaders of the early church were very sensitive to the leading of the Holy Spirit, and when He spoke they immediately detected His voice.

Left to himself Peter would never have preached the gospel to the Gentiles, but the Holy Spirit ordained that he should be the one to first open the door to them (Acts 15:7). The incident is recorded in

Acts 10 and rehearsed before his accusers in Jerusalem in chapter 11. Peter did not take kindly to the idea. It took a heavenly vision, repeated three times, to show Peter that he should obey the voice of the Lord. When he got back to Jerusalem he was called on the carpet by the apostles and elders. He defended his action through a blow-by-blow account of the happening and clinched the matter by saying, "The Spirit told me to go with them, making no distinction" (Acts 11:12).

Throughout mission history we repeatedly find this principle. Livingstone's first intention was to go to China, but God did not permit it; instead he went to Africa. William Carey thought he was heading for the South Seas, but the Holy Spirit changed his course and directed him to India. Adoniram Judson planned to work in India, but ended up in Burma. Looking back from our vantage point we can't imagine Livingstone in China or Carey in the South Seas. The Holy Spirit makes no mistakes. The great Pentecostal movement in Brazil started about the turn of the century when two laymen in Chicago were directed by the Holy Spirit to an unknown destination in Brazil. Like Abraham, they went out not knowing where they were going. Today the Evangelical churches in that part of the world are growing faster than anywhere else.

He Produces Missionary Results

Without spiritual power the Christian worker is helpless. God's word to Zerubbabel was: "Not by might, nor by power, but by my Spirit, says the Lord of hosts" (Zech 4:6). Jesus warned His disciples: "Apart from me you can do nothing" (Jn 15:5). Conversely Paul said, "I can do all things in him who strengthens me" (Phil 4:13).

If it is difficult to win men to Christ in a so-called Christian culture, how much more difficult is it to make converts in the non-Christian parts of the world?

When Jesus told His disciples to go into all the world and make disciples of all nations He gave them a humanly impossible task. There wasn't one chance in a thousand they would succeed, for the odds against them were overwhelming. They had no central organization, no financial resources, no influential friends, and no political machine. Arrayed against them were the ecclesiastical power of the Sanhedrin and the political and military might of the Roman Empire. In addition they had to face the religious fanaticism of the Jews and the cultural superiority of the Greeks. As for the empire-building Romans, they were enamored of power and were not likely to be impressed with a Savior who ended His life in weakness on a Roman cross. The idea that those eleven men could win the world for Christ was absurd. If missionaries the world over are ever to get results it will be because of the presence and power of the Holy Spirit. He plays a vital role in world evangelization.

1. He alone can convict the heathen of the truth of the Gospel. It is not exactly easy to win a person in our culture to personal faith in Jesus Christ. We all know how difficult it has been, at least until very recent years, to convert a Roman Catholic to the Protestant faith. It is even more difficult to convert an Orthodox Jew to Christianity. And yet in both cases we are not asking the person to deny or renounce his own faith. We are simply asking the Jew to accept Jesus of Nazareth as his long-expected Messiah. He is not expected to renounce Moses, Abraham, David, or any of the prophets or patriarchs. They belong to us as well as to him. In the case of the Roman Catholic, he already believes in Christ—His virgin birth, His sinless life, His atoning death, His bodily resurrection, and His ascension into heaven. We are simply asking him to believe that salvation is by grace through faith without human works. Even so, it is extremely difficult to convince him of that fact.

How different is the situation in the non-Christian world. Paul tells us that the Gentile nations of antiquity deliberately abandoned their knowledge of the one true God, and "changed the truth of God for a lie and worshipped and served the creature rather than the Creator" (Rom 1:25). When they gave up the knowledge of the true God they substituted gods of their own making. In time they came to erect vast and powerful religious systems which became part of Satan's kingdom of darkness (Mt 12:22-30; 2 Cor 4:4). These non-Christian religions have been around for a long time, all of them except Islam antedating Christianity by hundreds of years. They have their own saints, saviors, prophets, and teachers; their own sacred rivers and mountains, their rich and beautiful temples, shrines, stupas, and pagodas. They have their own doctrines of God, man, sin, and salvation. Far from living and dying in "heathen darkness," they believe they have the light. When the Christian missionary arrives on the scene with his Bible under his arm, they are not impressed.

Before a Buddhist or a Brahmin can be converted to Christ he must be persuaded that the Christian doctrines of God, man, sin, and salvation are true. If they are, then his religion—at least in part—must be false. That point he is not willing to concede. How is the Buddhist to be persuaded to give up his books and beads when his forefathers have used them from time immemorial? How can the Brahmin be persuaded to accept Christ when such an act would mean breaking

136

caste? How can the Muslim be persuaded of the deity and death of Jesus Christ when the Koran has denied these two doctrines for over twelve hundred years?

The Christian missionary will discover to his dismay that the insights he gained from Christian apologetics in seminary just don't impress, much less convince, the non-Christian in the Third World. No amount of logic, rhetoric, apologetics, or homiletics will persuade the Buddhist, the Hindu, or the Muslim of the basic truth of the Christian religion. That will come *only* through the illuminating power of the Holy Spirit. Man can approach God *only* through Christ, but man can come to a knowledge of Christ *only* through the Holy Spirit. "No man can say, 'Jesus is Lord!' except by the Holy Spirit" (1 Cor 12:3).

2. He alone can convict the heathen of the sinfulness of sin. In the gospel Jesus Christ is presented as the Savior from sin. He Himself said that He came not to call the righteous but sinners to repentance. They that are whole need not a physician, but they that are sick (Mt 9:12-13). But sick persons don't like to be informed they are sick. Sinners don't like to be told they are sinners; in fact, they resent the allegation.

If this is true in a so-called Christian culture, how much more true is it in a non-Christian culture. Most of the non-Christian peoples of the world have little or no sense of sin. In some languages there is no word for sin as we understand the term. To steal, or lie, or cheat is not a sin. It becomes sin only when it is exposed. Romans 1 and Ephesians 4 clearly teach that the non-Christian world is so steeped in sin that its peoples are "past feeling." They have come to love darkness rather than light because their deeds are evil (Jn 3:19). In other words, they have become naturalized in the unnatural. They sin without being aware of it. In fact Paul speaks of those who have gone so far as to "glory in their shame" (Phil 3:19).

The Chinese represent one-quarter of the human race. John Fairbank of Harvard has remarked that Confucius, their greatest sage, has had a stronger influence over a larger segment of the human race over a longer period of time than any other person in history. And Confucius taught that human nature is essentially good. By his definition, man is not a sinner. He is a noble creature who can achieve moral perfection by his own efforts. Mahatma Gandhi admired Jesus Christ and was very fond of the Sermon on the Mount, but he did not take kindly to the notion that man is a sinner. He was particularly irate when missionaries told the Indians they were sinners. He was especially critical of Reginald Heber's missionary hymn: "What though the spicy breezes blow soft o'er Ceylon's isle, where every prospect pleases and only man is vile." He declared: "We Hindus are *not* vile. We are an ancient and noble race and don't want outsiders telling us that we're sinners."

3. He alone can convert the heathen from the error of his ways. This is the last hurdle before conversion. With some people it is the greatest hurdle of all. It is not enough to acknowledge the truth of the gospel, or even to experience a sense of sin. The sinner must be willing to repent as well as believe. He must be willing to turn from his wicked way; only then can he return to the Lord (Is 55:6-7). He cannot hang on to his sin and embrace the Savior at the same time. If he is going to turn to God, he must give up his idols (1 Thess 1:9). He cannot add Christ to Krishna.

To many persons this is the greatest obstacle of all. They would gladly embrace Christ if they could retain their old way of life. Felix listened to Paul and "trembled," but he did not take the required step (Acts 24:25). Agrippa was "almost persuaded," but not quite (Acts 26:27-28). The Africans said to Bishop Hannington in 1885: "Your gospel is good. We would all accept it if you let us keep our wives and whiskey."

There are many educated people in the non-Christian world who are dissatisfied with their own religions. They have studied Christianity and are acquainted with the character and claims of Jesus Christ, but they cannot openly break with tradition and become outcasts from their own people. In China the great stumbling block was filial piety. In Japan it was emperor worship. In India it was the caste system. If somehow those persons could have become Christians without incurring the displeasure of family and friends, the Christian mission in those parts would have been much more successful.

Conversion is a very costly business in many parts of the mission field. The price is more than most people are prepared to pay. Only the power of the Holy Spirit can move the heart of a Hindu, or a Buddhist, or a Muslim to openly acknowledge Christ as Savior and Lord.

The Theological Imperatives of Missions

The worldwide mission of the Christian church is not an option but an obligation. We engage in mission not because we *wish* to, but because we *have* to. In the long run it boils down to a matter of obedience. The Christian is a person under orders. He is not his own; he has been bought with a price. Body, mind, and soul, he belongs to Jesus Christ. He is a soldier of Jesus Christ; as such his one duty is to obey his Commander-in-chief. To do otherwise is to be guilty of high treason.

It is the will of God that all men should be saved and come to a knowledge of the truth (1 Tim 2:4). This was the central purpose of the Incarnation. The Father sent the Son to be the Savior of the world (1 Jn 4:14). Jesus Himself declared that if He were lifted up from the earth He would draw all men to Himself (Jn 12:32). He also stated that the gospel of the kingdom *must* be preached in all the world; only then will the end come (Mt 24:14). And lest there be any doubt in the minds of His followers, He gave them the Great Commission in which He laid on them the obligation to preach the gospel to every creature (Mk 16:15) and to make disciples of all nations (Mt 28:19).

Moreover, Christianity by its very nature is a missionary religion. All those who accept its liberating message have an inner compulsion to share it with others. They cannot but speak the things that they have seen and heard (Acts 4:20). When ordered by their enemies to desist, they reply with the apostles: "We must obey God rather than

139

men" (Acts 5:29). And they are quite willing to suffer the consequences of their indiscretion. When they end up in jail, they preach the gospel to their fellow prisoners, and even the jailor himself is converted to Christ (Acts 16:29-33). Like the apostle Paul, they are forced to confess: "Woe to me if I do not preach the gospel!" (1 Cor 9:16).

The reasons for this are not hard to find. The issues are too great; the stakes are too high. Involved in the issue is the eternal destiny of the human race. "The wrath of God is revealed from heaven against all ungodliness and wickedness of men" (Rom 1:18). All men are created in the image of God. Because of this they possess an immortal soul that will live as long as God lives, either in fellowship with Him (Jn 14:1-3) or alienated from Him (2 Thess 1:5-9). For this reason it is imperative that all men understand and believe the gospel, for God has appointed a day in which He will judge the world in righteousness (Acts 17:31), and only those who turn to God from idols will be delivered from the wrath to come (1 Thess 1:9-10).

8

The Missionary Mandate

The missionary mandate is usually restricted to the last words of Christ as recorded in the closing verses of the Gospel of Matthew. This familiar passage is known as the Great Commission, and not without reason; for it contains the marching orders given by the risen Christ to His disciples on the eve of His departure from the world. These words surely form part of the mandate, but should not be regarded as the whole mandate. There is much more to it than that.

There are at least three dimensions to the missionary mandate, only one of which is the Great Commission. The missionary mandate in its fullness is seen in the character of God, the command of Christ, and the condition of mankind.

The Character of God

The Christian mission, like the gospel, originated in the heart of God. It is His work, not man's; and it grows out of His essential character. If God were any other kind of God, there would be no Christian mission. The revelation of God in the Scriptures is not confined to His existence, it includes the *kind* of God He is. Indeed, the Scriptures are not concerned to prove the existence of God; that is taken for granted. What the Bible reveals is the *character* of God. His person can never be divorced from His character.

141

The supreme arguments for missions are not found in any specific words. It is in the very being and character of God that the deepest ground of the missionary enterprise is to be found. We cannot think of God except in terms which necessitate the missionary idea. Though words may reveal eternal missionary duties the grounds are in the very being and thought of God, in the character of Christianity, in the aim and purpose of the Christian Church, and in the nature of humanity, its unity and its need.[1]

1. God is love. The Scriptures have much to say about the attributes of God. Two of them are closely linked with the underlying concept of the world mission of the church. The apostle John in his First Epistle makes two great declarations concerning the character of God: "God is light" (1:5) and "God is love" (4:16).

These two attributes have always been an integral part of the character of God, but they were not fully manifest to the world until the coming of Christ. After spending three wonderful years in the company of the Son of God, John expressed it well in these majestic words: "This is the message we have heard from him and proclaim unto you, that God is light and in him is no darkness at all" (1 Jn 1:5).

The same is true of the other attribute, love. John says: "In this the love of God was made manifest among you, that God sent his only Son into the world, so that we might live through him. In this is love, not that we loved him but that he loved us and sent his Son to be the expiation for our sins" (1 Jn 4:9-10).

These two attributes, revealing as they do the true character of God, constitute an important dimension of the missionary mandate.

The world belongs to God (Ps 24:1) and He loves that world (Jn 3:16). He is not willing that any should perish (2 Pet 3:9), but will have all men to be saved and come to a knowledge of the truth (1 Tim 2:4). Why? Because the human race is one big family—His family (Acts 17:26). Man was made in the beginning *by* God, *for* God; and it was God's intention that man should find his highest happiness *in* God. God made man in His own image so that He could have an object worthy of His everlasting love.

God is love. This is the central fact of the gospel. We look up through nature and discover that God is law, responsible and dependable. We look up through Christ and discover that God is love, slow to anger and plenteous in mercy, full of pity and compassion, ready always to forgive.

God's love, like Himself, is eternal, inscrutable, and immutable. He loves mankind with an everlasting love (Jer 31:3); and having

---

1. Robert E. Speer, *Christianity and the Nations* (New York: Revell, 1910), pp. 17-18.

once set His love on man, He can never let him go. No matter how long the prodigal has remained in the far country, he is always free to return to the Father's house; and on his return he will find the door open, the lamps burning, and the feast spread.

No one has expressed it more beautifully than Frederick Faber:

> There's a wideness in God's mercy
> Like the wideness of the sea;
> There's a kindness in His justice
> Which is more than liberty.
>
> For the love of God is broader
> Than the measure of man's mind,
> And the heart of the Eternal
> Is most wonderfully kind.

One of the greatest missionary books in the Old Testament is the book of Jonah. The meaning and the miracle of that episode are not found in the story of the "great fish," but in the mercy of God that spared the wicked city of Nineveh when king and people repented. Jonah knew all along that that was precisely what God was likely to do. That's why he refused to go to Nineveh in the first place. He had a sneaking suspicion that, given half a chance, God would forgive their sin and spare the city. Jonah knew enough about God to know He is essentially good and infinitely longsuffering, delighting not in the death of the wicked but desiring that man should turn from his wicked way and live.

This indestructible, all-inclusive love of God prompted Him to send Jesus Christ to be the Savior of the world (1 Jn 4:9). This is the Good News that constitutes the gospel. This great, glorious fact is the foundation of all missionary endeavor. Without it there would be no missionary mandate.

2. God is light. But that is not all there is to God's character. There is another side. God is light as well as love. "Light" in Scripture is a symbolic term standing for three things. Physically it stands for splendor or glory (2 Cor 4:6; Rev 21:23). Intellectually it stands for truth (Ps 43:3). Morally it stands for holiness (Rom 13:11-14). God is light; God is love. The two statements belong together.

God's love is a holy love. That is what makes it unique. It can never be compared with man's love. The difference between the two is not simply one of quantity, but one of quality as well. God's love is white as snow and pure as sunlight. Man's love, on the other hand, is a debased, corrupted form of love, streaked with selfishness and tainted with pride. This is why man has so much difficulty in understanding the true nature of love.

Everything pertaining to God speaks of the beauty of holiness. His law is perfect (Ps 19:7). His commandment is holy and just and good (Rom 7:12). His throne is a throne of holiness (Ps 47:8). His kingdom is a kingdom of righteousness (Mt 6:33). His scepter is a scepter of equity (Ps 45:6). The psalmist summed it all up in one sentence when he spoke of Jehovah as being righteous in all His ways and holy in all His works (Ps 145:17).

Associated with God's holiness is His wrath, which is revealed from heaven against "all ungodliness and wickedness of men" (Rom 1:18). If man rejects God's love, he shuts himself up to God's wrath (Jn 3:36). In our thinking about God we have tended to place these two attributes—love and wrath—in two separate compartments. His love, it is assumed, is reserved for His children, His wrath for His enemies. Not so. His love and His wrath cannot be separated. They are not two entities; rather they are two aspects of one entity— His holiness. His holiness glows with love, His love burns with holiness. He cannot express the one without at the same time expressing the other. His love goes out to the sinner just as much as to the saint, and for the same reason: both are creatures of His hand and therefore objects of His love. His anger is kindled against the saint as much as against the sinner, and for the same reason: He cannot tolerate sin no matter where it is found. When He punishes the sinner He acts in love; when He chastises the saint He likewise acts in love. The history of Israel in her declension and apostasy is ample evidence of that.

It has been said so often that it has become something of a cliché, but it is true nevertheless: God loves the sinner at the same time that He hates his sin. He loves righteousness *and* hates iniquity (Heb 1:9). The one is the corollary of the other. To love righteousness *is* to hate iniquity. This must be true in the very nature of the case. There is, therefore, no incompatibility between God's love and His wrath. His just wrath is an expression of His holy love.

If God were only love and not light, there would be no need of the Christian mission. He could save all men by a word, without faith or repentance. In that case there would be no need to preach the gospel. But Paul knew better. He declared, "Therefore, knowing the fear of the Lord, we persuade men" (2 Cor 5:11). He also said, "Woe to me if I do not preach the gospel" (1 Cor 9:16).

God's love makes it possible for the repentant sinner to be saved. God's holiness makes it inevitable that the unrepentant sinner will perish. Both are part of the gospel; both are part of the mandate. Without the love of God we would have no gospel. Without the wrath of

God there would be no need for the gospel. So the missionary mandate is rooted in the character of God, who is light and who is also love.

The Command of Christ

This, of course, refers to the Great Commission, which is recorded in all four Gospels and the first chapter of Acts. Here again the church has made the mistake of isolating one word—"go"—and building the entire missionary mandate on that. A closer look at the teachings of Christ will reveal the fact that He used not one but three words to express the relationship of the disciples to Himself and His mission. These words were "Come," "Follow," "Go." There is a sense in which everything Jesus said can be summed up in these three words. All three are really part of the Great Commission. Taken together they form an integral part of the missionary mandate.

1. The invitation to come. This was the word of invitation. It was addressed to the multitudes: to the publicans, harlots, lepers—in a word, to sinners. There is no more beautiful verse in the Bible than Matthew 11:28: "Come unto me, all who labor and are heavy laden, and I will give you rest." It was addressed to man in his alienation from God. The entire life of Christ on earth was a dramatic enactment of the call from Jehovah through Isaiah: "Let the wicked forsake his way and the unrighteous man his thoughts; and let him return to the Lord that he may have mercy on him, and to our God, for he will abundantly pardon" (Is 55:7). Men and women in all walks of life responded to the gracious invitation. They "came to Christ," and in coming they found exactly what He had promised—life and health, joy and peace, all based on the forgiveness of sins.

2. The command to follow. Having "come" to Christ, the person now becomes a believer. By an act of faith he has passed from death to life and is now a child of God, a member of Christ, and an inheritor of the kingdom of heaven.

Having responded to the invitation to come, he now hears a second word: "follow." As a believer, he is expected to take a second step and become a follower or disciple. Salvation is of grace by faith. It is a free gift. It does not depend on anything man can do. But discipleship is quite another matter. It is neither cheap nor easy; indeed, it is very difficult and very costly. In fact, in Jesus' day it was so costly that many people took offense when they heard the "hard sayings" of Jesus, and they went their way. Repeatedly Jesus said: "If any man would come after me, let him deny himself and take up his cross and follow me. . . . For whoever loses his life for my sake will find it" (Mt 16:24-25).

Matthew 11:28, which contains the Great Invitation, should never be divorced from Matthew 11:29-30—the Great Renunciation: "Take my yoke upon you, and learn from me; for I am gentle and lowly in heart, and you will find rest for your souls. For my yoke is easy and my burden is light." The Great Invitation was obviously addressed to the multitude. The Great Renunciation was demanded of those who had already allied themselves with Jesus but had gone no further. This verse is a challenge to the believer to become a disciple—one who follows Christ for the purpose of "learning" from Him.

In evangelical circles we hear more about salvation than discipleship. We have settled for a cheap and easy form of Christianity, and to add to our sense of spiritual well-being we have tossed in the concept of eternal security for good measure. Once saved, always saved. In the meantime we go our own way and do our own thing. A. W. Tozer called this "instant Christianity."

> It is hardly a matter of wonder that the country that gave the world instant tea and instant coffee should be the one to give it instant Christianity. . . . By instant Christianity I mean the kind found almost everywhere in gospel circles and which is born of the notion that we may discharge our total obligation to our own souls by one act of faith, or at most by two, and be relieved thereafter of all anxiety about our spiritual condition. We are saints by calling, our teachers keep telling us, and we are permitted to infer from this that there is no reason to seek to be saints by character. . . . By trying to pack all of salvation into one experience, or two, the advocates of instant Christianity flaunt the law of development which runs through all nature. They ignore the sanctifying effects of suffering, cross carrying and practical obedience. They pass by the need for spiritual training, the necessity of forming right religious habits and the need to wrestle against the world, the devil and the flesh. . . . Undue preoccupation with the initial act of believing has created in some a psychology of contentment, or at least of non-expectation. . . . It relieves them of the need to watch and fight and pray and sets them free to enjoy this world while waiting for the next.[2]

Tozer was right. Too often we have preached an emasculated gospel which has produced a watered-down version of Christianity. We have attached great importance to the positive aspects of the gospel—love, joy, and peace—but have said little about the less attractive features—alienation, humiliation, and persecution. Jesus warned His disciples

---

2. A. W. Tozer, *That Incredible Christian* (Harrisburg, Pa.: Christian Publications, 1964), pp. 23-25.

that they would be hated by all men, that they would encounter all kinds of opposition and tribulation. He went so far as to say that the day would come when "whoever kills you will think he is offering service to God" (Jn 16:2). Paul exhorted his converts to continue in the faith, warning them that "through many tribulations we must enter the kingdom of God" (Acts 14:22).

In our preaching we have challenged young people to "give their hearts to Christ" and led them to believe that this is the end and aim of the Christian life. We have said little or nothing about allegiance to the person of Christ, obedience to the will of Christ, or involvement in the cause of Christ. We have talked about self-fulfillment, Jesus talked about self-denial. Three times in one passage (Lk 14:25-33) He warned that if His followers were not prepared for self-denial in its severest form they *could not* be His disciples.

To be a disciple is to follow Christ. The whole idea underlying the word "disciple" is foreign to Western culture. The student in the West chooses the *school* to which he will go. He hopes he will find good teachers when he gets there, but that is of secondary importance. His loyalty is first to the school; it is called "school spirit." After graduation he becomes a loyal supporter of the school, but during four years in college he may never visit a single professor in his home.

For the real meaning of disciple we must go to India, where the disciple chooses a particular guru and proceeds to attach himself to his person, living under his roof, sitting at his feet, eating at his table, listening to his words, walking and talking with him in the bazaar or the marketplace, even helping with the household chores. In a word, he shares the total life of the guru. In the give-and-take of this intimate fellowship the disciple gradually takes on the character of his guru. Before long he finds himself thinking, talking, acting like him. When he gets through he is a carbon copy of the guru. That is discipleship.

This is what our Lord had in mind when He said, "Take my yoke upon you and learn from me." It is not enough to confess Christ as Savior. We must go on to acknowledge Him as our Teacher. We must attach ourselves to His person, enroll in His school, listen to His words, walk in His way, surrender to His will.

Slowly but surely we will undergo a complete transformation of life and thought. As a result we will come to have a new center of gravity, a new system of values, a new standard of morality, a new frame of reference, a new purpose in life. We are now His disciples because we have accepted His discipline. The two words come from the same root. As the discipline deepens, something of His spirit rubs off on us—the spirit of humility, sincerity, service, and sacrifice. We become a carbon copy of Him. That is discipleship.

3. The command to go. Now the disciple is ready for another word: "Go." He is not solely concerned for the cultivation of his own spiritual life, he must be concerned for others also. The time comes when he is ready to hear the word that will change him from a disciple to an apostle and send him into the world with the saving gospel of Jesus Christ. The true disciple will have the same compassion for the world that Jesus had. Indeed, this is one of the things he learns from his Teacher. Jesus was moved with compassion when He saw the multitudes as sheep without a shepherd, and He instructed His disciples to "pray the Lord of the harvest to send out laborers into his harvest" (Mt 9:38).

The central fact of the Christian faith is the Incarnation. Jesus leaves us in no doubt as to its purpose. "The Son of man came to seek and save the lost" (Lk 19:10). By His death and resurrection Jesus procured salvation for the entire human race. The glorious truth of the gospel is that "God was in Christ reconciling the world to himself" (2 Cor 5:19). That was the purpose of the Incarnation. Having achieved the victory over sin, death, and hell, Jesus returned to heaven; but before leaving He gave His disciples their marching orders for all time to come. "All authority in heaven and earth is given to me. Go therefore and make disciples of all nations" (Mt 28:18-19). In another passage He was careful to point out the vital connection between His mission and theirs. At His first meeting with the Twelve after His resurrection Jesus said: "As the Father has sent me, even so I send you" (Jn 20:21). The Great Commission is nothing new. It is part of the purpose of the Incarnation. As the Father sent Christ into the world on a mission of redemption, so Christ sends the church into the world on a similar mission.

By virtue of this third word—"Go"—the disciple now becomes an apostle, or, if you like, a missionary. The two words have the same root meaning, one derived from Greek and the other from Latin. In the early church they used the word "apostle." Today we use the term "missionary." The meaning is identical. An apostle, or a missionary, is simply a "sent one."

The order of these three words is important. One must first "come" to Christ before he can "follow," and one must learn to "follow" before he can "go." A great deal of frustration in Christian life and failure in Christian service has resulted from neglecting to observe the proper order of these words. Sincere people try to act like disciples without ever having become true believers. They try to order their lives by the Sermon on the Mount without being on speaking terms with the Savior of the Mount. There is nothing more frustrating than trying to cultivate a spiritual life that one does not possess. Likewise, there are those who undertake Christian service without ever having learned Christian discipline; and invariably they fail.

The missionary concept includes four ideas: the One who sends, the one who is sent, those to whom he is sent, and the message he is commanded to proclaim.

The One who sends is none other than Jesus Christ, who by virtue of His unquestioning obedience to the Father's will (Phil 2:8) is now invested with "all authority in heaven and on earth" (Mt 28:18). The Great Commission, then, is based on the supremacy and sovereignty of Jesus Christ, the Son of God, who in the Incarnation became the Son of Man, that through His death and resurrection He might become the Savior and Sovereign of the world. He is not only the Head of the church and the Lord of the harvest; He is also the Lord of history, the King of the nations, and the Arbiter of human destiny. Sooner or later all men must come to terms with Him. He and He alone has the right to demand universal allegiance.

The one who is sent is the disciple who has accepted both the doctrine and discipline of his Lord. He is commissioned to carry the gospel to the ends of the earth. In so doing he is prepared to hazard his life for the sake of the gospel. He knows both its preciousness and its power. He can share it with courage and conviction, knowing that "there is salvation in no one else, for there is no other name under heaven given among men by which we must be saved" (Acts 4:12).

And to whom is the missionary sent? In the Gospels the disciples were sent to the lost sheep of the house of Israel, but in the words of the Great Commission the apostles were to go into "all the world." They were to preach the gospel to "every creature." They were to make disciples of "all nations." The entire world was to be included and the message was to be addressed to all men. No distinction was to be made between Jew and Gentile, Greek and Roman. All men are lost; all men need to be saved; therefore all men must hear the gospel.

And what about the message? The message is the Good News: God loved the world; Christ died for all. Salvation is an accomplished fact. It is offered as a free gift. It can be a present possession. Salvation is bestowed by God on the principle of grace and received by man on the principle of faith (Eph 2:8). The early apostles and present-day missionaries share the same message: Jesus Christ and Him crucified (1 Cor 2:2). The missionary does not invent his message. He isn't even called on to defend it. His task is to proclaim it.

This gospel, preached in the power of the Holy Spirit, calls for a response. The hearer of the message is called on to repent and believe. In so doing he is saved. If he refuses, he faces certain condemnation (Mk 16:16). Missionary work is serious business. To one group of listeners the missionary becomes a fragrance from life to life, to another a fragrance from death to death. Little wonder that Paul exclaims, "Who is sufficient for these things?" (2 Cor 2:16). It is better for a person never to hear the gospel than having heard it to reject it.

The Condition of Mankind

This is the third dimension, and it constitutes an integral part of the missionary mandate. If the condition of mankind were other than it is, there would be little or no need for the Christian mission.

The needs of the world are deep-seated and of long standing. They cry out for amelioration. The church, if it is to be loyal to Christ, cannot pass by on the other side as the priest and the Levite did (Lk 10:31-32).

The church cannot be true to its own gospel if it turns a deaf ear to the cry of need, whatever that need may be. When Jesus saw the multitudes as sheep without a shepherd He was moved with compassion, and His compassion always issued in action. Peter described it in one beautiful phrase: "He went about doing good" (Acts 10:38). The Christian cannot do less.

There are those who contend that missionary work should be confined to the spiritual needs of the world; consequently the missionary has no business engaging in medical and educational work. The practice of our Lord and the teaching of the early church do not seem to support this view. At the beginning of His public ministry our Lord declared, "The Spirit of the Lord is upon me, because he has anointed me to preach good news to the poor. He has sent me to proclaim release to the captives, and recovering of sight to the blind, to set at liberty those who are oppressed, to proclaim the acceptable year of the Lord" (Lk 4:18). According to Matthew's Gospel Jesus came preaching, teaching, and healing (4:23), a threefold ministry corresponding roughly to the threefold nature of man: soul, mind, and body. It is from such passages that we get the expression, "The whole gospel for the whole man."

1. Man's spiritual needs. No Christian would wish to deny that man's deepest and greatest needs are spiritual. If man is made in the image of God and possesses an immortal soul that will live as long as God lives, either in fellowship with God or alienated from Him, it stands to reason that man's greatest need is to be saved. Certainly this was the teaching of Christ when He said, "What does it profit a man to gain the whole world and forfeit his life? For what can a man give in return for his life?" (Mk 8:36-37). The most profound question any man can ask during his life on earth is, "What must I do to be saved?" (Acts 16:30). On the answer to that question depends man's happiness here and hereafter.

The Scriptures clearly teach that mankind is alienated from God (Eph 4:18), hostile to God (Rom 5:10), and under the wrath of God (Jn 3:36). The sinner's only hope is to turn from his wicked way, repent, and believe the gospel. There is no other hope held out to him. He has no other option. It is, therefore, imperative for him to hear and understand the gospel.

The missionary's first concern, then, is to preach the gospel, to be instant in season and out of season, to seize every opportunity to press home the claims of Christ. The fact that most men are not conscious of their spiritual needs only serves to underscore the gravity of the situation. The most perilous aspect of man's lostness is the fact that he doesn't know he is lost (2 Cor 4:4). The fact that the "heathen" are lost and must hear the gospel in order to be saved is a major factor in the missionary mandate. If all men are not lost, or if God can somehow save them without a knowledge of Christ, the nerve of the Christian mission has been severed.

2. Man's intellectual needs. Man is not all soul. He has a mind as well. Consequently he has certain well-defined intellectual needs. If these are being met by other agencies, there is no need for the missionaries to duplicate the services provided by others. If, on the other hand, no one is caring for the intellectual needs of the people, the missionary is forced to do something about the situation. This is precisely what happened in Africa. When the missionaries first arrived they found more than eight hundred tribes, each with its own language. Not only were the people illiterate, their languages had never been reduced to writing. In that case the missionaries had no choice. They had to step into the breach and provide for the intellectual needs, first of their own converts and later of the people at large. What church can grow and become strong without a knowledge of the Word of God? The Bible must be translated into the vernacular, and the Christians must be taught to read their own language.

But more than that. Men's minds must be enlightened not simply in order to read the Bible but also to take their place in life and make their contribution to society. Man is a rational creature; his powers of mind and reason must be developed if he is to be the kind of well-integrated personality God intended him to be. So in every country missionaries opened schools, reduced languages to writing, taught the people to read, published literature, and opened a whole new world of thought and ideas to people previously content to spend their time eating, sleeping, and mating. Such people were not really living, they were merely existing.

3. Man's physical needs. Most of the Oriental religions, especially Hinduism and Buddhism, are world-renouncing. To them the body is a highly undesirable thing, something that stands in the way of man's spiritual quest. To cultivate his soul he must neglect, if not abuse, his body. Salvation does not embrace the body; that is something to be sloughed off when the soul enters Nirvana.

In contrast to all this is Christianity, which is a world-affirming religion. Jesus taught that man's most precious possession is his soul; and He warned that if that is lost, *all* is lost. But nowhere did Jesus deprecate either the body or its needs. He said, "Man shall not live by bread *alone*" (Mt 4:4); but he does need bread. In short, man has physical needs which are God-given. Jesus went so far as to sanction the act of David and his guerrilla band when they ate the shewbread, which was to be eaten only by the priests (Mt 12:4). So essential is the life and health of the body that, under certain circumstances, the elemental needs of human nature take precedence over religious ritual.

Repeatedly Jesus asked, "Will you be made whole?" The word "whole" comes from an old Anglo-Saxon root, *hal,* from which we get our words "health" and "holiness." In order to be "whole," man needs both health and holiness. In his mundane existence man needs a body; in the resurrection he will have a glorified body. No religion places more honor on the body than does Christianity. Hence we find Jesus cleansing the leper, healing the sick, feeding the hungry, even raising the dead. Sickness, pain, weakness, and death are all part of the kingdom of Satan that He came to destroy. When He sent out the Twelve and again the Seventy, He gave them instructions to heal the sick and cleanse the leper.

When the missionary took the gospel to the ends of the earth in the nineteenth century he too engaged in a healing ministry. It is true he did not work many miracles, but he took with him the findings and facilities of modern medicine and shared them not only with his converts but with others as well. He used modern medicine and surgery to bring health and healing to bodies until then racked with pain and deformed by disease.

Of course, others besides the missionary can minister to the intellectual and physical needs of the world; and this is being done more as the newly independent countries of the Third World introduce socialized medicine and universal, compulsory, free education. Consequently mission schools and hospitals are rapidly passing under government control. This is all to the good. The missionary should rejoice when he sees these things come to pass. Instead of bemoaning his "loss" he should rejoice that he is now being set free for the spiritual work that *only he can perform*. The spiritual needs of mankind will never be met by the governments, foundations, or corporations, however wealthy and benign they may become. Relieved of his medical and educational institutions, which in former years ate up so many of his human and material resources, today's missionary is free to concentrate on dispensing the True Bread which came down from heaven to give life to the world.

9

The Fate of the Heathen

Modern man finds it difficult if not impossible to accept the doctrine of eternal punishment. This doctrine becomes especially offensive when applied to the heathen who, having never heard the gospel, can hardly be blamed for rejecting it.

Before addressing ourselves to the fate of the heathen it will be helpful to discuss the lostness of man in general. Three questions are pertinent here. Is man lost or is he not? If he is lost, is he lost for time only or also for eternity? If perhaps he finds himself lost in the next life, will he have a second chance?

It is easy to ask these questions; it is not easy to answer them. Indeed, man does not have the answers to these questions, nor is he capable of finding them. Man's ultimate fate rests in the hands of God. Whether he is saved or lost depends entirely on Him. If God declares man to be lost, then he is lost. Left to his own intelligence and shut up to his own information, man has no way of knowing how he stands in the sight of God. Being a creature of time, he has no understanding of eternity. Being a denizen of earth, he has no knowledge of heaven— or of hell either, for that matter. It is, therefore, idle for him to speculate; it is dangerous for him to dogmatize. Concerning his own fate man knows only what God has been pleased to reveal. In that case, it is an act of consummate folly for him to reject that revelation.

Is Man Lost?

For the answer to that question we must turn to the Bible, the only book in the world that speaks to that point. And the answer we get comes through loud and clear: "Yes, man is lost." That statement embraces the entire human race. *All* men are lost. Jews and Gentiles, good men and bad, the pagans in America as well as the heathen in Africa—all have sinned and come short of the glory of God (Rom 3:23). All are children of wrath (Eph 2:3); all are under condemnation (Rom 3:19); all have a rendezvous with death (Rom 5:12; Heb 9:27). Upright, moral, decent men, such as Nicodemus and Cornelius—all are lost and need to be saved (Jn 3:3; Acts 11:13-14).

What does it mean to be lost? The Scriptures portray a dismal, dreadful picture of man in his lost condition. Man was made in the beginning *by* God *for* God, and God intended that man should find his highest happiness in fellowship with Him. But man disobeyed. With his eyes wide open and knowing full well the awful and inevitable consequences of his act, Adam put forth his hand and partook of the forbidden fruit. Instantly something happened; sin came into his life and God went out. From that day to this man has wandered to and fro as a spiritual vagabond on the face of the earth. He has sailed the seven seas; he has traveled to the ends of the earth; he has even visited the moon; he has conquered the wilderness and made the desert to blossom like the rose; he has founded empires and dynasties; he has built cities and castles; he has heaped to himself riches and honor; but for all that, his soul is an orphan still. In his heart there is what H. G. Wells called a "God-shaped blank" that nothing on earth can ever fill. His spirit, like Noah's dove, flits back and forth between "rough seas and stormy skies." He is totally unable to find what Jesus called "rest for the soul."

With the vertical connection broken, all horizontal connections are at loose ends. He is not only at odds with his Maker, but with his neighbor as well.

The Bible describes him as being dead in trespasses and sins (Eph 2:1). He has plenty of physical, intellectual, and social life; but he is completely devoid of spiritual life. He is alienated from the life of God (Eph 4:18), ignorant of the truth of God (Rom 1:25), hostile to the law of God (Rom 8:7), disobedient to the will of God (Tit 3:3), and exposed to the wrath of God (Jn 3:36). He has been separated from God so long that he has become naturalized in the unnatural, and actually loves darkness rather than light (Jn 3:19).

The virus of sin has penetrated into every part of his constitution.

His mind has been darkened (Eph 4:18), his emotions vitiated (Rom 1:26-27), and his will enslaved (Jn 8:31-36). In the words of the theologians, he is "totally depraved." Even his body has been affected by the Fall, so that it is now subject to weakness, sickness, pain, and finally death (Gen 3:19).

As a result of the Fall all men are now members of a sinful, fallen race. Every man is born in sin and shapen in iniquity (Ps 51:5). He enters the world with a corrupt, sinful nature and finds himself afflicted with an inborn, inevitable propensity to sin. He takes to sin like a duck takes to water. His members and faculties he employs as "instruments of wickedness" (Rom 6:13) and his five physical senses are inlets and outlets for sin (Col 2:21). A hundred times a day he commits sins of omission as well as commission. He sins in thought (Gen 6:5), word (Rom 3:13-14), and deed (Rom 1:29-32); and all his so-called good deeds are as filthy rags (Is 64:6).

Man is not a sinner because he sins; he sins because he is a sinner. It is just as natural for man to sin as it is for a dog to bark, or a bird to fly, or a fish to swim. It is part of his nature (Rom 7:18); it comes from his heart (Mt 15:19); and his heart is "deceitful above all things and desperately corrupt" (Jer 17:9). Or as Isaiah expressed it: "The whole head is sick and the whole heart faint. From the sole of the foot even to the head, there is no soundness in it, but bruises and sores and bleeding wounds; they are not pressed out, or bound up, or softened with oil" (Is 1:5-6).

Nowhere is the lostness of man more vividly portrayed than in the three parables spoken by Christ in Luke 15. There we have the lost coin, the lost sheep, and the lost son. J. Oswald Sanders says: "The coin was helplessly lost; the sheep was heedlessly lost; the son was wilfully lost."[1] Man has gone astray not like a bird but like a sheep (Is 53:6). He has no homing instinct. Left to himself he will always travel the downward road, further and further into the wilderness of sin (Lk 15:13).

Is Man Eternally Lost?

The question has meaning only if man possesses immortality. If man's existence is confined to this life and he dies like the beasts of the field, it is useless to talk about his being saved or lost for eternity. Man's destiny is linked with his origin. According to the biblical account, "The Lord God formed man of dust from the ground and

---

1. J. Oswald Sanders, *What of the Unevangelized?* (London: Overseas Missionary Fellowship, 1966), p. 27.

breathed into his nostrils the breath of life; and man became a living being" (Gen 2:7). Man is the only earthly creature who is said to have been made in the image of God (Gen 1:26). As such he must possess immortality.

The Bible nowhere tries to prove the immortality of the soul any more than it tries to prove the existence of God, for the simple reason that both ideas are part of the innate consciousness of the human race. There is no tribe, however primitive, that does not have some consciousness of a Supreme Being and some hope of life beyond the grave. Doubtless this was what the Preacher had in mind when he wrote: "He [God] has made everything beautiful in its time; also he has put eternity in man's mind" (Eccles 3:11).

The Bible clearly teaches that there are two destinies open to man. One involves everlasting happiness in the presence of God and the holy angels (Lk 15:10; Rev 22:3-5; 1 Thess 4:17), the other involves everlasting misery in the company of the devil and his angels (Mt 25:41). The New Testament speaks of two gates—one strait and the other wide; two ways—one broad and the other narrow; two destinies—one life and the other destruction (Mt 7:13-14). In the day of judgment the sheep will be separated from the goats (Mt 25:31-46), the wheat from the tares (Mt 13:36-43), the good from the evil (Jn 5:29). And in the resurrection there will be a separation between the just and the unjust (Acts 24:15).

The doctrine of everlasting punishment, though taught in the Scriptures, is challenged by many today. The chief quarrel with the doctrine is twofold. First, the very idea is said to be repugnant to the modern mind. No man in his right mind, they say, would consign his worst enemy to hell. Not even a Hitler deserves that kind of punishment. Second, it is impossible to reconcile everlasting punishment with the all-embracing love of God. Nels Ferré speaks for all universalists when he says:

> The very conception of an eternal hell is monstrous and an insult to the conception of last things in other religions, not to mention the Christian doctrine of God's sovereign love. Such a doctrine would either make God a tyrant, where any human Hitler would be a third degree saint, and the concentration camps of human torture the king's picnic grounds. That such a doctrine could be conceived, not to mention believed, shows how far from any understanding of the love of God many people once were, and, alas, still are.[2]

It must be acknowledged that the idea of everlasting punishment

---

2. Nels Ferré, *The Christian Understanding of God* (New York: Harper and Brothers, 1951), p. vii.

is repugnant to the modern mind. So what? That is not the only Christian doctrine that is unacceptable to the humanistic, naturalistic mind of the twentieth century. The Christian must choose between the modern mind and the mind of Christ; for after all, it was Christ who first taught this awful doctrine.

> Jesus Christ is the Person who is responsible for the doctrine of Eternal Perdition. He is the Being with whom all opponents of this theological tenet are in conflict. Neither the Christian Church nor the Christian ministry are the authors of it. The Christian ministry never would have invented the dogma; neither would they have preached it all the Christian centuries.[3]

The word "Gehenna" (hell) occurs twelve times in the New Testament; eleven times it came from the lips of Christ. It was not John the Baptist, or the apostle Paul, or Martin Luther, or John Knox who first coined the awful words we would prefer to drop from our present-day preaching: "the unquenchable fire," "the worm that dieth not," "outer darkness," "weeping and gnashing of teeth," "he is comforted and thou art tormented." These are not the wild, irresponsible words of some flaming evangelist who goes up and down the country preaching hell-fire and brimstone in an attempt to scare people into the kingdom. These words, terrible though they are, fell from the lips of the meekest Man who ever lived, the Friend of publicans and sinners, the Man who gave His life and shed His blood that men might be forgiven; and they were spoken, we may be sure, with a tear in the eye and a quiver in the voice.

No, we cannot evade the issue. Jesus taught the doctrine of everlasting punishment. He claimed to be the way, the truth, and the life; and we accept the claim. He knew the truth (Jn 2:24-25), He taught the truth (Jn 18:37), He lived the truth (Jn 1:14), He was the truth (Jn 14:6). Jesus Christ is the King of Truth. He cannot lie. What He says must be true. Whether we understand it or not, whether we like it or not is really beside the point. This makes no difference to the truth of any statement that comes from Him. If He said it, it must be true. Otherwise the concept of the lordship of Christ becomes meaningless.

It might not be out of place to remind ourselves that all we know about eternal life and heaven we learned from Christ. Likewise, all we know about death and judgment we obtained from the same source. What right have we to accept His teaching on the one and reject it on the other? If He is an authority on heaven, He is also an authority on hell.

---

3. William G. T. Shedd, *Dogmatic Theology* (Grand Rapids: Zondervan, 1953), II:680.

Some people talk as if love were the only truth Jesus ever taught. Nothing could be further from the facts. He taught love, all right. Indeed, He Himself was the ultimate expression of God's love (Jn 3:16). It is true that God loved the world and that Christ died for all. It is true that God is ready and willing to reconcile the rebel, forgive the sinner, and receive the prodigal back from the far country. But what if the rebel spurns God's love and persists in his rebellion? What if the sinner refuses forgiveness? What if the prodigal elects to remain in the far country?

Jesus taught the love of God as no one else has ever done. He also spoke of sin, wrath, death, and judgment. He recognized that there is such a thing as recalcitrant sin, and He did not hesitate to declare that if men will not accept the mercy of God they shut themselves up to the wrath of God (Jn 3:36). Christianity has two symbols, the cross and the throne. One speaks of love, the other of judgment. God does not force His love on anyone. On the contrary, every man must make his own choice. But let us make no mistake about it: the man who rejects God's love exposes himself to His wrath, and the one is commensurate with the other (Acts 17:30-31; Rom 2:3-5; 2 Thess 1:7-10).

Must Almighty God, Ruler of heaven and earth, tolerate rebellion in His universe forever? To ask the question is to answer it. Christ's picture of the final judgment is completely realistic. He was too good and too honest to fool us. What He told us about the judgment to come is the simple, naked, unvarnished truth of God; and we alter or reject it at our peril.

We do not preach the wrath of God because we like to, but because Jesus taught it. Being followers of Christ we have no choice. What preacher does not understand the feelings of C. S. Lewis when he wrote: "There is no doctrine which I would more willingly remove from Christianity than this [hell], if it lay in my power.... I would pay any price to be able to say truthfully: 'All will be saved.' "[4]

Mark that phrase: "If it lay in my power." That is the crux of the whole matter. It clearly does not lie in our power to remove hell, or any other doctrine, from the corpus of Christian truth. If Jesus Christ is Lord of all life, we should "destroy arguments and every proud obstacle to the knowledge of God, and take every thought captive to obey Christ" (2 Cor 10:5).

Those who reject Christ's teaching about everlasting punishment insist that the words He used are not to be taken at their face value. They are symbolic and not literal, and no longer mean what our fore-

---

4. C. S. Lewis, *The Problem of Pain* (New York: Macmillan Co., 1962), p. 118.

fathers of a cruder generation thought they meant. Be that as it may. If they are symbolic, they are symbolic of *something;* and whatever that something is, it must be unspeakably awful to require such symbols to express it. Take the most liberal view; place on these stinging words the most charitable construction they can possibly bear; one cannot by any stretch of the imagination deny the fact that they describe a form of punishment more severe than any human being would wish to bear.

Is There a Second Chance After Death?

Here again we are totally dependent for our information on the New Testament.

There is nothing in the teachings of Christ to suggest the possibility of a second chance after death. In fact, in the parable of the rich man and Lazarus (Lk 16:19-31) the very opposite is clearly taught. The rich man in Hades made two requests of Abraham. One was that Lazarus might be sent to cool his tongue with water, the other that he might be sent to warn his five brothers still on earth. Both requests were denied. In denying the first request Abraham explained the impossibility of any such arrangement: "Son, remember that you in your lifetime received your good things, and Lazarus in like manner evil things; but now he is comforted here, and you are in anguish. And besides all this, between us and you a great chasm has been fixed, in order that those who would pass from here to you may not be able, and none may cross from there to us" (Lk 16:25-26).

It is clear from this passage that death seals the fate of both believer and unbeliever. Repentance is possible only in this life; after death there is only remorse.

The author of the book of Hebrews says: "It is appointed for men to die once, and after that comes judgment"—not probation (Heb 9:27).

Are the Heathen Lost?

What about the heathen who have never heard the gospel and so cannot be charged with having rejected it? It is the fate of these individuals that has caused the most controversy. The doctrine of everlasting punishment is bad enough when applied to the hardened sinner who deliberately rejects the gospel, but what about those in non-Christian lands who never have a chance to accept Christ? Is it fair to punish them for rejecting a Christ of whom they are completely ignorant? Many of them are seeking souls and doubtless would believe if they had an opportunity. Are all these people going to be forever lost through no fault of their own?

Before we attempt to answer that specific question, it is necessary to discuss the condition of the heathen in general—again from the viewpoint of the New Testament. Certain truths are made clear.

1. The heathen were not heathen to begin with. They *became* heathen when they deliberately gave up their knowledge of God. "For although they knew God they did not honor him as God or give thanks to him, but they *became* futile in their thinking and their senseless minds were darkened. Claiming to be wise, they *became* fools, and exchanged the glory of the immortal God for images resembling mortal man, or birds, or animals, or reptiles" (Rom 1:21-23).

2. In their progressive apostasy the heathen did not lose all knowledge of God. They retained a knowledge of God's eternal power and deity which reached them through creation. "For that which can be known about God is plain to them, because God has shown it to them. Ever since the creation of the world his invisible nature, namely, his eternal power and deity, has been clearly perceived in the things that have been made" (Rom. 1:20).

3. The revelation of God through creation is supplemented by another revelation through nature or providence. Speaking to the primitive people of Lycaonia, Paul said, "He [God] did not leave himself without witness, for he did good and gave you from heaven rain and fruitful seasons, satisfying your hearts with food and gladness" (Acts 14:17). Modern man with his food stamps and welfare programs was not the first to discover the connection between food and felicity. God knew it all along and made provision for both. Farmers the world over realize how susceptible they are to the vagaries of the weather; but back of the weather is God, the Creator and Sustainer of the world of nature. Nearly every heathen society has some kind of ritual whereby it celebrates a good harvest. Alas, the thank offerings on such occasions are usually made to the earth god, not the God of heaven and earth. But the recognition is there. God has not left Himself without witness.

4. There is still another form of revelation given to the heathen: the human conscience. The heathen have neither the light of the law nor the light of the gospel, but they do have the light of conscience. Paul says, "When the Gentiles who do not have the law do by nature

161

what the law requires, they are a law to themselves, even though they do not have the law. They show that what the law requires is written on their hearts, while their conscience also bears witness and their conflicting thoughts accuse or perhaps excuse them" (Rom 2:14-15). Conscience is by no means a perfect instrument, and it can be abused to the point where it fails to function properly; but it still remains the divine monitor within the human breast. No man is so low in the moral scale that his conscience ceases to function.

This brings us to the crucial question: On what basis is the heathen to be judged? At this point there is a great deal of confused thinking. The popular argument goes something like this: There is only one way to be saved and that is through faith in Christ; the heathen, having never heard of Christ, cannot exercise faith; consequently he is doomed to everlasting punishment for something quite beyond his capability.

This line of thought is based on a false assumption that has no support in Scripture. The assumption is that all men will be judged on the same basis—namely, for failing to believe the gospel. Quite the contrary, Romans 2 makes it plain that all men will not be judged on the same basis. Rather they will be judged according to the light they had. In that chapter there are three groups: the Jew with the light of the law, the Gentile with the light of the gospel, and the heathen with the light of conscience. No man will be judged by light he did not possess. That would be grossly unfair. Every man possesses *some* form of light and he will be judged by that light and by no other.

The greater the light, the heavier the responsibility. The man who all his life lived in sound of the church bell but never entered the church door will have the hardest time of all. He will be judged in the blazing light of the full revelation of God's saving grace in Jesus Christ (2 Cor 4:4). He had Christian friends and neighbors. He possessed, or could easily have acquired, the Holy Scriptures, which are able to make him wise unto salvation (2 Tim 3:16). In his own home, on radio or television, he could have heard the gospel any Sunday in the year. The coins he carried in his pocket were inscribed with the words "In God we trust." What excuse does that man have for failing to come to terms with Jesus Christ? If he goes to hell he will have no one to blame but himself, and his remorse will be all the greater when he remembers the thousand and one opportunities for salvation he passed up.

The heathen on the other hand will have a much easier time. But he will not go scot-free. He had the light of creation, providence, and conscience; and he will be judged by that light. If he is finally condemned it will not be because he refused to believe the gospel, but because he failed to live up to the little light he had. In that case he too must bear the responsibility for his own destiny. God does not consign him to hell; he goes there because that is where he belongs.

If the heathen is judged by his works, how will he fare? The question has often been asked: Do any of the heathen live up to the light they have? The teaching of Scripture and the testimony of missionaries leave no room for hope in this regard. If the first chapter of Romans is an accurate picture of the heathen world, the individuals who make up that world are not likely candidates for salvation. The concept of the "noble savage" exists only in the mind of the skeptic. J. Hudson Taylor, who spent fifty years in China, said that in all that time he never met anyone who claimed to have lived up to the light he had. Moral failure is a universal phenomenon.

What about Cornelius, described in Acts 10? Though a Gentile, he is described as a devout person, one who feared God with all his house, who gave alms liberally to the people, and engaged daily in prayer. When Peter arrived in Caesarea his first words to Cornelius were: "Truly I perceive that God shows no partiality, but in every nation any one who fears him and does what is right is acceptable to him" (Acts 10:34-35).

What did Peter mean? What are the key words in this statement? The statement must be taken in its historical context. Peter had always believed this was true of the Jews. Now, for the first time in his life, he becomes aware of the fact that it is true regardless of race. The key words, then, are "in every nation."

Peter was not prepared to have anything to do with the Gentiles, good or bad, God-fearing or God-hating. Fraternization with them was totally unacceptable to Peter prior to this time. Now he learns better. Indeed, the real reason why the story of Cornelius is included in the book of Acts is not because of what the episode did for Cornelius but what it did for Peter. The story is really the "conversion" of Peter, not of Cornelius.

That Peter by these words did not mean to suggest that Cornelius was already a saved man comes out in his recital of the story on his return to Jerusalem. Peter's commission was to tell Cornelius words whereby he and all his house could be saved (Acts 11:14). Obviously, then, Cornelius was not saved prior to Peter's visit regardless of his piety and his prayers.

What about Romans 2:6-7, where Paul says: "For he will render to every man according to his works: to those who by patience in well-doing seek for glory and honor and immortality, he will give eternal life"? Do these verses hold out any hope that the "moral heathen" will one day win God's favor?

Paul Kanamori, the great Japanese evangelist of another day, had a very dear mother who was a devout Buddhist. Every morning she rose before dawn, lit the candles, burned incense, and prayed to Buddha. Alas, she died without ever hearing the gospel. Kanamori said that he expected to meet his mother in heaven. Sadhu Sundar Singh, the Indian Christian saint, also had a mother who longed and prayed and worked for salvation without ever hearing of Christ. Sundar Singh said that if he didn't find his mother in heaven he would request permission to go to hell to be with her.

One can admire the filial piety that prompted these two men to speak and feel the way they did. No person wants to think of his parents as being in hell. Momentous questions of this kind, however, cannot be answered on the basis of filial piety, family loyalty, or any other human sentiment. The Christian gospel says: "Everyone who calls on the name of the Lord will be saved" (Rom 10:13). Do we have the right to substitute the name of Buddha, or Vishnu, or Krishna for Christ? Most certainly not. "There is salvation in no one else, for there is no other name under heaven given among men by which we must be saved" (Acts 4:12). Jesus said, "I am the way, and the truth, and the life; no one comes to the Father but by me" (Jn 14:6). Paul says, "For no other foundation can anyone lay than that which is laid, which is Jesus Christ" (1 Cor 3:11). Again he says, "For there is one God, and there is one mediator between God and men, the man Christ Jesus" (1 Tim 2:5). The above statements are clear, cogent, and categorical. They admit of only one interpretation. All other passages which are less clear and which are capable of more than one interpretation must be exegeted in the light of these statements. This is the broad teaching of the New Testament. This is the general principle on which the Christian mission must operate.

Nevertheless, in the light of Romans 2:6-7 we must not completely rule out the possibility, however remote, that here and there throughout history there may have been the singular person who got to heaven without the full light of the gospel. In that case *God* is the sole Judge. He is sovereign in the exercise of His grace. We are not called on to pass judgment in such cases—if indeed they ever occurred. Here, as in many other instances, we must fall back on the sovereignty of God and say with Abraham, "Shall not the Judge of all the earth do right?" (Gen 18:25).

10

The Nature of the Christian Gospel

The missionary has but one message: the gospel. His supreme task is to communicate that gospel to the entire world. To be truly effective the communication must be in verbal form, spelled out line upon line and precept upon precept, until the hearer understands the message. Only then can he exercise intelligent, saving faith.

The missionary must have a clear understanding of his own gospel if he is to present it intelligently to others, especially to the non-Christians of the Third World. It is not enough to memorize certain gospel passages and pass them on in a mechanical fashion, hoping that somehow the Holy Spirit will honor His own Word and men will be brought to Christ.

What is the nature of the Christian gospel?

The Divine Origin

That the gospel is divine in its origin the apostle Paul makes crystal clear in several of his epistles. The Epistle to the Romans gives us the most scientific definition of the gospel. In the opening verse of that epistle Paul refers to the gospel as "the gospel of God." In Galatians he says: "The gospel which was preached by me is not man's gospel. For I did not receive it from man, nor was I taught it; but it came through a revelation of Jesus Christ" (Gal 1:11-12).

The gospel is not a human invention. Most of the philosophers of history developed their own systems of thought. They opened their schools, attracted disciples, and entered into dialogue with other philosophers. They asked their questions and propounded their theories. Their systems of thought were often named after them: Neo-platonism, Confucianism, Epicureanism, and others. Not so with the gospel. We speak of Pauline theology and we know what is meant by the term, but Paul would have repudiated the idea. He laid no claim to originality. Time and again he acknowledged his indebtedness to God: Father (Gal 1:15-16), Son (Gal 1:12), and Holy Spirit (1 Cor 2:9-14).

That Jesus Christ died under Pontius Pilate is a matter of history. That He died the just for the unjust to bring us to God is a matter of revelation which we would never have known had not God revealed it to us. Speaking of the essential facts of the gospel, Paul says: "I delivered unto you first of all that which I also received" (1 Cor 15:3). He says precisely the same thing when speaking of the Lord's Supper (1 Cor 11:23). Paul did not invent or develop his theology, he got it directly from the Lord.

1. God willed it in His sovereignty. Long before the creation of the world or the fall of man God devised a plan for the redemption of the human race, and at the heart of that plan was the cross of Christ (1 Pet 1:19-20). "Blessed be the God and Father of our Lord Jesus Christ, who has blessed us with every spiritual blessing in the heavenly places, even as he chose us in him before the foundation of the world, that we should be holy and blameless before him. He destined us in love to be his sons through Jesus Christ, according to the purpose of His will" (Eph 1:3-5).

2. God planned it in His love. God was under no obligation whatever to save the world. When He decided to do so, He acted in love. It is not enough that God is love (1 Jn 4:8). He went further and expressed that love in the gift of His Son (Jn 3:16). The first is simply a concept and so would not have saved anyone. The second was an event—and that made all the difference. The Christian mission is rooted in the love of God. Without that there would be no gospel and no mission.

3. God promised it in the Scriptures. Both Romans and Galatians make it clear that the gospel antedated the coming of Jesus Christ. Paul says that the gospel of justification by faith was "preached beforehand to Abraham" (Gal 3:8). The same emphasis is to be found in Romans. "Paul, a servant of Jesus Christ, called to be an apostle, set apart for the gospel of God, which he promised beforehand through the prophets in the holy scriptures" (Rom 1:1-2). And in Romans 4 Paul uses two Old Testament examples of justification by faith: Abraham and David.

4. God provided it in Christ. "The law was given through Moses; grace and truth came through Jesus Christ" (Jn 1:17). The clearest statement on this matter in the New Testament is Paul's words: "But now the righteousness of God has been manifested apart from the law, although the law and the prophets bear witness to it, the righteousness of God through faith in Jesus Christ for all who believe. . . . They are justified by his grace as a gift through the redemption which is in Christ Jesus, whom God put forward as an expiation by his blood" (Rom 3:21-25).

God then is the Author of salvation. From first to last it is His work. It is not man who seeks after God, it is a loving heavenly Father who waits to be gracious, who longs for the return of the prodigal and will never be satisfied until he comes back. Salvation, far from being a human achievement, is the gift of God. The gospel, far from being a human invention, was willed, planned, promised, and provided by God.

The Christocentric Content

The gospel has many facets but only one theme. This comes out repeatedly in the Acts of the Apostles. Immediately following his conversion in Damascus Paul preached Christ in the synagogues (Acts 9:20). In Athens he preached "Jesus Christ and him crucified" (1 Cor 2:2). Later on, he wrote to the Corinthians: "We preach not ourselves, but Jesus Christ as Lord" (2 Cor 4:5). The other apostles did the same. In the Temple and the synagogues of Jerusalem they preached Jesus and the Resurrection (Acts 2:24; 4:2; 4:33), so much so that they were accused of filling Jerusalem with their doctrine (Acts 5:28). Philip went down to Samaria and preached Christ (Acts 8:5). When he met the Ethiopian eunuch he "told him the good news of Jesus" (Acts 8:35).

The word "gospel" means Good News—the Good News that "God was in Christ reconciling the world to himself, not counting their trespasses against them" (2 Cor 5:19). It is the Good News that Jesus Christ "came into the world to save sinners" (1 Tim 1:15), that by His death and resurrection He "abolished death and brought life and immortality to light through the gospel" (2 Tim 1:10).

Count Zinzendorf, the greatest missionary statesman of the eighteenth century, left his stamp on Moravian missions in all parts of the world. He had rather definite ideas as to how the missionaries should go about their work of world evangelization. He gave them strict instructions to preach the gospel and forget theology—at least in the early stages. "The heathen," he insisted, "already know of the existence of God. What they need to hear about is the love of Christ."

Most of the great ethnic religions had human founders who were good and great men, but they were in no way indispensable to the religions they founded. Buddhism could exist in its essential form even if Gautama had never lived. The same can be said of Confucianism. Even Islam could get along without Mohammed, in spite of the creed which declares: "There is no God but Allah and Mohammed is his prophet." There was nothing unique about Mohammed and any of his followers could have become the "prophet."

Not so with Christianity. The Christian religion centers around a unique person—Jesus Christ. Remove Him from Christianity and there is nothing left but ethical teachings which can be duplicated in several of the other religions. The central fact of Christianity is the person of Christ. The crucial question is, "What do you think of the Christ? Whose son is he?" (Mt 22:42). Man's eternal destiny depends on the answer to that question. To the unbelieving Jews Jesus said, "I told you that you would die in your sins, for you will die in your sins unless you believe that I am he" (Jn 8:24). Jesus would say to Gautama, Confucius, Laotze, Zoroaster, and Mohammed what He said to the Jews of His day: "You are from below, I am from above; you are of this world, I am not of this world" (Jn 8:23).

The gospel is Christocentric in two ways: it pertains to both His *person* and His *work*.

1. His person. The New Testament teaches, and the early church believed, that Jesus Christ is a unique person having two natures, one human and the other divine. He is in truth "descended from David according to the flesh and designated Son of God in power according to the Spirit of holiness by his resurrection from the dead" (Rom 1:3-4). Paul speaks of Him as being originally "in the form of God" but "taking the form of a servant, being born in the likeness of men" (Phil 2:6-7).

The earliest and simplest Christian creed is expressed in the New Testament in four words: "Jesus Christ is Lord" (Phil 2:11). "Jesus," His human name, refers to His humanity. "Christ," His divine title, refers to His deity. The central figure of the New Testament was a unique person, the Son of God, who in the Incarnation became the Son of Man, that through His death and resurrection He might become the one and only Savior and Sovereign of the world.

The Incarnation was the greatest event in the history of the world. It remains to this day the greatest mystery of the Christian faith. Speaking of the Incarnation Paul said: "Great indeed, we confess, is the mystery of our religion; He [God] was manifested in the flesh" (1 Tim 3:16). It is quite impossible for the finite mind of fallen man to comprehend this great mystery.

In some mysterious way that we cannot possibly understand, God, the eternal, immortal, invisible One, wrapped Himself in the mantle of our humanity and appeared on earth in the humble guise of human flesh. God, the almighty One, became the Babe of Bethlehem and fled to Egypt to escape the wrath of an earthly potentate. God, the timeless One, broke into time and for thirty-three years was subject to the laws and limitations of time and space. God, the Architect of the universe, became the carpenter of Nazareth and mended broken furniture for the people next door. God, the Creator, Sustainer, and Possessor of all things, became a penniless preacher, dependent for His daily bread on the charity of others. Such was the mystery of godliness; God was manifest in the flesh.

And yet His deity did not overpower His humanity. Nor did His humanity defile or dilute His deity. Both came together in a perfect union which produced a unique person—the God-man. He was born as a man, lived as a man, died as a man, rose from the dead as a man, and ascended into heaven as a man. He did not shed the mantle of His humanity when He bade farewell to His disciples. He carried it with Him into heaven and today He is a man at the right hand of God.

At the same time He is "very God of very God." The deity of Christ is fundamental to the Christian faith. Whatever else we may or may not believe concerning Him, this is absolutely essential to both church and creed. Deny the deity of Christ and with it go the way of salvation, the forgiveness of sins, the resurrection of the body, and the life everlasting. Jesus Christ is both Son of God and Son of Man. Both facts are essential parts of the gospel.

2. His work. His unique person is not enough. The Incarnation made it possible for Jesus Christ to enter the stream of human history, but it alone does not constitute the gospel. Along with the Incarnation goes the Crucifixion. It too is an integral part of the gospel. It is not enough to preach Christ, we must preach Christ *crucified* (1 Cor 2:2). If Jesus had lived and taught and returned to heaven without going to the cross, there would have been no gospel. The Incarnation was not an end in itself, but a means to an end. It enabled Him not only to live and work and teach, but also to "bear our sins in his body on the tree" (1 Pet 2:24), to die "the righteous for the unrighteous that he might bring us to God" (1 Pet 3:18). And, of course, it did not end with the cross. Three days later He was raised from the dead "by the glory of the Father" (Rom 6:4), "by the power of an indestructible life" (Heb 7:16).

The early church in its teaching and the apostles in their witness insist on the centrality of Jesus Christ, Son of God and Son of Man, whose death and resurrection made possible the salvation of the world.

The Anthropocentric Outreach

If Christ is the theme of the gospel, man is the object of the gospel. There are other creatures in the universe besides man. Some are higher and others are lower than man. But the gospel is not for them.

So far as we know, the animals have only a very primitive kind of soul. They have no self-consciousness; certainly they have no God-consciousness. They are not immortal. When they die that is the end of them. They are not responsible moral agents; hence they are not candidates for salvation. As for the higher creatures, the angels, some have fallen from their high estate and are "kept by him [God] in the nether gloom until the judgment of the great day" (Jude 6). Hell is said to have been prepared for the devil and his angels (Mt 25:41). There is nothing in Scripture to suggest that salvation is possible for the fallen angels. The unfallen angels, confirmed in their goodness, have no need of salvation.

This leaves man the sole candidate for salvation. Man alone was made in the image of God (Gen 1:26-27). His immortality, derived from God, guarantees that man will live as long as God lives, either in fellowship with Him or alienated from Him. The divine image has been defaced by sin but not completely destroyed. The most primitive, degraded cannibal still bears the image of his Maker and is therefore a candidate for salvation. The greatest sinner who ever lived is not beyond redemption. Jesus came not to call the righteous but sinners to repentance (Mt 9:13). Indeed, "where sin increased, grace abounded all the more" (Rom 5:20). God's greatest glory is His grace, and He is never more glorified than when His grace reaches and reclaims the sinner.

Man in his sin is the object of God's pity and compassion. The two great truths of the gospel are: God loved the world; Christ died for all. The one is the corollary of the other. The first is the explanation of the second. The second is the expression of the first. The cross is God's way of saying to a prodigal world, "I love you; come home."

The Existential Approach

It meets man in all his need, right where he is in the midst of the human predicament. This note was sounded by Christ at the beginning of His public ministry when in the synagogue in Nazareth He applied to Himself the words of the prophet Isaiah: "The Spirit of the Lord is upon me, because he has anointed me to preach good news to the poor. He has sent me to proclaim release to the captives and recovering of sight to the blind, to set at liberty those who are oppressed, to proclaim the acceptable year of the Lord" (Lk 4:18-19).

The gospel claims to meet man's existential needs. "If any one *thirst* let him come to me and *drink*" (Jn 7:37). "Come to me all who *labor* and are *heavy laden,* and I will give you *rest*" (Mt 11:28). Again He said: "What man of you, if his son asks him for bread, will he give him a stone? Or if he asks for a fish, will he give him a serpent?" (Mt 7:9-10).

Jesus knew that all men are sinners and need forgiveness, and this He gave freely. He also knew that each man has his own problems, which are personal. He dealt with these also. To the paralytic Jesus said, "My son, your sins are forgiven." He also said: "Rise, take up your pallet and walk" (Mk 2:5-9). So the lepers were cleansed, the deaf were made to hear, the dumb were made to speak, and the blind had their sight restored.

This existential approach is seen in the teachings as well as the miracles of Jesus. Here again He deals with persons as individuals, each in his or her own peculiar situation. To Nicodemus, a religious leader with an impeccable reputation, He said: "You must be born anew" (Jn 3:7). To the immoral Samaritan woman He said: "Go, call your husband and come here" (Jn 4:16). He spent a night in the home of Zacchaeus, a rich and corrupt politician. Luke does not indicate what Jesus said to this man; but it is safe to assume that He put His finger on Zacchaeus' sore spot, for the latter repented with these words: "Behold, Lord, the half of my goods I give to the poor; and if I have defrauded any one of anything, I restore it fourfold" (Lk 19:8).

Jesus didn't waste words. He went right to the heart of each person's problem—and solved it.

Some people have criticized the gospel because it is man-centered and need-oriented. We accept the criticism and make no apology for it. That is precisely what the gospel is supposed to be. Jesus said: "Those who are well have no need of a physician, but those who are sick" (Mt 9:12). Most people came to Jesus from a sense of need rather than a sense of sin. The same is true today, especially on the mission field, where medical facilities and social services are either inadequate or nonexistent. We pay lip service to the concept of "the whole gospel for the whole man," but when some evangelist preaches a "utilitarian" gospel we are quick to condemn him. In His teaching, preaching. and healing ministry Jesus offered healing for the whole man—body, mind, and soul. His most frequent question was: "Wilt thou be made whole?"

Another criticism of the gospel is that it is a crutch designed for the weak. Red-blooded he-men have been known to scoff at the gospel, saying that religion is for women and children. Are we expected to apologize for the fact? Indeed not! What's wrong with women? My mother was a woman; so is my wife. I'm glad the gospel is for women! I'm glad it's for children too, for all of us were children at one time. Jesus seemed to have a tender spot for them. When the disciples were about to chase them away, He said: "Let the children come to me, and do not hinder them; for to such belongs the kingdom of heaven" (Mt 19:14). It would be a thousand pities if the gospel were "for men only." It *is* for the weak, the weary, the fearful, the fretful, the harlot, the publican, the sinner.

Does the Christian gospel speak to man in his existential situation? Does it offer any solution for what we call today "the human predicament"? Does it have anything to say to the black woman in the ghetto trying to hold together a family of seven children deserted by their father? Does it have anything to say to the rich man on his ranch whose marriage is on the rocks and whose daily life is a living hell? Or does the gospel simply promise us "pie in the sky by and by"?

The Communists have mocked the Christian church, calling religion "the opiate of the people." We know what they mean, and we repudiate the connotation as they understand it; but we should not be afraid or ashamed to acknowledge that there is an element of truth in the accusation. Opium is not a bad thing in itself. It has medicinal properties known to every physician. Missionaries without access to a doctor keep tincture of opium in their medicine chest and use it from time to time with good effect. Hundreds of millions of persons in all parts of the world are hurting, and the gospel is designed to heal their hurt. Horatius Bonar was speaking for every Christian when he wrote:

> I heard the voice of Jesus say,
>   "Come unto Me and rest;
> Lay down, thou weary one, lay down
>   Thy head upon My breast."
> I came to Jesus as I was,
>   Weary and worn and sad;

I found in Him a resting place,
And He has made me glad.

That is the glory of the gospel. It helps man where he hurts. In the words of John Newton, "It soothes his sorrows, heals his wounds, and drives away his fears." In the more picturesque words of the prophet, it gives him beauty for ashes, the oil of joy for mourning, and the garment of praise for the spirit of heaviness (Is 61:3). And if it fails to do that, it isn't the gospel at all.

The Dynamic Operation

The apostle in his Epistle to the Romans describes the gospel as the "power of God for salvation to every one who has faith" (1:16). No one can have a personal, vital encounter with Jesus Christ and not be radically changed at the center of his being. The demon-possessed Mary Magdalene; the immoral woman of Samaria; the corrupt politician, Zacchaeus; Saul of Tarsus, the archenemy of the church —all were confronted and conquered by Jesus Christ, and they were never again the same. There is nothing in all the world quite as powerful as the transforming friendship of Jesus Christ. To believe in Him is to pass from death unto life (Jn 5:24). Man's first and greatest need is not love, or truth, or freedom, but life. Jesus said, "I came that they may have life, and have it abundantly" (Jn 10:10). He spoke of the "living water" (Jn 4:10). He also spoke of the "bread of life" (Jn 6:48). Paul expressed it in another way: "For the law of the Spirit of life in Christ Jesus has set me free from the law of sin and death" (Rom 8:2).

Modern man is well aware that he is in a predicament from which he cannot extricate himself, but he doesn't seem to know the root cause of his predicament. He blames it on the system, the environment, the establishment—anything and everything but himself. He thinks that salvation lies in cleaning up the environment or changing the system or demolishing the establishment. Who polluted the environment? Who corrupted the system? Who devised the establishment? Man did! If the power structures are demonic, man made them so. He has only himself to blame. Sad to say, this is what he doesn't seem to understand.

Modern psychology, with its scientific insights into human behavior, has shed a good deal of light on the problem of human nature; but psychology has always found it easier to take the human personality apart than to put it together again. Not infrequently when psychiatrists come to the end of their resources they pat the patient on the back and exhort him to "live with his problem."

Jesus Christ never told anybody to "live with his problem." He always went to the root of the matter and changed the person at the center of his being. The real problem is in man not in his environment. To change the latter without changing the former is to treat the symptom and not the disease. Man needs to be converted—"born anew" is the term Jesus used (Jn 3:3). After conversion he is a different person. Paul expressed it most clearly when he said: "If any one is in Christ, he is a new creation; the old has passed away, behold, the new has come" (2 Cor 5:17).

This is not to say that conversion solves *all* of man's problems, after which he is carried to heaven on a flowery bed of ease. But it does mean that he is given a new power to face his problems and to cope with them. Nor does it mean that the gospel answers *all* of man's questions. But it has more and better answers than any other system of thought or religion. Among other things, it solves the problem of sin—both its penalty and its power. It throws light on the deepest mysteries of human existence, including the origin of the world, the destiny of man, the meaning of life here, and the prospect of life in the world to come. It also dispels man's greatest fear—his fear of death.

The Universal Appeal

This concept has been with us so long that we have come to take it for granted, but in Jesus' day it was a brand-new idea. The world of Jesus' day was a rigidly divided world. The Jews divided the world into two camps—the Jews and the Gentiles; and if you were a Gentile it was just too bad. The Greeks divided the world into two camps—the Greeks and the barbarians; and if you were a barbarian it was just too bad. The Romans divided the world into two camps—citizens and slaves; and if you were a slave it was just too bad.

Jesus refused to recognize any such polarization of the human race. His favorite title for Himself was "Son of Man," not "Son of David" or "Son of Abraham." The great word of the gospel is the word "whosoever." It was used by Jesus (Jn 3:16), Paul (Rom 10:13), and John (Rev 22:17). The gospel insists that God loved the world (Jn 3:16), that Christ died for all (2 Cor 5:15). In God's sight there is no difference between the Jew and the Greek or any other race or nationality, for "the same Lord is Lord of all and bestows his riches upon all who call upon him" (Rom 10:12).

This was the great mistake made by the Jews. They gradually came

174

to believe that they had a monopoly on the grace of God to the exclusion of all others (Mt 3:9). Jesus acknowledged that salvation was *from* the Jews (Jn 4:22), but not exclusively *for* the Jews (Mt 8:11). Though His public ministry was confined mainly to Palestine, He insisted that "the field is the world" (Mt 13:38); and when He gave His disciples their marching orders for the entire age, He instructed them to go into all the world, to preach the gospel to every creature, and to make disciples of all nations.

Four great things are implied in the universal appeal of the gospel. The fact of sin is universal (Rom 3:23); the offer of salvation is universal (Acts 2:21; 1 Tim 2:4; 2 Pet 3:9); the command to repent is universal (Acts 17:30); the invitation to believe is universal (Rom 10:9-11).

The Personal Application

In a *relative* sense there is such a thing as vicarious faith that one person can exercise on behalf of another (Mk 2:5); otherwise intercessory prayer would be impossible (Jas 5:13-16). But in an *absolute* sense every man must exercise faith on his own behalf. Every man is a moral agent responsible to God for his conduct. God's first question to Adam after he had sinned was, "Where are you?" (Gen 3:9). His question to Cain after he had killed Abel was, "What have you done?" (Gen 4:10). In both cases, God held the person responsible for his own sin.

It is, of course, true that men live together in communities and sin has social implications. Cities and even nations have come under the judgment of God because sin became so rampant in the community that everyone was involved. This comes out most clearly in the Old Testament where the prophets pronounced God's judgment on the nations, including Israel.

It is likewise true that whole communities can act in concert and in this way escape the judgment of God. Nineveh is a classic example of this. In our day we speak of a "people movement" which takes place when an entire tribe, perhaps under the leadership of its chief, decides to move en masse from animism and idolatry to Christianity. But even here the time comes when each individual in that tribe or clan must make his own personal decision to accept Christ.

Sin and guilt are primarily personal and individual. Faith and salvation are also personal and individual. Each man must decide his own destiny. He must decide whether to accept or reject Jesus Christ. When he repents, he repents for himself. When he believes, he believes for himself. The gospel makes it plain that each man comes to Christ on his own. The father cannot act on behalf of his son, nor the son on behalf of his father.

In his farewell address to the elders in Ephesus, Paul reminded them that for three years he did not cease day or night to admonish *every one* with tears (Acts 20:31). Grace has been given to *"each* of us according to the measure of the gift of Christ" (Eph 4:7). To the Colossians Paul wrote: "Him we proclaim, warning *every* man and teaching *every* man in all wisdom, that we may present *every* man mature in Christ" (Col 1:28). In the providence of God the day is coming when *every* knee will bow and *every* tongue will confess the universal lordship of Jesus Christ (Phil 2:10-11). Paul instructs us that "we must *all* appear before the judgment seat of Christ" (2 Cor 5:10), at which time *"each* man's work will become manifest" (1 Cor 3:13).

Every member of the human race is a single, separate entity with his own peculiar traits and temperament. He is different from all other members of the human race. As an individual he is a responsible moral agent, answerable in the final analysis to God. All sin, including what we call social sin, is sin against God (Ps 51:4; Lk 15:21); and every man is held responsible for his own sin. For this reason the gospel is personal in its application. It must be understood and received by the sinner as an individual, not simply as a member of a group.

The Revolutionary Implications

We hear a great deal today about revolution. It is probably the most overworked word in modern parlance; but the only people who take the word seriously are the Communists, and they have come the closest to achieving it. One reason why Communism has such an appeal is that we Christians have not taken seriously the revolutionary implications of our own gospel. Christianity is far more revolutionary than Communism is.

Today the "Young Evangelicals" are making a strong plea for what they call "radical Christianity." We may well ask ourselves, "Why the adjective?" In the beginning Christianity *was* radical by its very nature, and its proponents were known as men who "turned the world upside down" (Acts 17:6). In those days there was no need for the adjective "radical." Alas, Christianity has been so diluted that today it is a pale imitation of the real thing. In fact, if Jesus Christ were to come back today He would scarcely recognize His own followers. Ever since Constantine, the Western world has been so religious and the Christian church has been so worldly that it is almost impossible to tell the two apart.

There are two aspects to the gospel. There is the Good News that God was in Christ reconciling the world unto Himself (2 Cor 5:19). The essential core of the gospel relates to the death and resurrection of Jesus Christ, belief in which is sufficient for salvation (1 Cor 15:1-4). But there is more to the gospel than John 3:16 or Matthew 11:28. In its fullness the gospel embraces everything that Jesus ever taught. He made this clear in the words of the Great Commission: "Go therefore and make disciples of all nations, baptizing them in the name of the Father and of the Son and of the Holy Spirit, teaching them to observe *all that I have commanded you*" (Mt 28:19-20).

In the teachings of Jesus Christ there are many concepts far more revolutionary than anything ever advocated by Marx, Lenin, or Mao Tse-tung. The difference between Jesus and the other revolutionaries is that He applied His teachings to the individual and insisted that the Christian act like a Christian regardless of what the rest of the world thinks or does. The other revolutionaries attacked the power structures of the society and said little or nothing about the moral and ethical obligations of the individual. Christians, real Christians— radical Christians, if you like—were expected to act as the salt of the earth and the light of the world (Mt 5:13-16). How deplorable that so few Christians have paid any attention to the radical teachings of Jesus.

At the very heart of the Christian gospel is the concept of self-denial. Three times in the closing verses of Luke 14 Jesus said quite plainly that without utter and complete self-denial no man can be His disciple. Indeed, self-denial was at the heart of the Incarnation (Phil 2:5-8) and it came to full fruition in the Crucifixion (Jn 12:24). Self-denial is the exact opposite of the self-indulgence so characteristic of Western civilization.

Some of Jesus' sayings are so revolutionary that few Christians have bothered to take them seriously; others have regarded them as impractical and dismissed them as visionary. Some of these sayings include the following: "He who finds his life will lose it, and he who loses his life for my sake will find it" (Mt 10:39). "He who loves father or mother more than me is not worthy of me, and he who loves son or daughter more than me is not worthy of me" (Mt 10:37). "If any man would come after me, let him deny himself and take up his cross daily and follow me" (Lk 9:23). "Blessed are the meek, for they shall inherit the earth" (Mt 5:5). "It is more blessed to give than to receive" (Acts 20:35). "Love your enemies, do good to those who hate you, bless those who curse you, pray for those who abuse

177

you. To him who strikes you on the cheek, offer the other also; and from him who takes away your cloak do not withhold your coat as well. Give to every one who begs from you; and of him who takes away your goods, do not ask for them again" (Lk 6:27-30). It is ten times easier to shoulder a gun and overthrow a corrupt regime than to live by the Sermon on the Mount under any kind of system—socialism or capitalism.

Few Christians in affluent America have paid any attention to these sayings of Jesus: "A man's life does not consist in the abundance of his possessions" (Lk 12:15). "Do not lay up for yourselves treasures on earth . . . but lay up for yourselves treasures in heaven . . . for where your treasure is, there will your heart be also" (Mt 6:19-21). "When you give a dinner or a banquet, do not invite your friends or your brothers, or your kinsmen or rich neighbors, lest they also invite you in return, and you will be repaid. But when you give a feast, invite the poor, the maimed, the lame, the blind, because they cannot repay you" (Lk 14:12-14). "If I then, your Lord and Teacher, have washed your feet, you also ought to wash one another's feet" (Jn 13:14). "He who is greatest among you shall be your servant" (Mt 23:11).

These are revolutionary words! Not one professing Christian in a hundred takes them seriously. In theory we accept them, in practice we deny them. Jesus would have to say of us what He said of the hypocrites of His day: "This people honors me with their lips, but their heart is far from me; in vain do they worship me, teaching as doctrine the precepts of men" (Mt 15:8-9).

To His disciples Jesus said, "Why do you call me 'Lord, Lord,' and not do what I tell you?" (Lk 6:46). We have the same problem today. We do everything with Jesus except take Him seriously. We love Him, honor Him, serve Him, preach Him. We even worship Him. We do everything but *obey* Him.

The Exclusive Claims

Christianity claims to be the one and only true religion. The God of the Bible is the true and living God (1 Thess 1:9), and all other gods are dumb idols (1 Cor 12:2). There is only one Mediator between God and men, the man Christ Jesus (1 Tim 2:5). Jesus claimed to be the Son of God in a unique sense, and His words were so understood by His enemies (Jn 5:17-18). This claim was rejected by the Jews (Jn 10:31-33), and finally became the real cause of His crucifixion (Jn 19:7).

Equally important are the indirect claims found in the many

statements of Christ regarding His unique person and mission. We have it on His own testimony that He was older than Abraham (Jn 8:58), wiser than Solomon (Mt 12:42), and greater than Jonah (Mt 12:41). He declared that His words were spirit and life (Jn 6:63), would outlive heaven and earth (Mt 24:35), and would rise up in the last day to judge those who rejected His message (Jn 12:48). He claimed to possess all authority in heaven and on earth (Mt 28:18), including authority to forgive sins (Mk 2:10), to bestow eternal life (Jn 17:2), and to execute judgment (Jn 5:27). He declared Himself to be the resurrection and the life (Jn 11:25), and warned His enemies that if they put Him to death He would rise again the third day (Jn 2:19). Moreover, He said that there is a day coming when all who are in their graves will hear His voice and come forth, some to ever-lasting life and some to everlasting condemnation (Jn 5:28-29).

He claimed to know the mind of God (Mt 11:27), to speak the words of God (Jn 12:49), and to do the works of God (Jn 5:19). To the Jews He said, "I and the Father are one" (Jn 10:30). To Philip He said, "He who has seen me has seen the Father" (Jn 14:9). He spoke of the church as "my church" (Mt 16:18) and the kingdom as "my kingdom" (Jn 18:36). He promised that where two or three were gathered together in His name, He would be in the midst of them (Mt 18:20). He directed that prayer be offered (Jn 14:13), demons exorcised (Mk 16:17), and converts baptized (Mt 28:19) in His name.

He claimed to be the bread of life (Jn 6:48); the light of the world (Jn 8:12); the way, the truth, and the life; and He made it clear that He, and He alone, is the way to God (Jn 14:6).

His apostles seemed to understand the nature of His claims, for they made similar claims for Him in their teachings. Peter said: "There is salvation in no one else, for there is no other name under heaven given among men by which we must be saved" (Acts 4:12). The apostle Paul said: "No other foundation can any one lay than that which is laid, which is Jesus Christ" (1 Cor 3:11). Again he said: "There is one God and there is one mediator between God and men, the man Christ Jesus" (1 Tim 2:5). Though not one of the original Twelve, Paul was absolutely convinced of the claims of Christ and the truth of the gospel. For him there was only one gospel—the gospel of Christ. Any other gospel was not the gospel at all, and anyone—man or angel—who preached it was to be accursed (Gal 1:6-9).

Such an approach is totally unacceptable to the devotees of the various non-Christian religions. This is quite understandable. It also goes counter to modern thinking. Historians, philosophers, anthro-pologists, and even some theologians are predicting the ultimate unity of mankind under one government, subject to one world law, embracing one world culture, speaking one world language, and practicing one world religion. The one religion, of course, would have to be a combination of the best features of all the major faiths. This they insist is the wave of the future, and anyone who disagrees is hopelessly out of date.

The historian Nathaniel Peffer in his book, *The Far East,* has a chapter on missionary work in China. In it he makes the following statement:

> There was fundamentally something unhealthy and incongruous in the whole missionary idea. If the endeavor had been confined to primitive savages something could have been said for it. But to go out to a race of high culture and long tradition, with philosophical, ethical, and religious systems antedating Christianity, and to go avowedly to save its people from damnation as dwellers in heathen darkness—in that there was something not only spiritually limited but almost grotesque. Only men of inner limitation both intellectually and spiritually, can gratuitously thrust their beliefs on others on the assumption that they alone have the truth.[1]

The Christian missionary is not in a popularity contest, nor is he interested in "proving a point" or "thrusting his beliefs on others." Having himself found life in Christ, he has a passionate desire to share the Good News of the gospel with the whole world. Those who hear and believe the gospel are the first to confess that in their former state they *were* "dwellers in heathen darkness." D. T. Niles was correct when he said, "Evangelism is one beggar telling another beggar where he can find bread." In this case it is the bread of life.

The Divisive Results

We live today in a fractured world characterized by an almost universal desire for unity. In the world of politics every nation wants peace, but lasting peace cannot be achieved apart from justice. The same is true in the religious world. Everyone wants unity, but real unity cannot be achieved at the expense of truth. The World Council of Churches Fifth World Assembly in Nairobi in 1975 had as its theme "Jesus Christ Frees and Unites." It is certainly true that Jesus Christ frees. It is also true that He unites. But that is not the whole story. It is equally true that He divides, and if we are to be faithful witnesses we must be prepared to tell the whole truth.

Christmas cards with a religious motif usually make some reference

---

1. Nathaniel Peffer, *The Far East: A Modern History* (Ann Arbor: University of Michigan Press, 1968), p. 118.

to the words of the angel in Luke 2 about "peace on earth and good will to men." The idea is noble; moreover, it is true. But it is not the whole truth. Along with Luke 2 goes Matthew 10. Jesus warned His disciples: "Do not think that I have come to bring peace on earth; I have not come to bring peace, but a sword. For I have come to set a man against his father and a daughter against her mother . . . and a man's foes will be those of his own household" (Mt 10:34-36). To my knowledge this verse has never appeared on any Christmas card!

Missionaries have been severely criticized, especially by anthropologists, for taking their converts out of their natural habitat and alienating them from their friends and relatives, in this way making life unnecessarily hard for them, to say nothing of disrupting the social life of the community. Doubtless some missionaries have been unwise in this regard, but nine times out of ten it is neither the missionary nor the convert who is to blame for the alienation. The gospel of Jesus Christ is the divisive factor.

In the Acts of the Apostles Paul split every congregation right down the middle. Paul's gospel did *not* unite the synagogues of Galatia! In every case there were those who believed the gospel was true, and they followed him. There were others who believed, just as sincerely, that his message was false; and they fought him. On more than one occasion Paul almost lost his life. Everywhere he had to warn his converts that they must through "many tribulations" enter the kingdom of God (Acts 14:22). At the very end of his long and turbulent career he had to remind Timothy that "all who desire to live a godly life in Christ Jesus will be persecuted" (2 Tim 3:12).

The truth unites all who accept it. By the same token it alienates all who reject it. And those who reject almost always end up persecuting those who accept. Gladly would most converts remain with their tribe or clan provided they were given freedom to practice their new faith, but such is seldom the case. The community demands conformity and is prepared to punish anyone who gets too far out of line. In Islam there is the Law of Apostasy which permits the community to kill any member who defects from the faith. If the convert doesn't lose his life, he may well lose his job and even his family. It is not the Christian convert who rejects his Muslim friends and family, it is the Muslim family that repudiates him. The same is true of the other non-Christian religions: Hinduism, Buddhism, and Confucianism.

11

The Uniqueness of the Christian Faith

In a pluralistic world it is becoming increasingly difficult to maintain the uniqueness of the Christian faith. We have the problem right here on the home front, where Bible reading and the Lord's Prayer have been banned from the public school system because of the presence of a small minority of Jews, agnostics, and others for whom Christianity is not a viable option.

It is impossible to open the United Nations sessions with prayer, not because the illustrious delegates are atheists or agnostics, but because they represent all the major religions of the world, each competing for its place in the sun. If prayer is offered, to whom should it be addressed—God, Allah, Jesus, Buddha, Vishnu, Krishna, or someone else? Everyone, of course, believes his religion to be the best; but he runs into trouble when he tries to impose this point of view on others.

The notion that one religion is true and the others are—to a lesser or greater degree—false is hardly in keeping with the insights of anthropology. According to anthropology, religion is a purely social phenomenon, an integral part of culture. It is no longer considered in good taste to refer to certain cultures as "primitive" or certain religions as "pagan." To do so is to forfeit one's intellectual respectability in academic circles. Modern man is too sophisticated to speak in pejorative terms of other peoples or their cultures.

Even within Christendom the ancient landmarks are rapidly disappearing. In morality there is no such thing as sin; in theology there is no such thing as heresy. The only heresy is bigotry. Even the Supreme Court of the United States declares that it is impossible to define such terms as "pornography" and "obscenity"; so the movies and the magazines are filled with both, and it will not be long before they invade the television industry.

When we move into the non-Christian world, where the missionary has to operate, we find that the exclusive claims of Christianity are vigorously challenged by the non-Christian religions now undergoing an unprecedented resurgence. It is safe to say that the most offensive aspect of twentieth-century Christianity is its exclusiveness. Such a claim does not make sense to the Hindu, the Buddhist, or the Confucianist.

Most of the great ethnic religions of the world hold certain doctrines in common. Most of them believe in the existence of a Supreme Being. They possess sacred scriptures. They have a well-defined doctrine of salvation. They believe in life after death. They have a system of ethics. They have human founders for whom they make certain claims. They have a priestly caste and religious orders. But they are not, generally speaking, exclusive, except, of course, Islam. Hinduism is reputed to be the most inclusive of them all. Buddhism prides itself on being tolerant of other systems. Christianity and Islam are exclusive, the latter militantly so.

It is only fair to point out that while these non-Christian religions are tolerant in theory, they are not always so in practice. There are certain fundamental doctrines in Hinduism that are not open to debate. One of these is the doctrine that all matter, including *atman,* the individual soul, has no objective existence in fact. Another is that ultimate reality is spiritual and found only in *Brahman,* the world soul. Hinduism tolerates everything except conversion, and herein lies its inconsistency. If all religions are equally valid, as the Hindus maintain, why should they object when a Hindu becomes a Christian?

In this study we are not concerned to "prove" that Christianity is true or that the non-Christian religions are false. Nor are we saying that these other religions do not have *some* things in common with Christianity. We are simply trying to point out certain features of Christianity which, *taken together,* render it unique. Harry Emerson Fosdick, former high priest of American liberal theology, said on one occasion that there is nothing in Christianity that cannot be found in the other religions of the world. It is true that unusual births and strange resurrections are found in the non-Christian religions; but when one examines the details one is struck not with the similarities, but with the dissimilarities. What person in his right mind would want to suggest that the resurrection story in the Gospels is to be placed in the same category with the resurrections found in the mystery religions so common in the Roman world of Jesus' day? They have about as much in common as ancient witchcraft has with modern medicine.

The Character of God

The God of the Christian revelation, Jehovah or Yahweh, claims to be the one true God (Jn 17:3), Creator of heaven and earth (Is 40:28). Though His revelation was given through Israel and He was known as the God of Abraham, Isaac, and Jacob (Ex 3:6), He is never depicted as a tribal god. He is the King of all the earth (Ps 47:2). He is a great God and a great King above all gods (Ps 95:3), and all other gods are idols (Ps 96:5). There is no other god like Him (Ps 89:6). He deserves and demands the worship and service of all men (Deut 6:13-15).

1. He is an eternal being. He is self-existent (Ex 3:14) and therefore eternal (Deut 32:40). All else exists because He willed its existence (Col 1:16-17). He alone exists necessarily, from eternity to eternity (Jn 1:1).

2. He is a personal being. He is eternally separate and distinct from all other beings. He is conscious of Himself as the Eternal Ego (Prov 8:22-23). He possesses the power of self-determination. He can love (Jn 3:16) and be loved (Mt 22:37).

3. He is an infinite being. His attributes are infinite. He is *all* good (Ex 34:6), *all* wise (Rom 11:33), and *all* powerful (Is 40:18-26). He fills heaven (Is 66:1) and the earth as well (Ps 139:7-10). He is not merely more wise, more just, and more good than any other being; He is infinitely wise, infinitely just, and infinitely good. He is both immanent (Acts 17:27-28) and transcendent (Is 55:8-9) at the same time. His only limitations are those He has voluntarily imposed on Himself.

4. He is a moral being. The Greek gods were more immoral than their devotees. Not so Jehovah. He loves righteousness and hates iniquity (Heb 1:9). He is righteous in all His ways and holy in all His works (Ps 145:17). He is both light (1 Jn 1:5) and love (1 Jn 4:8). His love is a holy love. His holiness glows with love and His love burns with holiness. He is a holy God (Ex 15:11; Is 6:3) and demands holiness of all His people (Lev 19:2; Heb 12:14).

5. He exists in three persons—Father, Son, and Holy Spirit. They are three persons but only one God (Mt 28:19). All three persons are eternally coequal in wisdom, love, and power. Each has all the powers and prerogatives of the other two. All three persons have been and are engaged in the work of creation, redemption, and judgment.

6. He has revealed Himself to man. He is not a god afar off, who hides Himself. He rejoices in the inhabited world and delights in the sons of men (Prov 8:31). He has revealed Himself through general revelation, which includes creation (Rom 1:19-20) and conscience (Rom 2:14-15), and through special revelation, which includes the written Word (Heb 1:1) and the living Word (Jn 1:14).

No other religion has a god who possesses all these characteristics. The Christian God, therefore, is unique.

The Person of Christ

All the great religions, except Hinduism and Shinto, have their founders. Some of them were good and great men, but none of them belongs in the same category with Jesus Christ. He stands alone in solitary grandeur among the sons of men. By almost universal consent He was the greatest character who ever lived. Even non-Christians gladly acknowledge the influence of His life and teaching. Jean Paul Richter expressed it well when he said: "He, being the mightiest among the holy and the holiest among the mighty, lifted with His pierced hands the gates of empires off their hinges, turned the streams of centuries out of their channels, and today rules the world."

No other religion, including Islam, is so completely identified with the life and teaching of its founder. Christianity stands or falls with Jesus Christ. Without Him there would be no salvation, no gospel, no New Testament, and no Christian church.

The uniqueness of Jesus Christ finds expression in six things:

1. His virgin birth. This is clearly taught in two of the four Gospels. It is true that miraculous births are claimed for other religious leaders, but the details are so vulgar and grotesque as to make them suspect. In Jesus' case the miraculous element was reduced to an irreducible minimum—conception. After that, nature took over and Jesus was born nine months later as any other child is born.

He was neither a physical giant nor a mental prodigy. The record tells us that He "increased in wisdom and stature, and in favor with God and man" (Lk 2:52). If modern scholars have problems with

185

the virgin birth, they can derive comfort from the fact that both Mary and Joseph did too. We should also remember that the Gospel writer who gives us the most details concerning the birth of Christ is Luke, a physician. Moreover, the virgin birth was not added simply to embellish the story. It was a necessary part of the miracle of the Incarnation. It was essential to the preservation of His holy nature (Lk 1:35).

2. **His sinless character.** The matchless life of perfect love lived by Christ is a unique phenomenon in the history of the world. He was born without sin and He lived without sin. On this point we have the testimony of both friends (2 Cor 5:21; 1 Pet 2:22; 1 Jn 3:5) and foes (Lk 23:41; Jn 19:4-6). He was the only man who ever lived whose inner life was white as snow, pure as sunlight, strong as steel. Never once did He depart from the path of rectitude. Never once did He succumb to the world, the flesh, or the devil. He was the only person who ever loved God with all His heart and could say, "I delight to do thy will, O my God" (Ps 40:8).

3. **His atoning death.** Without sin Himself, He died for the sins of others. He died not as a prophet, or a reformer, or even a martyr. He died as a Savior, the *only* Savior of the world (1 Pet 3:18). He gave His life and shed His blood for the remission of sins (Mt 26:28). His death was part of God's eternal plan and purpose (Acts 4:27-28) and could be brought about only in God's way, in God's time, and with God's consent (Jn 19:11). In death as well as in life He occupied a solitary throne.

4. **His victorious resurrection.** Not only did He claim to be "the resurrection and the life" (Jn 11:25), He actually rose from the dead as He had predicted. The Resurrection accounts as given by the four evangelists bear all the earmarks of a true story. They are all the more remarkable because the disciples did not expect ever to see Jesus alive again; and even when His resurrection was reported to them, they refused to believe it until they saw Him with their own eyes. And when they finally preached "Jesus and the Resurrection" in the city that crucified Him they paid for it with their lives. To say that the disciples deliberately fabricated the story is sheer nonsense. To say that they believed something that didn't actually happen is also nonsense.

This historic event, one of the best authenticated facts in history, is of the utmost significance to the Christian faith. It is the foundation stone. Remove this stone and the whole superstructure crumbles. Christianity stands or falls on the Resurrection. Jesus' virgin birth, His sinless character, His atoning death—all these have no meaning apart from the Resurrection. Deny that and you have denied everything else.

5. His ascension into heaven. His entrance into the world was a miracle; His departure from the world was also a miracle. This is the way God intended it to be (Jn 16:28). Jesus did not intend to remain on earth indefinitely. He came simply to "tabernacle" among us (Jn 1:14). When His redemptive mission was accomplished it was fitting that He should return to heaven. The Resurrection and the Ascension are treated in the Pauline epistles as two phases of one climactic event by which God raised Him from the dead and exalted Him to His own right hand, far above all principality and power and might and dominion (Eph 1:20-21; Phil 2:9-10). He is now the Prince of life (Acts 3:15), the Lord of glory (1 Cor 2:8), and the Head of the church (Col 1:18). He sits at the right hand of God, the place of power, where He is a living, reigning Lord and Savior, able to save all who come to God by Him (Heb 7:25). All power in heaven and on earth has been given to Him (Mt 28:18).

6. His second coming to earth. The New Testament clearly teaches that Jesus Christ will return to the earth to rapture the church (1 Thess 4:16-17), to judge the world (Mt 25:31-46), and to establish His everlasting kingdom of justice and peace (Rev 19:11—20:4).

These six aspects of His life and person make Jesus a unique figure in the annals of history. Not one of these things can truthfully be said of any of the great figures of history or any of the founders of the non-Christian religions. Judged by human standards most of them were good; some were even great. But they should not be placed in the same category with Jesus Christ. Between Him and them there is a great gulf. They were of the earth, earthy. He is the Lord from heaven. They were human and sinful. He is divine and sinless. They died and were buried and their sepulchers are with us to this day. He died and rose again the third day in the power of an endless life. They could not save themselves, much less others. He voluntarily laid down His life a ransom for many and rose again that He might be the Lord of all life, the Master of men, the Judge of the living and the dead, and the Arbiter of human destiny.

The birth, life, death, and resurrection of Christ are all of one piece. They are like His seamless robe, woven from the top throughout. Remove any one of them and the whole fabric is destroyed. The influence of His character, the content of His teaching, the nature of His death—all these have no explanation apart from the Resurrection.

If the Gospel records had left Jesus in the grave the whole story would have turned out wrong. We should have felt intuitively that some sinister person had tampered with the facts. Such a story could not possibly have ended in that way. Everything that Jesus ever said or did would have led us to expect just such a glorious climax as the evangelists describe. Any other ending would be an anticlimax. Jesus is the only person who ever rose victorious over life; why should He not rise victorious over death? The uniqueness of the event is the most potent reason for accepting it, for it fits in perfectly with the rest of that unique life and completes the picture. Without it the story would not hang together.

By almost universal consent Jesus is the greatest character the world has ever seen. Even those who could not accept His deity—such as Gandhi—have hailed Him as the greatest religious genius that ever lived. Writing in the *Christian Herald,* Sholem Asch made this statement:

> Jesus Christ is the outstanding personality of all time. . . . No other teacher—Jewish, Christian, Buddhist, Mohammedan—is *still* a teacher whose teaching is such a guidepost for the world we live in. Other teachers may have something basic for an Oriental, an Arab, or an Occidental; but every act and word of Jesus has value for all of us.[1]

Another writer, Dr. Noah Porter, asks a pertinent question:

> How then can it be explained that forth from that generation came the loftiest and the loveliest, the simplest, yet the most complete ideal of a master, friend, example, Savior of human kind that the world has ever conceived; an ideal that, since it was furnished to man in the record, has never been altered except for the worse; a picture that no genius can retouch except to mar; a gem that no polisher can try to cut except to break it; able to guide the oldest and to soothe the youngest of mankind; to add luster to our brightest joys, and to dispel our darkest fears? Whether realized in fact or regarded only as an ideal, the conception of Jesus is the great miracle of the ages.[2]

The Doctrine of Salvation

All the great ethnic religions have a doctrine of salvation. Indeed, salvation is the ultimate purpose of all religions. They use various terms and advocate different ways, but they all purport to deliver man

---

1. Frank S. Mead, *The Encyclopedia of Religious Quotations* (Westwood, N.J.: Fleming H. Revell, 1965), p. 49.
2. Arthur T. Pierson, *Many Infallible Proofs* (Westwood, N.J.: Fleming H. Revell, n.d.), p. 226.

from the human predicament in which he finds himself. The doctrine of salvation in Christianity differs fundamentally from the salvation offered by other religions.

1. Salvation is the gift of God, not the work of man. In every other religion man seeks after God and tries by various ways and means to placate His wrath and secure His favor and protection. In Christianity it is God who seeks after man. Redemption is something accomplished by God and offered to man "without money and without price" (Is 55:1). Salvation is a free gift (Rom 6:23). The Christian doctrine of salvation runs counter to the universal notion that man, if he tries hard enough, can save himself.

2. Salvation is rooted in morality. God is a holy God. He cannot forgive sin simply by fiat. He cannot dispense mercy at the expense of justice. He must remain just at the same time that He justifies the sinner (Rom 3:26). He cannot save the sinner, however much He loves him, without first solving the moral problem of sin. The theology of redemption as taught in Scripture embraces several great laws or principles required by the holiness of God. (1) "The soul that sins shall die" (Ezek 18:20). (2) "Without the shedding of blood there is no forgiveness of sins" (Heb 9:22). (3) "For the life of the flesh is in the blood; and I have given it for you upon the altar to make atonement for your souls; for it is the blood that makes atonement, by reason of the life" (Lev 17:11). (4) "It is impossible that the blood of bulls and goats should take away sins" (Heb 10:4). (5) "He [Christ] entered once for all into the Holy Place, taking not the blood of goats and calves but his own blood, thus securing an eternal redemption" (Heb 9:12).

These five statements constitute the moral basis for the Christian doctrine of salvation. It is free, but not cheap. It cost God the lifeblood of His only Son. Now when God forgives sin He is not only good and kind (Tit 3:4), He is also faithful and just (1 Jn 1:9). No other religion offers a salvation that is rooted in morality and therefore consistent with the holiness of God.

3. Salvation is always deliverance from sin—both its penalty and its power. Other religions treat the symptoms, not the disease. Salvation for them is release from suffering, as in Buddhism; or from ignorance, as in Hinduism. In Christianity salvation goes deeper and gets at the root cause of suffering, ignorance, and all the other ills that afflict mankind. The human predicament is the result of sin; and all man's fears, doubts, and frustrations stem from it. To get rid of *them,* one must first get rid of *it.*

Jesus Christ by His atoning death and victorious resurrection met all the demands of a holy God against the sinner. Jesus Christ, acting on our behalf, accepted the penalty, paid the price, and settled the account. The sinner who repents and believes is forever set free from the law of sin and death (Rom 8:2). Here and now he enjoys "peace with God" (Rom 5:1) and for him there is "no condemnation" (Rom 8:1).

But that is not all. Salvation in Christianity includes deliverance from the power as well as the penalty of sin. This is made possible by the presence of the Holy Spirit in the life of the believer. If the Christian walks in the power of the Spirit he will not fulfill the lusts of the flesh (Gal 5:16). The power of sin has been broken. Sin has no more dominion over him, since he is not under law but under grace (Rom 6:14). He is given not just a new leaf but a new life. He is now "in Christ," which means that he is a "new creation" (2 Cor 5:17). Old things have passed away and all things have become new.

4. Salvation includes the whole man—body, soul, and spirit. When man fell, chaos was introduced into all parts of his constitution—spirit, soul, and body; mind, heart, and will. Theologians have called this "total depravity." Salvation, if it is to be effective, must attack and conquer sin in every part of man, not just his soul. This is precisely what Christian salvation does. It involves the whole man—spirit, soul, and body (1 Thess 5:23). It also includes the mind (Rom 12:2; Phil 2:5; 2 Cor 10:5), the heart (Rom 5:5; Col 3:15; Heb 10:22), and the will (Rom 7:9-25).

5. Salvation is a present possession as well as a future prospect. Christianity is the only religion which offers a here-and-now salvation. In all other religions the devotee must wait until the future life to discover whether or not he is a candidate for salvation. Buddhism and Hinduism teach the doctrine of *samsara*—reincarnation. One can only hope that his lot in the next life will be an improvement on this one. But he is never sure. He may go up in the scale of life or he may go down. Before he gets through he may have to pass through eight million incarnations. And when Nirvana is finally reached, what kind of salvation does he experience? The word "Nirvana" means to "blow out" like a candle. The five *khandhas,* or states of being, are dissolved, and the individual soul is lost in the universal soul. Like a drop of rain falling back into the ocean, it loses its separate identity. Not only is there no salvation for the body, but the personality itself is destroyed.

190

On the contrary, the Christian does not have to wait for the next life. Here and now he can enjoy the forgiveness of sins (1 Jn 2:12) and know that he has eternal life (1 Jn 5:13). Moreover, for the Christian salvation is also a future prospect. What he has now is only a foretaste of what's ahead. His body too is to be redeemed (Rom 8:23). In the resurrection he will be given a new body, a "spiritual" body (1 Cor 15:44), a "glorious" body (Phil 3:21), which will be free of sin and endowed with new powers and properties (1 Cor 15:42-44) quite beyond anything he has known in this life. Indeed, salvation will extend to the "whole creation" (Rom 8:22-25) and will involve a new heaven and a new earth, from which all trace and taint of sin will have been removed (Rev 21).

6. Salvation involves not only the individual but society as well. The gospel has social implications. "You shall love the Lord your God with all your heart . . . and . . . your neighbor as yourself" (Mt 22:37-39). The gospel is first personal, then social. Both are important. Traditionally the liberals have preached a social gospel and the conservatives a personal gospel. Both are right in what they include but wrong in what they omit. To preach one aspect of the gospel and omit the other is to preach an emasculated message.

The New Testament writers refused to settle for a dichotomy. In Paul's epistles, faith and love are frequently mentioned in the same verse (Col 1:4; 1 Thess 1:3). John brings the two together in his First Epistle (3:23). James insists that faith and works belong together, going so far as to say that without works, faith is dead (Jas 2:14-26). Genuine faith in Christ always leads to love for the brethren, but love does not stop with the brethren: it goes on to embrace the world in all its varied needs—physical, mental, material, and social, as well as spiritual. When the question is asked, "Am I my brother's keeper?" the Christian's answer is a resounding yes. He cannot, like the priest and Levite, pass by on the other side (Lk 10:31-32). The love of Christ will compel him to share his resources, however meager, with the world round about him. His Master "went about doing good" (Acts 10:38) and he can do no less (Gal 6:10). He has no illusions that by his own efforts he can bring in the kingdom; but as the "salt of the earth" and the "light of the world" he will do his best to permeate society with the principles of the gospel including social justice, civil rights, equal opportunity, brotherly love, and world peace.

Wherever missionaries have gone they have built churches, opened hospitals, operated schools, and in countless other ways have tried to follow in the steps of the Master, who had compassion on the multitudes, lifted the helpless, fed the hungry, healed the sick, cleansed the leper, and raised the dead.

Followers of non-Christian religions are now engaging in various kinds of social service and medical and educational work, but the impulse did not come from their religious beliefs. They have been forced into these activities by the competition afforded by Christian missionaries.

Each non-Christian religion has its own doctrine of salvation, but none of them can compare with the glorious salvation found in Jesus Christ.

The Holy Scriptures

All the great religions have their sacred books. Some of them are older than the oldest parts of our Old Testament. Some claim to be inspired, others claim to be revelations from God. Many of them contain fragments of high ethical teachings worthy of emulation. But when placed alongside the Christian Scriptures they leave much to be desired. Several important elements in the Christian Scriptures set them apart from all other so-called holy writings.

1. **The human element.** The Holy Spirit is the Author of the Bible, but the individual books were written by human writers. Altogether there are sixty-six books with some forty different authors, all of whom can be readily identified as historical persons. In the Old Testament we have such outstanding persons as Moses, David, Isaiah, Jeremiah, Ezekiel, Daniel, and others. In the New Testament we have Matthew, Mark, Luke, John, Paul, Peter, James, and Jude. Though they wrote under the inspiration of the Holy Spirit (2 Tim 3:16), each was permitted to retain his own vocabulary and style. Yet in spite of a vast array of writers stretching over a period of fifteen hundred years, there is in the Scriptures an amazing degree of unity.

2. **The historical element.** A large portion of both Testaments is taken up with history. Bible history is the history of Israel; nevertheless it is genuine history, not legend or myth. And there are frequent references to the other great nations of antiquity: Egypt, Babylon, Assyria, Persia, Greece, and Rome. The four Gospels, while biographical in content, include historical references. The book of Acts is made up entirely of history. Herod the Great, Herod Antipas, Herod Agrippa, Pontius Pilate, Caesar Augustus, Caiaphas, Gallio, and others are well-

known figures in Roman history. No other sacred scripture contains so many specific references to historical persons, places, and events.

3. The prophetic element. This is most prominent in the Old Testament. Coming events in Israel and in the Gentile world were foretold centuries before they came to pass. And this occurs not once or twice but many times. Genesis 15:13 predicted the four-hundred-year captivity of the Hebrews in Egypt. It also predicted their deliverance when the iniquity of the Amorites would be complete. Moses, in Deuteronomy 28, predicted the future of Israel, which included blessings if they obeyed and calamities if they disobeyed. It is most unusual for a people to record, much less predict, their failures and defeats. Jeremiah predicted that the Jews would be carried into Babylon, where they would remain in captivity for seventy years (Jer 25:8-11). He also predicted that after seventy years they would be restored to their own land (Jer 29:10). Both predictions came to pass.

Isaiah predicted the judgment of the heathen nations, and in each case the judgment came to pass. Hosea predicted that Israel would "dwell many days without king or prince, without sacrifice or pillar, without ephod or teraphim" (Hos 3:4). By all human reasoning the Jews as a people should long ago have perished from the earth, but they are still with us and in recent years have been restored to their homeland in Palestine. Daniel predicted the rise and fall of Babylon, Medo-Persia, Greece, and Rome with such detail and accuracy that liberal scholars insist that the book of Daniel is history and not prophecy! In the New Testament Jesus predicted the destruction of Jerusalem and the Temple (Mt 24:2), a prophecy that was fulfilled in A.D. 70.

4. The messianic element. The greatest of all predictions were those relating to the coming Messiah. The earliest reference is Genesis 3:15, where He is referred to as the seed of the woman. Later on further information was divulged. He was to be of the seed of Abraham (Gen 12:3), of the tribe of Judah (Gen 49:10), of the house of David (2 Sam 7:16). He was to be born of a virgin (Is 7:14) in the city of Bethlehem (Mic 5:2). His death by crucifixion was foretold in Psalm 22 long before crucifixion became an accepted form of execution. Many specific details of the crucifixion contained in that passage were fulfilled to the letter, as the Gospel writers were careful to point out.

5. The eschatological element. Voltaire said that history is nothing but a pack of tricks that we play on the dead. Matthew Arnold called history a "Mississippi of falsehoods." World history may not make sense to us, but it does to God. He is the King of the nations and He is the Lord of history. History is not moving in cycles, but unfolding persistently and progressively toward its appointed goal. Nations come and go, kingdoms rise and fall, civilizations wax and wane, all at His command (Dan 2:21).

God is both omnipotent and omniscient. He is in possession of all the facts. He is in control of every situation. He knows the end from the beginning and is working all things after the counsel of His own will (Eph 1:9-12). History will not run on forever. When it has run its appointed course God will step in and the curtain will close. This age will end with the coming of Jesus Christ. We know almost nothing of the details relating to the time and circumstance. We have been warned against setting dates, but the broad outlines have been drawn for us in the Scriptures. The world will not blow itself to smithereens nor will it end in a nuclear holocaust. At the end of the age Jesus Christ will return to establish His kingdom (2 Thess 1:5-10), the kingdom for which He told us to pray (Mt 6:10).

6. The dynamic element. We are accustomed to speaking of the "living Word" when referring to Christ and the "written Word" when referring to the Bible, and the distinction is a valid one; but we must not forget that the Bible is a living book (Heb 4:12). Jesus said, "The words that I have spoken to you are spirit and life" (Jn 6:63). The two agents that are used in the regeneration of the human soul are the Spirit of God (Jn 3:5) and the Word of God. When the living Spirit applies the living Word to the heart and conscience of the sinner, life is imparted to the dead soul and the person is born anew (Eph 2:1).

As a profligate young man, Augustine, walking in a garden in Milan, heard a voice saying to him: "Pick up the book and read." He opened the Bible and read:

> The night is far gone, the day is at hand. Let us then cast off the works of darkness and put on the armor of light; let us conduct ourselves becomingly as in the day, not in reveling and drunkenness, not in debauchery and licentiousness, not in quarreling and jealousy. But put on the Lord Jesus Christ, and make no provision for the flesh, to gratify its desires (Rom 13:12-14).

Augustine was immediately delivered from a life of sin and became the church's greatest theologian since Paul.

Martin Luther was gloriously liberated from a life of spiritual bondage when his mind was suddenly directed to the words "The just shall live by faith" (Rom 1:17, KJV), and he became the great leader of the Protestant Reformation.

As a young man Charles Spurgeon wandered into a country chapel and heard a semiliterate preacher read with some difficulty this text: "Turn to me and be saved, all the ends of the earth! For I am God and there is no other" (Is 45:22). The verse so gripped Spurgeon's soul that he was converted on the spot and went on to become one of England's greatest preachers.

Wherever the Bible has gone it has transformed men, nations, and cultures. It is by far the most influential book in the world, and year after year it continues to be the best seller. It has been translated into more than fifteen hundred languages and dialects and is now available, in whole or in part, to 98 per cent of the world's population. Among all the books of the world, religious and nonreligious, the Bible heads the list.

Voltaire wrote on one occasion: "A hundred years after my death you will not be able to find a Bible outside the museums." Exactly one hundred years later, the house in which Voltaire penned those words passed into the hands of the Geneva Bible Society and the walls were lined to the ceiling with Bibles.

There is a growing movement afoot to reduce all religions to a common denominator and to produce a composite religion that will be acceptable to peoples of all races and religions. Arnold Toynbee and others have suggested that this is the wave of the future. Some missionaries feel that they can no longer present Christ as the only Savior of mankind. They fear that such an approach will offend the sensibilities of the people they are trying to win.

This is a risk that must be taken. Paul spoke of the "offense" of the cross and the "scandal" of the gospel. It is something we must face up to with courage and candor. In the face of the resurgence of the non-Christian religions and the renaissance of the non-Christian cultures, we must continue in all humility and sincerity to preach the finality of Jesus Christ and the uniqueness of the Christian gospel.

PART FOUR

The Historical Context of Missions

Obviously history does not mean the same to God as it does to man. With Him "one day is as a thousand years, and a thousand years as one day" (2 Pet 3:8). Nevertheless, God is the God of history, and as such He is concerned with the events that go to make up the warp and woof of history.

The greatest of all historic events was the Incarnation, when God, the eternal Spirit, Maker of heaven and earth, wrapped Himself with the mantle of our humanity and appeared on earth in the humble guise of a helpless babe, dependent for His very life on His mother's milk. By that unique event, God, the timeless One, entered the stream of human history and for thirty-three years was subject to the laws and limitations of time and space. It is eminently fitting that everything before the Incarnation should be described as B.C.—Before Christ; and equally appropriate that all subsequent time should be referred to as A.D.—In the Year of our Lord.

God's plan of redemption is eternal. It is therefore both prehistoric and posthistoric. Nevertheless it is true that history is the context in which God is working out His redemptive purpose with regard to the human race. The Incarnation, the Crucifixion, the Resurrection, the Ascension, Pentecost, and the Second Advent are epochal events in the history of redemption. As such they have a direct bearing on the Christian mission.

12

Missions and the Resurrection

There can be no doubt that the Gospel writers portray the Resurrection as the great climactic event in the earthly life of Jesus Christ. And they present it as a historical fact, not as an "Easter story." We have more evidence for the resurrection of Jesus than for the death of Socrates. There is no evidence whatever that the story was fabricated. The disciples were there when it happened. It happened to them. And they knew whereof they spoke.

To say, as some do, that the disciples expected the Resurrection and that their expectations rose to such heights that the wish became father to the thought is to close one's eyes to the facts as recorded in the Gospels. We have only four authentic records—Matthew, Mark, Luke, and John—and all of them describe the Resurrection as fact, not fiction. There is no suggestion that the disciples ever expected Jesus to rise from the dead. Indeed, the opposite is true. They did not expect to see Him alive again; and when the Resurrection was first reported to them, they refused to believe it. Even after several personal appearances on the part of Jesus, there were still some who doubted (Mt 28:17).

There is a direct connection between the Resurrection and the Christian mission. It is expressed most clearly in the words of the angel addressed to Mary Magdalene and the other Mary on the first Easter Day: "Do not be afraid; for I know that you seek Jesus who was crucified. He is not here; for he has risen as he said. Come, see the place where he lay. Then go quickly and tell his disciples that he is risen from the dead" (Mt 28:5-7). *Come and see, go and tell.* The connection is obvious, essential, and imperative. *Come and see:* that is a challenge to investigate. *Go and tell:* that is a command to propagate. Having come and having seen the empty tomb, having been persuaded that the Lord was risen indeed, the disciples could not remain silent. They had to share the Good News with the world.

To accept the challenge but refuse the command is a contradiction. One cannot seriously believe in the Resurrection without at the same time believing in the Christian mission. The Christian mission goes back beyond Pentecost to the Resurrection, to the first recorded words of Jesus to His disciples after that world-shaking event: "Peace be with you. As the Father has sent me, even so I send you" (Jn 20:21).

What precisely is the connection between the Resurrection and the Christian mission?

The Historical Fact

The resurrection of Jesus Christ from the dead is one of the best-authenticated facts of ancient history. It is a fact, acknowledged by believer and unbeliever alike, that the tomb of Joseph of Arimathaea was empty on the first Easter morning. There are only two possible explanations for the empty tomb. Either Jesus rose from the dead in the power of an endless life, or His dead body was removed by someone else, either friend or foe. The latter explanation has been put forward many times, but the more closely it is examined the less credible it becomes.

For two thousand years the Christian church has preferred to accept the explanation of the angel: He is not here *for He is risen.* Consequently the challenge laid down by the church is: "Come and see. Visit the empty tomb. Read the sacred record. Interrogate the witnesses who had everything to lose and nothing to gain by perpetrating a lie. Get the facts before you make up your mind." It is noteworthy in this connection that the church's enemies never denied the Resurrection; they simply tried to explain it away. This thing, as Paul said, was not done in a corner. The facts are there for all to see. Consequently the church has nothing to fear from the investigation of science or the speculations of philosophy. In the Resurrection she has an impregnable fortress that no amount of rationalism, or skepticism, or humanism will ever blast from its foundation.

The fact of the Resurrection confirmed the faith of the disciples in three ways.

1. It confirmed their faith in the person of Christ. Throughout His entire ministry Jesus carried on a running battle with the Jewish leaders. There were many underlying causes for the feud, but they all boiled down to one thing—He claimed to be the Son of God and they denied the claim (Jn 5:18). This to them was sheer blasphemy and they set about to kill Him. When they first accused Him before Pilate, all their charges were of a political complexion. One by one Pilate brushed them aside and declared, "I find no crime in him" (Jn 19:4, 6). Finally, when they were backed into a corner, they came out with the real accusation: "We have a law, and by that law he ought to die, because he has made himself the Son of God" (Jn 19:7).

On more than one occasion, in a moment of high inspiration, the disciples had confessed Jesus to be the Son of God (Mt 16:16; Jn 6:69; 11:27); but it is doubtful if they understood the full import of their own words. As they watched their Master being led away by Roman soldiers to the place of crucifixion they must have had second thoughts about the identity of their Leader. If He was the Son of God, surely God would not allow Him to die on the cross between two malefactors. God was silent, strangely silent, on Good Friday. He did nothing to save His Son from the hands of His enemies, nor did Jesus ask for the twelve legions of angels that were at His disposal. God reserved His verdict for Easter morning. God doesn't often speak, but when He does His voice is as the sound of many waters. He doesn't often come down, but when He does the mountains tremble and the hills smoke. Mid rending rocks and quaking earth Jesus came forth from the grave in the power of an endless life, and by this one great cosmic event He gave proof to all who have eyes to see and ears to hear that He is the living Son of the living God. This is what Paul had in mind when he said that though Jesus was "descended from David according to the flesh," He was "designated Son of God in power according to the Spirit of holiness by his resurrection from the dead" (Rom 1:3-4).

This point of view is further strengthened by the experience of doubting Thomas, who refused to believe in the Resurrection even though his fellow apostles told him they had seen Jesus alive. But Thomas only said, "Unless I see in his hands the print of the nails, and place my finger into the mark of the nails, and place my hand in his side, I will not believe" (Jn 20:25). Eight days later Jesus met Thomas and said, "Put your finger here, and see my hands; and put out your hand, and place it in my side; do not be faithless but believing." Thomas answered Him: "My Lord and my God!" Never again did any of the disciples doubt that Jesus of Nazareth was the Son of God.

2. It confirmed their faith in the words of Christ. Jesus was the great Teacher. Much of His teaching was in parables, some of which even the disciples did not fully understand (Mt 13:36). They were dull of hearing and more than once Jesus had to rebuke them for their lack of faith and understanding (Mk 4:40; Lk 18:34). On one occasion He called them "fools" and chided them for being slow of heart to believe all that the prophets had spoken (Lk 24:25). When He first revealed to them His impending death in Jerusalem, Peter refused to come to terms with such a dire prediction, saying, "God forbid, Lord! This shall never happen to you" (Mt 16:22).

The disciples were basically men of faith, but their faith was far from perfect. At times it wavered, and even at best they had to confess with the distracted father of the epileptic son, "Lord, I believe; help my unbelief" (Mk 9:24). It is doubtful if the disciples fully understood or really believed some of the great sayings of Jesus. For instance did they grasp the full significance of such statements as: "I am the light of the world" (Jn 8:12); "I am the bread of life" (Jn 6:48); "I am the resurrection and the life" (Jn 11:25)? Indeed, it was in reply to Thomas' question, "Lord, we do not know where you are going; how can we know the way?" that Jesus said, "I am the way, and the truth, and the life" (Jn 14:6).

When Jesus said, "Destroy this temple and in three days I will raise it up," the disciples were quite nonplussed. When He told them plainly that He would rise again from the dead (Mt 16:21) they failed to take it in, for after the Crucifixion they all went to their own homes and Peter talked about going back to his old business of fishing (Jn 21:3). Certainly they did not expect ever to see Jesus alive again (Lk 24:21).

But the Resurrection changed all that. After they had met the risen Lord they saw things in a new light. All the dark, enigmatic sayings of Jesus suddenly took on new meaning. All the various pieces of the puzzle fell into place and the whole thing began to make sense. John brings this out very clearly: "When therefore he was raised from the dead, the disciples remembered that he had said this; and they believed the scripture and the word which Jesus had spoken" (Jn 2:22). For the first time they understood the full import of those words: "I am the resurrection and the life; he that believes in me, though he die, yet shall he live, and whoever lives and believes in me shall never die" (Jn 11:25-26).

3. It confirmed their faith in the mission of Christ. Jesus came not to reign but to serve (Mt 20:28), not to live but to die (Mt 16:21). This the disciples did not like. They refused to accept the idea of a suffering Messiah (Mt 16:22). They shared the national aspirations of their compatriots and clung to the hope of a conquering, reigning Messiah (Lk 19:11). Right up to the very end they hoped that Jesus would destroy the Roman yoke and establish His messianic kingdom (Acts 1:6). This being so, the Crucifixion was to them an unmitigated tragedy. They came to the conclusion that they had been mistaken and that they had backed the wrong man (Lk 24:21). Like John the Baptist, they thought they would have to wait for another Messiah (Mt 11:3).

The idea of a suffering Messiah was clearly in the Old Testament, but it was alien to their thinking, and so they rejected it. It was not until after the Resurrection, when on the way to Emmaus Jesus gave them a Bible lesson in Old Testament prophecy and opened their understanding that they might comprehend the Scriptures, that they came to accept it. "Was it not necessary," He said, "that the Christ should suffer these things and enter into his glory?" (Lk 24:26). And beginning with Moses and all the prophets He expounded to them in all the Scriptures the things concerning Himself. Then He said to them: "These are my words which I spoke to you, while I was still with you, that everything in the law of Moses and the prophets and the Psalms must be fulfilled" (Lk 24:44). Then He opened their minds to understand the Scriptures and said to them: "Thus it is written, that the Christ should suffer and on the third day rise from the dead, *and* that repentance and forgiveness of sins should be preached in his name to all nations" (Lk 24:46-47).

The Resurrection placed the Crucifixion in an entirely new light. Far from being a tragedy it was a triumph. It was part of God's eternal plan of redemption (Acts 4:27-28). The uniqueness of the Resurrection proved the uniqueness of the Crucifixion. Jesus did not die simply as a reformer, or as a prophet, or even as a martyr. He died as a Savior. He died "the righteous for the unrighteous, that he might bring us to God" (1 Pet 3:18). Paul says that "Christ died for our sins in accordance with the scriptures" (1 Cor 15:3).

All this became suddenly clear in the light of the Resurrection, for it proved once and for all that His mission was not to save His people from their enemies (Lk 1:71), but from their sins (Mt 1:21).

The apostles learned the lesson well. When after Pentecost they began preaching, they always presented Jesus of Nazareth as the suffering Messiah, whose sufferings ended in death, and whose death issued in resurrection (Acts 13:27-39). This was the message—the Good News—as preached by the apostles in the Acts.

The Existential Encounter

The Crucifixion was a devastating blow to the messianic expectations of the apostles, but it was more. It was a traumatic experience to them psychologically. It completely upset their spiritual equilibrium and left them in a state of shock. The three days that Jesus spent in the grave were the three darkest days they had ever experienced. Jesus, their long-anticipated Messiah, was dead, and they did not expect to see Him alive again. Suddenly the Resurrection changed everything, and in no time at all they were new men.

1. The Resurrection restored their peace. Just prior to the cross Jesus said to His disciples, "Peace I leave with you; my peace I give to you" (Jn 14:27). Twice in that discourse in the upper room He admonished them: "Let not your hearts be troubled" (Jn 14:1; 14:27). But in spite of all His comforting words their hearts were troubled and they were filled with fear. And well they might be, for there was no reason to believe that they too were not marked for destruction. If the Sanhedrin could get rid of Jesus, why not them? Jesus Himself had warned them that they could expect the same kind of fate as He (Mt 10:23-25; 20:23; Jn 15:20). Little wonder that when the disciples gathered in the upper room after the Crucifixion the doors were shut "for fear of the Jews" (Jn 20:19).

It was to that fearful group that Jesus appeared on the evening of the first Easter Day; and His first words to them were: "Peace be to you" (Jn 20:19). The peace they so sorely needed but had lost was restored to them by Jesus.

2. The Resurrection restored their joy. In that same discourse in the upper room Jesus also spoke of joy. He said: "These things have I spoken to you, that my joy may be in you, and that your joy may be full" (Jn 15:11). At the same time He was realistic enough to recognize that the Crucifixion was going to rob them of their joy. The very announcement of His impending departure had already filled their hearts with sorrow (Jn 16:6). He acknowledged as much when He said, "Truly, truly, I say to you, you will weep and lament, but the world will rejoice; you will be sorrowful" (Jn 16:20). It happened precisely as Jesus had said. They lost their joy. It was two joyless disciples that Jesus overtook on the road to Emmaus in Luke 24. When Jesus asked them for an explanation, "they stood still, looking sad" (v. 17).

But after the Resurrection, when they had seen and recognized their Lord, their whole outlook changed and the world looked a good deal brighter. John informs us that when Jesus met the disciples in the upper room and had spoken to them He showed them His hands and His side. "Then the disciples were glad when they saw the Lord" (Jn 20:20). The joy which they lost at the cross was restored to them tenfold by the Resurrection.

3. The Resurrection restored their courage. The disciples professed to be brave men when all was going well. Even when Jesus warned them of impending danger they refused to believe it would actually occur. Just before the cross He told them plainly they would be offended and the flock would be scattered when the shepherd was smitten (Mt 26:31-35). Peter vehemently denied that he would ever be offended. When told that he would deny his Lord, he repudiated the idea in no uncertain terms. He vowed that he would die with his Lord. And the other disciples did the same. But when the chips were down he did exactly what Jesus said he would do. Three times he denied Jesus, and on the third time around he tossed in a few familiar curse words to make the whole thing sound authentic. The men who vowed they would follow Jesus to the death completely lost their courage. John was the sole exception. He at least followed Jesus into the palace of the high priest.

But the Resurrection restored their courage. When Jesus met His disciples for the first time after the Resurrection they were huddled together in the upper room for fear of the Jews. This was the last time they cowered in fear. The sight of the risen, victorious Lord removed all fear of man and replaced it with the fear of God. One of the outstanding characteristics of the apostles in the Acts is their courage (4:13; 4:29; 5:40-42). They feared nothing, not even death itself (Acts 15:26).

These three qualities—peace, joy, and courage—are essential to missionary service. Fear is one of the most disintegrating forces in the human personality. It can paralyze a person to the point where he is incapacitated for any kind of constructive work. A timid, joyless, troubled missionary won't last long on the mission field.

The Theological Implications

Sometimes we have been so busy defending the historical fact of the Resurrection that we have overlooked its theological implications. The resurrection of Christ is more than a cold, hard fact of history. It is theology as well as history. As such it is the keystone of the

Christian faith. It was the altogether fitting climax to the matchless life of perfect love that we have come to identify with the person of Jesus Christ. The birth, life, death, and resurrection of Christ are all of one piece. They are like His seamless robe—woven from the top throughout. Remove any one of them and the whole fabric is destroyed.

Deny the Resurrection, and the birth of Christ, instead of being a beautiful miracle, becomes a biological monstrosity. Deny the Resurrection, and the teachings of Christ, instead of being the embodiment of the truth of God, become the pious platitudes of a provincial prophet. Deny the Resurrection, and the miracles of Christ, instead of being the natural, inevitable manifestations of His omnipotence, become the legerdemain of a master magician. Deny the Resurrection, and the death of Christ, instead of being the atoning death of the Lamb of God foreordained before the foundation of the world, becomes the untimely end of a religious reformer.

It is precisely at this point that Christianity differs from all the other religions. They had human founders. Judged by human standards, most of these men were good—some were even great. Just don't put them in the same category with Jesus Christ. Between Him and them there is a great gulf. They were of the earth, earthy. He is the Lord from heaven. They were human and sinful. He is divine and sinless. They died and were buried, and their sepulchers are with us to this day. He died and rose again in the power of an endless life.

1. The Resurrection has soteriological implications. The death and resurrection of Christ were cosmic events with universal significance. Speaking of His own crucifixion, Jesus said, "When I am lifted up from the earth, I will draw all men to myself" (Jn 12:32). Paul said, "As in Adam all die, so also in Christ shall all be made alive" (1 Cor 15:22).

Following the coming of the Holy Spirit at Pentecost, the apostles, in obedience to the Great Commission, launched the missionary enterprise of the early church. They went everywhere preaching the gospel. They had one and only one message: Jesus Christ. When they preached Christ, they preached the gospel; and when they preached the gospel, they preached Christ. Philip went down to the city of Samaria and "proclaimed to them the Christ" (Acts 8:5). When he encountered the Ethiopian eunuch, he told him "the good news of Jesus" (Acts 8:35). To the Jews in Antioch Peter declared: "Let it be known to you therefore, brethren, that through this man the forgiveness of sins is proclaimed to you" (Acts 13:38). In Thessalonica Paul declared: "This Jesus, whom I proclaim to you, is the Christ" (Acts 17:3).

In the apostolic preaching the Good News concerning Christ centered on two cardinal points: the Crucifixion and the Resurrection. Paul says, "For I delivered to you as of *first importance* what I also received, that Christ died for our sins in accordance with the scriptures, that he was buried, that he was raised from the dead on the third day in accordance with the scriptures" (1 Cor 15:3-4). To the Christians in Rome he declared that Christ was "put to death for our trespasses and raised again for our justification" (Rom 4:25).

Peter on the day of Pentecost lost no time in coming to the point: "Men of Israel, hear these words: Jesus of Nazareth . . . you crucified and killed by the hands of lawless men. But God raised him up, having loosed the pangs of death because it was not possible for him to be held by it" (Acts 2:22-24). And he concluded his message with these ringing words: "Let all the house of Israel know assuredly that God has made him both Lord and Christ, this Jesus whom you crucified" (Acts 2:36).

When questioned by the Sanhedrin regarding the healing of the lame man, Peter replied: "Be it known to you all and to all the people of Israel, that by the name of Jesus Christ of Nazareth, whom you crucified, whom God raised from the dead, by him this man is standing before you well" (Acts 4:10).

Paul was the most emphatic of all the apostles. To the Corinthians he wrote: "When I came to you, brethren, I did not come proclaiming to you the testimony of God in lofty words or wisdom. For I decided to know nothing among you except Jesus Christ and him crucified . . . that your faith might not rest in the wisdom of men but in the power of God" (1 Cor 2:1-5). As for the Resurrection, Paul determined that that too was part of his gospel and he preached "Jesus and the Resurrection" to the philosophers in Athens, even though he knew they didn't believe in any kind of resurrection and would regard him as a fool (Acts 17:18).

Saving faith in Jesus Christ included belief in the Resurrection. "If you confess with your lips that Jesus is Lord and believe in your heart that God raised him from the dead, you will be saved" (Rom 10:9). When he wrote to comfort the Thessalonian Christians who had recently lost loved ones, Paul said: "Since we believe that Jesus died and rose again, even so, through Jesus, God will bring with him those who have fallen asleep" (1 Thess 4:14). His strongest statement was written to the Corinthians. "If Christ has not been raised, your faith is futile and you are still in your sins. Then those also who have fallen asleep in Christ have perished" (1 Cor 15:17-18).

The early church attached paramount importance to the Resurrection. It was by virtue of the Resurrection that Jesus Christ became the Lord of glory, the Prince of life, the Judge of the living and the dead, and the Arbiter of human destiny. Sooner or later, either in this life or in the life to come, all men must come to terms with Him. He is the cosmic Christ. He is the universal Savior. He is the Son of God, who in the Incarnation became the Son of Man, that through His death and resurrection He might become the Savior of the world. All power in heaven and on earth is given to Him (Mt 28:18), and to Him every knee shall bow and every tongue shall confess that Jesus Christ is universal Lord (Phil 2:10-11).

2. The Resurrection has ecclesiastical implications. Jesus made several great predictions concerning Himself. Two of them are pertinent at this point. One was: "I will rise again" (Mt 16:21). The other was: "I will build my church" (Mt 16:18). Both were made on the same occasion, after Peter's great confession at Caesarea Philippi. They belong together. The second depends on the first. Had there been no Resurrection there would have been no church.

The phenomenon of the Christian church is inexplicable apart from the Resurrection. If the Christ event had ended with the cross there would have been no Christian church and no world mission. It was after the Resurrection and just prior to the Ascension that Jesus said to His apostles: "All authority in heaven and on earth has been given to me. Go therefore and make disciples of all nations, baptizing them in the name of the Father and of the Son and of the Holy Spirit" (Mt 28:18-19). The risen and exalted Lord is both the foundation (1 Cor 3:11) and the chief cornerstone (Eph 2:20) of the church. Paul says that God "raised him from the dead and made him sit at his right hand in the heavenly places, far above all rule and authority and power and dominion, and above every name that is named, not only in this age but also in that which is to come; and has put all things under his feet and has made him the head over all things for the church, which is his body, the fullness of him who fills all in all" (Eph 1:20-23).

The church is described by Paul as the "pillar and bulwark of the truth" (1 Tim 3:15), and the greatest of all truths is the truth of the Resurrection. He also declares: "If Christ has not been raised, then our preaching is in vain and your faith is in vain" (1 Cor 15:14).

It is worth noting in this connection that the two ordinances of the church—baptism and Communion—are both linked with the Resurrection. The former is clearly presented in the opening verses of Romans 6: "Do you not know that all of us who have been baptized into Christ Jesus were baptized into his death? We were buried therefore with him by baptism into death, so that as Christ was raised from the dead by the glory of the Father, we too might walk in newness of life. For if we have been united with him in a death like his, we shall certainly be united with him in a resurrection like his" (vv. 3-5).

In the ordinance of Communion we commemorate the Lord's death, the bread being the symbol of His body broken for us and the wine the symbol of His blood shed for the remission of sins. But His death would have had no atoning efficacy at all had it not been followed by the Resurrection. Moreover, when instituting the ordinance Jesus spoke of the coming of the kingdom. Luke says: "And he took a cup, and when he had given thanks he said, 'Take this, and divide it among yourselves; for I tell you that from now on I shall not drink· of the fruit of the vine until the kingdom of God comes'" (Lk 22:17-18). While the Resurrection is not specifically mentioned, it is clearly implied; for without the Resurrection there would have been no Ascension; and without the Ascension there could be no Second Coming, with which the Communion is clearly associated by Paul (1 Cor 11:26).

> In the Lord's Supper it becomes plain that association with Christ excludes every other association. Therefore Paul according to 1 Cor. 10 and 11 could use the Lord's Supper for the sharpest combat against heathendom, the association with demons, in short, the other kingdom. At the same time through the Lord's Supper the church again and again becomes the confessing church. Through this celebration she makes known to the world the once-for-all redemption.[1]

3. The Resurrection has eschatological implications. The Resurrection was the mighty act of God whereby He raised Christ from the dead and set Him at His own right hand, "far above all rule and authority and power and dominion, and above every name that is named, not only in this age, but also in that which is to come" (Eph 1:21).

Man in his hatred put Christ on the cross. Two secret disciples placed the dead body in the tomb. Friend and foe thought that was the end, but it wasn't. God intervened and in one majestic sweep raised Christ from the grave and set Him on the throne. This is known as the "exaltation." Paul describes it thus: "God has highly exalted him and bestowed on him the name that is above every name, that at the name of Jesus every knee should bow, in heaven and on earth and under the earth, and every tongue confess that Jesus Christ is Lord, to the glory of God the Father" (Phil 2:9-10).

The Resurrection ushered in a new age. "For as by a man came

---

1. Georg F. Vicedom, *The Mission of God* (St. Louis: Concordia Publishing House, 1965), p. 130.

death, by a man came also the resurrection of the dead. For as in Adam all die, so also in Christ shall all be made alive" (1 Cor 15:21-22). Christ is the "firstfruits," the prototype of the new humanity. Jesus Christ is not only the Head of the church (Eph 1:22), He is also the King of kings and the Lord of lords (1 Tim 6:15). The universal lordship of Jesus Christ is an accomplished fact, not a vague and distant hope (Acts 2:36). It was accomplished by an act of God, not an act of man (Acts 2:36).

Part of the church's witness to the world is to declare and demonstrate the lordship of Jesus Christ over all creation. All authority in heaven and on earth has been given to Him. It is because of this that the church is called on to carry the gospel into all the world, to preach the gospel to every creature, and to make disciples of all nations.

This gospel of the death and resurrection of Christ must be preached to the ends of the earth and to the end of time. "This gospel of the kingdom must be preached throughout the whole world as a testimony to all nations; *and then the end will come*" (Mt 24:14). We know from other parts of Scripture that the end will involve the rapture of the church (1 Thess 4:13-18), the judgment of the nations (Mt 25:31-46), the destruction of the wicked (2 Thess 1:7-9), the binding of Satan (Rev 20:1-3), and the establishment of the kingdom (Rev 11:15).

The end will be a time of blessing for the church but a time of judgment for the world, when God's wrath against sin will be poured out on the earth. In the meantime, the church's chief task is to preach the gospel, to beseech men to be reconciled to God (2 Cor 5:20). The proclamation of the gospel is a matter of life or death, depending on how it is received (2 Cor 2:14-16). The message of the gospel involves judgment as well as salvation. Why? Because "God has fixed a day on which he will judge the world in righteousness by a man whom he has appointed, and of this he has given assurance to all men by raising him from the dead" (Acts 17:31).

So the Resurrection is tied in with the Second Coming. The fact of the first is the guarantee of the second. By raising Jesus Christ from the dead and exalting Him to His own right hand, God has announced to the world that He has committed all judgment to the Son (Jn 5:22). When Jesus Christ comes the second time it will not be in weakness and obscurity but in power and majesty. He will come not to save but to judge. It is by virtue of the Resurrection that Jesus Christ can be both Savior and Judge. All men must meet Him in one or the other of these two roles. To acknowledge His lordship is to be saved. To reject it is to be lost.

13

Missions and the Ascension

Of all the major events in the life of Christ, the Ascension is the most neglected. As could be expected, those who do not believe in the Resurrection have no room in their thinking for the Ascension. Authors like Bruce Barton *(The Man Nobody Knows),* who leave Jesus on the cross, can hardly be expected to show any interest in the Ascension. For all such people there never was an Ascension, so why talk about it? But even among evangelicals the doctrine of the Ascension has not been given the attention it deserves. One widely acclaimed book on Bible doctrine dismisses the Ascension in forty words! We hear much more about the Resurrection and the Second Coming than we do about the Ascension.

So important was the Ascension to the early church that when it came to choosing a successor to Judas Iscariot, one of the qualifications was that he should have been a witness with the apostles not only of the Resurrection but also of the Ascension (Acts 1:22).

The Ascension was the natural, inevitable, and altogether fitting conclusion to the life of the Son of God on earth. Jesus never intended to remain among us indefinitely. John tells us: "The Word became flesh and dwelt among us" (Jn 1:14). Jesus Christ came into the world for a specific purpose, and when that purpose was accomplished nothing more could be done by prolonging His stay. Indeed, had He remained with us in physical form we should have been impoverished rather than enriched. It is to our advantage that He returned to heaven.

The Resurrection and the Ascension were not two separate events;

in the New Testament they are looked on as one event which took place in two stages. The Lord's first recorded word on Easter morning, addressed to Mary, was: "Do not hold me . . . for I am ascending to my Father and your Father, to my God and your God" (Jn 20:17). He was even then on His way.

In Ephesians 1 Paul takes Jesus from the grave to the glory in one grand sweep. "He [God] raised him from the dead and made him sit at his right hand in the heavenly places" (v. 20). The interval between the Resurrection and the Ascension was in the nature of a stopover, during which the Master rounded up the defeated disciples and gave them further instructions regarding the kingdom of God. He stayed with them only long enough to comfort their hearts, confirm their faith, and give them their marching orders. That done, He continued His upward way to the throne of the universe, which He had voluntarily abdicated some thirty-three years before.

The Historical Phenomenon

Of the four Gospel writers only two—Mark and Luke—mention the Ascension, and that in very few words. The fullest account is found in the opening verses of the Acts of the Apostles where Luke, in his usual beautiful style, describes the climactic event which brought to a close the earthly life of the Son of God.

The final departure of the Lord Jesus was not altogether unexpected. On more than one occasion Jesus had intimated that His sojourn among men was not a permanent thing. "Do you take offense at this? Then what if you were to see the Son of Man ascending where he was before?" (Jn 6:61-62). This was an early warning of His impending departure. Later on, as the time drew near, He mentioned it more frequently to the inner circle. In His last discourse in the upper room He told them plainly that He was getting ready to leave them. "I came from the Father and have come into the world; again, I am leaving the world and going to the Father" (Jn 16:28).

It is doubtful if the disciples grasped the significance of these words. They seemed to fall on dull, if not deaf, ears, just as His prediction of His death and resurrection had done (Mt 16:21-23). This seems fairly clear from the question they asked on their last occasion together on the very day of the Ascension: "Lord, will you at this time restore the kingdom to Israel?" (Acts 1:6).

In spite of all that Jesus had told them concerning the spiritual character of His kingdom, the necessity of His departure, and the coming of the Holy Spirit, it is apparent that they still cherished hopes of an earthly kingdom based on temporal power. That the disciples shared in considerable degree the national aspirations and messianic hopes of their religious compatriots is obvious to every student of the New Testament. Right up to the end they could not disabuse their minds of that narrow nationalism which had characterized the Jewish nation ever since the days of the Babylonian captivity. The tragic events of Passion Week were a devastating blow, but the Resurrection had revived their hopes. Hence the question.

The Ascension took place on the slopes of the Mount of Olives overlooking the familiar little town of Bethany, a mile or two away, where Jesus on many occasions had received hospitality in the home of Martha and Mary. How many disciples were on hand to witness the event is not known. That the number was not confined to the eleven apostles is clear from Peter's words in Acts 1:21-22. Perhaps many, if not all, of the one hundred and twenty mentioned in Acts 1:15 were present. Certainly Mary Magdalene would not want to miss such a momentous occasion, nor would Jesus' mother, Mary, nor His brother James. Perhaps Mary and Martha and their brother Lazarus went up from Bethany. Be that as it may, Luke tells us in his Gospel that when the last farewell words were said, Jesus lifted up His hands and blessed them. The benediction pronounced, the familiar Figure began to ascend, slowly and deliberately, in full view of the wondering disciples. Up, up, up He went, until a cloud closed in on Him and He was lost to view. In this manner the earthly life of the Son of God came to an end. He left the world as silently and secretly as He had entered it, unknown to all but a handful of His own chosen ones.

The bewildered disciples stood there with upturned faces, watching and wondering, not knowing quite what to make of the event. During the previous forty-day period they had become accustomed to sudden appearances and just as sudden disappearances, but this was evidently something of a different nature. It was not the kind of parting that took place when He suddenly vanished during the evening meal from the sight of the two disciples with whom He had journeyed on the way to Emmaus (Luke 24). There was an air of finality about this departure which they had not sensed before; and their minds were, for the moment, somewhat confused. After the cloud had received Him out of their sight they continued to gaze heavenward, not knowing what this strange happening could mean. When they emerged from their reverie it was to find two men in white apparel standing by their side, who addressed them in these words: "Men of Galilee, why do you stand looking into heaven? This Jesus, who was taken up from you into heaven, will come in the same way as you saw him go into heaven" (Acts 1:11).

This angelic announcement set their minds at rest on two points. First, it confirmed the fact of the Ascension. This was no temporary withdrawal into the nearby unseen world, to be followed several days later by another meeting elsewhere, as they had become accustomed to. Instead, it was the final departure of their risen Lord to the right hand of the Majesty on high. His earthly career was definitely over and He had passed into the heavens to appear in the presence of God, and so His disciples could expect no further appearances. They had had their last sight of Jesus in the flesh. Hereafter they would worship and serve Him in spirit and truth. Second, the angels foretold the Second Advent. He had gone for good, yet not for good; for heaven would receive Him only until "the time for establishing all that God spoke by the mouth of his holy prophets from of old" (Acts 3:21). He had gone to the Father's house to prepare a place for them, and when the preparations were complete He would come again to receive them to Himself (Jn 14:1-3).

While this was taking place on the earthly side, what, we may wonder, was transpiring on the heavenly side? Imagine the scenes of joy and exultation in heaven when the mighty Conqueror returned victorious from the conflict! He had glorified God on the earth and had finished the work God had given Him to do. He had been obedient unto death, even the death of the cross, and had thereby won for man eternal redemption. As the Captain of our salvation He had defeated Satan and destroyed his power. He had gone down into Hades and had emerged again leading captivity captive. He had invaded the kingdom of darkness and was returning to heaven laden with the spoils of war. If "heaven's arches rang and the angels sang" when He left the "ivory palaces" to come into the world, what must have been the angelic acclamations when He returned to heaven in a glorified body, still bearing the scars of battle, "red with the wine of war."

Is it too much to imagine that the heavenly hosts came out to meet the conquering King and escort Him on His triumphal way—up the steps of light, through the pearly gates, down the golden streets, singing as they went:

> Lift up your heads, O gates!
>   and be lifted up, O ancient doors!
>   that the King of glory may come in.
>
> Who is the King of glory?
>   The Lord, strong and mighty,
>   the Lord, mighty in battle!
>
> The Lord of hosts,
>   he is the King of glory! (Ps 24:7-10).

When Jesus returned to His place at the Father's right hand He did so, not simply as the Son of God, but also as the Son of Man, who during His earthly life had perfectly glorified God by His unqualified obedience. In the Incarnation Jesus Christ brought heaven down to earth and revealed God to man. In the Ascension He took earth up to heaven and introduced humanity into the Godhead. When He sat down at the right hand of the Majesty on high, human nature appeared in heaven for the first time. In the Incarnation He became bone of our bone and flesh of our flesh. Though a divine Person, He acquired a human nature; and that human nature He carried with Him into heaven. It may now be said that He "wears our nature on the throne."

One of the great mysteries of the Incarnation is that Jesus did not shed the mantle of His humanity when He returned to heaven. He took it with Him when, as the Forerunner of redeemed humanity, He entered heaven's gates. He is there today as our High Priest, able to sympathize with our weaknesses. Thus His identification with humanity is not only complete but permanent. A full generation after the Ascension Paul referred to Him as "the *man* Christ Jesus" (1 Tim 2:5). And where He has gone, we will surely follow (Jn 13:36). Even now, as the Captain of our salvation, He is bringing many sons to glory (Heb 2:10).

The Moral Necessity

When Jesus first announced His impending departure, the disciples, not unnaturally, were filled with sorrow and fear. His personal presence had meant so much to them that they did not see how they could ever get along without Him. But Jesus insisted that His departure, far from being a catastrophe, would actually be a blessing in disguise. "Nevertheless I tell you the truth: it is to your advantage that I go away" (Jn 16:7). There were two reasons for this. One was the coming of the Spirit and the other was the constitution of the church.

1. The coming of the Spirit. There are two passages in John's Gospel that indicate a necessary connection between the departure of the Lord and the coming of the Holy Spirit. When Jesus at the Feast of Tabernacles spoke of "rivers of living water" flowing from the believer, John adds this editorial explanation: "Now this he said about the Spirit, which those who believed in him were to receive; for as yet the Spirit had not been given, because Jesus was not yet glorified" (Jn 7:39). The same thought is expressed in chapter 16 when Jesus said:

"If I do not go away, the Counselor will not come to you; but if I go, I will send him to you" (v. 7).

It seems clear from these two passages that there was some necessary connection between Christ's return to the right hand of the Father, where His former glory was restored to Him (Jn 17:5), and the coming of the Holy Spirit at Pentecost. Just what this connection was we do not know. Scripture is content to state the fact without offering an explanation. We can only conclude that this necessity arose from some peculiar relationship existing among the three persons of the Holy Trinity.

It would seem that in the divine economy each of the three persons of the Trinity has His own role to play in the redemption of the world. There are certain works that can best be executed by the Father, others by the Son, and still others by the Spirit. When the Son had finished His work on the earth (Jn 17:4) He returned to heaven, thus making way for the coming of the Spirit (Jn 16:7).

This exchange between the second and the third persons of the Trinity would in no wise work to the disadvantage of the church. In fact, quite the opposite is true. Jesus said: "He who believes in me will also do the works that I do; and greater works than these will he do, because I go to the Father" (Jn 14:12). Just as the dispensation of the Son was an advance over that of the Father (Mt 11:11; 13:17), so the dispensation of the Spirit is an advance over that of the Son.

What these "greater works" are is clear from the Acts of the Apostles. If results are any criterion, the apostles accomplished more after Pentecost than they did during their three years with Jesus. There was nothing in the ministry of Christ comparable in size and scope to the dramatic results achieved by Peter in Jerusalem, Philip in Samaria, Barnabas in Antioch, or Paul in Ephesus. Nor did these "greater works" cease with the apostles. Their successors, like themselves, were known as "men who turned the world upside down." They continued the work in true apostolic succession and achieved similar results, not because of any "apostolic succession" but because they carried out their ministry in the power of the Holy Spirit.

Church history is replete with examples of the "greater works" promised by Christ and made possible by the ministry of the Holy Spirit. Whenever the Holy Spirit has been free to do His own thing the church has been revived, the gospel preached in power, and sinners by the thousands converted to Christ. John Wesley and George Whitefield in England, Jonathan Edwards and Charles Finney in this country, Dwight L. Moody in America and Britain, and more recently Billy Graham in all six continents have demonstrated that it is not by might nor by power, but by the Spirit of God that these "greater works" are accomplished. For the immense success of the gospel and the phenomenal growth of the Christian church there is but one explanation—the explanation given by Peter at Pentecost: "This Jesus God raised up, and of that we all are witnesses. Being therefore exalted to the right hand of God, and having received from the Father the promise of the Holy Spirit, he has poured out this which you see and hear" (Acts 2:32-33). How deplorable that the church so often throughout history has sold its birthright for a mess of pottage, substituting the traditions of men for the Word of God and the methods and techniques of the world for the power of the Holy Spirit.

2. The constitution of the church. Another reason for the Ascension is found in the kind of church envisaged by our Lord. The Christian church is not a man-made organization but a living organism, and between the two there is a world of difference. The church as founded by Christ is a mystical body (Eph 5:21-32) with a heavenly calling (Heb 3:1) and a heavenly destiny (Phil 3:20). It is described in Scripture in various images: a "spiritual house," a "holy temple," a "royal priesthood." Its chief function is not to accumulate material wealth, acquire temporal power, or peddle political influence, but to manifest the glory of the risen and glorified Christ.

As envisaged by Christ, the church was to be spiritual rather than physical in character and universal rather than local in scope. To achieve this kind of church it was imperative that Christ's physical presence be withdrawn and be replaced by the unseen presence of the Holy Spirit. It is not difficult to imagine what would have happened to the church had Jesus remained on earth in bodily form. In that case He must of necessity have established His headquarters in some geographical location. The choice of such a world capital would have been extremely difficult and would have led to endless altercation on the part of both the church and the state. Of all the cities of the ancient world, Jerusalem would have been able to press the strongest claim. Had Jerusalem been chosen, it would have been well-nigh impossible to overcome the nationalistic tone and temper of that city, which for a thousand years had been the center of Jewish worship. In such an atmosphere the church, instead of launching out on its divinely appointed program of world evangelization, would have found itself bound hand and foot by the graveclothes of Judaism, quite unable to fulfill its duty or destiny as the light of the world and the salt of the earth.

So long as Jerusalem remained the capital of the Christian world, the apostles would have been loath to venture far afield. Jesus' physical presence in that center would have exerted a mighty centripetal influence over their hearts and minds. Wherever they went, their eyes would have always been turned toward the Holy City; and the farther away they traveled, the deeper would have been their sense of separation. They would never have been able to feel at home anywhere else. They would have always been returning to the home base to make reports and receive instructions. Moreover, the churches founded by them in foreign lands would naturally have looked up to Jerusalem as the mother church and would have referred all their important matters to that center, thus weakening their own position and retarding the development of a strong indigenous church.

More detrimental still would have been the adverse effect of the personal presence of Jesus in Jerusalem on the life and faith of the church members. What Christian would have been able to resist the temptation to go in person to Jerusalem to get a glimpse of the divine presence? The sick and infirm, failing to get an answer to their prayers, would have sold their lands and goods and flocked to Jerusalem in droves that they might know the virtue of His healing touch. Under such conditions it would have been only a matter of time before Jerusalem was reduced to the vulgar status of Mecca, and the Jordan River would have become to Christians what the Ganges River is to Hindus. Thus the Christian religion would have been localized, secularized, and paganized. No longer would Christians the world over be able to sing:

> The healing of His seamless dress
> Is by our beds of pain;
> We touch Him in life's throng and press
> And we are whole again.

For that it would have been necessary to go in person to Jerusalem. We would have been in the same predicament as Martha when she chided Jesus for His delay: "Lord, if you had been *here,* my brother would not have died" (Jn 11:21). Jesus could not be in two places at the same time, so Lazarus died—or so Martha thought.

Nor would the sick be the only pilgrims to Jerusalem. Sinners seeking pardon, backsliders in the throes of conviction, doubters with their doubts—all these and more would converge on Jerusalem by land, sea, and air to have their problems solved and their needs met. Such a state of affairs would be ruinous to the spiritual character of the Christian church.

It was not by accident that every vestige of Christ's human life perished from the earth. Not a single thing that belonged to Him, or was used by Him, has come down to us. The stable in which He was born, the house in which He lived, the cross on which He died—all have long since crumbled into dust. No one knows for sure the location of Calvary or the site of the empty tomb. He wrote no books, erected no monuments, endowed no institutions. He didn't even leave us a picture of Himself. For this we can be profoundly thankful. The idolatry of the Middle Ages is a standing reminder of the innate fondness of the human heart for pictures, images, relics, icons, and other objects of veneration. We can only praise God for the wisdom which removed Jesus from the scenes and associations of His mundane existence and exalted Him to a place of power at the right hand of God, thus making possible a religion at once spiritual and universal. At the Ascension the curtain dropped on His earthly life; after that His followers were called on to live by faith, not by sight.

The Spiritual Significance

The Ascension has a direct bearing on three major groups: the individual believer, the Christian church, and the world at large.

1. The exalted Christ and the individual. The New Testament clearly teaches the priesthood of all believers and insists that every child of God has free and immediate access to his heavenly Father. Faith is the only prerequisite to fellowship with God (Heb 11:6) and the only basis for our standing before God (Gal 2:16). All this is made possible by the fact that Jesus Christ is now seated at the right hand of God the Father Almighty, where His presence provides every believer with a Mediator, an Advocate, and a High Priest.

(1) *Christ as our Mediator.* Sin alienated man from God and produced in man a sense of separation. Man, therefore, has always felt the need for someone to come between him and God to effect, if possible, a reconciliation. Job, upright though he was, cried out in despair: "If I wash myself with snow, and cleanse my hands with lye, yet thou wilt plunge me into a pit, and my own clothes will abhor me. For he is not a man, as I am, that I might answer him, that we should come to trial together. Would that there were an umpire between us who might lay his hand upon us both" (Job 9:30-33).

What is needed is someone who can lay his hand on God and man and bring them together. But where is such an "umpire" to be found? Certainly not among the sons of men, for all men have sinned and come short of the glory of God (Rom 3:23). Certainly not among the angels of heaven, for they possess neither the nature of God nor the nature of man. How then could they lay hold on both and bring them together? There is only one Person who meets all the conditions and possesses all the qualifications—the Man Christ Jesus. Paul says: "For there is one God and there is one Mediator between God and men, the man Christ Jesus" (1 Tim 2:5).

Being in the form of God (Phil 2:6), He was able to lay hold on God. Being a partaker of flesh and blood (Heb 2:14), He was able to lay hold on man. And these two He brought together at the cross, where He laid the foundation for His mediatorial work. That His redemptive work was successful is seen in the fact that the Father raised Him from the dead and exalted Him to His own right hand as a Prince and Savior. There He sits today, the one and only Mediator between God and men; and all who come to God must come through Him (Jn 14:6).

(2) *Christ as our Advocate.* The Christian has three great enemies: the world, the flesh, and the devil. As long as we are in the body we are exposed to the constant attack of the devil. Satan is called in Scripture the "accuser of the brethren" (Rev 12:10). In this capacity he seeks to defame, if not destroy, the believer. Jesus lifted the curtain on the unseen world and revealed Satan as the great adversary. "Simon, Simon," He said, "Satan demanded to have you, that he might sift you like wheat, but I have prayed for you that your faith may not fail" (Lk 22:31-32).

From the very beginning Satan has attempted to destroy God's handiwork, both in creation and in redemption. Even after his vassals have been transferred from the kingdom of darkness to the kingdom of light, Satan continues to carry on his destructive work. He pursues the Christian into the very presence of God and there accuses him of all kinds of misdemeanors. Just as David withstood the threats of Goliath when he came out day after day to defy the armies of Israel, so Christ, great David's greater Son, by virtue of His victory over sin and death, defeats the sinister designs of the adversary and delivers the Christian from falling before his accusations. Paul expressed it well: "Who shall bring any charge against God's elect? It is God who justifies; who is to condemn? It is Christ Jesus who died, yes, who was raised from the dead, who is at the right hand of God, who indeed intercedes for us" (Rom 8:33-34).

The purpose of Christ's redemptive work on the cross was that we might be redeemed "from all iniquity" (Tit 2:14). This includes deliverance from the power as well as the penalty of sin (Rom 6:12-14). Hence John could write: "My little children, I am writing this to you that you may not sin." But he knew that believers *do* sin; so he added: "But if any one *does* sin, we have an advocate with the Father, Jesus Christ the righteous" (1 Jn 2:1). The word "advocate" here is the same as the word "counselor" in John 14:26. The term is a legal one and refers to one who takes his place alongside another for the purpose of helping him by pleading his cause. Thus the believer has two Counselors or Advocates—Jesus Christ at the right hand of God, and the Holy Spirit in his heart.

When the believer sins he does not forfeit his life in Christ. The Christ who died for him on the cross is the One who pleads for him on the throne. The believer is summoned to sinlessness of life at the same time that he is assured of the forgiveness of God. Both are made possible by Jesus Christ.

Satan doubtless thought he could destroy Peter, but he failed to reckon with Peter's Advocate, Jesus Christ. The difference between the fate of Judas and the fate of Peter is found in Jesus' words: "I have prayed for you."

> He ever lives above,
> > For me to intercede;
> His all-redeeming love,
> > His precious blood to plead;
> Before the throne my Surety stands,
> My name is written on His hands.

> Five bleeding wounds He bears,
> > Received on Calvary;
> They pour effectual prayers,
> > They strongly plead for me.
> "Forgive him, oh, forgive," they cry,
> "Nor let that ransomed sinner die."

(3) *Christ as our High Priest.* Under the Old Testament economy it was the duty of the high priest to look after everything pertaining directly or indirectly to the religious life of the community. Morning and evening he led the people in their daily sacrifices. Persons suspected of having leprosy went to him for inspection and cleansing. Individuals who contracted ceremonial defilement went to him for purification. Transgressors went to him to confess their sins and offer sacrifice. By him prophets were anointed and kings crowned. All manner of people looked to the high priest for sympathy and succor.

What Aaron and his successors were to the people of their day, Jesus Christ is to His people today. He has all the qualifications they had and more besides. Being divine, He has both the will and the power to achieve His purpose in and through His people. Being human, He has a perfect understanding of human nature. He knows our frame and remembers that we are dust. He is the ideal High Priest, for He combines knowledge with experience. In the days of His flesh He was tempted in all points as we are. He was made perfect through suffering; and because He suffered, being tempted, He is able to succor those who are tempted (Heb 4:14-16).

Just as the needy Israelite went to Aaron with all his trials and tribulations, so we are invited to "draw near to the throne of grace that we may receive mercy and find grace to help in time of need" (Heb 4:16). He knows. He loves. He cares. There is nothing too great for His power and nothing too small for His love. He ever lives to make intercession for us. Much is made today of the "finished work" of Christ on the cross, but the New Testament also speaks of the "unfinished work" of Christ on the throne. Simply put, the first would not be complete without the second. This is what Paul had in mind when he spoke of our being "saved by his life" (Rom 5:10).

These three phases of the continuing work of Christ at the right hand of the Father are of special interest to the missionary who lives and works in a non-Christian environment, with all the discouragements and disappointments inherent in his vocation. He himself draws strength from the fact that he is not alone. At any hour of the day or night he has immediate access to the throne of grace. Like Paul, he is "afflicted in every way, but not crushed; perplexed, but not driven to despair; persecuted, but not forsaken; struck down, but not destroyed" (2 Cor 4:8-9). When his beloved converts lapse into immorality and idolatry, he does not despair. He knows that they too have an Advocate with the Father who will plead their cause, and a High Priest who understands both their fears and their folly and prays for them, even as He prayed on one occasion for Peter.

2. **The exalted Christ and the church.** The unique relationship between the ascended Christ and the church is one of the great mysteries of the New Testament. Paul says: "He [God] raised him from the dead and made him sit at his right hand in the heavenly places ... and made him the head over all things for the church, which is his body, the fullness of him who fills all in all" (Eph 1:20-23). What makes the church a unique institution in the earth? Not her long history, her beautiful liturgy, her magnificent cathedrals, her ancient traditions, her material wealth, her political power; rather, it is the presence and power of Jesus Christ. Paul says: "He [Christ] is the head of the body, the church; he is the beginning, the firstborn from the dead, that in everything he might be pre-eminent" (Col 1:18).

The word "church," as used by Paul, embraces the entire household of faith, regardless of denominational barriers or theological differences. Every believer redeemed by His blood, kept by His power, and indwelt by His Spirit is a member of the universal church. Local churches have their deacons and elders; large denominations have their bishops and moderators; but the invisible church, which is His body, has only one Head, Jesus Christ. It is He who maintains her life, promotes her growth, and directs her activities.

When Christ ascended on high He gave to His church certain gifts in the form of apostles, prophets, evangelists, pastors, and teachers (Eph 4:11); but these individuals, no matter how eminent in holiness or successful in service, were never intended to usurp the headship of the church. At best they were but ministers for the perfecting of the saints, for the building up of the body of Christ (Eph 4:12). The church has only one Lord. He is the Chief Shepherd; all others are undershepherds. He is the Bishop of our souls; all others are pastors. He is the Lord of the harvest; all others are laborers. He is the church's one foundation; all others are stones fitly framed together. He is the Head of the body; all others are members one of another.

This being so, the church has no visible head on earth. Her Head is in heaven. Her life is hid with Christ in God. She is linked to Him by indissoluble bonds of life and love. She will have no other lover, she will follow no other leader. She will recognize no other voice, she will acknowledge no other authority. To ascertain the mind of Christ, to manifest the life of Christ, to execute the will of Christ— this is the supreme concern of the church in every age. The church that bows down to popes and prelates is substituting the traditions of men for the commandments of God.

It is impossible to overestimate the effects of the Ascension on the missionary work of the church. The churches founded by Paul throughout the Roman Empire were taught to look directly to their risen, exalted Head in heaven, not to Jerusalem, Antioch, Ephesus, or Rome. Each church was linked directly with its living Lord and encouraged to develop, under the guidance of the Holy Spirit, its own mode of worship, its own pattern of growth, its own method of evangelism, and its own form of fellowship. Even when "fierce wolves" threatened the church in Ephesus, Paul was content to commend the believers to God and to the Word of His grace (Acts 20:32). In this way the churches throughout the world were able to be truly independent, indigenous churches, free to express their Christian faith in forms compatible with their traditional culture.

One of the great problems facing the Roman Catholic Church in the Third World is its ecclesiastical connection with the Vatican in Rome. Catholic churches throughout the world must acknowledge the supreme authority of the pope. There is no such thing as a national Catholic church. The Catholic churches in Brazil, Uganda, and Japan are all an integral part of the *Roman* Catholic Church, with no real autonomy of their own. This is one reason why the Catholic Church has been singled out for special attention in Communist countries.

3. The exalted Christ and the world. Christ's exaltation to the right hand of God constitutes Him the undisputed Lord of the universe. By an act of God He was exalted "far above all rule and authority and power and dominion, and above every name that is named, not only in this age but also in that which is to come" (Eph 1:21).

When Jesus Christ began His earthly existence He is said to have "emptied himself" (Phil 2:7). When His sojourn on earth was over He again took to Himself those divine powers and prerogatives which He had voluntarily laid down. But there was more to the Ascension than that. Besides restoring His original glory, the Ascension also conferred on Him certain additional glories which He acquired as Son of Man. These glories were the Father's reward for His life of complete obedience (Phil 2:9-11). His exaltation from the lowest hell to the highest heaven was the Father's answer to the ignominious treatment He received at the hands of wicked men. In His humiliation He descended to unimaginable depths of suffering and shame. In His ascension He ascended to unprecedented heights of power and glory.

It was in anticipation of His impending ascension that Jesus said to His disciples: "All authority in heaven and on earth is given to me. Go *therefore* and make disciples of all nations" (Mt 28:18-19).

By virtue of His death and resurrection Jesus Christ is the one and only Savior of the world (Acts 4:12). By virtue of His ascension He is now the one and only Sovereign of the universe (1 Tim 6:15). Because of this, every knee shall bow to Him and every tongue shall confess that Jesus Christ is Lord to the glory of God the Father (Phil 2:10-11).

The Christian missionary does well to bear these facts in mind when he encounters opposition in a pluralistic world that accuses him of cultural imperialism. The missionary has no need to be defensive or apologetic. Christianity is not the white man's religion, any more than the sun is the white man's sun. The ancient Chinese had a proverb: "There is only one sun in the sky; there is only one emperor on the earth." There *is* only one sun in the sky and it is not the monopoly of any one people or race. It belongs to the whole world and all mankind enjoys both its light and its heat.

The missionary does not say to the Hindu or the Buddhist: "You must believe *my* book. You must accept *my* gospel. You must embrace *my* religion." The Christian has no corner on these things. They are God's gifts to the world for whom Christ died. Rather the missionary says: "The gospel is for *both* of us. The Bible is as much *yours* as mine."

The God and Father of our Lord Jesus Christ is not the white man's God. He is the Creator and Sustainer of the world and doesn't "belong" to any particular race. As for Jesus, He is not an Anglo-Saxon; certainly He is not an American. He is the Son of Man and as such He has universal appeal. He is the cosmic Christ. He is the universal Lord. He is the Christ of the Indian road, the African road, and every other road.

14

Missions and Pentecost

Although the birth of Christ is celebrated by all branches of the Christian church, the birthday of the church itself receives little attention. Only a few Christian churches take the time to commemorate this historic event. Year after year Pentecost Sunday comes and goes almost unnoticed by Christendom. Certainly it receives nothing like the attention given to Christmas and Easter.

Jesus made four great declarations: I will rise again; I will send My Spirit; I will build My church; I will come again. The first two are already accomplished facts. The third is now going on. And the fourth is yet to come.

The Holy Spirit was in the world long before the Pentecost event. He was present and active at creation when He moved on the face of the waters (Gen 1:2). He was involved in the Flood when God warned that His Spirit would not strive with man forever (Gen 6:3). And throughout the Old Testament He came upon the prophets and caused them to proclaim the Word of God. But there is a sharp distinction between the forerunners of Christ *inspired* by the Holy Spirit and the followers of Christ *baptized* with the Spirit.

The Spirit, of course, is the same Holy Spirit, the Third Person of the Trinity; but His coming at Pentecost marked an epoch in His working in the world. Pentecost was a unique event and introduced an entirely new order of spiritual reality.

The Inauguration of a New Age

There have been three distinct ages, or dispensations, in the history of redemption. The first age was that of the Father and covers the entire period of the Old Testament. The second age was that of the Son. It was the shortest of the three and lasted only some thirty years when Jesus Christ was here in the flesh. The events of that age are recorded in the four gospels. The third age is that of the Spirit. It began at Pentecost, has continued to the present, and will continue until the age ends with the Second Coming of Christ. The Acts of the Apostles is the one book in the Bible that gives the details concerning the inauguration of this third age.

> It is evident that the present dispensation under which we are is the dispensation of the Spirit, or of the Third Person of the Holy Trinity. To Him, in the divine economy, has been committed the office of applying the redemption of the Son to the souls of men by the vocation, justification, and salvation of the elect. We are therefore under the personal guidance of the Third Person as truly as the apostles were under the guidance of the Second.[1]

It is clear from Scripture that there are distinct differences between these three ages. Obviously the age of the Father differed radically from that of the Son. Jesus implied as much when He said: "Truly I say to you, among those born of women there has risen no greater than John the Baptist; yet he who is least in the kingdom of heaven is greater than he" (Mt 11:11). The privileges of the age ushered in by Christ were immensely greater than those of the previous age. Likewise a major difference between the age of the Son and that of the Spirit is implied in the words of Jesus when He said to His disciples, sorrowing at the prospect of His impending departure: "Nevertheless I tell you the truth: it is to your advantage that I go away, for if I do not go away, the Counselor will not come to you; but if I go I will send him to you" (Jn 16:7).

The most important event recorded in the Acts of the Apostles is the coming of the Holy Spirit at Pentecost. That event overshadows all others. Without it all the other wonderful happenings would be without adequate explanation. Indeed, without Pentecost the other events would never have taken place.

1. The Holy Spirit was promised by the Father. The work of redemption is from first to last the work of the Triune God—Father,

---

1. Henry E. Manning, quoted by A. J. Gordon, *The Holy Spirit in Missions* (Harrisburg, Pa.: Christian Publications, 1968), p. 8.

Son, and Holy Spirit. The salvation of the world was planned by the Father, provided by the Son, and implemented by the Holy Spirit. The promise of the Messiah was made by God through the Old Testament prophets. The promise of the Spirit was made by God through Christ in the Gospels. As Christ came to glorify the Father (Jn 17:4), so the Holy Spirit came to glorify Christ (Jn 16:14). When Jesus Christ was on earth the Father's word was: "This is my beloved Son, with whom I am well pleased; listen to him" (Mt 17:5). Now that the Holy Spirit is on the earth the divine injunction is: "He who has an ear, let him hear what the Spirit says to the churches" (Rev 2:7). Salvation consists in returning to God the Father (Is 55:7). Christ is the way to the Father; there is no other way (Jn 14:6). And how do men come to Christ? They come to Christ through the Holy Spirit. "No one can say 'Jesus is Lord!' except by the Holy Spirit" (1 Cor 12:3).

It is widely assumed that Jesus gave only *one* command to His disciples prior to the Ascension. That was the command recorded by Matthew to go into all the world and make disciples of all nations. That command, known as the Great Commission, has for the last two hundred and fifty years been the missionary mandate of the Christian church. Actually, Jesus gave *two* commands, not one. The other was a command not to "go" but to "tarry." They were told to tarry in the city of Jerusalem until they were endued with power from on high (Lk 24:49). In both the closing verses of Luke's Gospel and the opening verses of the Acts reference is made to that command.

The promise was referred to as "the promise of the Father" (Lk 24:49; Acts 1:4), but it was communicated to the disciples by Jesus. The "power from on high" in Luke's Gospel was identified in the Acts with the "baptism with the Holy Spirit." John the Baptist had baptized with water, but they were to be baptized with the Holy Spirit. This was to be an entirely new experience designed to equip them for the monumental task of world evangelization. Consequently their instructions were clear: "Tarry in Jerusalem *until* you are endued with power from on high." Jesus intimated that the anticipated event would occur "before many days" (Acts 1:5).

In obedience to Jesus' command the disciples waited in Jerusalem. They numbered one hundred and twenty in all. For ten days they waited and prayed. And on the Day of Pentecost the power from on high fell upon them and they were all baptized with the Holy Spirit. They had received the promise of the Father and were now prepared to begin their missionary task.

2. The Holy Spirit was given by Christ. There was a necessary and direct connection between the ascension of Christ and the coming of the Holy Spirit. At the Feast of Tabernacles in Jerusalem, Jesus said: "If any man thirst, let him come to me and drink. He who believes in me, as the scripture has said, 'Out of his heart shall flow rivers of living water.' " And John adds this word: "Now this he said about the Spirit, which those who believed in him were to receive; for as yet the Spirit had not been given, because Jesus was not yet glorified" (Jn 7:37-39).

Why the Spirit could not come until Jesus had ascended is not stated. We can only believe that there was some necessary connection between the two events. The age of the Son had to be culminated before the age of the Spirit could be inaugurated. In support of this concept are the words of Peter in his first sermon on the Day of Pentecost: "This Jesus God raised up, and of this we all are witnesses. Being therefore exalted at the right hand of God, and having received of the Father the promise of the Holy Spirit, he has poured out this which you see and hear" (Acts 2:32-33).

During the days of His flesh Jesus was the Executive Director of the Godhead here on earth. During that time the disciples were expected to love Him (Jn 21:15-17), follow Him (Mt 4:19), and obey Him (Lk 6:46). When the Holy Spirit came at Pentecost He became the Executive Director of the Godhead here on earth. Now the disciples are expected to live and walk in the Spirit (Gal 5:25), to work (Gal 3:3), witness (Acts 1:8), and worship (Phil 3:3) in the Spirit.

The relationship between Christ and the Spirit is very close. The Spirit given by Christ at Pentecost is called the "Spirit of Christ" (Rom 8:9). He is also referred to as the "Spirit of His Son" (Gal 4:6). So intimate is the relationship that Paul states: "Now the Lord is the Spirit" (2 Cor 3:17). There is no jealousy, much less rivalry, between the Second and Third Persons of the Holy Trinity. The Holy Spirit was active in the earthly ministry of Jesus, and the risen Christ is now active in the ministry of the Spirit. God the Father anointed Jesus with the Holy Spirit and power (Acts 10:38), and the risen Christ anointed His church with the Holy Spirit and power (Acts 1:8). As Christ carried out His ministry in the power of the Holy Spirit, so the church carries out her ministry in the same power.

Because this gift was Christ's gift, it was given only to the church, not to the world. The world could not receive the Spirit (Jn 14:17) because it had rejected Christ (Jn 1:10-11). Philip the evangelist was mistaken about the "conversion" of Simon Magus and proceeded to baptize him, but the Holy Spirit made no such mistake. Simon wanted the power of the Spirit without the life of Christ, but he could not have the one without the other. The Spirit is the Spirit of Christ and is given only to those who believe in, and belong to, Him.

3. The Holy Spirit was received by the church. The coming of the Holy Spirit at Pentecost was a unique event. It marked the beginning of the new age, which has now lasted for almost two thousand years. However, it was not the only occasion on which the Holy Spirit was "received." Luke records three other occasions on which the Holy Spirit was "received" by various groups. The other groups include the Samaritans in Acts 8, the Gentiles in Acts 10, and the disciples of John in Acts 19.

In each case the group is described as "receiving" the Holy Spirit. The accompanying signs were not always the same. In the case of the Samaritans the emphasis is on the laying on of the apostles' hands. No mention is made of speaking in tongues. In the case of Cornelius, there appears to have been no laying on of hands. While Peter *was still speaking* the Holy Spirit "fell on all who heard the word" (Acts 10:44). This was immediately followed by speaking in tongues. In the case of the disciples of John the Baptist, Paul laid his hands on them and the Holy Spirit came on them; and they spoke with tongues and prophesied (Acts 19:6).

It is obvious that the apostles attached utmost importance to the "receiving" of the Holy Spirit. It was the touchstone of genuine Christian experience. They expected it to happen, and when it didn't they inquired about it. In the city of Ephesus Paul found a small group of "disciples" who attracted his attention. There must have been something sufficiently different about this group to prompt Paul to inquire about their spiritual condition. His question is most instructive. He didn't ask whether they believed in Christ but whether, having believed, they had received the Holy Spirit. The surest sign of believing in Christ was receiving the Holy Spirit; hence the question. They replied that they had never so much as heard that there was a Holy Spirit. Paul then shared with them the truth of Christ and exhorted them to believe in Him. After that he baptized them in the name of the Lord Jesus, then he laid hands on them and they "received" the Holy Spirit.

Still the Pentecost event remained the norm for all subsequent "receiving" of the Holy Spirit. When Peter returned to Jerusalem from his visit to Cornelius he was questioned about his "irregular" behavior in preaching the gospel to Gentiles. After giving a blow-by-blow account of the episode, Peter added: "As I began to speak, the Holy Spirit fell on them *just as on us at the beginning....* If then God gave the same gift to them *as he gave to us when we believed* in the Lord Jesus Christ, who was I that I could withstand God?" (Acts 11:15-17).

When the leaders in Jerusalem heard that, they could argue

no further. They simply concluded: "Then to the Gentiles also God has granted repentance unto life." This was clearly a momentous decision on the part of the church leaders. The fact that the Holy Spirit fell on Cornelius and his company *in the same manner* as He had fallen on the Jewish church in Jerusalem at Pentecost was proof positive that the whole thing was of God and not of man. And the elders and apostles in Jerusalem were wise enough to accept the sovereign working of the Holy Spirit. That clinched the matter for them.

The early church was fully aware of the nature of the "gift" it had "received." Peter on the Day of Pentecost described it as the fulfillment of the prophecy of Joel 2:28-32. On another occasion he recalled that it was the fulfillment of the promise made by Christ: "John baptized with water, but you shall be baptized with the Holy Spirit" (Acts 11:16). It was the natural outcome of the exaltation of Christ to the right hand of the Father (Acts 2:33). It was Christ's gift to His church and could be received only by those who shared His life (Acts 8:21-23). Consequently it was unknown outside the church. Unbelievers who tried to duplicate the gift were severely punished. A classic example was Simon Magus (Acts 8). Another example involved the seven exorcists in Ephesus who tried to invoke the name of Jesus in an effort to cast out evil spirits (Acts 19).

The Formation of a New Organism

The new organism was, of course, the Christian church. Jesus had said: "On this rock I will build my church", (Mt 16:18); but the actual formation of the church did not begin until Pentecost, when one hundred and twenty disciples were baptized by the Holy Spirit into the Body of Christ.

We talk today about "joining the church." This may be the way people join the local, visible organization known as the church. It is not the way to become members of the invisible, universal church, the Body of Christ. Luke says: "The Lord added to their number day by day those who were being saved" (Acts 2:47). As for the others, "none of the rest dared join them" (Acts 5:13). Only believers were added, and they were added to the *Lord,* not the *church* (Acts 5:14). And how were they added to the Lord? There was, and is, only one way. Paul says: "By one Spirit we were all baptized into one body— Jews or Greeks, slaves or free—and all were made to drink of one Spirit" (1 Cor 12:13). Again Paul says: "There is one body and one Spirit, just as you were called to one hope that belongs to your call, one Lord, one faith, one baptism, one God and Father of us all, who is above all and through all and in all" (Eph 4:4-6).

The church is not a voluntary association of believers. Peter, James, and John didn't get their heads together and decide to organize a church. They and their fellow believers waited in the upper room for the outpouring of the promised Holy Spirit, and when that event took place they were all baptized into the one Body of Christ. The church, therefore, is not an organization; it is an organism that derives its life and character from its living Head. Far from being just another institution, it is the "dwelling place of God in the Spirit" (Eph 2:22). "Do you know," says Paul, "that you are God's temple, and that God's Spirit dwells in you?" (1 Cor 3:16).

The apostle Peter likens believers to "living stones . . . built into a spiritual house." Because they are members of the Body of Christ they are also members of one another. The church then is a community of believers who enjoy a common life, share a common faith, and cherish a common hope.

It is fair to ask: What kind of church was the early church? Its chief characteristics as described by Luke in the Acts were threefold.

1. **It was a God-fearing church.** In the Wisdom literature of the Old Testament the people of Israel were taught that the fear of the Lord is the beginning of wisdom. This is a universal principle just as valid under the new dispensation of grace as it was under the old dispensation of law. The God and Father of Jesus Christ is not essentially different from the God of Abraham, Isaac, and Jacob. In all ages He is righteous in all His ways and holy in all His works. He demanded holiness of His people in the Old Testament and He demanded the same of His people in the New Testament.

There are, of course, two kinds of fear—one good and the other bad. The latter is based on a preoccupation with the majesty, holiness, and wrath of God. It is a slavish form of fear that drives its victim to despair. It is definitely pathological. The other is a warm, rational form of fear that is based on a recognition that while God is a thrice-holy God whose word is law and whose law cannot be broken with impunity, He is also a loving heavenly Father whose lovingkindness is better than life and whose tender mercies are over all His works. This kind of fear engenders trust and leads to worship. This is not the fear of Sinai but of Calvary. It is rooted in grace, not law. It is a noble, wholesome, liberating form of fear without which true worship is impossible.

There were good reasons why the early church was a God-fearing church. Three of them are prominent in the Acts of the Apostles.

(1) *The church realized the presence of God.* The early church had no pictures, images, icons, or statues. Indeed, for at least two hundred years it didn't bother to acquire property or erect buildings. Such external accouterments were in no way essential to the service of Christ or the worship of God. It was universally understood that God does not dwell in temples made with hands (Acts 17:24), for God is spirit and those who worship Him must worship in spirit and truth (Jn 4:24).

Far from dulling their sense of the presence of God, this fact helped to sharpen it. God was not some far-off Being "out there," whose presence had to be invoked by incantations of one kind or another. The church *itself* was the dwelling place of God through the Spirit. Thus the Spirit of God was able to impinge Himself directly on the hearts and minds of the believers, who themselves were indwelt by Him. So real was the presence of the Spirit that when the Jerusalem council finished its work and recorded its decision, it did so in these words: "It has seemed good to the Holy Spirit and to us" (Acts 15:28). So powerful was the presence of God in the early church that unbelievers entering the church were convicted of their sins, and falling on their faces declared that God was really in their midst (1 Cor 14:25).

What happened only once to Jacob was a daily occurrence in the early church. After his vision of God at Bethel, Jacob cried out: "Surely the Lord is in this place; and I did not know it. . . . How awesome is this place! This is none other than the house of God, and this is the gate of heaven" (Gen 28:16-17). The early church needed no beautiful cathedrals with stained glass windows to remind them of the presence of God. Wherever they met—in homes, in caves, in prisons, or in the open air—they were immediately conscious of the presence of God. To them, every place was a place of prayer and every house was the house of God. They remembered the words of Jesus: "Where two or three are gathered together in my name there am I in the midst of them" (Mt 18:20). They would have found it quite natural to sing with Henry Twells:

> What if Thy form we cannot see?
> We know and feel that Thou art here.

(2) *The church experienced the power of God.* All power ultimately derives from God and belongs to God. This applies to redemption as well as to creation. David was right when he said: "Once God has spoken; twice have I heard this: that power belongs to God" (Ps 62:11).

The classic example of divine power in the Old Testament is the Exodus. Time and again in later years Israel was reminded of the great power of God by which they were delivered from the bondage of Egypt. In the New Testament the classic example of divine power is the resurrection of Christ. Not only did the church commemorate the Resurrection as a historical event, but its members were taught to believe that the resurrection power of Christ was available to them (Eph 1:19-21). Writing to the Romans, Paul said: "If the Spirit of him who raised Jesus from the dead dwells in you, he who raised Christ Jesus from the dead will give life to your mortal bodies also through His Spirit which dwells in you" (Rom 8:11).

No one can read the Acts of the Apostles and not be impressed with the power manifest in the life and witness of the early Christians, who preached with power, prayed with power, and worked miracles with power. And the power was not theirs, but God's. "With great power the apostles gave their witness to the resurrection" (Acts 4:33). It was said of Stephen that he was full of grace and power, and did great wonders and signs among the people, so that his enemies could not withstand the wisdom and the spirit with which he spoke (Acts 6:8-10). So powerful was the preaching of Paul in Antioch in Pisidia that the next Sabbath day almost the whole city assembled to hear the word of God (Acts 13:44). Similar results were seen in other cities where he ministered, so much so that Paul and his companions were known as "men who turned the world upside down" (Acts 17:6). And their prayers were as powerful as their preaching. Peter was delivered from martyrdom at the eleventh hour through the intercession of the church (Acts 12). After one prayer meeting in Jerusalem "the place in which they were gathered together was shaken; and they were all filled with the Holy Spirit" (Acts 4:31).

And what can be said about the mighty signs and wonders that accompanied their message? A forty-year-old man, lame from birth, was healed by Peter; and all Jerusalem was agog with excitement. A crackdown was ordered by the council; but the more repressive the measures, the more the movement grew. The apostles were sent to prison, but the next day they were back in the Temple preaching Jesus and the Resurrection. Finally in desperation the council was obliged to confess: "What shall we do with these men? For that a notable sign has been performed through them is manifest to all the inhabitants of Jerusalem, and we cannot deny it" (Acts 4:16). Little wonder that "the number of the disciples multiplied greatly in Jerusalem, and a great many of the priests were obedient to the faith" (Acts 6:7).

(3) *The church witnessed the judgment of God.* Judgment is God's "strange" work (Is 28:21). It is not something in which He takes pleasure (Ezek 18:23). Nevertheless He cannot be indifferent to moral distinctions. Every institution, including the church, stands

under the judgment of God. Indeed, Peter reminds us that judgment *begins* with the household of God (1 Pet 4:17). If the church is to enjoy fellowship with God it must be on His terms, not ours. He loves righteousness and hates iniquity, and He expects His children to do the same. When they fail they too fall under the judgment of God.

The church of Jesus Christ sustains a unique relationship to God. It is a community of God's own people, forever separate and distinct from the world (Jn 17:9, 16; 2 Cor 6:14-18), with higher standards, purer motives, and nobler aspirations. God has ordained that this redeemed community should be a "chosen race, a royal priesthood, a holy nation" (1 Pet 2:9). Only thus can the community declare the wonderful deeds of Him who called its members out of darkness into His marvelous light.

It is in the light of these facts that we must evaluate the episode involving Ananias and Sapphira in Acts 5. This couple was struck dead when Peter pronounced judgment on them. Their only offense was trying to appear more generous than they actually were, and then telling a lie to back it up. While Peter was still interrogating Ananias, he fell down dead at Peter's feet. Three hours later, when his wife appeared on the scene and told the same story, she too fell down dead. One wonders what would become of today's church if that kind of judgment were meted out. Doubtless its membership would be reduced in short order!

The church in Jerusalem survived the ordeal and was better for it. It was a timely reminder that it is a "fearful thing to fall into the hands of the living God" (Heb 10:31), for He is a "consuming fire" (Heb 12:29). Like the episode of Nadab and Abihu at the beginning of another dispensation (Lev 10), the judgment of God on Ananias and Sapphira was intended to be a signpost clearly indicating *for all time* the kind of holiness God requires of His people.

With such a dramatic object lesson before it, the early church could hardly be anything else but a God-fearing church. Not only was this strange event good for the church, it had a salutary effect on outsiders as well. Luke says: "Great fear came upon the whole church, and upon all who heard of these things." As for the outsiders, "none of the rest dared join them, but the people held them in high honor. And more than ever believers were added to the Lord, multitudes both of men and women" (Acts 5:11-14).

2. It was a Christ-centered church. When the disciples were first informed of the impending departure of Christ, they were filled with sorrow (Jn 16:6); but the coming of the Holy Spirit at Pentecost changed all that. Far from being an absent Lord, Jesus was now universally present with the church in all places. No longer was the church dependent on His physical presence. Through the ministry of the Holy Spirit He became to them a living, bright reality. The daily life of the entire church revolved around a center of gravity—the risen and exalted Christ.

(1) *He was the center of their fellowship.* While Jesus was still with them in the flesh, He had said: "Where two or three are gathered in my name there am I in the midst of them" (Mt 18:20). This was not a promise but a simple statement of fact, which suddenly became a conscious reality after Pentecost. It was the unseen but real presence of Jesus Christ in the church that made the church what it was.

It was said of the early Christians that they "devoted themselves to the apostles' teaching and fellowship, to the breaking of bread and the prayers" (Acts 2:42). This fellowship had two dimensions— vertical and horizontal. They enjoyed fellowship with one another, to be sure; but they also enjoyed fellowship with their risen Lord. Indeed, the latter was the basis of the former. It was their common allegiance to Christ that brought both Jews and Gentiles together in Christian fellowship. The apostle John refers to both forms of fellowship in the prologue to his First Epistle where he says: "That which we have seen and heard we proclaim also to you, so that you may have fellowship with us; and our fellowship is with the Father and with his Son Jesus Christ" (1 Jn 1:3).

The early Christians "went to church" primarily to meet the Lord, only secondarily to greet one another. And their fellowship with one another was all the sweeter because their fellowship with Him was deep and abiding. All phases of their life and work were related to Him. They preached (Acts 4:18), prayed (Jn 16:23-24), baptized (Acts 8:16), worked miracles (Acts 4:10), and cast out demons (Acts 16:18), all in His name. When they gathered for worship they sang His praise (Col 3:16). When they broke bread they commemorated His death and looked forward to His return (1 Cor 11:26). Their life was bound up with His life (Col 3:1-3); and everything they did, they did in "the name of the Lord Jesus" (Col 3:17). Their identification with Christ was so close that they came to be known as "Christians"—Christ's ones (Acts 11:26).

(2) *He was the theme of their preaching.* The early church had only one message: Jesus Christ. Both His person and His work were essential elements in that message. As to His person, He was both the Son of God and the Son of Man. His humanity made it possible for Him to die, and His deity gave salvific efficacy to His death; otherwise it would have been nothing more than the untimely end of a religious reformer. To the early church, Jesus of Nazareth was a unique person.

He was both God and Man. By His death and resurrection He became the one Mediator between God and men (1 Tim 2:5).

The apostles preached the gospel to many different kinds of people: Jews, Gentiles, Samaritans, sophisticated and primitive people. Their approach was different in each case. With the Jews they began with Abraham, Moses, or David and quoted extensively from the Old Testament. With the Gentiles they began with creation and talked about God's providential care of mankind. With the intellectual elite of Athens, Paul adopted a rational approach, appealing to their minds and quoting from their philosophers. It mattered not where they began; they always ended up with Jesus Christ, His atoning death, and victorious resurrection. That to them was the gospel, and they preached it without variation wherever they went. And the message never failed to bring results.

(3) *He was the object of their faith, hope, and love.* It took the disciples some time to come to faith in Christ, and along the way they encountered many setbacks. Some could not accept His "hard sayings" and went their way (Jn 6:66). Those who stayed with Him to the end were persuaded that He was indeed "the way, and the truth, and the life" (Jn 14:6). When asked if they too would forsake Him, Peter replied: "Lord, to whom shall we go? You have the words of eternal life; and we have believed, and have come to know, that you are the Holy One of God" (Jn 6:68-69). Later on, when commanded by their enemies to recant, they refused. When cast into prison, they prayed and sang praises. When threatened with death, they looked forward with joy to a martyr's crown. Nothing could shake their faith in Jesus Christ. By that faith they were determined to live, and for that faith they were prepared to die. And many of them did just that.

The faith of the early disciples was much more than an intellectual exercise. It had emotive as well as cognitive content. Their faith begat love, and their love in turn deepened and strengthened their faith; and Jesus Christ was the object of both. There was a time when Saul of Tarsus hated the name of Christ and all it stood for. After his encounter with the living Christ, he said: "Whatever gain I had, I counted as loss because of the surpassing worth of knowing Christ Jesus my Lord. For his sake I have suffered the loss of all things, and count them as refuse, in order that I may gain Christ" (Phil 3:7-8).

When warned by his friends not to go to Jerusalem for fear of impending danger, Paul replied: "What are you doing, weeping and breaking my heart? For I am ready not only to be imprisoned but even to die at Jerusalem for the name of the Lord Jesus" (Acts 21:13). The secret of Paul's passionate love for Christ lay in the words: "The Son of God, who loved me and gave himself for me" (Gal 2:20). To his dying day Paul could not forget what he owed to the love of Christ, and he in turn loved Christ even unto death.

Jesus Christ was also the object of their hope. Grace they had already received (Jn 1:16). Glory was still ahead of them (Jude 24). Through Christ, says Paul, "we have obtained access to this grace in which we stand, and we rejoice in our hope of sharing the glory of God" (Rom 5:2). They had seen the glory of God in the face of Jesus Christ (2 Cor 4:6), and already Christ in them was their hope of glory (Col 1:27). Day by day they all, with unveiled face, beholding the glory of the Lord, were being changed into His likeness from one degree of glory to another (2 Cor 3:18). But they looked forward to the day when they would appear with Christ in glory (Col 3:4), not only to see Him and be with Him, but to be like Him (1 Jn 3:2). This hope burned like a beacon against the dark horizon of the days in which they lived. It, more than anything else, enabled them to endure the vicissitudes of privation and persecution. They knew that their present afflictions were both slight and momentary and were preparing them for an eternal glory beyond all comparison, because they looked not to the things that are seen but to the things that are unseen; for the things that are seen are transient, but the things that are unseen are eternal (2 Cor 4:17-18). So certain was their hope that they could say with Paul: "For to me to live is Christ, and to die is gain" (Phil 1:21).

3. **It was a Spirit-filled church.** The Holy Spirit was present in the early church not as a guest but as the Host. He was not "invited" by the church, He invaded it. He took possession of the church, directing and controlling all its activities, so that the church in His hands became an instrument through which its Head, Jesus Christ, could accomplish His purpose.

The term "filled with the Holy Spirit" is misunderstood by many people. To them it conjures up the image of a vessel filled to the brim. In order to be filled with one substance it must be emptied of all other substances. So in order to be "filled" with the Holy Spirit, a person must be "emptied" of sin and self and all other substances that would interfere with the "filling" of the Holy Spirit. This, of course, is an erroneous view.

When the apostles spoke with other tongues at Pentecost the phenomenon caused quite a stir among the people. "All were amazed and perplexed, saying one to another, 'What does this mean?' But others mocking said, 'They are filled with new wine'" (Acts 2:12-13). In this chapter we have two expressions: "Filled with the Holy Spirit" and "filled with new wine." To be filled with new wine does not mean that every nook and cranny of the digestive system is "filled with wine." It simply means that the person is no longer in control of his own mental faculties but is under the control of an outside influence—wine. To be filled with the Holy Spirit carries the same meaning. It does not mean that every part of a person's body, or even his mind, is "filled" with the Holy Spirit. The idea carries no quantitative connotation. It simply means that all the powers of his personality are under the control of an outside influence—the Holy Spirit. A similar comparison between the influence of the Holy Spirit and that of wine is made by Paul in Ephesians 5:18.

When the New Testament speaks of the church being filled with the Holy Spirit it means that the Spirit was present in the church in all the fullness of His divine power, inspiring its worship (Phil 3:3), administering its affairs (1 Cor 12:1-11), directing its activities (Acts 13:1-3), energizing its service (Acts 6:3-5), and effectuating its witness (Acts 4:31). In that sense it was a Spirit-filled church.

If the Holy Spirit is in complete control of the church, we should expect Him to reproduce in the church His own essential characteristics. Certain features are clear in the book of Acts.

(1) *Life.* The Holy Spirit is the Spirit of life. Through His regenerating power He has set the believer free from the law of sin and death (Rom 8:2). The chief work of the Holy Spirit is to confer life, and this He does by the preaching of the Word. The Spirit of God applies the Word of God to the heart, mind, and conscience of the sinner and thereby produces life. In this way the sinner is "born anew" (Jn 3:3), after which he is a "new creation" (2 Cor 5:17). The theological term for this experience is "regeneration" (Tit 3:5). Every true believer possesses this new life (Rom 8:9-10). It is the mark of sonship (Rom 8:14).

Reproduction clearly is the law of life—spiritual as well as physical. When God said to Adam and Eve, "Be fruitful and multiply and replenish the earth," He was giving them a mandate that inhered in their physical nature. Rather than being an external command, it was, as Harry R. Boer points out, an "organic law." This law

> enters into the very fiber of man's being [and] penetrates and permeates his entire constitution. It is the *nature* of man to be reproductive.... This command is obeyed, the law is observed, by all men everywhere and at all times. Awareness of it is not at all necessary in order to obey it. Men obey this law because their very nature, their whole being, drives them to obey it. Not to live in accordance with this law is to deny the human nature with which man was created.[2]

2. Harry R. Boer, *Pentecost and Missions* (Grand Rapids: Eerdmans, 1961), p. 121.

It is this fact that explains the spontaneous, irresistible character of the witness given by the early church. One looks in vain for any reference to the Great Commission. The church needed no such external command. It had been endowed with the life of Christ, conferred by the operation of the Spirit; and in the power of that life its members went out to win the world to Christ. There was no attempt to corral or coerce. The only compulsion came from within. When forbidden to teach or preach in the name of Christ, the apostles replied: "We cannot but speak of what we have seen and heard" (Acts 4:20).

During the period of modern missions the Great Commission has repeatedly been employed as a "big stick" to prod a lifeless church to missionary action. Used in this way it is both good and bad.

> The prominence of the Great Commission in the modern period of the Church's history is a sign of vigor and health in so far as it was put forward by men burdened by the undischarged task of the Church. It is a sign of spiritual decadence in so far as emphasis on the binding character of the Great Commission was made necessary by the indifference of the Church to her calling, and by her blindness to the responsibilities which the law of her being placed upon her.[3]

(2) *Liberty.* Paul speaks of the "glorious liberty" of the children of God (Rom 8:21), and warns the Galatian Christians, in danger of reverting to the Mosaic law, to stand fast in the liberty wherewith Christ had made them free (Gal 5:1). Life and liberty belong together. Both are found only in Christ and are conferred on the church by the Holy Spirit.

Wherever the Holy Spirit is in control of the church, there is bound to be liberty; for "where the Spirit of the Lord is, there is liberty" (2 Cor 3:17, KJV). This is seen most clearly in the early church and can be traced in every revival of true religion throughout history. The Holy Spirit is not only the great Initiator, He is also the great Innovator. As such He must be free to go His own way, make His own plans, and do His own thing; and the church that goes along with Him will find itself celebrating a new and glorious form of freedom in all phases of its life and work.

Michael Green, author of *Evangelism in the Early Church,* in his address at the Lausanne Congress in 1974, said:

> Many of you commented that my paper was thin in the strategy of the early Christians. You are right. You see, I don't believe they had much of a strategy. . . . Which of the advances in mission sprang from the planners in Jerusalem? The Gospel spread out in

---

3. Ibid., p. 129.

an apparently haphazard way as men obeyed the leading of the Spirit, and went through doors that He opened.[4]

After mentioning several episodes in the book of Acts, Green went on to say:

All these developments are specifically attributed in Acts to the Holy Spirit who led men, usually very ordinary men, little men, sometimes against their will even—and certainly without the planning of their leaders, to break fresh ground in this way. So while it is right to set our sights high, and aim to spread the Gospel throughout the globe in this generation, we must remember that it is Christ, not Lausanne, that holds the key of David. It is He alone who shuts and no man opens; who opens and no man shuts. We must not organize Him out of the picture.[5]

That is an ever-present temptation—to organize Him out of the picture, or worse still, to put Him in a theological strait jacket, and tell Him what He may do or how He may act in a given time or situation. When the Holy Spirit works in His own sovereign way, things are apt to get "out of hand"—at least by our definition. We much prefer the tried-and-true methods that have the sanction of tradition; and in defense we quote Paul's words about doing "all things decently and in order" (1 Cor 14:40), forgetting that all too often we identify "decency" with our particular brand of church "order"!

History is replete with examples of the church's proclivity to ignore or neglect the presence and power of the Holy Spirit and to employ carnal means to achieve spiritual results. During the first century her rallying cry was: "Where the Spirit is, there is liberty"; but by the second century it had changed to: "Where the bishop is, there is authority." The problem is still with us. We haven't yet learned our lesson.

In a frantic attempt to make up for this lack, we do as the church has done in all its history. We resort to organization, promotion, authority, theologies, moralism, and unholy alliances with governments and business to get the church's job done. . . . Our failure in mission is the terrible judgment which we have brought upon ourselves. . . . No institutional development, promotional campaign, or consolidation with secular powers can take the place of the covenanted community's waiting for the Holy Spirit. Out of the Spirit's power, and that power alone, comes the church's witness. Institution, promotion, and alliances may help or hinder, as the case may be, but none can provide the dynamic of the Spirit's presence. None can give rise to the mission of the church among

---

4. *Let the Earth Hear His Voice,* ed. J. D. Douglas (Minneapolis: World Wide Publications, 1974), p. 174.
5. Ibid.

men. Only the Spirit can bring to men through the church the creative, redemptive mission of God.[6]

(3) *Unity*. Jesus Christ is the basis of all Christian unity. "The church's one foundation is Jesus Christ her Lord." John Wesley expressed it well: "If your heart beats with my heart in love and loyalty to Jesus Christ, give me your hand." This spirit of unity, based on the person of Christ, was made possible by the coming of the Holy Spirit. It was He who at Pentecost united all believers in a single body—the Body of Christ. The church does not, and cannot, create that unity. She can only maintain it (Eph 4:3); and, sad to say, she hasn't always done a good job at that.

In the opening verses of Acts 2 the word "all" occurs three times. They were "all" with one accord in one place. The Holy Spirit filled "all" the house where they were sitting. They were "all" filled with the Holy Spirit. Thus from the very beginning the note of unity was sounded. Following Pentecost they were all together and had all things in common. They even sold their possessions and shared their goods with all, as every person had need. They continued daily in the Temple with one accord; and breaking bread from house to house, they ate their food with gladness and singleness of heart (Acts 2:44-46).

Not only among the disciples in Jerusalem was this kind of unity in evidence, but also among the various churches. The church in Antioch sent famine relief to the poor saints in Jerusalem. The churches of Macedonia and Achaia did the same.

Unity is not an end in itself; it leads to fellowship. Michael Green speaks of the remarkable fellowship found in the early church:

> Master and slave ate together. Jew and Greek ate together: unparalleled in the ancient world! Their fellowship was so vital that their leadership could be drawn from different races and cultures and colors and classes. Here was a fellowship in Christ which transcended all natural groupings and barriers. There was nothing like it anywhere—and there still isn't.[7]

The Beginning of a New Movement

Emil Brunner said that the church exists by mission as fire exists by burning. This is a welcome statement to come from a theologian, for ordinarily theologians have had a blind spot when it comes to the Holy Spirit and missions.

---

6. John E. Skoglund, *To the Whole Creation* (Valley Forge, Pa.: Judson Press, 1962), p. 80.
7. *Let the Earth Hear His Voice*, p. 175.

There can be no understanding of the Holy Spirit apart from missions. Yet, serious students of theology have often missed this point. Go, for example, to a theological library and examine the books catalogued there under "Holy Spirit." If the library is really complete it will have more than 1,200 titles. Almost without exception, the relation of the Holy Spirit to mission is missing. Everything else under the sun except that which is primary seems to be attributed to the Holy Spirit.[8]

Roland Allen, more than a century ago, lodged a similar complaint.

In our day this revelation of the Holy Spirit in Acts has been strangely overlooked. We have been content to read Acts as the external history of the church: we have used it as a happy hunting ground for arguments on behalf of different theories of church government. For each of these theories we have sometimes claimed the authority of the Holy Spirit on the strength of one or two isolated sentences, or even of a single word introduced incidentally by St. Luke. . . . But in tithing the mint and the rue of the Acts we have passed over mercy and the love of God. The great fundamental, unmistakable teaching of the book has been lost. Our best writers on the Holy Spirit have been singularly blind to it.[9]

Nor have the church historians done any better. For the most part church history is concerned with Christian doctrine, ecclesiastical machinery, church feuds, schismatic movements, ecumenical councils, papal bulls, imperial decrees, religious wars, the exercise of discipline, the formulation of creeds, the suppression of heresy, and other episodes and movements relating to the survival and success of the church as a gigantic religious institution. Little or nothing is said about the preaching of the gospel, the translation of the Scriptures, the conversion of non-Christian peoples, or the extension of the kingdom into all parts of the world. Little wonder that the worldwide mission of the church has traditionally been the responsibility of a tiny minority of church members.

It is difficult to understand how theologians can study the Acts of the Apostles and completely miss its main thrust. Almost without exception everything recorded by Luke relates directly or indirectly to the proclamation of the gospel and the growth of the church. Scant attention is given to James, the leading elder in the Jerusalem church, while the labors and travels of lesser lights are recorded in great detail—Stephen, Philip, Timothy, Silas, Barnabas, and John Mark. Philip and Stephen are first introduced as deacons, but nothing is said of their ministry in that capacity. Both became evangelists; and that, for Luke, is important.

---

8. Skoglund, *To the Whole Creation*, p. 76.
9. Roland Allen, *The Ministry of the Spirit* (Grand Rapids: Eerdmans, 1962 edition), p. 20.

Even events which in themselves were not essentially missionary in character are given a missionary twist by Luke. He no sooner gets through with the feud between the Hellenists and the Hebrews than he observes: "And the word of God increased; and the number of the disciples multiplied greatly in Jerusalem, and a great many of the priests were obedient to the faith" (Acts 6:7). He dutifully records the sin of Ananias and Sapphira and the awesome judgment that followed; but immediately he goes on to add: "And great fear came upon the whole church. . . . None of the rest dared join them, but the people held them in high honor. And more than ever believers were added to the Lord, multitudes both of men and women" (Acts 5:11-14).

The only major event in the Acts which appears to be ecclesiastical in character is the Jerusalem council in chapter 15; but even that had a direct bearing on the growth of the church, and the encyclical letter drawn up by the council was addressed to the Gentile churches in Syria and Cilicia, founded doubtless by Paul and Barnabas in the course of their missionary activities. And the decision reached on that historic occasion was definitely designed to strengthen the hands of those two great missionary leaders.

Luke mentioned various persecutions but was always careful to point out how they resulted in a further expansion of the church. All the churches mentioned in the Acts, except the Jerusalem church, were mission churches, founded by Paul or others as a result of their evangelistic endeavors. Luke does not stop to discuss or describe the internal organization of these churches, beyond noting that Paul organized elders in every city. Paul is given more space than all the other persons put together, yet Luke is interested only in Paul's *missionary* activities. Paul was a theologian as well as a missionary, but Luke says practically nothing of him as a church organizer or a Christian thinker. He doesn't mention one of the many epistles written by Paul, nor does he go back to describe the problems of the churches founded by Paul. "This can only be because his attention was wholly fixed on one thing: the preaching of the gospel in ever wider fields, the progress of his hero towards the capital of the world."[10]

Luke gives great prominence to the church in Antioch but says nothing of the face-to-face confrontation between Peter and Paul in that city. He does, however, go into great detail in describing the "conversion" of Peter in Acts 10 when he was bidden by the Holy Spirit to preach the gospel for the first time to a Gentile. And he *repeats* the story in abbreviated form in chapter 11. Why the repetition? Because that event opened the door of faith to the Gentiles.

10. Ibid., p. 15.

Pentecost not only marked the birthday of the church, it also was the beginning of the Christian mission.

> When we discuss the relationship of Pentecost to the witnessing Church we must qualify the Church in the sharpest possible manner as being *in her nature* a witnessing community and that she is this precisely because she derives her life from the Pentecost event. Witnessing is not one of many functions or activities of the Church; it is of her essence to witness, and it is out of this witness that all her other activities take their rise.[11]

In those early days the church *was* mission in every sense of the word, and its first responsibility was to make disciples of all nations. To this end it devoted all its energies.

This comes out clearly in the description of Pentecost in Acts 2. It is clear from that account that the church was intended by Christ to be a witnessing community. A sound came from heaven like the rush of a mighty wind, and it filled all the house where they were sitting. And there appeared to them tongues as of fire, resting on each one of them. And they were all filled with the Holy Spirit and began to speak in other tongues, as the Spirit gave them utterance.

The tongues were tongues "as of fire." Obviously this signified a complete cleansing such as Isaiah experienced at the time of his call. He complained that he was a man of unclean lips and dwelt in the midst of a people of unclean lips. One of the seraphim touched his mouth with a burning coal from the altar and said: "Behold, this has touched your lips; your guilt is taken away, and your sin forgiven." After hearing the voice of the Lord saying, "Whom shall I send?" Isaiah replied: "Here am I. Send me" (Is 6:6-8).

The symbolism of tongues is most instructive. Why tongues? Why not hands, or feet? The tongue is the medium of communication. When these "tongues" rested on them, they were filled with the Holy Spirit and began to speak with other *tongues* as the Spirit gave them *utterance*. As a result Jews and proselytes from all parts of the Roman Empire heard for the first time in their own tongue the wonderful works of God.

For two thousand years Christian scholars have been debating the nature of this miracle. Was it a miracle of "speaking" or one of "hearing"? Was the gift of "tongues" in Acts 2 the same as the gift of "tongues" in 1 Corinthians 14? Was the gift intended to be temporary or permanent? And so the debate continues with no conclusive results. During all this time we have missed the whole point of the story. Instead of being an inspiration for Christian witness for all time, it

---

11. Ibid., p. 100.

has become a theological bone of contention. What was intended to unite the church in witness has only served to divide it in theology. We have done with the miracle of Pentecost what we did with Jonah in the Old Testament. We made the whole story hinge on the miracle of the "great fish" and completely lost sight of the greater miracle of the infinite mercy and compassion of God.

As Luke develops his theme, three important trends appear in his narrative, each of them fitting in perfectly with his overall design—the worldwide expansion of the Christian church.

1. Paul replaced Peter. The apostle Peter is the dominant figure in Acts 1–12, after which he is mentioned only once, in chapter 15. Beginning with chapter 13 Paul moves into the picture and occupies the center of the stage through chapter 28, the end of the book. These two men had little in common except their allegiance to Jesus Christ. Their paths crossed on at least three occasions: on Paul's first visit to Jerusalem after his conversion (Gal 1:18), at the Jerusalem council (Acts 15), and in Antioch (Gal 2:11-17).

Peter was one of the twelve apostles. Not without reason he has been called the "prince of the apostles." He was a Galilean, a fisherman by trade, and probably came from peasant stock. His formal education was doubtless quite meager. Like most Jews of his day, Peter was a bigot and refused to have anything to do with uncircumcised Gentiles. He and his wife kept a kosher kitchen even after Pentecost. Left to himself he would never have preached the gospel to any but the Jews. It required a special vision, repeated three times over, to convince him that the gospel should be shared with the Gentiles. It is true that he was present at the Jerusalem council and played a major role in the decision to give Gentile converts equal status with Jewish Christians; but to the end he remained an apostle to the circumcision, and doubtless was more at home with Jews than with Gentiles. The fact is, his first epistle was addressed to the "exiles of the Dispersion" (1 Pet 1:1).

Paul, on the other hand, was an unusual individual—an ardent Jew, and a proud and loyal citizen of Rome. He was a native of Tarsus, the capital of Cilicia, one of the three great university centers of the day. Unlike Peter he was a member of the Diaspora. Though brought up in a predominantly Greek city, he clung tenaciously to the faith of his fathers. As a Pharisee he was exceedingly zealous for the law. He received his rabbinical training in Jerusalem at the feet of Gamaliel.

In his pre-Christian days Paul hated the name of Christ and did everything in his power to exterminate the Christian church. As head of the Gestapo of that day he rounded up the Christians in all the synagogues in Jerusalem and imprisoned them, and when they were condemned to death he cast his vote against them. In his unrelenting fury he pursued them to foreign cities. On one such mission to Damascus he was confronted and conquered by the living Christ. Immediately he set about to build again the things he had destroyed. Everywhere he preached Jesus and the Resurrection.

By background, training, and temperament he was destined to become the apostle to the Gentiles, though he never ceased to love his own people with a consuming passion. In fifteen short years he founded churches in four important provinces of the empire—Asia, Galatia, Macedonia, and Achaia.

Paul more than any other one person left his stamp on the Christian church. He better than anyone else understood the gospel of grace and the glorious truth of justification by faith without the works of the law. Without the towering figure of Paul it is doubtful if the early church would have been able to throw off the swaddling clothes of Judaism. Without his missionary endeavors Christianity might never have become the universal religion it is today.

2. Antioch replaced Jerusalem. It is impossible for present-day Christians to realize what Jerusalem meant to the Jews of Jesus' day, including the apostles. For a thousand years Jerusalem had been the soul and center of the worship of the one true God, Maker of heaven and earth. It was the one place on earth where God had "set His name." Jerusalem was not only the city of the kings, it was the site of the Temple. Only there could sacrifices be offered to Jehovah. The Jews of the Diaspora made an annual pilgrimage to Jerusalem, and those who couldn't make the journey paid the Temple tax.

Jesus honored Jerusalem by visiting it on three, possibly four, Passovers during His public ministry. His last days were spent there. He died outside its walls and was buried there. After the Resurrection He met His disciples in Jerusalem. He ascended to heaven from the Mount of Olives, just east of the city; and to that city He was expected to return.

Jerusalem was equally important to the church. Pentecost took place there. So did the first sermon and the first miracle. In those early days Christianity was regarded by its adherents as a reform movement within Judaism and by its enemies as a heretical sect to be destroyed. The church in Jerusalem soon became the mother church to which the other churches looked for guidance. The early Christians, including the apostles, continued to frequent the Temple. Much of their teaching was done there. So attached to the city were the apostles that when persecution drove the Christians from Jerusalem, they remained behind.

As a result the church in Jerusalem was more Jewish than Christian in flavor. The disciples there were known as "Jews that believed" rather than as "Christians." As late as A.D. 58 they were still worshiping in the Temple, keeping the law, and even taking vows. Jerusalem was also the home of the Judaizers who dogged the steps of Paul and played havoc with the mission churches established by him in the Gentile world.

Antioch was an altogether different kind of city, less conservative and more cosmopolitan, with a cultural climate more conducive to the spread of the new faith. So it came about that with the advent of the apostle Paul, the center of spiritual gravity shifted from Jerusalem to Antioch.

Antioch, situated at the crossroads of the Mediterranean world, was the third city in the empire. From its beginning in 300 B.C. it had a cosmopolitan population, including a colony of Jews. During the Greek period it was a wealthy and sophisticated metropolis in which Greek civilization flourished alongside Oriental culture and religion. During the Roman period, which began in 64 B.C., the city was enlarged and beautified along Roman lines and began to enjoy the *Pax Romana* which later on was to provide much-needed protection for the Christian missionaries. Antioch was the only city, other than Athens, in which Paul preached the gospel without precipitating a communal riot. Because of its efficient Roman administration it enjoyed a degree of public order not possible in a turbulent city like Jerusalem.

Moreover, the presence in Antioch of the mystery cults, with their doctrines of salvation, regeneration, and life after death, did much to prepare the way for the reception of similar concepts in Christianity. As a result Antioch in the first century was characterized by an eclectic intellectual spirit which produced an environment definitely conducive to the reception of the gospel.

> In all these ways Antioch differed fundamentally from the other cities outside Palestine in which the Christian mission might have found a start, and the whole history of the city, prior to the time of Christ, had given it a unique character as a place in which the followers of the Way could begin their expansion.[12]

Luke's remark that the disciples were first called Christians in Antioch is in keeping with all we know of the cultural and religious climate of that illustrious city.

---

12. *The Interpreter's Dictionary of the Bible* (New York: Abingdon Press, 1962), I:147.

Under the teaching of Barnabas and Paul the church in Antioch increased in strength and numbers until it rivaled, and later replaced, Jerusalem as the mother church of Christendom. When Paul and Barnabas received their call to missionary service it was in the church in Antioch, not Jerusalem; and from that point on Antioch became a rendezvous of Christian missionaries as they traveled back and forth across the Roman world. From Antioch the gospel spread westward into Galatia, Asia, and Europe; northward into Armenia, Pontus, and Bithynia; and eastward by way of Damascus and Edessa into Mesopotamia. Later on Antioch became the seat of an archbishopric. The famous Ignatius was Bishop of Antioch in the early part of the second century.

3. The Gentiles replaced the Jews. Christianity began as a reform movement within Judaism. Jesus was a Jew; so were all twelve of the apostles. The book of Acts opens with a hundred and twenty timid disciples—all of them Jews—meeting secretly in an upper room for fear of their enemies. A generation later the gospel had been preached as far west as Rome, and there was a thriving Christian church in almost every city of significance in the eastern part of the empire. What began as a Jewish sect in A.D. 30 had grown into a world religion by A.D. 60.

Along the way there was no clean break with Judaism. For a time Christianity remained closely tied to Judaism. It took many years to develop its own image to the point where it was recognized as a separate religion.

It was only natural that in time the Gentiles would come to outnumber the Jews, for the simple reason that the Jews represented only about 7 per cent of the population. Moreover, the Gentiles proved more receptive to the gospel. Most of Paul's audiences were made up of Jews, proselytes, and Gentiles. Most of his converts came from the two latter groups. In every city it was the Jews and their leaders who opposed Paul and his message—so much so that in Antioch in Pisidia Paul said, "It was necessary that the word of God should be spoken first to you. Since you thrust it from you, and judge yourselves unworthy of eternal life, behold we turn to the Gentiles" (Acts 13:46). The same thing happened in other cities as well.

The strongest statement on this matter is found in Paul's letter to the Thessalonian church. Speaking of his own beloved people, the Jews, he said: "Who killed both the Lord Jesus and the prophets, and drove us out, and displease God and oppose all men by hindering us from speaking to the Gentiles that they might be saved—so as always to fill up the measure of their sin. But God's wrath has come upon them at last" (1 Thess 2:15-16).

After a time the church ceased in her efforts to convert the Jews. The Christians grew impatient with their recalcitrant spirit and came first to hate and then to persecute them. "Such an injustice as that done by the Gentile church to Judaism is almost unprecedented in the annals of history. . . . The daughter first robbed her mother, and then repudiated her."[13] Consequently Christianity never took root in Jewish, or even in Semitic, soil. Like Buddhism, it died out in the land of its birth and came to bloom in distant parts.

Nor did Judaism survive in Palestine beyond A.D. 135, when the fanatical Jews under Bar Cocheba made their last desperate attempt to regain their freedom. After three flaming years and more than a million casualties the Jews were crushed, not to rise again until the twentieth century.

> From this moment they entered their Middle Ages. . . . No other people has ever known so long an exile, or so hard a fate. Scattered into every province and beyond, condemned to poverty and humiliation, unbefriended even by philosophers and saints, they retired from public affairs to private study and worship. . . . Judaism hid in fear and obscurity while its offspring, Christianity, went out to conquer the world.[14]

This does not mean that God has completely forsaken His ancient people. Paul makes that quite clear in Romans 11, where he says: "I ask, then, has God rejected his people? By no means!" (v. 1). There always has been, and always will be, a believing remnant. Their present "rejection" is partial and temporary and is an integral part of God's plan and purpose for the world. "Through their trespass salvation has come to the Gentiles" (v. 11). Paul goes on to say: "If their rejection means the reconciliation of the world, what will their acceptance mean but life from the dead?" (v. 15). The rejection of the Jews was occasioned by their unbelief, but Paul intimates that their unbelief will not last forever. He says: "If they do not persist in their unbelief, [they] will be grafted in, for God has the power to graft them again" (v. 23). He concludes his argument by saying: "So *all* Israel will be saved. . . . For the gifts and call of God are irrevocable" (vv. 26-29).

---

13. Adolf Harnack, *The Mission and Expansion of Christianity* (New York: Harper and Brothers, 1962), p. 69.
14. Will Durant, *Caesar and Christ* (New York: Simon and Schuster, 1944), p. 602.

15

Missions and the Second Coming

Christianity is a historical religion founded on the life, work, and teachings of a historical person, Jesus Christ, who entered the stream of human history in the days of Caesar Augustus and died under Pontius Pilate. The church which He founded is a historical institution. It had its beginning at Pentecost and will run its course until the Second Advent. Between these two points the chief task of the church is to proclaim the universal lordship of Jesus Christ, helping in this way to prepare for His return. This task was given to the church by her Lord. The mandate is clear: Preach the gospel to every creature; make disciples of all nations; occupy till I come.

Harry R. Boer reminds us that "the church and her missionary task must be seen eschatologically." He goes on to say:

> The Church lives between the first and second coming of Christ. She is conscious of being the uniting element between these two events, and she must express herself in terms of this consciousness. The Church is an interim phenomenon and her characteristic activity in the interim period is missionary activity. Judging by the Pentecost account we may say that both Church and missions are creations of the Holy Spirit and are both taken up as essential elements in the divine plan for the world.[1]

The New Testament lays down two terminal goals for the church and its mission. One relates to time, the other to space. The first is a

---

1. Harry R. Boer, *Pentecost and Missions* (Grand Rapids: Eerdmans, 1961), p. 62.

matter of history and runs to the end of the age. The second is a matter of geography and extends to the ends of the earth. Both goals were obscure to the early church. It is doubtful if the apostles themselves were fully aware of all the ramifications of the phrase "the ends of the earth." To them the "earth" was the Roman Empire, and even Paul in his day stated that the gospel had been preached to "every creature under heaven" (Col 1:23). Paul and his fellow apostles could hardly have known much about the world east of the Khyber Pass. Certainly they were totally unaware of the Eskimos of Greenland, the Indians of North America, and the aborigines of Australia.

Today we know better. The seven seas have been charted in depth as well as length and breadth; as for the six continents, every square mile has been photographed many times by satellites that are even now orbiting the earth. Indeed, we know more about the geography of the moon than the early apostles knew about the geography of the earth.

With regard to the end of the age there was even more obscurity. Our Lord warned His disciples against setting dates or making any prognostications. And when the disciples asked their last question, "Lord, will you at this time restore the kingdom to Israel?" He replied, "It is not for you to know times and seasons which the Father has fixed by his own authority" (Acts 1:6-7). He went so far as to state that even He did not know the time of His return (Mt 24:36).

Jesus did, however, command them to take the gospel to the ends of the earth—wherever that might be; and He promised to be with them until the end of the age—whenever that might be.

The End of the Age

Acts 1:6-7 clearly indicates that God is interested in the unfolding of history. History is under His control. He knows the end from the beginning (Rev 22:13) and is working all things after the counsel of His own will (Eph 1:11). He has a plan and purpose for the Jews (Rom 9–11), the Gentiles (Acts 15:14; Rom 11:25), and the church (Eph 5:25-27).

When Jesus gave the Great Commission to His apostles He said quite plainly that the mandate was to extend to the end of the age (Mt 28:20). The Christian mission was not to terminate with the apostolic age. Neither was it to end with the Dark Ages, or the Renaissance, or the Reformation, or the Evangelical Awakening. It was to continue to the end of the age.

It seems clear that the early Christians expected the Lord to return in their lifetime. The wish no doubt was father to the thought. Certainly the apostles entertained this hope. Otherwise why were they so loath to leave Jerusalem? Luke informs us that when the church in Jerusalem suffered a devastating persecution at the hands of Saul of Tarsus, the believers were all scattered throughout the region of Judea and Samaria, *except* the apostles (Acts 8:1). And when they did manage to go outside of Jerusalem they always found their way back again with all haste.

When the Samaritans first received the gospel (Acts 8) the church in Jerusalem sent Peter and John to Samaria to look over the situation to make sure that the new departure was in line with official policy. As soon as their mission was accomplished they made a beeline back to Jerusalem (Acts 8:25). The same thing happened after Peter preached the gospel for the first time to a Gentile—Cornelius. Immediately we find him back in Jerusalem making his report to the leaders there (Acts 11:2).

When Paul and Barnabas wanted a definitive statement regarding the status of the Gentile Christians and their relationship to the law of Moses, they referred the matter to the apostles who were then still in Jerusalem (Acts 15:2).

How are we to explain the reluctance of the apostles to leave Jerusalem for any length of time? Doubtless it was because they expected the return of the Lord momentarily, and they did not want to be caught in Antioch or Ephesus or Corinth when that event occurred. They wanted to be on hand to meet and greet Him and to be sure of an important portfolio in His cabinet. We now know that the early church was mistaken on this point. Christ did not return in their lifetime. Almost two thousand years have come and gone and the church is still here. But it will not be here forever. Just as it had a beginning at Pentecost (Acts 2), so it will have an end when Christ returns (1 Thess 4:13-18).

In the meantime there would be wars and rumors of wars and all kinds of opposition and persecution. The disciples would be hated of all men. The missionary enterprise would be fraught with all kinds of difficulties and dangers. The messengers of the cross would be hunted and hounded from pillar to post. They would be scourged in the Jewish synagogues and beaten by Roman officials, and some of them would lay down their lives for the sake of the gospel. But the mandate would never be rescinded nor the mission aborted. If the disciples were persecuted in one city, they were not to call off the operation but proceed to the next city. This is exactly what Paul did. In every city but one he was met with sticks and stones, and even there (Athens) he was scorned and scoffed at by the philosophers, who regarded him as a "babbler" (Acts 17:18).

Neither the mischief of men nor the machinations of the devil were to deter them. They were taught to believe that they were engaged in a holy war with an implacable foe who would not surrender without a life-and-death struggle (Eph 6:10-12; 1 Pet 5:8). Casualties would occur and reverses come, but they were to press on in full confidence that the Captain of their salvation would be with them *to the end of the age.* Many battles would be lost, but the war would be won. On that point there was no doubt (Rom 8:35-39; 2 Cor 2:14).

We do well to bear this in mind when the modern prophets of doom are sounding the death knell of the Christian mission. The days are dark and doors are closing in various parts of the world. Some timid souls fear that we are about to witness the demise of the world-wide missionary enterprise. When Mahatma Gandhi was carrying on his "Quit India" campaign against the British during World War II, it looked to many as if the missionary body would have to evacuate India along with the British Raj when independence came. When the situation in Zaire blew up in our faces in the 1960s, some Christians at home were ready to recall the missionaries from that troubled land. When Jomo Kenyatta, the ex-leader of the Mau Mau Rebellion, became prime minister of Kenya in 1963, the missionaries feared the worst. They had their suitcases all packed, ready to leave at a moment's notice. But in all three countries the dust has settled and the missionaries are still there. After almost sixty years of oppression and persecution the Soviet Government has not been able to crush the church in the U.S.S.R. There are more evangelical Christians in Russia today than at any time in her long history.

Dictators come and go, kingdoms rise and fall, civilizations wax and wane; but the worldwide mission of the church will continue to the end of the age in spite of all the vicissitudes of world history. When one door closes, another will open. If Western missionaries become *personae non gratae,* non-Western missionaries will be raised up to take their place. If *all* expatriate missionaries are expelled from a given country, there will be the indigenous church to carry on. If the indigenous church is forced to go underground, there will still remain the Spirit of God, who dwells not in temples made with hands but in the hearts of His people. It is one thing to get rid of the visible church, it is quite another to get rid of the Almighty God. Heaven is His throne and earth is His footstool. It is impossible to banish Him from any part of His domain. The Christian mission is here to stay—until the end of the age, however long that may be.

The Second Coming has always been a strong incentive for the worldwide mission of the church. The first sentence in the "Principles and Practice" of the China Inland Mission (now Overseas Missionary Fellowship) reads as follows: "The China Inland Mission was formed under a deep sense of China's pressing need, and with an earnest desire, constrained by the love of Christ and the hope of His coming, to obey His command to preach the Gospel to every creature."[2] Missionary leaders such as Rowland Bingham, Charles Studd, Grattan Guinness, and others all found the Second Coming to be a great incentive to missionary work. So have others of the more modern period. Georg F. Vicedom says:

> Through the mission the church must do nothing less than prepare for the arrival of Jesus. The end can only come when the message of the Kingdom is proclaimed to all nations as a sign over them (Matt. 24:14). Therefore the Holy Ghost leads the church step by step into the mission to the heathen as a fact of the last times and thus prepares for the arrival of Jesus.[3]

Oscar Cullmann says virtually the same thing:

> The genuine primitive Christian hope does not paralyze Christian action in the world. On the contrary, the proclamation of the Christian Gospel in the missionary enterprise is a characteristic form of such action, since it expresses the belief that "missions" are an essential element in the eschatological divine plan of salvation. The missionary work of the Church is the eschatological foretaste of the kingdom of God, and the Biblical hope of the "end" constitutes the keenest incentive to action.[4]

If this is so, then this present age is pre-eminently one of proclamation. Nowhere is this clearer than in the writings of the apostle Paul. We think of him as a theologian; he considered himself always to be an apostle—a missionary. Before he was born he was called by God's grace to preach Christ among the Gentiles (Gal 1:15-16). He never ceased to marvel at the grace of God that had made him a chosen vessel.

Through the preaching of the gospel the Gentiles could become fellow heirs and members of the same body, and partakers of the promise of Christ Jesus (Eph 3:6). Paul's greatest privilege was to preach the "unsearchable riches of Christ" to the Gentile world (Eph 3:8). He went so far as to say that "Christ did not send me to baptize but to preach the gospel" (1 Cor 1:17). Little wonder that he exclaimed, "Woe to me if I do not preach the gospel!" (1 Cor 9:16).

---

2. Frank Houghton, *The Fire Burns On* (London: Lutterworth Press, 1965), p. 233).
3. Vicedom, *Mission of God*, p. 42.
4. Oscar Cullmann, "Eschatology and Missions in the New Testament" in *The Theology of the Christian Mission,* ed. Gerald H. Anderson (Nashville: Abingdon Press, 1961), pp. 42-43.

His only fear was that after preaching to others he himself should be disqualified (1 Cor 9:27). But such fear was unfounded, for at the close of his life he could testify to the fact that he had fought the good fight, he had finished the race, he had kept the faith (2 Tim 4:7). Consequently he could look forward with joy to the near return of Jesus Christ, when his converts would be his hope and joy and crown of rejoicing (1 Thess 2:19).

The Ends of the Earth

In the second place the Christian mission is to extend to the ends of the earth. The last words spoken by Christ on the day of the Ascension indicate that God's redemptive purpose embraces the whole world. The mission was to *begin* in Jerusalem, but it was to *extend* to Judea and Samaria, and ultimately to the ends of the earth (Acts 1:8).

The rationale for this is not difficult to discover. The world belongs to God. "The earth is the Lord's and the fulness thereof, the world and those who dwell therein" (Ps 24:1). "In the beginning God created the heavens and the earth" (Gen 1:1). Following the Flood God promised Noah He would maintain on this earth those physical and atmospheric conditions essential to life. "While the earth remains, seedtime and harvest, cold and heat, summer and winter, day and night, shall not cease" (Gen 8:22). In His sovereignty He governs the world. "The Lord has established his throne in the heavens, and his kingdom rules over all" (Ps 103:19). In Him we live and move and have our being (Acts 17:28). Day by day He opens His hand and supplies the need of every living thing (Ps 145:16). Moreover, one day He will judge the world (Acts 17:31). All men, good and bad, will stand before Him to be judged (Jn 5:29); and all nations, great and small, will do the same (Mt 25:32). In the meantime God intends to redeem the world. "For God sent the Son into the world, not to condemn the world, but that the world might be saved through him" (Jn 3:17).

Peter says that God is not willing that any should perish but that all should come to repentance (2 Pet 3:9). Paul speaks of God as the "Savior of all men" (1 Tim 4:10). John refers to Jesus Christ as the "Savior of the world" (1 Jn 4:14). Jesus Himself said, "The field is the world" (Mt 13:38). He also said, "I, when I am lifted up from the earth, will draw all men to myself" (Jn 12:32). Christianity, in contrast to Judaism, contains a note of universality. At the heart of the gospel is the glorious Good News: God loved the *world* (Jn 3:16). Christ died for *all* (2 Cor 5:14). *Whosoever* shall call on the name of the Lord shall be saved (Rom 10:13).

This being so, it naturally follows that the church's mandate includes the command to take the gospel to the ends of the earth. It must not be restricted to the Jew or the Gentile, the Roman or the Greek. The field is not Judea, or Palestine, or even the Roman Empire. The field is the world; and by the "world" Jesus meant the *entire* world—East and West, ancient and modern, Christian and non-Christian. The world is one world—His world. The human race is one family—His family. And the purpose of God will not be fulfilled until every segment of that family has been confronted with the claims of Jesus Christ.

The early church was slow in coming to this conclusion. Even the apostles, who might have been expected to take the lead, were themselves reluctant to share the gospel with the Gentiles. It required a special vision, repeated three times, to persuade Peter of his obligation to share the gospel with men of other races. It was an epochal event in the history of the church when Peter came to the conclusion that "God shows no partiality, but *in every nation* any one who fears him and does what is right is acceptable to him" (Acts 10:34-35).

The church in Jerusalem never managed to throw off the graveclothes of Judaism. On Paul's fifth and last visit to that city, about A.D. 58, the church there was still more Jewish than Christian in flavor. The disciples were known as "believing Jews" (Acts 21:20). The church members in Jerusalem were still keeping the law, frequenting the Temple, and taking vows a full generation after Pentecost (Acts 21:20-26).

Paul more than anyone else was responsible for the widespread proclamation of the gospel in the first century. At the time of his conversion he was commissioned by God to be the apostle to the Gentiles (Acts 9:15) and he gloried in his office (Rom 11:13). He traveled farther (Rom 15:24) and worked harder than all of the other apostles (1 Cor 15:10). In less than fifteen years he planted churches in four of the most populous provinces of the empire: Asia, Galatia, Macedonia, and Achaia. He was always teaching and preaching "the glorious gospel of the blessed God" (1 Tim 1:11).

He had one message: Jesus Christ and Him crucified (1 Cor 2:2), and wherever he went he called men to repentance and faith (Acts 20:21). It was always his ambition to preach the gospel where Christ had not been named, lest he should build on another man's foundation (Rom 15:20). Toward the end of his life he could say, "From Jerusalem and as far round as Illyricum I have fully preached the gospel of Christ" (Rom 15:19). Having preached in the major cities of the eastern part of the empire, he set his sights on Spain (Rom 15:24). If Clement of Rome's reference to Paul having preached the gospel in "the extreme west of the empire" refers to Spain, then Paul probably realized his ambition, though the New Testament is silent on this point. According to a strongly held tradition in the Syrian Orthodox Churches in South India, the apostle Thomas took the gospel to India in A.D. 52. He labored for ten years in the north, around Lahore, and ten years in the south, near Madras. Certainly there is evidence to prove that the Christian church has existed in India since the third century.

In the second and third centuries the gospel spread into all parts of the Roman Empire. During the second century Christianity continued to make steady gains, particularly in the east. Christians were especially numerous in Asia Minor, where the pagan temples were reported by Pliny, the governor of Bithynia, to be "almost deserted." It was not until the third century, when the empire began to break up, that large numbers of people turned to Christianity. In North Africa conversions were so numerous as to approximate a mass movement. By the close of the third century the two greatest strongholds of the faith were Asia Minor and North Africa. In the east, Edessa was well on its way to becoming the first state to make Christianity the official religion.

Following the conversion of Constantine Christianity entered a period of unprecedented expansion. During the fourth century the number of Christians multiplied by some 400 per cent. Sad to say, what the church gained in wealth and numbers, it lost in piety and power.

Between A.D. 500 and 1200 Christian missionaries—many of them monks—roamed all over Europe, teaching and preaching the gospel and establishing monasteries which became centers not only of light and learning but also of missionary activity. Missionaries from Ireland took the gospel to Scotland, Britain, and the continent. In time English missionaries joined their Irish brethren and helped with the conversion of Europe. The most illustrious names include Patrick, Columba, Aidan, Cuthbert, Augustine, Boniface, Anskar, Columbanus, Willibrord, Rimbert, Constantine, and Methodius. Christianity was introduced into Norway from England and into Sweden from Germany.

Later on kings and princes, following their conversion, lent both power and prestige to the movement to Christianize Europe. Some of them, such as Charlemagne, combined military conquest with religious persuasion. By A.D. 800 the Holy Roman Empire was finally well established. By 1200 the "Christianization" of Europe was complete, but not always by proper methods or with desirable results.

Christianity spread far beyond the borders of the Roman Empire. In the fourth century it penetrated into Ethiopia. In the seventh century the great Nestorian Church took the gospel to China, where it flourished for some two hundred years before dying out. A second attempt to plant Christianity in the great Chinese Empire was made by the Franciscans in the thirteenth century. A third attempt was made by the Jesuits in the seventeenth century. Beginning with the era of Vasco da Gama the Roman Catholic Church, working closely with the rulers and explorers of Portugal and Spain, took Christianity to the New World and the East Indies. The greatest numerical success was achieved in the Philippines and in South America.

It took the Protestant churches of Europe almost two hundred years to launch their overseas missionary enterprise. One would have expected the spiritual forces released by the Reformation to prompt the Protestant churches to take the gospel to the ends of the earth during the period of world exploration and colonization which began about 1500, but such was not the case.

There were several factors at work in the situation, but the most important was the theological factor. The Reformers, spiritual giants though they were, had a blind spot when it came to world missions. They taught that the Great Commission pertained only to the original twelve apostles; that the apostles fulfilled the Great Commission by taking the gospel to the ends of the then known world; that if later generations were without the gospel, it was their own fault—a judgment of God on their unbelief; that the apostolate—with its immediate call, peculiar functions, and miraculous powers—having ceased, the church in later ages had neither the authority nor the responsibility to send missionaries to the ends of the earth.

It is true that they believed the Word should be preached to all men everywhere. From time to time they even used the term "heathen," but by "heathen" they meant the unbelievers—Jews, Turks, Muslims, and agnostics—within the *corpus Christianum*. They did not apparently envisage the possibility of carrying the saving gospel of Christ to the "heathen" in Africa and Asia. When men like Hadrian Saravia and Justinian von Welz began to crusade on behalf of world evangelization they incurred the wrath of the ecclesiastical hierarchy of the Lutheran churches. Calvin taught that the kingdom of Christ is neither to be advanced nor maintained by the industry of man. World mission is the work of God alone.

Justinian von Welz wrote three treatises in which he advocated the missionary obligation of the church, called for the organization of a missionary society (Lovers of Jesus) to get the job done, and proposed the opening of a training school for missionary candidates. But he was like the voice of one crying in the wilderness. Nobody paid any attention to him except to excoriate him for his heretical views.

When William Carey in the 1790s published his *Enquiry into the*

Obligation of Christians to Use Means for the Conversion of the Heathen, he too met with strong opposition. When he proposed at a ministerial meeting in Northamptonshire, England, that they discuss the implications of the Great Commission, the moderator retorted, "Young man, sit down. When God pleases to convert the heathen He will do it without your aid or mine."

The first Protestant mission began in 1705 when two Lutheran missionaries, Ziegenbalg and Plütschau of the Danish-Halle Mission, took the gospel to India in 1705. In 1732 the Moravians launched their overseas missionary enterprise by sending missionaries to the Virgin Islands. Other fields were opened in rapid succession: Greenland (1733), Surinam (1735), South Africa (1737), North American Indians (1740), Jamaica (1754), and Antigua (1756). Between 1732 and 1760 some 226 Moravian missionaries began work in ten foreign countries.

It was not until the nineteenth century—called by Latourette "The Great Century"—that the Protestant churches in England and North America took the Great Commission seriously and began to send missionaries to all parts of the non-Christian world. William Carey led the way in 1792. As a direct result of his influence other missionary societies came into being: the London Missionary Society (1795), the Scottish and Glasgow Missionary Societies (1796), the Netherlands Missionary Society (1797), the Church Missionary Society (1799), the American Board of Commissioners (1810), and the American Baptist Missionary Society (1814).

Equally important was the formation of the Bible societies—the British and Foreign Bible Society (1804), the National Bible Society of Scotland (1809), the Netherlands Bible Society (1814), and the American Bible Society (1816)—which were responsible for the translation, publication, and distribution of the Scriptures in all parts of the mission field. In the early decades of the nineteenth century, on both sides of the Atlantic, one denomination after another formed its own foreign mission board. By the end of that century Christianity had become established on a worldwide basis, with missionaries in every country of the world that would receive them.

The twentieth century has witnessed a continued surge of missionary interest and activity. Today there are some 55,000 Protestant missionaries and more than twice that number of Roman Catholic missionaries in all parts of the world. Wherever they have gone they have made converts, established churches, opened hospitals, and maintained schools, besides engaging in all kinds of humanitarian service. Certainly the greatest achievement of all is the Christian church.

The raw material out of which the church has been built differed from place to place. It included the Brahmins of India, the scholar-gentry of China, the samurai of Japan, the Hottentots of Africa, the Eskimos of Greenland, the aborigines of Australia, the Indians of Amazonia, the headhunters of New Guinea, the cannibals of the South Seas.

All walks of life and all classes of men were included in the gospel invitation. Old and young, rich and poor, literate and illiterate, medicine men, fakirs and philosophers, princes and paupers, scholars and scavengers—all were welcomed into the Christian fold; all became members of the Body of Christ.

Far from dying out, the missionary movement of our day is experiencing a new surge of life and a new sense of direction and purpose. For the first time since Pentecost it is now possible to speak responsibly of completing the task of world evangelization in a single generation. We have the tools and the techniques, the men and the money. Old forms of missions are disappearing, but in their place new forms are emerging. In all parts of the world exciting things are happening. People are turning to Christ in ever-increasing numbers. The gospel is being preached to a worldwide audience on an unprecedented scale. People are responding not by the thousands but by the tens of thousands. It is estimated that in Africa 20,000 persons are turning to Christ every day. For the time being at least there is a worldwide hunger for spiritual reality that can be attributed only to the working of the Holy Spirit. It is not identified with any one charismatic personality—not even Billy Graham; nor is it the monopoly of any one denomination. It runs the entire gamut from the Plymouth Brethren to the Roman Catholic Church.

In some major areas of the world we have suffered reverses. China is a classic example. In other areas, such as India and Southeast Asia, we are barely keeping up with the population growth rate; but in Latin America and Africa the Christians are increasing two and three times faster than the population.

During the past 270 years phenomenal progress has been made. Today the Christian church is to be found in almost every country. There are still countries from which Western missionaries are barred; but there are very few without a Christian church, and none without a Christian witness. For the first time in history the Christian church is a truly universal institution. And it is growing faster in the Third World than in North America or Europe. Indeed, the center of gravity may be shifting from the West to the East.

One of the most exciting aspects of the modern missionary movement is the way in which the "younger" churches of the Third World are assuming responsibility for the evangelization of the world—both theirs and ours. The first All-Asia Mission Consultation ever held was convened in Seoul, Korea, in 1973. The initiative for the Consultation came entirely from the Asians themselves. Twenty-five delegates from fourteen countries unanimously adopted the following statement:

> We appeal to the Christian churches in Asia to be involved in the preaching of the Gospel, specially through sending and receiving Asian missionaries to strengthen the witness to the saving power of Christ. We are compelled by the Holy Spirit to declare that we shall work towards the placing of at least two hundred new Asian missionaries by the end of 1974.[5]

In keeping with the new emphasis was the first All-Asia Student Missionary Convention, Urbana style, in Baguio (Philippines) in December 1973, attended by eight hundred students from all parts of Asia. At a missionary conference in Korea in 1974 some two hundred young people readily responded for missionary service. Today there are well over three thousand Third World missionaries, serving mostly but not exclusively in the Third World. Some of them have become missionaries to the Western world.

Along with gospel preaching and church planting goes Bible translation. As of December 31, 1974, the Scriptures had been translated into 1,549 languages and dialects. The complete Bible is available to 90 per cent of the world's population. The New Testament is available to another 5 per cent, and Scripture Portions to still another 3 per cent. This leaves only 2 per cent of the world's people without any portion of the Word of God. This 2 per cent represents some three thousand tribes—most of them rather small—yet to be reached. Wycliffe Bible Translators, now working in over six hundred tribes, is rapidly closing the gap. They hope to complete the job by 1985, by which time every known tribe in the world will have some portion of the Word of God in its own language. In the meantime Gospel Recordings, Incorporated, has produced several million gospel records in almost four thousand dialects.

And what shall be said about gospel radio broadcasting? There are now some sixty-five radio stations owned and operated by Christian missions in all parts of the world. Most of them are small and minister within a limited radius, but some of them are very powerful and are broadcasting the gospel message literally around the clock and around the world. Some of these stations, with a million watts of power, are so powerful that even medium-wave transmissions can blanket an entire continent. Cheap transistor radios made in Japan have made it

---

5. *Missionary News Service,* September 17, 1973.

possible for tens of millions of illiterate people to hear the gospel for the first time in their own language.

C. Stacey Woods, former General Secretary of the International Fellowship of Evangelical Students, wrote in 1972:

> I see two worldwide, contradictory crosscurrents strongly flowing: First, there is the rushing torrent of godlessness, sensuality, secularism, and violence, which is increasing everywhere. Second, there is what many of us believe may be the final great movement of God's Spirit just before the Day of God's grace ends and the awesome Day of the Lord begins.[6]

Without a doubt world history is approaching a climax. Historians and sociologists are talking about the demise of Western civilization. Others fear that some madman may blow the world to smithereens by a nuclear holocaust. But Christians who believe that Jesus Christ is the Lord of history as well as the Head of the church are not given to this kind of pessimism. So far as they are concerned, these are days of great opportunity. The doors that are open are *wide* open. People the world over are responding to the gospel as never before. The fields are white unto harvest. Bill Bright, president of Campus Crusade for Christ, after returning from a world tour in 1973 said: "The more I see of what God is doing in the world, the more I am convinced that we stand today, *at this very hour,* on the threshold of the greatest spiritual advance the world has ever witnessed."[7]

The theme of the Lausanne Congress in July 1974 was "Let the Earth Hear His Voice." Over three thousand participants from 150 countries returned home to do just that. When the number of the elect is made up and the church is complete it will include in its membership those from "every tribe and tongue and people and nation" (Rev 5:9). That day is rapidly approaching, if indeed it is not already upon us.

In the Olivet Discourse our Lord brings together two important concepts: the end of the age and the ends of the earth. "This gospel of the kingdom will be preached throughout the whole world, as a testimony to all nations; and then the end will come" (Mt 24:14). For almost two thousand years the church has been praying "Thy kingdom come," without fully realizing the import of the words. Too often, especially in times of persecution, Christians have looked forward to the Second Coming as the event that would remove them from the world with all its "sin and want and sorrow," forgetting that the glorious climactic event cannot come to pass until the purposes of God for this age of grace are worked out to His satisfaction rather than for our consolation. The end of the age will come when the gospel

6. C. Stacey Woods, *Asia Pulse* III, no. 3 (April 1972): 101.
7. Bill Bright, *Christmas Letter,* 1973.

has been preached to the ends of the earth. There seems to be some necessary connection between the two. Missiology and eschatology belong together. Eschatology will not be realized until missiology has been fulfilled.

The words of Revelation 22:17 are pertinent here: "The Spirit and the Bride say, 'Come.' And let him who hears say, 'Come.' And let him who is thirsty come, let him who desires take the water of life without price." The Spirit and the Bride join their voices in a great advent cry, "Come, Lord Jesus." At the same time both issue the gospel invitation to a thirsty world: "Whosoever will, let him take the water of life freely."

> The heart of the missionary must maintain this double direction if it is to be kept from discouragement on the one hand and from dreaminess on the other. The uplifted gaze without the outstretched hands tends to make one visionary; the outstretched hands without the upward look tends to make one weary. Ever more must "the patience of hope" walk with equal footsteps with "the labor of love" until the Lord shall come.[8]

8. A. J. Gordon, *The Holy Spirit in Missions* (Harrisburg, Pa.: Christian Publications, reprint 1968), p. 162.

PART FIVE

The Spiritual Dynamics
of Missions

All kinds of forces have been at work in the Christian mission. Some of these have been divine; others have been human; and still others have been demonic. The church is the one institution to which Jesus Christ delegated the responsibility for the evangelization of the world. In this capacity the church has found herself caught in the crossfire of the forces emanating from both human and demonic sources. Even within the church there have been conflicting forces. Some of these have been dedicated to the Christian mission; others have been adamantly opposed to it. Still others, content to take a neutral stance, have done nothing to advance or retard the cause of Christ around the world. And even the forces that have traditionally been in favor of the Christian mission have not always been employed in the wisest way or to the greatest advantage.

Throughout history the church has known periods of advance and decline. She has not always been obedient to her Lord, and even in the best of times she has failed to realize her full potential as the salt of the earth and the light of the world. As we approach the end of the age she would do well to take inventory of her spiritual resources to make sure that she is employing them to the fullest degree.

16

The Opposition of Satan

The Christian has three implacable foes: the world, the flesh, and the devil. The New Testament has a good deal to say about all three. The Christian is warned to be on his guard against the corruption of the world (1 Cor 6:9-11), the lusts of the flesh (Gal 5:19-21), and the wiles of the devil (Eph 6:11).

The wiles of the devil are of special concern to the missionary. Paul recognized his thorn in the flesh as a "messenger of Satan" to harass him (2 Cor 12:7). He wrote to the Thessalonian believers: "We endeavored the more eagerly and with great desire to see you face to face; because we wanted to come to you—I Paul, again and again—but Satan hindered us" (1 Thess 2:17-18). *Satan hindered us* has been the story of Christian missions ever since the first century. The missionary, more than most Christian workers, is engaged in a holy war with the unseen powers of darkness.

Satan was not always the monster of iniquity that he is today. When first created he was full of wisdom and perfect in beauty. Not content with being the highest created intelligence in the universe, Satan decided that he would usurp the throne of God. His declaration of defiance was expressed in five *I will's:* "I will ascend to heaven above the stars of God. I will set my throne on high. I will sit on the mount of assembly in the far north. I will ascend above the heights of the clouds. I will make myself like the Most High" (Is 14:13-14). This was outright treason, something God could not tolerate. As a result Satan was cast out—"brought down to Sheol to the depths of the Pit."

From that day to this, two kingdoms have existed side by side: the kingdom of God and the kingdom of Satan.

Two Kingdoms

These two kingdoms, one of light (Jn 12:36) and the other of darkness (Col 1:13), are mutually antagonistic. They have absolutely nothing in common (2 Cor 6:14-17). A state of war, known as the conflict of the ages, has always existed between them (Eph 6:10-12); it will continue to exist until one finally overcomes the other (Rev 11:15). Every member of the human race belongs to one or other of these two competing kingdoms. When conversion takes place the individual is said to pass from darkness to light and from the power of Satan to God (Acts 26:18; Col 1:13; 1 Pet 2:9).

The conflict between these two kingdoms came to a head during the earthly ministry of our Lord. Whenever He came into personal contact with demon possession He cast out the demon and set the victim free. The Pharisees, unable to deny the fact of His power, ascribed its source to Satan, Beelzebub, the prince of the demons (Mt 12:24). Jesus replied: "Every kingdom divided against itself is laid waste.... If Satan casts out Satan, he is divided against himself; how then will his kingdom stand?" In verse 29 He adds: "How can one enter a strong man's house and plunder his goods, unless he first binds the strong man?"

Here we have three things: the strong man, the strong man's house, and the strong man's goods. We are left in no doubt regarding their identity. The strong man obviously is Satan, the prince of the demons. The strong man's house is the vast world system over which Satan presides. The strong man's goods are the souls of men, held captive by Satan (Acts 26:18; 2 Tim 2:26).

This earth has been the scene of Satan's greatest achievements. Unable to usurp God's authority in heaven, he decided to destroy God's handiwork on earth. This he did in the Garden of Eden when he persuaded man to join him in his rebellion against God. When Adam and Eve fell they not only sinned against the goodness and authority of God, they joined Satan in his war against the Most High.

It was God's original intention that man should be fruitful and multiply and replenish the earth, in this way extending His dominion over the whole earth. Instead, it was the kingdom of Satan that was extended throughout the world, for when we come to the New Testament we read that "the *whole world* is in the power of the evil one" (1 Jn 5:19). Satan is described as "the god of this world" (2 Cor

4:4), in which capacity he demands man's worship. He is also called "the prince of the power of the air" (Eph 2:2), and as such he demands man's service. He demanded both of Jesus in the wilderness, but Jesus replied: "You shall worship the Lord your God and him only shall you serve" (Mt 4:10).

This world over which Satan reigns as god and prince belongs really to God. He created it (Gen 1:1), He sustains it (Gen 8:22; Acts 14:17), and He intends to redeem it (Jn 3:17; Rev 21:1-5). "The earth is the Lord's and the fulness thereof, the world and those who dwell therein" (Ps 24:1). Satan assuredly is here; but he is an outsider, an invader, and, therefore, a usurper. The power structure that he has established in the world has no legitimacy in fact or in law. His government is a puppet government and all his emissaries are quislings. But even Jesus acknowledged that, rightly or wrongly, Satan is a king and has a kingdom (Mt 12:26).

As long as Satan remains in power, this planet is "occupied territory" in the eyes of God. Let us make no mistake about it: Satan is mankind's Enemy Number One, the strong man whose power must be broken if his house is to be invaded and his captives set free. Martin Luther expressed it well:

> For still our ancient foe
> Doth seek to work us woe;
> His craft and power are great,
> And, armed with cruel hate,
> On earth is not his equal.

When General Douglas MacArthur, after losing the Battle of Bataan, left the Philippines and transferred his headquarters to Australia in 1942, he made a broadcast to the Filipino people which ended with the famous words: "I will return!" During his absence the invading Japanese army overran the archipelago, imposing its iron will on the helpless victims of its ruthless aggression. Two and a half years later MacArthur, true to his word, waded ashore with the first wave of U.S. Marines at Leyte. In a matter of hours the good news spread fast and far: "MacArthur has returned!" War widows wept for joy. Strong men trembled with emotion. College students gathered in little groups to discuss the momentous news. MacArthur was on his way! Liberation was at hand! Freedom—man's most precious heritage—was to be theirs once more.

In a similar way, only on a grander scale, Satan invaded this planet in the dawn of human history, and for four thousand years held mankind in bondage and darkness. As the archenemy of God and man he marched to and fro throughout the earth "working his woe." Men and nations bowed before him. Kings and princes trembled at his word. Thrones and kingdoms rose and fell at his behest (Is 14:16-17). From the beggar on the dunghill to the king on his throne, all men everywhere jumped at the crack of his whip. The strong man, "armed with cruel hate," kept his house; and his goods were safe.

Then one day, at the height of his power, something happened. A Warrior from another world, the Captain of our salvation, made a landing at a place called Bethlehem and established a beachhead. Immediately the fight was joined. Satan fought with all the fury at his command. Herod, the tool of the evil one, struck the first blow. The movement went underground and didn't emerge until thirty years later in the wilderness of Judea. There, for the very first time, Satan came face to face with a Man who was his equal—nay, his superior; a Man in whose moral armor he failed to find a single flaw; a Man in whose perfect humanity he searched in vain for a single weakness. Three times, with consummate skill, he hurled his fiery darts. One by one they fell to the ground, shattered in a thousand pieces. Just as all Israel shouted with a great shout when Goliath lay dead at David's feet, so all heaven, we can visualize, broke into acclamations loud and long when Jesus Christ made the first successful attempt to bind the strong man.

That was but the first of many encounters, but it was the proof and promise of victory all along the line. The holy war was by no means over, but that first decisive battle marked the turning of the tide. Had that battle been lost, all hope of final victory would have vanished. Had the last Adam failed as did the first Adam, the human race would have lost its one and only Champion. Who then would have been able to bind the strong man, to enter his house, and deliver his captives?

One stated purpose of the Incarnation was to "destroy the works of the devil" (1 Jn 3:8). Disease, death, and demons are all part of the kingdom of Satan that Jesus came to destroy; that is why He "went about doing good and healing all who were oppressed by the devil" (Acts 10:38).

The conflict of the ages reached its climax at the cross. It was there that Jesus Christ administered the fatal blow to the enemy of our souls. It was through death that He destroyed him who had the power of death, that is, the devil, and delivered all those who through fear of death were subject to lifelong bondage (Heb 2:14-15).

Paul tells us that it was on the cross that Jesus Christ "disarmed the principalities and powers and made a public example of them, triumphing over them in it" (Col 2:15). Ellicott in his Commentary makes an excellent point on this passage: "Taking his metaphor from a Roman triumph, St. Paul represents Him as passing in triumphal majesty up the sacred way to the eternal gates with all the powers of evil bound as captives behind His chariot before the eyes of men and angels."

By His resurrection Christ threw another chain around the strong man, again demonstrating His complete power over Satan and proving that life, not death, is the last word. By rising from the dead in the power of an endless life He robbed death of its sting and the grave of its victory (1 Cor 15:55). Forty days later He ascended into heaven and took His place at the right hand of the Majesty on high (Heb 1:3), far above all "rule and authority and power and dominion" (Eph 1:21).

Because of that great historic event, the church for two thousand years has been a singing church.

> To Thee, and to Thy Christ, O God,
> We sing, we ever sing;
> For He invaded Death's abode
> And robbed him of his sting.
> The house of dust enthralls no more,
> For He, the strong to save,
> Himself doth guard that silent door,
> Great keeper of the grave.
>
> To Thee, and to Thy Christ, O God,
> We sing, we ever sing;
> For He hath crushed beneath His rod
> The world's proud rebel king.
> He plunged in His imperial strength
> To gulfs of darkness down;
> He brought His trophy up at length,
> The foiled usurper's crown.

The Temptation, the Crucifixion, the Resurrection, the Ascension— all were steppingstones in Christ's triumphal march to victory over Satan. One steppingstone remains, the Second Advent. When that event takes place, the King of kings and Lord of lords will come forth riding on the wings of omnipotence, with the armies of heaven following in His train, to administer the *coup de grâce*. Clothed in a garment dipped in blood, He will judge and make war. His eyes will be as a flame of fire. On His head will be many crowns. Out of His mouth will issue a sharp sword. At the rumble of His chariot the pillars of the earth will shake. At the rustle of His wings all opposition will melt away. At the sight of His glorious banners His enemies will bite the dust. Satan will be seized, bound with a great chain, and cast into the bottomless pit, where he will remain for a thousand years (Rev 20:1-3).

That climactic event still lies in the future. In the meantime the church has been given a job to do. Before the Captain of our salvation took His final departure He commanded His disciples to go into all the world, to preach the gospel to every creature, and to make disciples of all nations (Mt 28:19-20).

These are fighting words. They are tantamount to a declaration of war on Satan, who, though a defeated foe in the purpose of God, is nevertheless still very much alive and active in the world. This cruel tyrant, who has held the world in darkness and bondage ever since the dawn of history, is not likely to relinquish his hold without a life-and-death struggle. He will do everything in his power to guard his house and keep his goods. This world is still "occupied territory" and Satan is still its god and prince. The apostle Paul warns us that "we are not contending against flesh and blood, but against the principalities, against the powers, against the world rulers of this present darkness, against the spiritual hosts of wickedness in heavenly places" (Eph 6:12).

Opposition in the Early Church

Satan in his opposition to the church of Jesus Christ assumes one of two guises. Sometimes he goes about as a "roaring lion" (1 Pet 5:8), in which case his purpose is to destroy. At other times he assumes the form of an "angel of light" (2 Cor 11:14), in which case his aim is to deceive. Either way he, as the archenemy of God and man, stands ready to oppose any and all attempts to invade his territory or to liberate his captives. This comes out very clearly in the Acts of the Apostles, where we have the record of four instances when the gospel messengers encountered demonic opposition; and each time it "happened" to coincide with a fresh attempt on the part of the church *to penetrate deeper into enemy territory.*

When the gospel was first preached to the Samaritans (Acts 8), Simon Magus, a sorcerer, stood in the way and tried to match his power with that of the apostles. When he discovered that this was impossible, he offered Peter money to give him the superior power which he had seen displayed by Philip. Peter, sensing the gravity of the situation, pronounced a curse on Simon Magus: "Your silver perish with you, because you thought you could obtain the gift of God with money! You have neither part nor lot in this matter, for your heart is not right before God. . . . I see that you are in the gall of bitterness and in the bond of iniquity" (Acts 8:20-23).

At the outset of Paul's first missionary journey we have a similar situation. When the proconsul of Cyprus showed an interest in the Christian gospel, Elymas, a sorcerer, tried to turn him aside. Paul, recognizing the demonic nature of the opposition, did not hesitate to pronounce a curse on him: "You son of the devil, you enemy of all righteousness, full of all deceit and villainy, will you not stop making crooked the straight paths of the Lord?" (Acts 13:10). As a result of the apostolic curse, Elymas was struck blind for a time.

The third episode took place immediately after Paul set foot in Europe. As he went back and forth to the place of prayer in Philippi, a demon-possessed slave girl, who brought her masters much gain by soothsaying, mocked Paul and his companions, crying: "These men are servants of the most High God, who proclaim to you the way of salvation" (Acts 16:17). She kept this up for many days until Paul could stand it no longer, whereupon he turned to the spirit and said, "I charge you in the name of Jesus Christ to come out of her." And it came out that very hour.

The last event of this kind took place in Ephesus, the center of the worship of the great goddess Artemis (Diana). Pilgrims from all over the Roman Empire journeyed to Ephesus to participate in this pagan form of worship. So deeply entrenched was this religious system that it required "extraordinary" miracles by the hand of Paul to make any impression on the city. Sick people were healed and demon-possessed persons were delivered.

As might be expected, the devil fought back. Itinerant Jewish exorcists undertook to duplicate the miracles performed by Paul, using the name of the Lord Jesus in their incantations. But the evil spirit called out: "Jesus I know and Paul I know; but who are you?" (Acts 19:15). At this point the demon-possessed man leaped on the exorcists and overpowered them so that they fled out of the house naked and wounded.

It is important to notice that in all four episodes the opposition to the gospel was not human but demonic. Also it occurred precisely when the gospel was introduced *for the first time* into parts of the world until then under the undisputed sway of Satan. In each case the confrontation was sharp and bitter, and ended in victory for the kingdom of God. Paul was speaking from his own experience when he said that we wrestle not against flesh and blood but against demonic powers (Eph 6:12).

Under these circumstances it was inevitable that the devil would use his emissaries—sorcerers and other demon-possessed persons—to

273

withstand the apostles. He would not suffer his kingdom to be invaded by the messengers of the cross. Every convert to the Christian faith weakened Satan's hold on his own territory, and if enough converts were made they would pose a threat to his entire kingdom.

Opposition Today

The Christian life is a warfare, and every Christian is expected to take his stand against the wiles of the devil (Eph 6:11). But the Christian missionary, by the very nature of his work, finds himself in a highly exposed part of the battlefield, where the Christian forces are thin and where the firepower of the enemy is the heaviest.

We used to divide the world neatly into two parts, Christian and non-Christian; but since we in the West are now talking about a "post-Christian era" we have some misgivings regarding our former categories. The so-called Christian world is becoming less and less Christian with every passing year; and some countries in the so-called non-Christian world—China, for example—put us to shame when it comes to morality, private and public. Also, not all the demonic forces are to be found in the Third World. Spiritism is rampant in France, Brazil, and other countries of the free world; and right here in our own country there are now Satan churches where worship is intentionally offered to Satan.

Nevertheless, it is a fact that in many parts of the world the Christian missionary comes face to face with demonic systems which for thousands of years have been an integral part of the kingdom of Satan. As a soldier of the cross he is a threat to this kingdom of evil. The missionary's ultimate quarrel is not with humanism, nationalism, Communism, or any other earthly system, but with Satan himself. Back of the religious, political, and economic power structures of the world is the prince of the power of the air, who is determined to "work his woe" on mankind as long as he possibly can. Because the missionary's task is to open their eyes, to turn them from darkness to light and from the power of Satan to God (Acts 26:18), he naturally becomes the object of special attack on the part of the devil.

This is especially true of pioneer missionaries who are called on to lead the assault on the kingdom of darkness in the faraway places of the earth. They are particularly vulnerable in the early days before a base of operations can be established. The attack may be physical, mental, or spiritual in character. It may involve the missionary himself or the first converts. In either case the attack can be devastating in the early stages of the operation.

When the Evangelical Alliance Mission first entered Irian Jaya in 1952, it sent two missionaries, Erickson and Tritt, on an exploratory trip into the unknown jungle territory. One day, for no apparent reason, the two men were brutally murdered by their native carriers. Who is to say that this was not the result of demonic influence?

When the Overseas Missionary Fellowship, following the evacuation of China, decided to send missionaries into north Thailand in the early 1950s, they found the tribespeople completely bound by Satan. Every home had its own demon shelf where the family worshiped every day. To make the bondage even greater, the principal cash crop was opium, and this meant that everyone was addicted to the drug, the little children imbibing it with their mothers' milk. In the face of overwhelming odds the missionaries, some of them veterans from the China field, penetrated the mountain regions in search of the tribespeople still without any knowledge of the gospel. Slowly and painfully they went forward on their knees, covered by a barrage of prayer in the homelands. Even so there were casualties. In 1959 Lillian Hamer and in 1960 Roy Orpin were ambushed and shot to death on the mountain trails. Humanly speaking there was no known motive for the slayings. Was this the work of Satan?

Mental depression is another favorite method of attack. Discouragement is the most lethal weapon in the devil's arsenal. Spiritual giants, immune to all other forms of attack, have been known to succumb to depression. J. O. Fraser, a mighty man of God, labored alone in Lisuland in southwest China. Owing to the primitive conditions, his life and work were incredibly hard. After five hard years without a convert, Fraser was ready to quit.

> A strange uncertainty began to shadow his inward life. All he believed and rejoiced in became unreal, and even his prayers seemed to mock him as the answers faded into nothingness. . . . Deeply were the foundations shaken in those days and nights of conflict, until Fraser realised that behind it all were "powers of darkness" seeking to overwhelm him. He had dared to invade Satan's kingdom, undisputed for ages. At first vengeance had fallen on the Lisu inquirers, an easy prey. Now, he was himself attacked —and it was war to the death, spiritually.[1]

It stands to reason that new converts will be singled out for special attention, for they have had the audacity to make a clean break with the past, destroying their idols and burning all the paraphernalia connected with pagan worship. One such convert known to the author suddenly went blind the day after he took his stand for Christ. Another

---

1. Mrs. Howard Taylor, *Behind the Ranges* (London: Lutterworth Press, 1944), pp. 89-90.

Christian, living in a region where the worship of the fire god was common, had his haystack catch fire several times. Others have had their children suddenly fall ill. Still others have lost their cattle by some strange disease. Missionary annals are filled with such accounts, attesting to the fact that Satan is a hard taskmaster who seldom fails to fight back when his kingdom is invaded.

17

The Wrath of Man

In the Christian mission we must differentiate between the opposition of Satan, which is demonic, and the wrath of man, which is human. In Psalm 2 we read: "Why do the nations conspire, and the peoples plot in vain? The kings of the earth set themselves, and the rulers take counsel together, against the Lord and his anointed, saying, 'Let us burst their bonds asunder, and cast their cords from us.' "

When Jesus sent out the twelve apostles on their first missionary journey He warned them: "Beware of *men;* for they will deliver you up to the councils, and flog you in their synagogues" (Mt 10:17). So violent was the opposition going to be that Jesus compared the apostles to "sheep in the midst of wolves" (Mt 10:16), hardly a pleasant prospect. Mao Tse-tung said on one occasion that a revolution is not an invitation to a tea party. Jesus said virtually the same thing about the Christian mission. Indeed, He went so far as to say, "The hour is coming when whoever kills you will think that he is offering service to God" (Jn 16:2). Doubtless He had Saul of Tarsus in mind when He spoke those words (Acts 26:9-11; 23:1).

The two kinds of opposition—human and demonic—can never be completely divorced, for man is often the tool of the devil; but there is an essential difference between the two and we should be aware of it.

How the Wrath of Man Is Expressed

There are many ways in which the wrath of man can be expressed.

277

At least five were experienced by the early church, and all of them can be found in the modern missionary movement. They may vary from time to time in nature and intensity, but basically they represent man's hostility to the gospel of Jesus Christ.

1. Religious fanaticism. In New Testament times the Jews were a classic example of this kind of wrath. It was they who persecuted Jesus and later His disciples. For the most part the common people heard Him gladly, but the Jewish leaders were unrelenting in their opposition. All the major parties—Pharisees, Sadducees, Herodians, and scribes—did their best to destroy Him and finally succeeded, with a little help from Pilate. They would not enter the kingdom themselves, nor would they allow others to enter. Consequently Jesus reserved His most scathing denunciations not for the publicans and sinners, but for the self-righteous leaders whom He described as blind leaders of the blind (Mt 15:14).

Jesus warned His disciples that persecution would come not from the Roman senate but from the Jewish synagogue (Mt 10:17; Jn 16:2). Saul of Tarsus, for a time the leader of the opposition, spearheaded the persecution of the Christian church. Hating the very name of Christ with a deep, dark, pathological hatred, he entered every synagogue in Jerusalem, apprehended men and women, and cast his vote to put them to death (Acts 26:10). Not satisfied with cleaning up Jerusalem with its 460 synagogues, he carried his persecution to foreign cities.

Later on, following his conversion, Paul got a taste of his own medicine. For the remainder of his life he was never free from persecution. Death was his daily companion (Rom 8:36). On more than one occasion his life was spared only by the timely intervention of local Roman officials (Acts 18:12-16; 19:35-41; 21:31-32). Though he never returned hate for hate (Acts 28:19) and yearned for the salvation of his own people (Rom 9:1-3), he did on one occasion speak out against the religious fanaticism of the Jews. His words were sharp but true. He said they "killed both the Lord Jesus and the prophets, and drove us out, and displease God and oppose all men by hindering us from speaking to the Gentiles that they might be saved" (1 Thess 2:15-16).

In our own day the Christian mission encounters religious intolerance in many parts of the world, but it is found in its most virulent form in Islam—the most fanatical of all religions. As mentioned before, in Islam there is the Law of Apostasy which permits the community to kill any member who defects from the faith. This law goes a long way toward accounting for the paucity of converts from Islam. The law is not always applied, but its very existence acts as a strong deterrent.

In most Muslim countries conversion is an exceedingly dangerous undertaking and only the bravest souls have the requisite courage to face the prospect. Discipleship is so very costly that few are willing to pay the price. A veteran missionary to the Middle East had this to say: "So confined is the Muslim that in some countries of the Middle East a follower of Islam who changed his religion would in effect be tearing up his birth certificate, citizenship papers or passport, voting registration, and work permit; and would become like a man without a country."[1]

Though more tolerant than Islam, both Hinduism and Buddhism have strenuously opposed the Christian faith in the great continent of Asia. Few converts from these religions have escaped persecution. They have been driven from their homes by their own parents, denied access to the village well, and generally treated as outcasts from society.

2. Racial prejudice. In our day racial prejudice is generally regarded as the sin of the white race. Admittedly our guilt in this respect is very great, but we are by no means alone in our guilt. The fact of the matter is that there is not a single sizable society on earth where racial prejudice is not present in one form or another. Every country has its second-class citizens, usually members of a minority group, who continue year after year to suffer various forms of discrimination. Closely allied with racial prejudice, and indeed an integral part of it, is a sense of cultural superiority. The dominant group is usually more sophisticated as well as more wealthy and more powerful than the minority group.

In New Testament times racial prejudice was the hallmark of the Greeks. They were the intellectuals of the day; philosophy was born with them. As Emerson said, "Plato is philosophy and philosophy Plato." And speaking of *The Republic* he added, "Burn the libraries, for their value is in this book." Little wonder that the Greeks had an inflated opinion of themselves. Civilization was *Greek* civilization, and anyone who didn't share that civilization was treated as a barbarian. We are still wondering how one small race could be so prolific in ideas, so dynamic in action, and so massive in achievement. The secret is to be sought not so much in the temper of the times as in the temperament of the Greek—his inquiring mind, his restless spirit, and his zest for life.

According to the New Testament there are two classes that are difficult to win for Christ: the wealthy (Lk 18:24-25) and the wise

1. R. Park Johnson, *Middle East Pilgrimage* (New York: Friendship Press, 1958), p. 142.

(1 Cor 1:18-29). The reason is that both wealth and wisdom have a tendency to produce in a person a sense of self-sufficiency which engenders pride and renders him independent of God. It is the antithesis of the spirit of humility and trust required for conversion (Mt 18:3). Sophistication is definitely an asset when we are dealing with men, but it is a liability when we come to deal with God (Mt 11:25).

The classic example of cultural pride is seen in Paul's experience in the Areopagus (Acts 17:16-34), where he preached the gospel to the philosophers of Athens. His message was well prepared and well delivered. It was cogent, conciliatory, and captivating. It was designed to disarm their prejudice, satisfy their curiosity, and impart to them the truth concerning God's activity in creation, redemption, and judgment. It was a brilliant address, punctuated with references to their poets and couched in philosophical terms likely to appeal to their intellectual interests. They listened attentively until he mentioned the Resurrection; at that point they laughed him to scorn. The very idea was repugnant to the Greek mind. It was too primitive, too puerile, too plebeian for their way of thinking.

The experience at Athens was probably Paul's most traumatic one as a preacher of the gospel. He was accustomed to sticks and stones (Acts 14:19) hurled at him by rabble-rousers (Acts 17:5), and on his body he bore the stigmata of Jesus (Gal 6:17); but this was the first time his mind was scarred by slurs hurled at him by intellectuals. He was obviously greatly distressed. He intimates as much in his letter to the Corinthians, where he says, "I was with you in weakness and in much fear and trembling; and my speech and my message were not in plausible words of wisdom, but in the demonstration of the Spirit and power, that your faith might not rest in the wisdom of men but in the power of God" (1 Cor 2:3-5).

This doesn't sound at all like the great fearless apostle Paul who had nothing but disdain for physical danger (Acts 21:13). The statement is all the more remarkable when we recall that Paul's journey took him directly from Athens to Corinth (Acts 18:1).

The modern counterpart to this is found in the ancient civilizations of Asia, particularly China and India. These peoples are proud of their cultural heritage and are in no hurry to give it up. They regard their civilization as superior to ours in everything but technology, and they are not persuaded that technology is an unmixed blessing.

The Brahmins of India are the social and intellectual elite, who look with jaundiced eye on the lower castes, particularly the Sudras, who are the workers and artisans. The lowest of the Sudra subcastes are the carpenters and the fishermen. Jesus was a carpenter and some of the apostles were fishermen. Little wonder that the Brahmins have found it difficult to embrace a religion whose Founder and early leaders were so far down in the social scale.

And what can be said about the Confucian scholars of China? China is justly proud of her long history, advanced civilization, and enormous population. In all three she leads the world. For well over a thousand years China shed the light and luster of her ancient civilization over most of Asia. She lent to everyone, she borrowed from no one. Even Japan owes much of her civilization to China. So far as the Chinese were concerned there was only one civilized country in the world—the Middle Kingdom. All others were beyond the pale; hence they were regarded as "barbarians." During the Dark Ages, when the light of learning had all but disappeared from Europe, Changan, the capital of the T'ang Dynasty, was probably the most sophisticated city in the world. With such a history and civilization, China can be forgiven if she entertained ideas of her own greatness.

When George III tried in 1793 to open trade with China, the emperor wrote him a letter turning him down flat: "Strange and costly objects do not interest me. . . . Our celestial Empire possesses all things in prolific abundance, and lacks no product within its own borders. I . . . have no use for your country's merchandise."[2]

When the missionaries with their blond hair, blue eyes, and white complexion arrived in China they were called "foreign devils." Everywhere they were opposed by the scholar-gentry class, who regarded them as a threat to their position and prestige as leaders in society. With every weapon at their command they tried to undermine their influence. Most of the antiforeign outbreaks were the direct result of the opposition of the Confucian scholars. When they were challenged to study the Christian religion they replied: "Nothing doing; we'd sooner go to hell with our Confucius than go to heaven with your Jesus."

China has come a long way in the last two hundred years, but the idea of cultural superiority in Asia dies hard. As recently as 1955 U Nu, then prime minister of Burma, in an address before the National Press Club in Washington, D.C., said:

> First of all Burma has a long history. We had a great and flourishing civilization in Burma, based on one of the great religions of the world, Buddhism, at the time when William the Conqueror was crossing the English Channel. This civilization, passed on to us by our forebears, has now become our national heritage. It is our way of life. We prefer it to any other way of life on this earth. We are not prepared to exchange it for any other way of life.

There can be no doubt about it: a cultural superiority complex

2. Helmut G. Callis, *China: Confucian and Communist* (New York: Henry Holt, 1959), p. 168.

has had enormous detrimental effect on the spread of the gospel, especially in Asia.

3. National chauvinism. In the New Testament this kind of opposition came from the Romans. They were great empire builders. Their legions roamed the Mediterranean world, chasing the pirates from the seas and the robbers and bandits from the land. Their laws were of a high order. Their jurisprudence is the foundation of our Western legal system. The *Pax Romana* which they imposed on 60 million people was both benign and beneficial.

Roman society was divided into two large camps: citizens and slaves. Gibbon estimates that slaves accounted for half the population in the time of Christ. Others have placed the ratio as high as three slaves to every free man. Be that as it may, slaves were sufficiently numerous to form a significant segment of Roman society. In the Roman Empire a person was either a free man with all the rights and privileges pertaining thereto, or he was a slave without any rights at all. Many of the early Christians were slaves.

The Romans were naturally proud of their great empire with all its pomp, pageantry, and power. Even Paul was proud of his Roman citizenship, and on more than one occasion it stood him in good stead when persecution broke out. Nevertheless nationalism prompted the Romans to regard the Jews as the "second race" and the Christians the "third race" in the empire.

On not a few occasions nationalism proved inimical to the progress of the gospel. Twice Paul and his gospel were rejected for no other reason than that he and his message were regarded as Jewish. In Philippi, which was a Roman colony, Paul and Silas were dragged into the marketplace before the magistrates. The accusation made against them was: "These men are Jews and they are disturbing our city. They advocate customs which it is not lawful for us Romans to accept or practice" (Acts 16:20-21).

Whether Paul's doctrine was good or bad, true or false, was beside the point. It was *foreign,* and therefore unacceptable.

In Thessalonica he had a similar experience. Here again he incurred the displeasure of the Roman citizenry. The charge was, "These men who have turned the world upside down have come here also, and Jason has received them; and they are all acting against the decrees of Caesar, saying that there is another king, Jesus" (Acts 17:6-7).

Patriotism ran high in the Roman Empire. Everyone was compelled to confess, "Caesar is lord." It was precisely at this point that the Christians found themselves in trouble. They adamantly refused to engage in emperor worship. During the first two centuries every kind of torture was used to extract such a confession from them, but to little avail. Every known method of execution was employed, but few recanted. They went cheerfully to prison, to the mines, and into exile. Not a few became martyrs.

The issue was particularly troublesome because it had political as well as religious overtones. "The rejection of the imperial cultus was a crime which came under the head of sacrilege as well as of high treason, and it was here that the repressive measures taken by the state against Christianity almost invariably started."[3]

Nationalism is without doubt the greatest problem facing the Christian mission today. During the nineteenth century missionaries had all kinds of liberty for the preaching of the gospel throughout Africa and Asia. Not so today. With the collapse of the colonial system nationalism has taken over and walls are being erected in all parts of the world. Some countries have already closed their doors to foreign missionaries; others are exerting pressure on the national churches to support military regimes of the left or right. Indigenous cultures are being revived and refurbished, and national Christians are viewed with suspicion if they fail to participate in all phases of the renaissance.

Almost everywhere Christianity is regarded as a Western importation. Throughout Asia it is called a "foreign religion." In Africa it is known as the "white man's religion." National Christians are very sensitive on this point. They have a sincere desire to be good Christians and loyal citizens at the same time, but the odds are against them. This is especially true in countries with a state religion. In Thailand, for instance, to be a genuine Thai one must be a Buddhist. To be a Christian, even a patriotic one, is to be a second-class citizen.

This kind of situation exists even in countries where religious liberty is guaranteed by the constitution. In many countries of the Third World religious liberty is being eroded. Jails are filled with political prisoners, some of whom are church leaders. This is true in Asia, Africa, and Latin America.

4. Economic interests. Here the businessman enters the picture. Most businessmen believe that "honesty is the best policy." Without it the whole credit system, with its corollary, instalment buying, would collapse overnight. But the businessman does not want anything, including honesty, to interfere with his profits. When that happens he will fight back—every time.

---

3. Adolf Harnack, *The Mission and Expansion of Christianity* (New York: Harper and Brothers, 1962), p. 69.

We have two examples of this in the Acts of the Apostles, and Paul figured in both. In Philippi the opposition came from the unscrupulous businessmen who trafficked in the souls and bodies of their demon-possessed victims. When Paul exorcised the demon from the slave girl, she was of no further use to her owners. It was when the owners saw that their profits were dropping that they seized Paul and Silas and dragged them into the marketplace (Acts 16:19).

The second incident occurred in Ephesus when the silver merchants ganged up on Paul because his preaching threatened their business enterprise. They called a meeting of the merchants' guild and said: "Men, you know that from this business we have our wealth. And you see and hear that not only at Ephesus but almost throughout all Asia this Paul has persuaded and turned away a considerable company of people, saying that gods made with hands are not gods. And there is danger not only that this trade of ours may come into disrepute but also that the temple of the great goddess Artemis may count for nothing" (Acts 19:25-27). So enraged were these silversmiths that they precipitated a citywide riot that almost cost Paul his life.

Things are better now, but in the early days of the modern missionary movement there was no love lost between the merchant and the missionary. In the seventeenth and eighteenth centuries the great East Indian Companies had a virtual monopoly on ocean travel and world trade. Missionaries were at the mercy of these powerful mercantile firms. Often they were denied passage on their ships. On occasion they were not permitted to live or work in their domains. The British East India Company stated:

> The sending out of missionaries into our Eastern possessions is the maddest, most extravagant, most costly, most indefensible project which has ever been suggested by a moonstruck fanatic. Such a scheme is pernicious, imprudent, useless, harmful, dangerous, profitless, fantastic. It strikes against all reason and sound policy. It brings the peace and safety of our possessions into peril.

The proliferation of adjectives in the above statement is just a smoke screen. The real reason for the vitriolic statement is found in the last sentence—"the peace and safety of our possessions." Peace and safety were not an end in themselves but a means to an end. The end was profit, and they made plenty of it; and woe betide anyone who got in the way.

Then, as now, there was considerable exploitation on the part of Western businessmen. The missionaries, by their presence if not by their protests, were a thorn in the side of the exploiters. Whether it was the opium trade in China, the slave trade in East Africa, the liquor traffic in West Africa, or the shameful exploitation of indentured labor in the Pacific Islands, the missionaries were the only ones to raise a protest; and in so doing they made more enemies than friends in the business community. Referring to the situation in the Pacific, Robert Hall Glover wrote:

> While among these Europeans there were some whose lives were irreproachable, for the most part they were dissolute and un-principled, and left a shameful trail wherever they went. They reveled in the heathen immorality, imported rum wherewith to frenzy the natives, and firearms to add to the horrors of tribal warfare, they deceived and exploited the Islanders and were guilty of the grossest excesses and cruelties.

> Dr. John G. Paton estimated that 70,000 Islanders had been taken from their homes by these slave hunters. The fearless fight which this noble missionary and his fellows waged against this iniquitous traffic won for them the sworn enmity of the unscrupulous traders, to whom may be traced most of the libelous tales about mission-aries which furnish the stock arguments of critics of foreign missions.[4]

Coming closer to our own time, we must recognize that the "Dollar Diplomacy" practiced by Uncle Sam in Latin America in the early part of this century and the economic exploitation still perpetrated in that part of the world have done nothing to enhance the image of the American missionary there. He too is a *gringo*.

5. **Political instability.** There was not much of this in the Roman Empire during the first three centuries of the Christian era. The *Pax Romana* guaranteed the maintenance of law and order throughout the empire, and this greatly facilitated the preaching of the gospel in the apostolic age. However, Roman peace did not extend to every nook and cranny of the empire. There were regions where local bandits lived off the land and were a menace to travelers. Paul speaks of various kinds of peril in a long list of dangers he encountered in the course of his missionary work (2 Cor 11:23-27). Among them he mentioned "danger from robbers." Doubtless more than once he was called on to "take joyfully the spoiling of his goods." John the Baptist was beheaded not for any crime but because he had the courage to speak out against wickedness in high places. Stephen was stoned and thus became the first recorded martyr. Herod Agrippa beheaded James for no better reason than that he decided to vex the church. Peter came close to sharing the same fate (Acts 12). Paul was kept in prison

---

4. Robert Hall Glover, *The Progress of Worldwide Missions* (New York: Harper & Brothers, 1939), p. 303.

285

for two years in Caesarea when Roman justice broke down and Felix succumbed to the temptation of bribery (Acts 24:26).

Jesus warned His disciples that there would be wars and rumors of wars until the end of the age. The missionary enterprise, however, must continue to function within the context of world history regardless of how turbulent that history becomes. The nineteenth century, like the first three centuries, was one of comparative peace—a peace imposed on Africa and Asia by the great imperial powers of Europe. China was, of course, a notable exception. This colonial peace continued right down to World War II. Since then the world picture has altered drastically. In thirty short years some ninety nations have received their independence and joined the United Nations. Most of these are located in the Third World, where the Christian mission has traditionally operated. Here and there small pockets of colonialism remain —Hong Kong, Macao, Panama Canal Zone, Gibraltar, Guantanamo Bay—but these cannot continue forever.

The advent of independence, good and proper though it was, has raised serious problems for the Christian mission and the national churches. Both we and they are going through a period of adjustment, and the end is not yet.

In Africa alone over forty colonies have achieved independence, but only two or three have enjoyed political stability. The others have all experienced some kind of coup, successful or abortive. Civil warfare has raged in Nigeria, Zaire, Sudan, Angola, and Burundi. Church and mission property has been destroyed; church leaders have been killed; others have been imprisoned. Civilian war casualties have been extremely high and war refugees have been numbered in the hundreds of thousands.

The most explosive situation was in Zaire, which got its independence in 1960. On three occasions the situation blew up and three times the missionaries had to evacuate under difficult conditions. On the third occasion many of them didn't quite make it. They were hunted down by the Simbas and killed as they tried to escape. In some cases their bodies were hacked to pieces and thrown to the crocodiles. Over two hundred missionaries lost their lives, the vast majority being Roman Catholics. The question remains to haunt us: Were they killed because they were missionaries? If so, they became martyrs for the faith. Or were they killed because they were foreigners and therefore identified with the Belgian colonial regime? At the Urbana Missionary Convention in 1967 a short memorial service was held for the missionaries killed by the Simbas; but no one was quite sure just what to call them—martyrs, heroes, or simply victims of a civil war.

Teachings of Christ Regarding the Wrath of Man

The wrath of man is a strange thing and it assumes many forms. It has plagued the Christian mission since its inception and it will be with us to the end. Somehow, in the last quarter of this twentieth century we must learn to live not only with tension and terror, but also with danger and death. The servant is not above his Lord, and the missionary is not above his Master.

When Jesus Christ sent out the Twelve (Mt 10), He took the pains to warn them of the kind of opposition they were likely to encounter. He pulled no punches. He told them frankly what kind of treatment they could expect at the hands of a cruel, hostile world. In the course of His discourse He laid down several principles which are as valid today as they were in the first century.

1. Conflict in the Christian mission is inevitable. Jesus said, "Do not think that I have come to bring peace on earth; I have not come to bring peace, but a sword" (Mt 10:34). Again He said, "In the world you have tribulation" (Jn 16:33). Paul taught his converts that the only way into the kingdom is "through many tribulations" (Acts 14:22). He wrote to the fledgling mission church in Thessalonica: "When we could bear it no longer . . . we sent Timothy . . . to establish you in your faith and to exhort you that no one be moved by these afflictions. You yourselves know that this is our lot. For when we were with you, we told you beforehand that we were to suffer affliction; just as it has come to pass" (1 Thess 3:1-4).

In the early church, persecution was the common experience of all Christians. Peter wrote: "Beloved, do not be surprised at the fiery trial which comes upon you to prove you as though something strange were happening to you" (1 Pet 4:12). And Paul goes so far as to say that "all who desire to live a godly life in Christ Jesus will be persecuted" (2 Tim 3:12).

Missionaries have been accused of removing their converts from their cultural milieu, ostracizing them from their friends and relatives, and thus unnecessarily exposing them to persecution. The truth is that it is not the convert who declares war on his family but the family that declares war on him. The new convert is not required to make any change in his life style except where it comes into open and direct conflict with the teachings of Christ. At that point he has no choice. He must make a clean break with immorality and idolatry—the two great sins of the pagan world—and in so doing he necessarily

alienates the affection of his family and friends. If the idolatrous cere-
mony is one that involves the whole clan or village, then he incurs
the wrath of the entire community. It is the price he must pay in order
to be true to Christ.

Family harmony and clan solidarity are most desirable goals and
should be preserved with all vigor, but never at the expense of truth.
No one recognized this more clearly than Jesus. His words are plain:
"I have come to set a man against his father and a daughter against
her mother, and a daughter-in-law against her mother-in-law; and a
man's foes will be those of his own household" (Mt 10:35-36).

The new convert doesn't have to rail against idolatry; he has only
to refuse to engage in it and he will be in trouble. This is written so
large on the pages of the New Testament and occurs so consistently
throughout mission history that it is difficult to see how it can possibly
be overlooked.

**2. Conflict will involve the disciples in personal danger—perhaps
death.** This principle was clearly enunciated by our Lord. "Beware of
men," He said, "for they will deliver you up to councils, and flog you
in their synagogues, and you will be dragged before governors and
kings for my sake, to bear testimony before them and the Gentiles"
(Mt 10:17-18). He went on to say: "Brother will deliver up brother
to death, and the father the child, and children will rise up against
their parents and have them put to death, and you will be hated by
all for my name's sake" (Mt 10:21-22).

How prophetic these words were can be seen from the experience
of Paul and the other apostles. There was hardly a city in which Paul's
ministry did not terminate in a citywide riot that almost cost him his
life. Damascus, Jerusalem, Antioch, Iconium, Lystra, Philippi, Thessalonica, Berea, Corinth, Ephesus—in all of them Paul found that "bonds
and afflictions" awaited him. Our Lord warned us that preaching can
be a dangerous occupation. It was for Stephen, James, Paul, and a
host of others.

The dangers involved included the converts as well as the evangelists. The gospel by its very nature is revolutionary and, therefore,
divisive. The missionary knows that by his preaching of the gospel he
will surely stir up trouble for himself and his converts. Even here in
America, when a Jew becomes a Christian or a Roman Catholic becomes a Protestant there is likely to be a family feud. In non-Christian
cultures the opposition is much greater. A Hindu cannot become a
Christian without incurring the displeasure of his family and friends.
To convert a Muslim to Christianity is almost impossible, for no
Muslim is permitted by his community to change his religion. To do so

is to become an apostate to the faith and a traitor to the country.

In every generation the church has had its martyrs. Stephen led the way, followed by James. Peter and Paul were beheaded in Rome under Nero. If tradition can be trusted, John was the only one of the twelve apostles to die a natural death. The others all met a violent end.

3. Danger or even death is no reason to halt the missionary enterprise. Again we go back to Matthew 10 and listen to the words of our Lord: "Do not fear those who kill the body but cannot kill the soul. . . . When they persecute you in one town, flee to the next. . . . He who finds his life will lose it, and he who loses his life for my sake will find it" (28, 23, 39).

The twelve apostles learned their lesson well, as the New Testament attests. They suffered persecution without retaliating, asking only that they might have the courage to endure (Acts 4:29). They took joyfully the spoiling of their goods, knowing that their real treasures were in heaven (Heb 10:34). They faced beatings and imprisonment with a cheerfulness that left their persecutors completely nonplussed (Acts 4:16). They refused to be intimidated even by death. And those who were called on to seal their testimony with their blood asked only that their enemies be forgiven (Acts 7:60).

Paul's last visit to Jerusalem involved such a high degree of risk that the Christians in Caesarea did their tearful best to dissuade him from proceeding on his way. With characteristic impatience he brushed them aside, saying, "What are you doing, weeping and breaking my heart? For I am ready not only to be imprisoned but even to die at Jerusalem for the name of the Lord Jesus" (Acts 21:13).

Such was the missionary zeal of those first century Christians. With no weapon but truth and no banner but love, they pressed on day after weary day, fording rivers, climbing mountains, crossing deserts, teaching and preaching the most revolutionary message the Roman world had ever heard, until the mighty empire cracked wide open and the emperor bowed the knee to Jesus Christ.

This same missionary passion managed to leap the gap of the centuries and became impregnated in the hearts of the missionary giants of the nineteenth century. William Carey, Adoniram Judson, Hudson Taylor, David Livingstone, Mary Slessor, and a host of others became the true successors of the twelve apostles.

4. Whatever the danger, they could always count on Christ's presence. All power in heaven and in earth was given to Him and He would be with them to the end of the age (Mt 28:18-20). Nothing could happen to them that had not first happened to Him (Jn 15:18).

289

Facing almost inevitable shipwreck, Paul bade his fellow travelers be of good cheer, saying, "For this very night there stood by me an angel of the God to whom I belong and whom I worship" (Acts 27:23). At his trial in Rome all his fellow workers forsook him, but he said, "The Lord stood by me and gave me strength" (2 Tim 4:17).

Missionaries by the thousands have lived and died for Jesus Christ. None was ever forsaken. The presence of the living Christ was so vivid to them that life or death was a matter of indifference. If they lived, they went on serving Christ. If they were killed, they went home to heaven in a blaze of glory. There is no better way to live, and no finer way to die.

> Finding, following, keeping, struggling,
>   Is He sure to bless?
> Saints, apostles, prophets, martyrs,
>   Answer, "Yes."

18

The Role of the Church

There are two aspects to the Christian mission: the divine and the human. In part two, we discussed the first; now we turn to the second. The Scriptures plainly teach the sovereignty of God. They just as plainly teach the responsibility of man. Properly understood, there is no conflict between these two concepts.

God is omnipotent, by which we mean that He is able to do anything that is in accord with His own nature, which is essentially holy. He is the sovereign Lord of the universe and works everything after the counsel of His own will, by His own power, and for His own glory. Of one thing we are sure: God is a moral Being, righteous in all His ways and kind in all His doings (Ps 145:17). His choices and decisions are always determined with reference to these eternal principles of righteousness, goodness, and truth of which His own nature is the eternal and absolutely perfect expression. His only limitations are those that He *chooses to place upon Himself.*

Miracle and Mandate in Creation

In all three of His works—creation, redemption, and judgment—God works according to His own plan and purpose. He is the self-existing, all-sufficient Supreme Ruler who upholds all things by the word of His power. Yet for reasons fully understood only by Himself, He has agreed to place certain limitations on the exercise of His own sovereignty. He has ordained that certain prerogatives belong solely to Him. He has likewise ordained that certain responsibilities belong solely to man. In the work of creation described in Genesis 1 and 2 this division of labor is clearly seen. A simple diagram will illustrate the point.

GOD'S PART—MIRACLE	MAN'S PART—MANDATE
God created the heavens and the earth and prepared the latter for the advent of man.	Man was told to cultivate the garden and subdue the earth.
God created the first forms of plant and animal life.	Once created, these plants and animals reproduced "each after its own kind."
God created the first pair, Adam and Eve, in His own image.	By his own powers of procreation man was able to multiply and replenish the earth.

In each instance God's work involved supernatural power. In no instance did man's work involve supernatural power. The miracle, therefore, belongs to God; the mandate belongs to man.

Obviously man was the apex of God's creation. He was God's masterpiece. It was God's intention that man should live in conformity to the law of God and work in harmony with the purposes of God. God took man into partnership with Himself and made him His representative on the earth. To this end God gave him dominion over the fish of the sea, the fowl of the air, and the beasts of the field. All were placed under the rule and at the service of man. In making this arrangement God was, as it were, sharing a little of His sovereignty with man. In this sense man was crowned with glory and honor (Ps 8:5).

After the Flood God promised Noah that He would maintain on the earth certain physical and atmospheric conditions essential to the preservation of life (Gen 8:22), but this was on the assumption that man would do his part. He would sow the seed in the spring; only then would he reap a harvest in the fall. General Booth of the Salvation Army said: "It takes two to grow a potato—God and the farmer." God could, of course, grow potatoes on His own; but He has never been known to do so. He has provided the sun, the soil, the rain, and the seed. He will do no more. Man must assume his responsibility. He must prepare the soil; he must sow the seed; he must harvest the crop. That is a law that runs uniformly throughout all of nature, and woe betide the farmer who ignores or defies the law.

God is most prodigal when it comes to dispensing His grace. He is most economical when it comes to exercising His power. If man can do the job on his own, God allows him to do so. Indeed, God insists that man use all the resources at his command. Only when these have been employed and have failed does God step in and work a miracle. There are those who deny that God ever works miracles. There are others who think that God should always work miracles and thus relieve them of the obligation to put forth any great effort on their own behalf. God *created* the earth; then He turned it over to man and instructed him to *subdue* it. The first required a miracle, for it was obviously beyond the power of man to achieve. The second was not a miracle; rather it constituted a mandate.

It stands to reason that there are some things that God does all on His own. It's just as well, because there isn't much that we can do to help Him. The seasons come and go and the tides rise and fall without any help from man. The stars in their courses and the planets in their orbits, the earth on its axis—all are maintained and controlled by His almighty power. Man is quite helpless to do anything in those areas.

If there is a human or natural way for God to achieve His purpose, however, He will go that route; and He expects man to follow. In so doing He confers on man a high honor as well as a great obligation, for then man becomes a coworker with God (1 Cor 3:9). It is a staggering thought that God has taken man into partnership with Himself.

This is true in the realm of redemption as well as in the realm of creation. The Old Testament is replete with examples of divine-human cooperation. God always achieves His purpose, but seldom without the active cooperation of His people. When God decided to destroy the world with the Flood He commanded Noah to build the ark. When He decided to liberate His people from the bondage of Egypt He commissioned Moses to be their emancipator. When the theocracy gave way to the monarchy God raised up David, a man after His own heart, who did all His will. When God found it necessary to punish His people He used a heathen king, Nebuchadnezzar, to carry them into captivity. When He saved His people from national destruction He saw to it that Queen Esther was on the throne at the right time. When He wanted to restore His people to the Promised Land after the Captivity He raised up Ezra, Nehemiah, and Zerubbabel.

Miracle and Mandate in Redemption

When we turn to the New Testament we find the same division of labor in the realm of redemption that we noted in the early chapters of Genesis with regard to creation. Here again we find both miracle and mandate, the miracle being the work of God and the mandate being the work of man. The miracle involved three historic events—the incarnation of Jesus Christ, His atoning death, and His bodily resurrection.

The greatest event in the history of the world occurred when God visited this planet in the person of His Son, when He wrapped Himself round with the mantle of our humanity and appeared on earth in the humble guise of a tiny babe wrapped in swaddling clothes and cradled in a manger. In the Incarnation the Son of God became the Son of Man, that through His death and resurrection He might reconcile the world to Himself (2 Cor 5:19).

The New Testament is very clear concerning the purpose of the Incarnation. Jesus said: "The Son of man came to seek and to save the lost" (Lk 19:10). Paul said: "Christ Jesus came into the world to save sinners" (1 Tim 1:15). John said: "The Father has sent His Son as the Savior of the world" (1 Jn 4:14).

The salvation of the human race could not be effected by any other means. It required nothing less than the death and resurrection of the Son of God. The Gospels record with some detail the three-year public ministry of Christ, but the main emphasis is obviously on the last week—Passion Week—which ended with the Crucifixion. His prime purpose in coming into the world was not to live but to die.

The Crucifixion involved two kinds of suffering. During the first three hours on the cross Jesus' sufferings were physical, inflicted by the hand of man. They were an expression of man's hate. During the second three hours His sufferings were spiritual, inflicted by the hand of God. They were an expression of God's wrath. The former He bore without a murmur. Indeed, He rose triumphant above them and prayed for His tormentors. But the latter—the spiritual sufferings—were of an entirely different character. Because they were spiritual they entered into the very sinews of His soul. It was during those three hours that His soul was made an offering for sin (Is 53:10). Peter said: "He himself bore our sins in his own body on the tree" (1 Pet 2:24). Paul went further and said that the sinless One was actually made "to be sin" on our behalf (2 Cor 5:21). Here we come face to face with the mystery—miracle, if you like—of the Atonement. In some mysterious way that we cannot understand, Jesus Christ on the cross was so thoroughly and completely identified with us and our sin that He is said to have been "made sin for us." No theologian has ever been able to plumb the depths of that expression.

> We do not know, we cannot tell
> What pains He had to bear;

But we believe it was for us
He hung and suffered there.

There was none other good enough
To pay the price of sin;
He only could unlock the gate
Of heaven, and let us in.

The third great event was the Resurrection. If the gospel story had ended with the Crucifixion there would have been no salvation, no gospel, no church, and no mission. But it didn't end there; it went on to include the Resurrection. In the New Testament the death and resurrection of Christ are linked together. Paul said He was "put to death for our trespasses and raised for our justification" (Rom 4:25). These two events belong together. Both are essential to the gospel (1 Cor 15:3-4).

The fact that nobody else ever rose from the dead is no reason for rejecting the Resurrection, for it is one of the best authenticated facts of history. But the Resurrection was not the only unique thing about Christ. Everything about Him was unique. His virgin birth, His sinless character, His atoning death, His victorious resurrection, and His glorious ascension into heaven—all were unique. He was the only one who ever rose victorious over life. Why should He not rise victorious over death? It is unthinkable that Jesus, who claimed to be the resurrection and the life and who raised others from the dead, should Himself finally succumb to its power. Everything Jesus ever said or did would lead us to expect a resurrection. If He didn't rise from the dead, He should have!

So much for the miracle of redemption. What about the mandate? This is where the apostles came in. Jesus came to *provide* redemption, not to *preach* it. The preaching is part of the mandate and for that reason belongs to the disciples. That is why Jesus did not remain on earth more than forty days after the Resurrection. So far as we know, Jesus never engaged in public ministry after His resurrection. His redemptive mission, that part of it which involved a miracle and for which He was responsible, was accomplished and He returned to heaven, from where He had come.

But before He left He gave the disciples the missionary mandate, the Great Commission, as recorded in one form or another in all four Gospels and repeated by Luke in Acts 1:8. He had done His part, now they had to do theirs. His part was to *provide* the gospel, theirs was to *proclaim* it. They *could* not provide it, He *would* not proclaim it.

So important was this lesson that Jesus began teaching it to His disciples long before the Crucifixion. From among His many disciples

He chose twelve apostles that they might learn to bear His yoke (Mt 11:29) and ultimately come to share His mission (Jn 20:21). On these twelve men He lavished most of His time, thought, counsel, and prayer. He was training them for the part they were destined to play later on in His redemptive mission. He taught them to pray. He sent them out to preach. He gave them power to heal the sick and to cleanse the lepers. They cast out demons in His name.

Even in the working of His miracles He saw to it that His disciples were identified with Him. On certain occasions He used their resources rather than His own. When performing the very first miracle He enlisted the help of others. He could easily have made the wine out of nothing, but He chose to take water and convert it into wine. And where did He get the water? From a nearby well. The servants could not turn the water into wine, but they could fill the waterpots with water and thus make it possible for Jesus to work the miracle. Jesus insisted on others doing what they could before He employed His power to do what they could not.

Again, when He fed the five thousand He was careful to solicit their cooperation. He performed the miracle in such a way as to teach them another lesson in divine-human cooperation. He began by asking for an inventory of their resources. They were meager, to be sure— five loaves and two fishes. The disciples complained that they were insufficient. But they were finally persuaded to turn them over to Him. And with *their* resources He worked the miracle and the people were fed. He simply multiplied the loaves and fishes they had provided. He could easily have created food out of nothing or turned the stones into bread. Instead He chose to work with and through His disciples, thereby teaching them an important lesson.

The greatest of all miracles was the raising of Lazarus from the dead. Surely Jesus would work this miracle entirely on His own. But no; there were two things the others could do, and Jesus insisted that they do them. One preceded the miracle and the other followed, but both were part of the lesson He wanted to get across to them. So He said to Martha: "Roll away the stone." Why the command? Could He not have raised Lazarus with the stone in its place? Failing that, could He not have rolled away the stone by Himself, either by word or deed? Then why all the bother to get Martha in on the act? Because here, as on other occasions, He wanted to teach the lesson of divine-human cooperation.

After Lazarus was raised from the dead there was one more act to the drama. So Jesus commanded: "Loose him and let him go." Again, Jesus could have done this by Himself with little or no effort, but He wanted to drive home the all-important lesson that they must be prepared to do everything that is humanly possible; then and only then will He perform the miracle.

The Missionary Mandate

Did the disciples learn the lesson well? For the answer we need only turn to the Acts of the Apostles. The miracle of redemption had been completed and Jesus had returned to heaven. The disciples, who in the Gospels were timid, fearful, stupid, and unbelieving, were now full-fledged apostles. The Holy Spirit had come and they had been endued with power from on high. As a result they now manifested a new insight into Scripture (Acts 2:16, 25-28, 34-35), a new courage in witnessing (Acts 4:13, 31), a new power in service (Acts 5:12-16), and a new initiative in action (Acts 5:1-11; 6:1-7).

They realized that the end of the miracle was the beginning of the mandate. Jesus Christ had gone, but the Holy Spirit had come; and in His power they were prepared to take the gospel to the ends of the earth. They began, as Jesus told them, in Jerusalem; and before long they were accused of filling the city with their doctrine (Acts 5:28). From Jerusalem the gospel spread to Judea and Samaria, and in a few years there were churches throughout all Judea, Galilee, and Samaria (Acts 9:31). Peter preached Jesus Christ to Cornelius and thus opened the door of the gospel to the Gentiles (Acts 10). Later Paul appeared on the scene and became the greatest gospel preacher of all time.

It is clear from the Acts that the church was fully aware of the missionary mandate. In those days the church *was* mission. The history of the early church is the history of missions. The entire book of Acts, with the possible exception of chapter 15, deals directly with the proclamation of the gospel and the extension of the kingdom into all parts of the empire. And even chapter 15 has an indirect bearing on missions, for it records the momentous decision of the church to allow the Gentiles into the church as first-class citizens.

The apostles were eyewitnesses of the *miracle* of redemption (1 Jn 1:1-3). They were there when it happened (2 Pet 1:18), and to a man they were persuaded that God was in Christ reconciling the world to Himself (2 Cor 5:19). They were equally sure that the *mandate* of redemption rested on them and that God had committed to them the ministry of reconciliation. Everywhere they went their testimony was the same. "We are ambassadors for Christ, *God making his appeal through us.* We beseech you on behalf of Christ, be reconciled to God" (2 Cor 5:20).

The glorious fact of the gospel is that whoever calls on the name of the Lord shall be saved (Rom 10:13). But Paul asks: "How are men to call upon him in whom they have not believed? And how are they to believe in him of whom they have never heard? And how shall they hear without a preacher?" (Rom 10:14). That is logic, not rhetoric; and the logic is devastating. God has ordained that men should be saved through the preaching of the gospel, even though the gospel may be folly to the Greeks and a stumbling block to the Jews (1 Cor 1:23).

There is not a single line in the book of Acts to suggest that God saves human beings without employing human agents. On the contrary there are several examples of God going to great lengths to secure the active cooperation of one or another of His servants.

The Ethiopian eunuch in chapter 8 is a classic example. A proselyte to Judaism, he had been to Jerusalem to worship in the Temple. While there he had acquired a copy of the Old Testament and was on his way home, still without a knowledge of Christ. Philip the evangelist was called away from a citywide crusade in Samaria and directed by the Holy Spirit to go south into the desert to intercept the eunuch as he traveled back to Ethiopia. Philip found the eunuch reading Isaiah 53. His first question was: "Do you understand what you are reading?" and the reply was, "How can I except someone guides me?" (Acts 8:30-31). In this case even a copy of the Scriptures was not sufficient. He needed someone to explain them to him. This Philip did. The eunuch believed, was baptized, and went on his way rejoicing.

Perhaps the most notable example of the human agent in Christian witness is that of Peter and Cornelius in chapter 10. Cornelius was a Roman centurion, a proselyte to Judaism, and doubtless a seeker after truth. His prayers and his alms prompted God to act on his behalf and make it possible for him to hear the gospel. And how did He do it? He sent an angel all the way from heaven to Caesarea, and when he got there all he could do was give Cornelius the name and address of a *man* who would tell him the gospel. The angel had no mandate to preach—just to inform Cornelius where he could find a preacher.

What about Saul of Tarsus? At first sight it would seem that he was an exception to the rule. But this is more apparent than real. Actually there were at least two human agents used in the conversion of Saul. One was Stephen and the other was Ananias.

Saul's first contact with Stephen came long before the latter was stoned (Acts 7:58). It is almost certain that these two men had more than one face-to-face confrontation in the synagogue of the Cilicians in Jerusalem (Acts 6:9). That Saul was a member (doubtless an elder) of that particular synagogue is a safe assumption. He hailed from Tarsus, the most important city in Cilicia. It is unthinkable that he was not a member of the synagogue made up of his compatriots from that province. If so, he must have been among those who "disputed with Stephen." It is said that Stephen preached with such convincing power that the leaders of the synagogue were unable to hold their own against him. Saul, as a leading rabbi, must have felt the sting of Stephen's words.

But that was not all. When Saul was struck blind at Damascus (ch. 9) a local Christian, Ananias by name, was commissioned by God to contact him, restore his sight, baptize him, and introduce him to the local church. So the mighty Saul of Tarsus, later to become the great apostle Paul, was initiated into the Christian faith by a humble, unknown disciple in Damascus.

The question naturally follows: Is this an invariable rule? If so, what happens when the church falls down on the job and missions are allowed to languish? What about the heathen who have never heard? Are they all lost? The final answer must rest with God, the Judge of all the earth (Gen 18:25), who is righteous in all His ways and holy in all His works (Ps 145:17). It would not be correct to say that Almighty God *cannot* impinge His saving truth directly on the minds of men with sufficient force to bring them to Himself; but we have no reason *from the Scriptures* to believe, or even to assume, that He ever does so. By precept and example the New Testament clearly teaches that the mandate to preach the gospel and make disciples of all nations has been given to the church, and only the church can assume and fulfill that mandate.

Some people have taken comfort from the hope that if one person falls down on his missionary obligation, God will raise up someone else to take his place. There is nothing in Scripture to warrant such a false hope. Jesus has told us that God has given to every man his own work (Mk 13:34). Nowhere does the New Testament suggest that God has His back-up team to step into the gap when the original team fails to follow through. Every Christian has been appointed to his own task. If he is pulled out of line to fill the gap left by some delinquent, what happens to his work?

Then there are those whose understanding of God's sovereignty leads them to believe that come what may, God will achieve His purpose, with or without man's help. God will take care of the heathen, they say. This was the prevailing view among the Reformers and the churches they established in Europe. For almost two hundred years there was practically no missionary outreach from Protestant Europe. As late as William Carey's day the church continued to have a blind spot in regard to world missions. When Carey, in a ministerial meeting, urged the brothers to undertake the conversion of the heathen world, he was politely told by the moderator: "Young man, sit down! When God decides to convert the heathen He will do so without your help or mine."

The moderator was dead wrong. God converted the heathen in India, but *not* without Carey's help. Carey spent almost forty years in India, during which time he helped to translate the Scriptures into thirty-five of the languages of that part of the world. Those thirty-five languages and the people who spoke them had been in existence for several thousand years. The complete Scriptures had been in existence for almost eighteen hundred years, but never until the nineteenth century were those Scriptures made available to those people. And without Carey, and the others who followed him, those people would still be without a knowledge of Christ.

To say, "God will take care of the heathen," and leave it there is to close one's eyes to the clear statements of the Bible and the hard, cold facts of history. The question is not whether God will take care of the heathen, but *how* He does it. He has made it abundantly clear in His Word that it is His will and purpose to care for the heathen *through the church*. The *miracle* of reconciliation was accomplished by the death and resurrection of Christ. The *ministry* of reconciliation has been committed to the church. If the church for any reason fails to fulfill its God-given ministry, the church, and not God, must bear the blame. The church cannot abrogate its responsibility and throw the burden back on God. World evangelization *can* be achieved by human means and manpower. It is both futile and foolish to expect God to achieve by supernatural means what the church can accomplish by human means.

19

The Place of Miracles

Both Judaism and Christianity claim to be supernatural religions. This being so, we should expect miracles to occupy a prominent place in both. This is exactly what we find. The greatest miracle in Judaism was the Exodus from Egypt, which culminated in the crossing of the Red Sea. Repeatedly this unique historic event is referred to in the Old Testament. Jehovah never grew weary of reminding Israel that it was by His strong hand and outstretched arm that He delivered them from the bondage of Egypt. That was the beginning of their national existence as a free people.

Similarly, the greatest miracle in Christianity was the resurrection of Jesus Christ from the dead. That too was a historic event which ushered in a new age. It was the crowning event in the earthly life of our Lord. It was in the power of the Resurrection that the apostles went out to win the world for Christ. Wherever they went they preached "Jesus and the Resurrection."

Miracles in the Ministry of Christ

Miracles played a major role in the ministry of our Lord. In the four Gospels thirty-five separate miracles are described in some detail. In addition He performed many more miracles that are not recorded (Jn 20:30). These miracles demonstrated Christ's power over man, nature, and demons.

There are three words used for miracle in the New Testament. One is the word "sign"; another is "wonder"; the third is "power" or "mighty work." All three of these words are brought together in Hebrews 2:4 and Acts 2:22. Any definition of the term "miracle" would have to include all three ideas. A suggested definition might be: A miracle is a demonstration of supernatural power designed to excite wonder and at the same time to constitute a sign.

A study of the four Gospels will reveal that the miracles of Christ had a fourfold purpose.

1. To authenticate His messianic claim. The Jews of Jesus' day found it exceedingly difficult to accept His claim to be the long-expected Messiah predicted by the Old Testament prophets. He didn't look, sound, or act like a Messiah. His humble origin; His quiet, unassuming manner; His identification with publicans and sinners; His emphasis on meekness, humility, submission, and self-abnegation; His adamant refusal to resort to political action to bring in the kingdom— all these served to confuse the Jews to whom He came preaching the kingdom of God. Finally, in desperation they came to Him and said, "How long will you keep us in suspense? If you are the Christ, tell us plainly." Jesus answered them: "I told you, and you do not believe. The works that I do in my Father's name, they bear witness to me" (Jn 10:24-25).

2. To inculcate faith in the individual. The Gospel of John traces the development of faith in the disciples and unbelief in the Jews. Seven distinct miracles are recorded by John in his Gospel. In each case the miracle serves to strengthen the faith of the disciples (2:11; 4:53; 6:14; 11:45). So powerful an impression was created by the raising of Lazarus that the enemies of Jesus said: "What are we to do? For this man performs many signs. If we let him go on thus, every one will believe in him" (Jn 11:47-48). It goes without saying that not everyone was led to faith in Christ by the miracles. Jesus Himself acknowledged that there are some people who will not be convinced even if the message were conveyed by one who had been raised from the dead (Lk 16:31).

The fact remains that many persons were brought to faith in Christ by the miracles they saw. Indeed, this was the reason given by John for including the seven miracles in his Gospel (Jn 20:31).

3. To induce national repentance (Mt 11:20-24). Jesus presented Himself first to the nation of Israel (Jn 1:11). To them He made the most amazing proposition ever made to any people. It was called the "kingdom of God." It demanded, among other things, repentance. Both John the Baptist and Jesus called for repentance (Mt 3:2; 4:17), but without success. There were individuals, of course, who repented and became part of the kingdom; but the nation as a whole remained unmoved.

The miracles performed by Jesus were different from all others. Never before in the history of Israel had there been such a mighty outpouring of divine grace and power (Jn 15:24). He had every reason therefore to expect that such an overpowering demonstration of God's goodness would lead the nation to repentance. When it failed in its purpose He was obviously disappointed. He remembered that the pagan city of Nineveh had engaged in an act of corporate repentance at the preaching of Jonah; and behold, here was one far greater than Jonah! He went so far as to say that if the mighty works that were done by Him in the cities of Galilee had been done in Tyre and Sidon those cities would have repented (Mt 11:21).

4. **To alleviate human suffering.** The great preponderance of Jesus' miracles were of a humanitarian nature and were designed to meet some specific human need. Jesus never performed a miracle merely to impress people with His great power. In fact, He leaned over backward not to create that impression. Matthew tells us that He went about Galilee healing "every disease and every infirmity among the people" (Mt 4:23).

Teaching, preaching, healing—these were the three main elements in His public ministry. They were intended to meet the needs of the whole man. If men are to enjoy abundant life in the kingdom of God they must be made whole—redeemed from the physical, moral, and spiritual jeopardy of sin. That is what Christ meant by salvation. Peter summed it up beautifully in one short sentence: "He went about doing good" (Acts 10:38).

He healed people because they needed healing. His great heart of love could not bear to see people suffer without doing all in His power to relieve it. And there were no strings attached to His gifts. There was no compulsion in His service. He was not dispensing charity, He was manifesting love. He was not concerned with visible results; those He was content to leave with God. If the recipients of His grace repented and turned to God, they were doubly blessed. Their bodies were healed and their souls were saved. But we know that such persons were comparatively few. The majority were content with the loaves and fishes. They were not interested in the heavenly manna or the living water. Of the ten lepers that were cleansed, only one returned to give God thanks (Lk 17:17).

But this did not greatly perturb Jesus. He went about doing good because this was the will of God for Him. Moreover, goodness is its own reward. So He worked His miracles of healing whether or not the beneficiaries repented. His messianic mission included not only the preaching of the gospel but humanitarian service as well. When John the Baptist expressed doubts about the messianic mission of Jesus, his messengers were told: "Go and tell John what you hear and see: the blind receive their sight and the lame walk, lepers are cleansed and the deaf hear, and the dead are raised up, and the poor have good news preached to them" (Mt 11:2-6). Jesus never used miracles as a bait to get people to believe. He hoped they would believe. He was disappointed when they didn't believe. He never made repentance a prerequisite to physical healing; though He did say on one occasion, "Sin no more, that nothing worse befall you" (Jn 5:14).

Miracles in the Early Church

Did miracles cease with the Ascension? The answer must be: No. In His last discourse with His disciples Jesus said, "Truly, truly, I say to you, he who believes in me will also do the works that I do; and greater works than these will he do, because I go to the Father" (Jn 14:12).

Here Jesus clearly states that miracles were not to cease with the Ascension but were to continue into the church age. In fact, He spoke of "greater works" than He Himself had performed.

There are those who believe the "greater works" to be spiritual rather than physical. The conversion of the soul, they affirm, is a greater miracle than the healing of the body. This may be true, but it in no way invalidates the statement as it stands. Granted, for the sake of argument, that the "greater works" refer to spiritual healing, what are we to do with the first part of the statement: "He who believes in me will also do the works that I do"? These "works" were surely miracles of healing; and these, said Jesus, were to continue.

When we examine the record in the Acts of the Apostles we find that miracles played an important role, especially in the early chapters that deal with the ministry of Peter among the Jews (3:6-8; 4:30; 5:12; 9:32-42). Nor were the apostles the only ones to work miracles. Philip in the city of Samaria not only preached the word, he also performed miracles (Acts 8:7).

The miracles in the early church served much the same purpose as they did in the ministry of Jesus—the inculcation of faith. In almost every instance the miracle is followed by a statement to the effect that "many believed" (Acts 5:14; 9:42).

It is doubtful if Christianity would have survived, much less succeeded, in the Roman Empire without the miracles. Christianity was a new faith trying to compete with the mystery religions which were rampant at that time.

> In the New Testament, the strongest impressions seem to have been made by miracles. . . . Again and again it was a miracle which brought interest and conviction. The visions which preceded the conversion of Cornelius, the blinding of Elymas the sorcerer which convinced the Proconsul Sergius Paulus that Paul and Barnabas could invoke a mightier spirit than he could, the earthquake followed by the magnanimous conduct of the prisoners which led to the baptism of the Philippian jailer and his household, are only some of the many which come immediately to mind.[1]

The early church recognized that the conflict between Christ and Caesar was really a spiritual one. The apostles were not contending "against flesh and blood, but against the principalities, against the powers, against the world rulers of this present darkness, against the spiritual hosts of wickedness in the heavenly places" (Eph 6:12). It is not surprising then that we read of power struggles between the forces of light and the forces of darkness. Several such confrontations are recorded in the Acts, and in each case the superior power of Christianity was demonstrated by a miracle (13:6-12; 16:16-18; 19:11-16).

There are some who discount the importance of miracles in the spread of the gospel. To support their position they point to the fact that miracles are prominent in the early chapters of the Acts of the Apostles when the gospel was preached primarily to the Jews; but later on when the gospel was taken to the Gentile world by Paul, miracles either ceased or were drastically reduced in number.

If the Acts were the only literature we possessed, this point of view would be difficult to refute; but fortunately we have Paul's epistles, and from them we learn many things which Luke did not include in the Acts. Most of Paul's sufferings recorded in 2 Corinthians 11:21-27 are completely overlooked by Luke. Obviously Luke's account of the expansion of the church in the apostolic age is fragmentary.

That the incidence of miracles did not diminish in the fourth and fifth decades of the first century is clear from Paul's account of his own ministry in the Gentile world. Toward the end of his life Paul could say: "For I will not venture to speak of anything except what Christ has wrought through me to win obedience from the Gentiles,

---

1. Kenneth Scott Latourette, *The First Five Centuries*, vol. 1, *A History of the Expansion of Christianity* (New York: Harper & Brothers, 1937), p. 119.

by word and deed, by the power of signs and wonders, by the power of the Holy Spirit, so that from Jerusalem and as far round as Illyricum I have fully preached the gospel of Christ" (Rom 15:18-19). It is a safe assumption that Paul worked many more miracles than the few recorded by Luke in the book of Acts. And what is true of Paul is doubtless true of the other preachers of the gospel (Gal 3:5).

Did the Miracles End with the Apostles?

Bible expositors who take a strong dispensational stand teach that the power to perform miracles was given only to the twelve apostles, and when they passed away miracles naturally ceased. The miracles had served their purpose—namely, to authenticate both the message and the messengers. Moreover, by that time the New Testament books had all been written and the canon, for all practical purposes, was closed. The need, therefore, for miracles had disappeared. The truths of Christianity had been fixed by the apostles and enshrined in their inspired writings. The church now possessed the full corpus of truth; and because the truth is self-authenticating, miracles were no longer needed. Some of these expositors go so far as to maintain that since the death of the apostle John down to the present time there has not been a single bona fide miracle in the history of the church.

There are three problems with this point of view.

1. **Nowhere does the New Testament clearly state that miracles were to cease with the apostles.** The passage usually cited in support of this view is 1 Corinthians 13, where Paul contrasts the permanence of love with the impermanence of prophecy, tongues, and knowledge. These, he says, will pass away; but love will endure forever. Paul does not say *when* these things will pass away, but the "then" and "now" (used twice) in verse 12 surely give us a clue. It is obvious that Paul is contrasting our present earthly state with our future heavenly estate, not the apostolic age with the postapostolic age. One of the three gifts that is to pass away is knowledge. If Paul had in mind the end of the apostolic age, then knowledge along with tongues and prophecy should have ceased with the last apostle; but nobody believes that. It is difficult to see how even tongues and prophecy should have ceased when both were given originally for the edification of the entire church (1 Cor 14:5, 12, 26). We must conclude, then, that there is nothing in the New Testament to support the view that miracles were intended only for the apostolic age.

The writings of the church fathers, especially the apologists, are

306

filled with references to the power of Jesus Christ over all the forces of evil. Tatian, Cyprian, Tertullian, and Origen all make ample reference to the signs and wonders wrought by the church in the name of Christ. There were two dimensions to this power. "It involved healing and exorcisms, and this was a factor of incalculable importance for the advance of the gospel in a world which had inadequate medical services and was oppressed with belief in demon forces of every kind."[2]

It is quite impossible for modern Christians to fully understand and appreciate the extent to which daily life in the Roman Empire was dominated by the fear of demons.

> The whole world and the circumambient atmosphere were filled with devils; not merely idolatry, but every phase and form of life was ruled by them. They sat on thrones, they hovered around cradles. The earth was literally a hell, though it was and continued to be a creation of God. To encounter this hell and all its devils Christians had command of weapons that were invincible. Besides the evidence drawn from the age of their holy scriptures, they pointed to the power of exorcism committed to them, which routed evil spirits, and even forced them to bear witness to the truth of Christianity.[3]

It is clear from the teaching of the New Testament and the writings of the church fathers that the power to perform miracles was not restricted to the twelve apostles. Therefore it doesn't make sense to insist that miracles ceased with the passing of the last apostle.

2. The twelve apostles were not the only ones to perform miracles. Apparently the power to perform miracles was fairly widespread in the early church. Philip was a deacon and he performed miracles in connection with his very effective ministry in the city of Samaria (Acts 8:6). Saul of Tarsus had his sight restored by a humble disciple in Damascus named Ananias (Acts 9:17-18). James in his epistle instructs invalid church members to resort to the church rather than the doctor for physical healing. "Is any among you sick? Let him call for the elders of the church, and let them pray over him, anointing him with oil in the name of the Lord; and the prayer of faith will save the sick man" (Jas 5:14-15).

3. If the gospel needed the support of miracles in apostolic days, why not in later times? If Christianity as preached by the apostles needed the authentication of miracles to get it established in the Roman

---

2. Michael Green, *Evangelism in the Early Church* (Grand Rapids: Eerdmans, 1970), p. 188.
3. Adolph Harnack, *The Mission and Expansion of Christianity* (New York: Harper and Brothers, 1962), pp. 131-32.

Empire, why would the early missionaries to China, India, and Japan not need the same kind of support when they tried to establish Christianity for the first time in a strange and hostile empire?

Indeed, it would seem that the need for miracles was greater in the Chinese Empire than in the Roman Empire. Paul and his colleagues had many favorable factors completely missing in China. Paul had no cultural barrier to cross, no strange and difficult language to learn, no passport to worry about. Travel was easy and comparatively safe. Audiences were not hard to find. The synagogues established by the Jews of the Diaspora provided him with a unique opportunity which he never failed to embrace. The Jews had already prepared the way for the spread of the gospel by introducing into the Mediterranean world the concept of monotheism, the practice of morality, the institution of the Sabbath, and the expectation of a coming Savior. Moreover, the Old Testament had long since been translated into Greek, the *lingua franca* of the Roman world.

Besides all this, Paul enjoyed the protection of the Roman authorities. On more than one occasion they saved him from death at the hands of his compatriots. Paul was a good Jew and a proud Roman citizen. Politically, religiously, and culturally he felt at home wherever he went.

All this was in stark contrast to the situation in China, where the missionaries were regarded as "barbarians" and treated accordingly. On four separate occasions Christianity was introduced into China. In each instance it flourished for a time but withered when persecution broke out. If the Christian message needed the authentication of miracles anywhere, surely it was in China, the home of the oldest, highest, and most enduring civilization in history.

Christianity as Truth and Power

Two things are necessary to establish Christianity in virgin territory, especially where the climate is unfavorable and the soil is unproductive.

1. **A declaration of truth.** Christianity is a revealed religion with solid cognitive content. It contains certain propositional truths, the sum total of which is called by Paul "the truth of the gospel" (Gal 2:5). Paul and the other apostles believed that in the gospel they possessed *the* truth concerning God, man, sin, and salvation. Paul believed that when he preached the gospel, he was preaching the truth. So sure was he of his conviction in this matter that he could pronounce a curse on anyone—man or angel—who dared to preach what he called

"another gospel" (Gal 1:8). He testified to the Ephesian elders that during his three years among them he "did not shrink from declaring the whole counsel of God" (Acts 20:27).

No New Testament writer is clearer than John when it comes to the proclamation of the gospel. In the prologue to his First Epistle he says: "That which was from the beginning, which we have heard, which we have seen with our eyes, which we have looked upon and touched with our hands—the life was made manifest and we saw it and testify to it, and proclaim to you the eternal life which was with the Father and was made manifest to us—that which we have seen and heard we proclaim also to you" (1 Jn 1:1-3).

The Christian gospel with its propositional truths must be proclaimed in no uncertain terms. It must be articulated line upon line and precept upon precept so that intelligent, saving faith can be exercised. The truth of the gospel must be proclaimed with such clarity and cogency that the hearers will be obliged to make up their minds for or against Jesus Christ.

It is fair to ask: Is a declaration of the truth *all* that is required when Christianity is introduced to a non-Christian people for the first time? Is abstract truth *always* self-authenticating? Paul admits that the Jews demand a sign and the Greeks seek after wisdom (1 Cor 1:22). When he preached the gospel he endeavored to meet the needs of both groups. He wrote: "We preach Christ crucified, a stumbling block to Jews and folly to Gentiles; but to those who are called, both Jews and Greeks, Christ the *power* of God and the *wisdom* of God" (1 Cor 1:23-24).

2. **A demonstration of power.** Western thought is concerned with truth and the Western mind is intrigued by reason. Hence our emphasis on logic. We vainly imagine that if we can win the argument we will win the adversary. The Oriental mind, on the other hand, is not primarily interested in truth, still less in logic. Christian theology has emphasized truth to the neglect of power; the Oriental religions have emphasized power to the neglect of truth. Both are right in what they include but wrong in what they omit. Religion to be viable must be vital as well as valid.

Paul was both a theologian and a missionary. He was a better theologian because he was a missionary, and he was a better missionary because he was a theologian. The missionary in him kept the theologian from being completely preoccupied with truth, and the theologian in him kept the missionary from being solely enamored of power. As missionary-theologian Paul maintained a healthy balance between truth and power. Little wonder that he was the greatest missionary and the greatest theologian of the Christian church.

This balance is clearly seen in his statement to the sophisticated Corinthians, who were in danger of exalting knowledge at the expense of power. "When I came to you, brethren, I did not come proclaiming to you the testimony of God in lofty words or wisdom. For I decided to know nothing among you except Jesus Christ and him crucified. And I was with you in weakness and in much fear and trembling; and my speech and my message were not in plausible words of wisdom, but in *the demonstration of the Spirit and power,* that your faith might not rest in the wisdom of men but in the power of God" (1 Cor 2:1-5).

The gospel is not only the truth of God (Col 1:5), it is also the power of God (Rom 1:16). Both ideas were present in the proclamation of the gospel in the book of Acts. "And the multitudes with one accord gave heed to what was said by Philip, when they *heard* him and *saw* the signs which he did" (8:6). We have a similar situation with Paul at the outset of his first missionary journey. "Then the proconsul believed when he *saw* what had occurred [a miracle] for he was astonished at the *teaching* of the Lord" (13:12). It was a demonstration of power that led to his acceptance of the truth.

The Lord in His ministry encountered a good deal of unbelief. He recognized the intellectual problems inherent in the acceptance of the gospel and was willing to accommodate Himself to hardness of heart on the part of His hearers. We have a remarkable example of this in Mark 2. When they brought to Him a man sick of the palsy Jesus said to him: "My son, your sins are forgiven." But the scribes standing by objected: "Why does this man speak thus? It is blasphemy! Who can forgive sins but God alone?" So Jesus answered: "Which is easier, to say to the paralytic, 'Your sins are forgiven,' or to say, 'Rise, take up your pallet and walk'? But that you may know that the Son of man has authority on earth to forgive sins"—he said to the paralytic —"I say to you, rise, take up your pallet and go home." The result was that they were all amazed and glorified God, saying, "We never saw anything like this" (Mk 2:12).

The statement about the forgiveness of sins was a declaration of truth, but because it was in the realm of the metaphysical it could not be proved—or disproved. It was not susceptible to tangible proof. But the miracle that followed was a different matter. That they could see and understand, and they could not refute it. The interesting thing is that Jesus, knowing their thoughts, was willing to go the second mile and provide the kind of proof they could appreciate.

Truth and power—they are both part of the gospel; and what God has joined together let no man put asunder. It is very instructive that when Jesus gave the Great Commission to the apostles and told them to go into all the world and make disciples of all nations, He prefaced the command with the statement: "All power in heaven and in earth is given unto me. Go ye therefore" (Mt 28:18-19).

The Situation in Modern Missions

After 250 years of missions in Asia only about 3 per cent of the population are professing Christians, and that includes all who name the name of Christ. What is the reason for the paucity of results? There are many factors that enter into the picture, but the greatest single factor has been our lack of spiritual power.

In that part of the world we came into conflict with the great ethnic religions of antiquity, most of which antedate Christianity by hundreds of years. They have their sacred scriptures, which they regard as inspired. They have their founders, philosophers, gurus, bodhisattvas, saints, saviors, and sages. They have their ornate temples, pagodas, shrines, and stupas. They have their sacred rivers and mountains. Through the centuries they have acquired land, wealth, power, and prestige. Their devotees, numbered in the hundreds of millions, believe their religion to be true and all other religions to be false in part or in whole.

Into this religious milieu comes the Christian missionary preaching Jesus Christ as *the* way, *the* truth, and *the* life. Upon examination it is discovered that this Jesus, who is reputed to be the Savior of the world, was born in a stable, lived in obscurity among a captive people, plied His trade as a carpenter, and died the death of a common criminal. In His short lifetime He wrote no books, endowed no institutions, and erected no monuments. In fact, He did nothing to perpetuate the memory of His own name. And at the end He was betrayed by one of His disciples, disowned by another, deserted by His friends, mocked by His enemies, and finally rejected by the leaders of His own nation. When it was all over He was buried in a borrowed grave by two disciples who didn't have the courage to confess him openly. His followers claimed that He rose from the dead after three days; but that obviously is a myth, for nobody else before or since ever rose from the dead.

How is the missionary to persuade the Hindu, or the Buddhist, or the Confucianist that this Jesus is indeed the Son of God, who in the Incarnation became the Son of Man that through His ignominious death on the cross He might become the Savior of the world? Merely by saying so? Hardly. For thousands of years these non-Christians have believed that their religion is true. Now they are asked to acknowledge that it is false or at least partly false, and that this strange, new religion is true.

If it required "special" miracles by the hand of Paul to make any impression on the vast idolatrous system in Ephesus (Acts 19:11), how could the Christian missionary in India or China expect to succeed without them? Is it any easier to convert an impeccable Brahmin priest or a proud Confucian scholar than to convert the Philippian jailor or the proconsul of Cyprus or the idolaters of Ephesus? These people were all brought to faith in Christ when a declaration of truth was accompanied by a demonstration of power. It is in Romans that we find the clearest definition of the *truth* of the gospel that Paul called "my gospel." Yet it is in that same epistle that Paul declares: "I am not ashamed of the gospel for it is the *power* of God for salvation to everyone who has faith" (Rom 1:16).

The Role of Medical Missions

One of the truly bright spots in the Christian mission has been the medical work carried on by practically every mission in the world. The doctors and nurses who manned the medical institutions deserve the highest praise. They sought diligently to minister to both the physical and the spiritual needs of the patients, some of whom became Christians. But many mission leaders have come to the conclusion that the returns from our institutional work—educational as well as medical—have not been commensurate with the enormous investment in men and money.

When Thomas Aquinas visited the Pope in Rome, the Holy Father showed him the Vatican with all its wealth and remarked: "The day is gone when my predecessor had to say, 'Silver and gold have I none.'" "Yes," replied Aquinas, "and the day is also gone when your predecessor could say, 'In the name of Jesus of Nazareth rise up and walk.'"

The accusation can be leveled at all branches of the Christian church of our day. We have all kinds of power—ecclesiastical, economic, social, and political; but we have precious little spiritual power. We can no longer say: "In the name of Jesus of Nazareth rise up and walk." So when we took the gospel to the non-Christian world we opened hospitals and used modern scientific medicine to do what the early church accomplished largely by miracles. The hospitals helped, to be sure; but there was no clear demonstration of spiritual power to back up the gospel message. The people were impressed with our medical skill and were deeply grateful for our compassion and concern, but in their eyes there was no *necessary connection* between the message of the evangelist and the medical skill of the doctor.

Medical missions are not wrong nor should they be discontinued. Neither should they represent the sole method of healing. There is no conflict between divine healing and medical science. Luke was a physician and accompanied Paul on his missionary journeys. It is inconceivable that Luke did not use his medical skill on at least some occasions. It is also a fact that Paul performed miracles without the help of Luke—and it was Paul's miracles and not Luke's medicine that won the day. It is unlikely that Paul included Luke's medical successes in the "sights and wonders" referred to in Romans 15:19.

As it was in the first century, so it is today. The greatest victories are won where the truth of the gospel is backed up with a demonstration of power. In 1973 Jacques Giraud, a French evangelist, was invited to conduct an evangelistic campaign in Abidjan, the capital of the Ivory Coast. The services were held in the municipal soccer stadium. Each day 30,000 people crowded into the facility. During the first week the evangelist preached on the power of Jesus to *heal*. Hundreds responded and were healed. The meetings became the talk of the town. During the second week he preached on the power of Jesus to *save,* warning them that the salvation of the soul is far more important than the healing of the body. Hundreds responded and over 1500 were baptized. Two thousand letters were received requesting prayer or offering testimony to what God had done. The Bible Society sold out its entire stock: 12,000 New Testaments, 2,000 Bibles, and 20,000 Gospels. Never in the history of the Ivory Coast was so much Christian literature sold in so short a time.

Rightly or wrongly, the people of the Third World identify religion with power. They live close to nature and the veil between the seen and the unseen world is very thin. The natural and the supernatural are both a very real part of human existence. Consequently they don't have all the hang-ups that we in the West have when it comes to religious experience. In their traditional religions they have the medicine man, the witch doctor, and the sorcerer to whom they go in times of drought, disease, disaster, and death. They are of a very practical turn of mind. If religion works, they want it; if it doesn't, they don't. They are not interested in a religion that merely promises them "pie in the sky by and by." They want something that will meet their needs and solve their problems here and now.

It is regrettable that the modern missionary movement, with few exceptions, has failed to demonstrate the *power* as well as the *truth* of the gospel.

313

20

The Power of Prayer

In one of His parables Jesus taught His disciples that men "ought always to pray and not to lose heart" (Lk 18:1). Heart failure is Killer No. 1 in the physical realm; it is also Killer No. 1 in the spiritual realm. Discouragement is the most powerful weapon in the devil's arsenal. It is a weapon he has used with great dexterity and effectiveness from the beginning of time. Moses, David, Elijah, and Jeremiah all had their times of discouragement when they were ready to throw in the towel. Even today more men leave the ministry because of discouragement than for any other single reason.

There are three good reasons why we should pray without ceasing. First, prayer is always *possible*. There are times when, because of sickness or other circumstances over which we have no control, we are unable to engage in the usual forms of Christian service. But it is always possible to pray. Satan can build a wall around us and seal us off from all contact with fellow Christians, but he can never build a roof over our heads and cut us off from fellowship with God. Second, prayer is always *proper*. There is no conceivable situation in which prayer is out of place. It matters not whether the circumstance be one of pleasure or pain, birth or death, joy or sorrow; prayer is always right and proper. Third, prayer is always *profitable*. It always pays to pray. "The prayer of a righteous man has great power in its effects" (Jas 5:16). One of the most astounding statements Jesus ever made is, "If you ask anything in my name, I will do it" (Jn 14:14). Time spent in prayer is never wasted. After a lifetime of service in Burma,

Judson could say, "I never prayed sincerely and earnestly for anything, but it came at some time."[1]

Prayer in the Life of Christ

"Nowhere does a man betray the quality of his spiritual life more clearly than in his praying."[2] Here, as in every other aspect of our lives, Jesus Christ is our great example. He was the first and great Missionary (Heb 3:1), and prayer played a vital role in His earthly life and ministry. Although He was the Son of God and possessed all authority in heaven and on earth, He lived a life of complete dependence on God. Prayer to Him was indeed His "vital breath," His "native air." Ten times in the Gospel of Luke we find Him in the act of prayer. Before choosing His twelve apostles, He spent the entire night in prayer (Lk 6:12). When He fed the five thousand, He prayed (Lk 9:16). When He raised Lazarus from the dead, He prayed (Jn 11:41-42). Three of His seven sayings on the cross were prayers. From first to last He lived a life of prayer, and by so doing He left us an example that we should do likewise.

> Was prayer fundamental in his life and work or was it just one of his many activities? We have no doctrinal statement about this in the New Testament, but from some passages we can conclude that our Lord not only needed prayer, but that all his words and deeds, his miracles and teachings were answers to prayer and grew out of his continual and perfect inner prayer life.[3]

In the New Testament there is a direct connection between prayer and missions. Jesus not only prayed before choosing His twelve apostles, but He instructed His disciples to pray "the Lord of the harvest to send out laborers into His harvest" (Mt 9:38). The mission is God's mission. He originated the idea. He controls the operation. He provides the power. He chooses the workers and sends them out. Some are sent to sow and others to reap (Jn 4:35-38). But all are sent by Him—in answer to the church's prayer.

Prayer in the Early Church

When we study the formative years of the early church as

---

1. Robert E. Speer, *Missionary Principles and Practice* (New York: Revell, 1902), p. 476.
2. J. Oswald Sanders, *Spiritual Manpower* (Chicago: Moody Press, 1965), p. 207.
3. *Let the Earth Hear His Voice*, ed. J. D. Douglas (Minneapolis: World Wide Publications, 1974), p. 1185.

described in the Acts of the Apostles we get a definite impression that the early church was both a missionary church and a praying church. The ten days between the Ascension and Pentecost were spent in prayer (Acts 1:14). The apostles were told by Jesus to remain in Jerusalem until they were endued with power from on high (Lk 24:49). They were not specifically told to pray, but to wait; but what better way to spend the waiting time than to pray? Pentecost, the birthday of the church, was ushered in by a ten-day period of prayer.

The coming of the Holy Spirit in all His fullness did nothing to lessen their dependence on prayer. In fact, it heightened their sense of dependence; so we find the church engaged almost continually in prayer. Immediately following Pentecost, we are told, the disciples "devoted themselves to the apostles' teaching and fellowship, to the breaking of bread and the prayers" (Acts 2:42). After that we find Peter and John going up to the Temple "at the hour of prayer" (Acts 3:1). After their first encounter with persecution, Peter and John went back to the upper room and with the infant church found solace in prayer (Acts 4:23-24). When the first big internal crisis occurred, again the apostles and the church resorted to prayer (Acts 6:4). Peter received the greatest vision of his life in a few moments of prayer on the housetop in Joppa while the noonday meal was being prepared (Acts 10:9). It would appear that prayer was the disciples' chief occupation, and to it they repeatedly returned. When Barnabas and Saul were set apart for their missionary work, the church in Antioch was engaged in prayer (Acts 13:1-3).

And what can be said of the apostle Paul? We think of him as a great missionary and theologian, but he was first and last a man of prayer. The first thing recorded of him after his conversion was "Behold, he is praying" (Acts 9:11). In his last letter, written shortly before his death, he wrote to Timothy: "I remember you constantly in my prayers" (2 Tim 1:3). He said the same about the converts that he won and the churches he founded in all parts of the Roman world (Rom 1:9-10; Eph 1:15-16; Phil 1:3-4; Col 1:9; 1 Thess 1:2; 2:13). His very life was bound up with the life of his converts. He rejoiced when they stood fast (1 Thess 3:6-10) and grieved when they went astray (2 Cor 2:1-4). Indeed, he went so far as to say: "Now we live if you stand fast in the Lord" (1 Thess 3:8). Day and night, with many tears, he remembered them in his prayers. Nor did he think he had any monopoly on the privilege or power of prayer. He attached equal importance to the prayers of his converts, and on more than one occasion asked them to pray for him (Eph 6:19; 2 Thess 3:1; Rom 15:30).

Prayer is one of the spiritual weapons in the Christian's armory as outlined by Paul in Ephesians 6:10-20. He reminds his readers that "we are not contending against flesh and blood, but against the principalities, against the powers, against the world rulers of this present darkness, against the spiritual hosts of wickedness in the heavenly places." It is imperative that the Christian, especially the missionary, in the forefront of the battle for the souls of men, be clothed in the "whole armor of God." Included in the armor is the weapon of prayer. "Pray at all times in the Spirit with all prayer and supplication. To that end keep alert with all perseverance, making supplication for all the saints, and also for me, that utterance may be given me in opening my mouth boldly to proclaim the mystery of the gospel, for which I am an ambassador in chains; that I may declare it boldly, as I ought to speak." Even the great, courageous apostle felt the need of moral support that comes from intercessory prayer. The success of his mission depended on the prayer support of his converts.

Writing later to his favorite colleague, Timothy, then in charge of the church in Ephesus, he urged that "supplications, prayers, intercessions, and thanksgivings be made for all men, for kings and all who are in high positions, that we may lead a quiet and peaceable life." Why was law and order so important? So that the church might enjoy a period of peace and prosperity? No; but because God "desires all men to be saved and to come to the knowledge of the truth" (1 Tim 2:1-4). Peace and tranquility are not an end in themselves, they are a means to an end—the proclamation of the gospel and the salvation of the lost. Peace, not war, is conducive to the work of evangelism; therefore pray for peace.

It has often been said that the blood of the martyrs is the seed of the church. That is true, but only up to a certain point. A little persecution is a good thing for the church; but widespread, prolonged persecution, especially the kind engendered by the state, has often proved debilitating, sometimes devastating. Other things being equal, the church thrives best in a peaceful climate that is conducive to growth.

This is precisely what happened during the period of peace following the conversion of Saul of Tarsus. With his conversion the organized persecution of the churches ceased, and Luke includes a pertinent footnote in Acts 9:31: "So the church throughout all Judea and Galilee and Samaria had peace and was built up; and walking in the fear of the Lord and in the comfort of the Holy Spirit it was multiplied."

Prayer in Modern Missions

No one can study the development of the modern missionary movement and not be impressed with the extent to which prayer and missions have gone hand in hand. "In no realm does the primacy of prayer shine forth more regally than in the story of missionary progress. Every fresh putting forth of missionary energy has been preceded by believing prayer. The seed of the missionary enterprise has been planted and has germinated in the hearts of believing, praying disciples."[4]

The modern missionary movement was born in a revival of prayer. Justinian Welz was one of the few persons to raise a prophetic voice on behalf of missions in the seventeenth century. In one of his essays he wrote:

> Whoever will be used in the worthy activity of spreading the evangelical faith must be diligent in prayer in all his doings. If he wishes to undertake this office, he must begin with prayer. If he wishes to accomplish anything glorious, he must adhere to it with persistent prayer to his dearest master, Jesus Christ. If anything is to reach a blessed conclusion, he must seek to attain it through devout prayer. Yea, all his doing must be concluded in humble prayer. It is prayer that can encourage a heart to begin Christian work. It is prayer that emboldens a man amid the dangers of a journey. It is prayer that hinders the persecutor and lays a bit in his mouth. It is prayer that gives power to the preached word to bring it about. It is prayer that compels heretics to hearken to the gospel and pure doctrine. It is prayer—only prayer—that softens the stony heathen heart and makes it fit to obey Christ.[5]

Justinian Welz was a voice crying in the wilderness. Few people paid any attention to him; consequently the beginning of the modern missionary movement had to await the arrival of the Pietist Movement under the leadership of Jacob Spener and August Francke. The outstanding feature of the Pietist Movement was the cultivation of the inner life by Bible study and prayer.

The modern missionary movement may be said to have begun in earnest with the Moravians. When a group of exiled Moravians under Christian David arrived in Saxony in 1722, Count Zinzendorf gave them shelter on his estate, later known as *Herrnhut*—the Lord's Watch. The colony developed rapidly as additional exiles arrived, built homes and workshops, dug wells, laid out roads, established orphanages, and erected a meeting house and school. Under the dynamic leadership of Zinzendorf, *Herrnhut* became the nerve center of a worldwide missionary movement unique in the history of the church.

It all began with prayer. A three-month revival at *Herrnhut* in the summer of 1727 led to the establishment of a round-the-clock prayer

4. Helen B. Montgomery, *Prayer and Missions* (West Medford, Mass.: The Central Committee of the United Study of Foreign Missions, 1924), p. 75.
5. James A. Scherer, *Justinian Welz: Essays by an Early Prophet of Mission* (Grand Rapids: Eerdmans, 1969), pp. 70-71.

watch, seven days a week, by twenty-four Single Brothers and twenty-four Single Sisters. This prayer watch continued without interruption for *one hundred years!* Their first mission (1732) was to the Negro slaves on the Danish island of St. Thomas in the Virgin Islands. Greenland was next in 1733. "Within twenty years of the commencement of their missionary work the Moravian Brethren had started more missions than Anglicans and Protestants had started during the two preceding centuries."[6]

About the same time the Holy Spirit was moving among the churches in England. In 1723 Robert Millar, a Presbyterian minister in Paisley, wrote *A History of the Propagation of Christianity and the Overthrow of Paganism,* in which he advocated intercession as the primary means of converting the heathen. This book was soon followed by the rise of Methodism, whose first society was formed in 1739. The great Methodist revival, which spread rapidly over the English-speaking world, was the first evidence of the church's interest in world missions. It began in the hearts of a little group of students in Oxford University who met regularly for prayer and Bible study. The idea soon caught on. Prayer groups began meeting all over the British Isles. Their chief petition was for the conversion of the heathen world.

In 1746 a memorial was sent to Boston inviting the Christians there to enter into a seven-year "Concert of Prayer" for missionary work. The memorial evoked a ready response from Jonathan Edwards, who the following year issued a call to all believers to engage in intercessory prayer for the spread of the gospel throughout the world.

Some thirty years later, in 1783, Edwards' pamphlet was introduced to the churches in England by John Sutcliff in the Northamptonshire Ministerial Association. Following the reading of the pamphlet, a motion was made that all Baptist churches and ministers set aside the first Monday of each month for united intercession for the heathen world. It read:

> Let the whole interest of the Redeemer be affectionately remembered, and the spread of the Gospel to the most distant parts of the habitable globe be the object of your most fervent requests. We shall rejoice if any other Christian societies of our own or other denominations will unite with us, and we do now invite them to join most cordially heart and hand in the attempt. Who can tell what the consequences of such a united effort in prayer may be.[7]

---

6. Charles H. Robinson, *History of Christian Missions* (New York: Scribners, 1915), p. 50.
7. Montgomery, *Prayer and Missions*, p. 78.

The "consequences" were not long in coming. In 1792 William Carey sailed for India under the Baptist Missionary Society. Other societies were formed in rapid succession: the London Missionary Society (1795), the Scottish and Glasgow Missionary Societies (1796), the Netherlands Missionary Society (1797), and the Church Missionary Society (1799).

In the meantime on this side of the Atlantic the Spirit of God was moving among a group of students at Williams College in Williamstown, Massachusetts. Samuel J. Mills and half a dozen other students met frequently for prayer, Bible study, and discussion regarding a mission to the heathen world. One day on their way to prayer they were caught in a thunderstorm and took shelter in the lee of a nearby haystack. There they had their usual time of prayer for the conversion of the heathen. When the storm was over, Mills stood up and said: "We can do it if we will." They then resolved to become America's first foreign missionaries and signed a pledge to that effect.

Prayer and Revival on the Mission Field

The first mission field of the London Missionary Society in 1795 was the Society Islands in the Pacific Ocean. Eighteen members of the first party of thirty landed on Tahiti. After an encouraging beginning the situation worsened. King Pomare turned against the missionaries. Some were killed, others fled, and some died of disease. In 1804 the king died and was succeeded by his son, Pomare II, who was even more cruel than his father, and harassed and persecuted the missionaries to the point where they began to despair.

Just when the situation looked hopeless, friends back in London called for a special meeting to pray specifically for the conversion of King Pomare. That was in July 1812. That same month the king was converted and became an ardent supporter of Christian missions. At his own expense he built a large church where, in the presence of four thousand of his subjects, he was baptized. In a comparatively short time Tahiti became predominantly Christian.

Hudson Taylor, founder of the China Inland Mission, was above all else a man of prayer. His philosophy of the Christian life was summed up in four phrases: There is a living God; He has spoken in His Word; He means what He says; He always keeps His promise. Taylor gave fifty years of loving service to the people of inland China. During that time the sun never rose in China without finding Hudson Taylor on his knees. For over one hundred years the China Inland Mission (now the Overseas Missionary Fellowship) has followed the principle laid down by its founder—moving men through God by prayer alone. In 1889 the mission prayed for one hundred new workers and got them. In the depth of the Depression (1932-33), when other missions were retrenching, the mission prayed for two hundred new workers—and got them!

Hudson Taylor is often referred to as the "father of faith missions," but that honor really goes to John Evangelist Gossner, a German pastor in Berlin, who at the age of sixty-three founded the Gossner Mission in 1836. During the remainder of his life Gossner, by prayer alone, sent out and supported two hundred missionaries, including wives. At his funeral it was said of him that "he prayed mission stations into being, and missionaries into faith; he prayed open the hearts of the rich, and gold from the most distant lands."

Pastor Louis Harms, founder of the Hermannsburg Mission, over a period of thirty years recruited and supported 350 missionaries who planted a church of more than 13,000 members. In his journal he wrote: "Last year, 1857, I needed for the mission fifteen thousand crowns, and the Lord gave me that and sixty over. This year I need double, and the Lord has given me double and one hundred and forty over."

On the whole, Christian missions have not been very successful on the great continent of Asia. After 250 years of Protestant missionary work, and a much longer period of Roman Catholic missions, slightly less than 3 per cent of the population are professing Christians. One bright spot, however, has been Korea. There church growth has been described as "wildfire." By far the strongest churches in Asia are in Korea, and the growth continues unabated. Several factors have contributed to this phenomenal growth, but the greatest single factor would have to be the great revival of 1907.

For five months prior to that time both missionaries and native Christians had been meeting daily for prayer, seeking for a deeper, more satisfying experience of the abundant life in Christ. On January 14 the Holy Spirit fell on the seven hundred Christians gathered in Pyongyang for the annual Bible classes conducted by the missionaries. There is no doubt that the revival was the direct result of five months of earnest prayer.

The revival lasted for two weeks, during which all other work was suspended and the Christians gave themselves to prayer, confession, and restitution. The revival spread to Seoul and other cities of Korea and beyond the borders of Korea into Manchuria and China. To this day the church in Korea has a quality of spiritual life seldom seen in other parts of the world. Many of the churches have an early morning prayer service *every day of the year,* with several hundred in attendance. There is no doubt that the vitality of the Korean church can be traced directly to the revival of 1907 and the enormous volume of prayer engendered at that time.

Three things have always gone together: prayer, revival, and missions. If church history has taught us anything it is that a moribund church can never engage in the task of worldwide missions. It must be revived in order to be ready for its chief task. And revival doesn't "just happen." It is always preceded by a period of prolonged and earnest prayer. This is just as true today as it was two hundred or two thousand years ago.

As recently as August 1972 the church leaders in the Ivory Coast set aside two hours each morning for prayer. The missionaries were not invited to these meetings. Indeed, they were unaware that they were going on. The prayer meetings lasted for several months. When Richard Harvey, Christian and Missionary Alliance pastor, visited the Ivory Coast in November, revival broke out. Missionaries, pastors, and church leaders were all involved. There was a great breaking and melting, and church and mission were united as never before. Six months later a French evangelist, Jacques Giraud, held a six-week evangelistic campaign in the Ivory Coast and thousands were swept into the kingdom.

We generally think of William Carey as the father of modern missions, and everyone knows of his monumental work in India; but few know about his invalid sister at home who stood behind him in daily intercession for many years. Everyone knows of Hudson Taylor and the great China Inland Mission he founded, but few are aware of the fact that both his mother and his sister at home were prayer warriors of the first order and gave themselves unstintingly in prayer on his behalf.

J. O. Fraser labored in Lisuland in southwest China as a pioneer missionary in the 1920s. He did everything in his power to reach those primitive people with the gospel, but there was no response. Finally, in desperation he wrote home to his praying friends:

> The church of Protestant countries is well able to nourish the infant church of the Orient by a steady and powerful volume of intercessory prayer.... I am not asking you to give "help" in prayer as a sort of sideline, but I am trying to roll the *main responsibility* of this prayer warfare on you. I want you to take the BURDEN of these people on your shoulders. I want you to wrestle with God for them.... Anything must be done rather than let this prayer-service be dropped or even allowed to stagnate.[8]

8. Frank Houghton, *The Fire Burns On* (London: Lutterworth Press, 1965), p. 153.

It was not long after this that prayer was answered. The breakthrough came and thousands of Lisu became Christians.

Prayer, the Perennial Source of Power

Intercessory prayer is fast becoming a lost art in the Christian church. Many churches no longer have a midweek prayer service, and those that do must be content with the "faithful few" who turn up rain or shine. But even they don't seem to have any great burden for the evangelization of the world. The prayers offered at such meetings usually revolve around the physical and material needs of the local congregation. Only now and again, when some tragedy strikes the mission field, do the folks at home get down to the business of praying for missions around the world. "The evangelization of the world in this generation depends first of all upon a revival of prayer. Deeper than the need for men, deeper far than the need for money; deep down at the bottom of our spiritless life is the need for the forgotten secret of prevailing, worldwide prayer."[9]

What the Christian mission needs more than anything else today is a revival of prayer. Our generation has lost its sense of dependence on God. We have more knowledge, expertise, tools, money, committees, land, and buildings than the church in any previous age. We have ecclesiastical power, economic power, and political power—everything but spiritual power. We are like the church of Laodicea: rich, prosperous, and needing nothing (Rev 3:17)—or so we imagine. Human effort and ingenuity have displaced prayer. This is especially true of American Christians, who tend to be activists. We would sooner work than think, converse than commune, plan than pray. So we multiply committees and organizations and then spend most of our time and effort keeping the organizations working and the committees busy. To be energetic, we think, is to be effective. Little time is left for prayer, especially intercessory prayer. All the while God is trying to tell us that it is not by might nor by power but by His Spirit (Zech 4:6).

> Whatever else a careful reading of vital mission history tells us, it is this: behind every outburst of real mission in the life of the church, we find a company or companies of believing men and women who have prayed until the Spirit of God has come upon them; then in the Spirit's power they have gone out to witness the mighty acts of God. In every instance the new movement to mission parallels the waiting, praying group of disciples in the Jerusalem upper room at Pentecost. The church can find its mission

9. Speer, *Missionary Principles*, p. 478.

in no other way than through earnest men and women in small companies praying and waiting until the Holy Spirit comes upon them with power.[10]

The Christian missionary is engaged in a life-and-death struggle with the powers of evil. The warfare in which he is engaged is pre-eminently spiritual. In this kind of warfare his most powerful weapon is prayer. Happy is the missionary who has standing behind him a faithful band of prayer warriors who know the secret of prevailing prayer and give themselves to this holy exercise on a daily basis.

A very encouraging sign in recent years has been the emphasis mission leaders are placing on intercessory prayer. Many mission boards now publish a monthly prayer bulletin that goes out to all their supporters. These bulletins contain a specific prayer request for every day of the month. Some boards have gone so far as to appoint a full-time prayer secretary to their headquarters staff. These secretaries coordinate the entire prayer ministry of the mission. Other missions hold weekend prayer conferences, when at least half the time is given over to intercession on behalf of world missions.

Christians at home, as much as missionaries on the field, have a vital role to play in the evangelization of the world. "If intercession is truly the all-important foundation of our entire work, then you at home who pray with us and intercede for us are fulfilling a ministry in God's work as vital and indispensable as that of the busiest missionary in the most demanding situation."[11]

---

10. John E. Skoglund, *To the Whole Creation* (Valley Forge, Pa.: Judson Press, 1962), p. 88.
11. John Stam, "The Praying Church," *Latin America Evangelist* (September-October 1975), p. 9.

Bibliography

Adeney, David H. *The Unchanging Commission*. Chicago: Inter-Varsity Press, 1955.

Allen, Geoffrey, *Theology of Missions*. Naperville, IL: Allenson, 1963.

Allen, Roland. *The Ministry of the Spirit*. Grand Rapids: Eerdmans Publishing Co., 1962.

———. *Missionary Methods: St. Paul's or Ours?* Grand Rapids: Eerdmans Publishing Co., 1962.

Andersen, Wilhelm. *Toward a Theology of Missions*. London: SCM Press, 1955.

Anderson, Gerald K. *Asian Voices in Christian Theology*. Maryknoll, NY: Orbis Books, 1976.

———. *Christian Mission in Theological Perspective*. Nashville: Abingdon Press, 1967.

———. *The Theology of the Christian Mission*. New York: McGraw Hill, 1961.

Beyerhaus, Peter. *Missions: Which Way? Humanization or Redemption*. Grand Rapids: Zondervan Publishing House, 1971.

———. *Shaken Foundations: Theological Foundations for Mission*. Grand Rapids: Zondervan Publishing House, 1972.

Blauw, Johannes, *The Missionary Nature of the Church*. New York: McGraw Hill, 1962.

Boer, Harry R. *Pentecost and Missions*. Grand Rapids: Eerdmans Publishing Co., 1961.

Bonino, Jose Miguez. *Doing Theology in a Revolutionary Situation*. Philadelphia: Fortress Press, 1975.

Boyd, E. H. S. *An Introduction to Indian Christian Theology*. Madras: Christian Literature Society, 1969.

Carver, William O. *The Bible a Missionary Message*. New York: Revell, 1921.

————. *Missions in the Plan of the Ages*. Nashville: Broadman, 1951.

Champion, Richard, et al. (eds.). *Our Mission in Today's World*. Springfield, MO: Gospel Publishing House, 1968.

Cook, Harold R. *An Introduction to the Study of Christian Missions*. Chicago: Moody Press, 1954.

Costas, Orlando E. *The Church and Its Mission: A Shattering Critique from the Third World*. Wheaton, IL: Tyndale House, 1974.

Douglas, J. D. (ed.). *Let the Earth Hear His Voice: International Congress on World Evangelization, Lausanne, Switzerland*. Minneapolis: World Wide Publications, 1975.

Forman, Charles W. *A Faith for the Nations*. Philadelphia: Westminster Press, 1957.

Glover, Robert H. *The Bible Basis of Missions*. Chicago: Moody Press, 1964.

Gordon, A. J. *The Holy Spirit in Missions*. Harrisburg, PA: Christian Publications, 1968.

Green, Michael. *Evangelism in the Early Church*. Grand Rapids: Eerdmans Publishing Co., 1970.

Gutierrez, Gustavo. *A Theology of Liberation*. Maryknoll, NY: Orbis Books, 1973.

Hahn, Ferdinand. *Mission in the New Testament*. Naperville, IL: Allenson, 1963.

Hartt, Julian N. *Towards a Theology of Evangelism*. New York: Abingdon Press, 1955.

Henry, Carl F. H. and Mooneyham, W. Stanley (eds.). *One Race, One Gospel, One Task: World Congress on Evangelism—Berlin 1966* (2 vols.). Minneapolis: World Wide Publications, 1967.

Hillis, Don W. (ed.). *The Scriptural Basis of World Evangelization*. Grand Rapids: Baker Book House, 1965.

Johnston, Arthur P. *World Evangelism and the Word of God*. Minneapolis: Bethany Fellowship, 1974.

Kantonen, T. A. *The Theology of Evangelism*. Philadelphia: Muhlenberg Press, 1954.

Kato, Byang. *Theological Pitfalls in Africa*. Kisumu, Kenya: Evangel Publishing House, 1975.

Koyama, Kosuke. *Waterbuffalo Theology*. London: SCM Press, 1974.

Kraemer, Hendrik. *The Christian Message in a Non-Christian World*. New York: Harper & Brothers, 1938.

Lawrence, J. B. *The Holy Spirit in Missions*. Atlanta: Home Mission Board, 1947.

Lindsell, Harold (ed.). *The Church's Worldwide Mission*. Waco, TX: Word Books, 1966.

————. *An Evangelical Theology of Missions*. Grand Rapids: Zondervan Publishing House, 1970.

Love, Julian Price. *The Missionary Message of the Bible*. New York: Macmillan, 1941.

McGavran, Donald. *Crucial Issues in Missions Tomorrow*. Chicago: Moody Press, 1972.

———— (ed.). *Eye of the Storm*. Waco, TX: Word, Inc., 1972.

McQuilkin, J. Robertson. *How Biblical Is the Church Growth Movement?* Chicago: Moody Press, 1973.

Montgomery, Helen B. *Prayer and Missions*. West Medford, MA: Central Committee on the United Study of Foreign Missions, 1924.

Morgan, G. Campbell. *The Missionary Manifesto*. Grand Rapids: Baker Book House, 1970.

Neill, Stephen. *Creative Tension*. London: Edinburgh House Press, 1959.

————. *The Unfinished Task*. London: Lutterworth Press, 1957.

Newbigin, Lesslie. *A Faith for This One World*. London: SCM Press, 1961.

————. *The Finality of Christ*. Richmond, VA: John Knox Press, 1969.

————. *The Household of God*. New York: Friendship Press, 1953.

————. *One Body, One Gospel, One World*. London: William Carling, 1958.

————. *Trinitarian Faith and Today's Mission*. Richmond, VA: John Knox Press, 1963.

Niles, Daniel T. *The Message and Its Messenger*. Nashville: Abingdon Press, 1966.

————. *The Preacher's Task and the Stone of Stumbling*. New York: Harper & Brothers, 1958.

————. *Upon the Earth*. New York: McGraw Hill, 1966.

Orchard, Ronald K. *Missions in a Time of Testing*. Philadelphia: Westminster Press, 1964.

Perry, Edmund. *The Gospel in Dispute. The Relation of Christian Faith to Other Missionary Religions*. Garden City, NY: Doubleday, 1958.

Peters, George W. *A Biblical Theology of Missions*. Chicago: Moody Press, 1972.

Power, John. *Mission Theology Today*. Maryknoll, NY: Orbis Books, 1971.

Rooy, S. H. *Theology of Missions in the Puritan Tradition*. Grand Rapids: Eerdmans Publishing Co., 1965.

Rowley, H. H. *The Missionary Message of the Old Testament*. London: Carey Press, 1944.

Sanders, J. Oswald. *How Lost Are the Heathen?* Chicago: Moody Press, 1972.

SEDOS (ed.). *Foundations of Mission Theology*. Maryknoll, NY: Orbis Books, 1972.

Shorter, Aylward. *Theology of Mission*. Notre Dame, IN: Fides Publishers, 1972.

Skoglund, John E. *To the Whole Creation*. Valley Forge, PA: Judson Press, 1962.

Smith, Eugene L. *God's Mission—and Ours*. Nashville: Abingdon Press, 1961.

Soper, Edmund D. *The Biblical Background of the Christian World Mission*. New York: Abingdon-Cokesbury Press, 1951.

Speer, Robert E. *The Church and Missions.* New York: Doran, 1926.

————. *The Finality of Jesus Christ.* New York: Revell, 1933.

Sundkler, Bengt. *The World of Mission.* Grand Rapids: Eerdmans Publishing Co., 1965.

Taylor, John V. *The Go-Between God: The Holy Spirit and the Christian Mission.* London: SCM Press, 1972.

Tippett, Alan R. *Church Growth and the Word of God.* Grand Rapids: Eerdmans Publishing Co., 1970.

————. *Verdict Theology in Missionary Theory.* Lincoln, IL: Lincoln Christian College, 1969.

Toynbee, Arnold. *Christianity Among the Religions of the World.* New York: Charles Scribner's Sons, 1957.

Vicedom, Georg F. *The Mission of God.* St. Louis, MO: Concordia Publishing Co., 1965.

Visser t'Hooft, W. A. *No Other Name.* Philadelphia: Westminster Press, 1963.

Wagner, C. Peter. *Latin American Theology: Radical or Evangelical?* Grand Rapids: Eerdmans Publishing Co., 1970.

Warren, Max A. C. *The Gospel of Victory.* London: SCM Press, 1955.

————. *The Uniqueness of Jesus Christ.* London: Highway Press, 1969.

Webster, Douglas. *Unchanging Mission: Biblical and Contemporary.* Philadelphia: Fortress Press, 1965.

————. *Yes to Mission.* New York: Seabury Press, 1966.

Winter, Ralph D. (ed.). *The Evangelical Response to Bangkok.* South Pasadena, CA: William Carey Library, 1973.

Wolff, Richard. *The Final Destiny of the Heathen.* Lincoln, NE: Back to the Bible Broadcast, 1961.